Law in the EU's Circular Energy System

NEW HORIZONS IN ENVIRONMENTAL AND ENERGY LAW

Series Editors: Kurt Deketelaere, *Professor of Law, University of Leuven, Belgium and University of Dundee, Scotland* and Zen Makuch, *Reader in Law, Barrister, Imperial College, London, UK*

Environmental law – including the pressing considerations of energy law and climate change – is an increasingly important area of legal research and practice. Given the growing interdependence of global society and the significant steps being made towards environmental protection and energy efficiency, there are few people untouched by environmental and energy lawmaking processes.

At the same time, environmental and energy law is at a crossroads. The command and control methodology that evolved in the 1960s and 1970s for air, land and water protection may have reached the limit of its environmental protection achievements. New life needs to be injected into our environmental protection regimes – perhaps through the concept of sustainability in its environmental, economic and social forms. The same goes for energy policy and law, where liberalization, environmental protection and security of supply are at the centre of attention. This important series seeks to press forward the boundaries of environmental and energy law through innovative research into environmental and energy law, doctrine and case law. Adopting a wide interpretation of environmental and energy law, it includes contributions from both leading and emerging international scholars.

For a full list of Edward Elgar published titles, including the titles in this series, visit our website at www.e-elgar.com.

Law in the EU's Circular Energy System

Biofuel, Biowaste and Biogas

Edited by

Lucila de Almeida

Abreu Chair of ESG Impact, NOVA School of Law and Centre for Research on Law and Society (CEDIS), Portugal; Part-time Professor, Florence School of Regulation, Robert Schuman Centre for Advanced Studies, European University Institute, Italy

Josephine van Zeben

Professor and Chair, Law Group, Wageningen University, the Netherlands

NEW HORIZONS IN ENVIRONMENTAL AND ENERGY LAW

Edward Elgar PUBLISHING

Cheltenham, UK • Northampton, MA, USA

Published by
Edward Elgar Publishing Limited
The Lypiatts
15 Lansdown Road
Cheltenham
Glos GL50 2JA
UK

Edward Elgar Publishing, Inc.
William Pratt House
9 Dewey Court
Northampton
Massachusetts 01060
USA

A catalogue record for this book
is available from the British Library

Library of Congress Control Number: 2023946638

This book is available electronically in the **Elgar**online
Law subject collection
http://dx.doi.org/10.4337/9781802205879

MIX
Paper | Supporting responsible forestry
FSC® C013604

ISBN 978 1 80220 586 2 (cased)
ISBN 978 1 80220 587 9 (eBook)

Printed and bound by CPI Group (UK) Ltd, Croydon, CR0 4YY

Contents

PART III CROSS-SECTORAL ISSUES

Figures

Tables

Contributors

Edwin Alblas, Assistant Professor, LAW Group, Wageningen University, the Netherlands.

Mirta Alessandrini, Lecturer, LAW Group, Wageningen University, the Netherlands.

Álvaro Antón Antón, Associate Professor, CEU Cardenal Herrera University, Spain.

Aalt Bast, Professor, Department of Pharmacology & Toxicology and University College Venlo, Maastricht University, the Netherlands.

Lin Batten, PhD Student, Law Group, University of Strathclyde, Glasgow, Scotland.

Alie de Boer, Assistant Professor, Food Claims Centre Venlo, Maastricht University, the Netherlands.

Geert van Calster, Full Professor, KU Leuven, Belgium and practising member of the Belgian Bar.

Elisa Cavallin, PhD Researcher at Hasselt University, Belgium.

Ilaria Conti, Head of Gas Hydrogen and Decarbonisation, Florence School of Regulation, Italy.

Benjamin Gomado, Student, Graduate Program Global Engineering, University of Colorado Boulder, USA; Control and Automation Engineer, Sewerage Systems Ghana Company Limited; Solar PV Design and Technical Site Intern Engineer, SunPower Power Innovations Ghana Limited.

Allard Knook, Professor of State Aid, Utrecht University, the Netherlands; and Head Public Sector Legal and Partner, PwC, the Netherlands.

Phillip Lugmayr, Policy Officer, European Commission DG CLIMA, Belgium.

Maria Olczak, Research Associate, Florence School of Regulation, Italy.

Andris Piebalgs, Part-time Professor, Florence School of Regulation, Italy.

Alberto Pototschnig, Part-time Professor and Deputy Director, Florence School of Regulation, Italy.

Madhura Rao, PhD Candidate, Food Claims Centre Venlo, Maastricht University, the Netherlands.

Piero Carlo dos Reis, Policy Officer, European Commission DG CLIMA, Belgium.

Agnieszka Smoleńska, Assistant Professor, Institute of Legal Studies, Polish Academy of Sciences, Poland.

Maciej M Sokołowski, Assistant Professor, the University of Warsaw, Poland; Guest Professor (Global), Keio University, Japan.

Abbreviations

AIB	Association of Issuing Bodies
BAT	best available techniques
BAT_AEELS	efficiency level associated with the best available techniques
BREFS	Best Available Techniques Reference
BSE	bovine spongiform encephalopathy
CE	Circular Economy
CEAAG	Climate, Environment and Energy Aid Guidelines
CH_4	methane emissions
CHP	Combined Heat and Power
CINEA	European Climate, Infrastructure and Environment Executive Agency
CJEU	Court of Justice of the European Union
CNG	Compressed Natural Gas
CO_2	carbon dioxide
CORSIA	Carbon Offsetting and Reduction Scheme for International Aviation
DA	Delegated Acts
DNSH	Do no significant harm
EC	European Commission
ECA	European Court of Auditors
ECJ	European Court of Justice
EEA	European Environment Agency
EEAG	Energy and Environmental State Aid Guidelines
EEB	European Environmental Bureau
EECS	European Energy Certificate System
EF	Emission factors
EFSI	European Fund for Strategic Investments

EIB	European Investment Bank
EIC	European Innovation Council
EoL	End-of-life
ERGaR	European Renewable Gas Registry
ESIS	Energy System Integration Strategy
ESR	Effort Sharing Regulation
ETD	Energy Tax Directive
ETS	Emissions Trading System
EU	European Union
EUA	European Union Emission Allowance
EoW	End-of-waste
FAME	fatty acid methyl ester
FAO	Food and Agricultural Organization of the United Nations
FBO	food business operator
FIP	feed-in premium
FIT	feed-in tariff
GBER	General Block Exemption Regulation
GC	Green Certificate
GFL	General Food Law
GHG	greenhouse gas
GMP	Global Methane Pledge
GO	Guarantees of Origin
GRO	Guarantees of Renewable Origin
ICAO	International Civil Aviation Organization
IEA	International Energy Agency
IED	Industrial Emissions Directive
ILUC	indirect land-use change
IPCC	The Intergovernmental Panel on Climate Change
LDAR	leak detection and repair programmes
LNG	liquid natural gas
LULUCF	land-use, land-use change and forestry
MEO	Market Economy Operator
MFF	Multiannual Financial Framework

MRV	monitoring, reporting and verification
MS	Member State
N_2O	nitrous oxide
NDC	Nationally Determined Contributions
NECP	National Energy and Climate Plan
NO_x	Nitrogen Oxides
NRP	National Recovery Plan
OECD	Organisation for Economic Co-operation and Development
PM	Particulate Matter
PPP	polluter pays principle
RED	Renewable Energy Directive
RENEWFM	EU renewable energy financing mechanism
RES	Renewable Energy Source
RES-T	renewable energy in the transport sector
RFNBOs	Renewable Fuels of Non Biological origin
RRF	Recovery and Resilience Facility
SAF	sustainable aviation fuels
SEIP	Sustainable Europe Investment Plan
SO_x	sulphur oxides
TFEU	Treaty on the Functioning of the European Union
TGC	tradable green certificates
VAT	value-added tax
W2E	waste to energy
WFD	Waste Framework Directive

1. The EU's circular energy system and the Green Deal

Lucila de Almeida and Josephine van Zeben

I. TOWARDS AN EU CIRCULAR ENERGY SYSTEM

The European Green Deal,[1] presented by the European Commission in December 2019, sets out the European Union (EU)'s growth strategy in light of climatic and environmental challenges. It aims to create a 'fair and prosperous society, with a resource-efficient and competitive economy' that 'decouples'[2] economic growth from resource use and achieves net zero emissions by 2050.[3] This transition is meant to be 'just and inclusive' by putting 'people first', ensuring attention to all the EU's regions and their differences and guaranteeing public participation at every stage.[4]

The Green Deal is premised on the successful marriage of the EU's environmental and climate goals with its economic and social goals. The decarbonisation of the energy sector is an especially crucial piece of the resulting puzzle. Energy production and use account for over 75% of the EU's greenhouse gas (GHG) emissions. The decarbonisation of the energy system requires a fundamental transformation – from a production structure mainly based on

---

1 European Commission, 'The European Green Deal' COM (2019) 640 ('Green Deal').

2 The element of decoupling growth from resource use (also known as 'green growth') must be seen as fundamentally different from 'degrowth'; the focus remains on sustaining a certain standard of living through economic growth and competitiveness *in line with* environmental objectives where possible. Though there are some features of the Green Deal that signal a more fundamental shift beyond green capitalism, thus far, the Green Deal is mostly considered to be a new version of the green growth narrative ('critical green growth model'), rather than a clear break with this tradition. See in detail, Marinus Ossewaarde and Roshnee Ossewaarde-Lowtoo, 'The EU's Green Deal: A Third Alternative to Green Growth and Degrowth' (2020) 12 Sustainability 9825, doi:10.3390/su12239825.

3 Green Deal (n 1) at 1.

4 ibid.

fossil fuels to one powered by renewables[5] – necessitating changes to how EU society provides, transports and consumes energy. However, disagreements exist over how this system should be transformed by 2050 to accomplish the EU's net zero emissions ambitions.[6]

Within 2016's Clean Energy Package,[7] the Commission prioritised the decarbonisation of electricity generation under the assumption that electrification would play a significant role in the energy transition. The Green Deal, instead, expands the energy transition to the gas and transportation sectors, where renewable fuels and gases are presented as alternatives for the decarbonisation of the gas sector,[8] and more sustainable liquid fuel options for air, water and road transportation in contrast to fossil fuels as oil and natural gas.[9] In addition to the goals of the Green Deal, the Russian invasion of Ukraine (February 2022) and the resulting ongoing armed conflict have motivated the adoption of even more ambitious targets regarding the decarbonisation of the energy sector, as well as the acceleration of oil and gas phase-out as a matter of security of supply.

The potential and ambition to decarbonise the EU's power supply stands in stark contrast with the practice of the EU's energy mix. In February 2022, almost three-quarters of the EU energy system came from fossil fuels. Oil dominates in the EU energy mix (35%), followed by natural gas (24%) and coal (14%). The share of renewables is growing but still plays a more limited role (14%), as does nuclear (13%).[10]

In July 2020, the European Commission released two Communications to kick-start changes to the energy sector: the 'EU strategy for Energy System Integration'[11] and the 'Hydrogen strategy for a climate-neutral Europe'.[12] Our focus here is on the former: the Energy System Integration Strategy (ESIS),

---

5 ibid 31.

6 Many modelling studies perform scenario analysis to provide insights into a variety of future pathways depending on variables such as technological developments, consumer preferences and political choices. See George Zachmann and others, *Decarbonisation of Energy, Publication for the Committee on Industry, Research and Energy (ITRE)* (European Parliament 2021), 24.

7 European Commission Communication, 'Clean Energy for All Europeans' COM (2016) 840, 8.

8 Green Deal (n 1) 6.

9 ibid 11.

10 Data are made available by Eurostat, here: https://ec.europa.eu/eurostat/statistics-explained/index.php?title=Energy_statistics_-_an_overview#Final_energy_consumption

11 European Commission, 'Powering a climate-neutral economy: an EU strategy for Energy System Integration' COM (2020) 299 ('ESIS').

12 European Commission, 'A hydrogen strategy for a climate-neutral Europe' COM (2020) 301. The hydrogen strategy details the EU plans for the development of renew-

which lays the foundation for fundamental changes to the planning and operation of the energy system – across multiple energy carriers, infrastructures and consumption sectors – with a view to delivering 'low-carbon, reliable and resource-efficient energy services at the lowest possible cost for society'.[13] To achieve this goal, ESIS sets out three sub-aims, which importantly include the creation of 'a more circular energy system, with energy efficiency at its core'.[14]

The Communication on ESIS represents the formal introduction of the notion of a 'circular energy system' into the energy policy framework. Despite not defining it, the Commission lists two 'key actions' to build a more circular economy model of production in an integrated energy system.[15] The first concerns waste heat from industrial sites, data centres or other sources, which could be reused on-site or via a district heating and cooling network.[16] The second involves the conversion of biological waste and residues into biofuels and biogas. The latter plays a central role in the EU's circular energy system as applied in this volume, precisely in order to '[i]ncentivise the mobilisation of biological waste and residues from agriculture, food and forestry sectors and support capacity-building for rural circular energy communities through the new Common Agriculture Policy, Structural Funds and the new LIFE Programme'.[17]

The ESIS introduces a circular energy system that uses biological waste for energy production. This articulation of a circular energy system is highly comparable to the most commonly used definition of a circular economy (CE), namely a model of production and consumption which involves reusing, repairing, refurbishing and recycling existing materials for as long as possible.[18]

---

able hydrogen production, transportation and consumption, which is a type of renewable gas from non-biological origins.

[13] ESIS (n 11) 2.

[14] ibid 2. The other two sub-aims are (2) to ensure 'greater direct electrification and end-use sectors'; and (3) 'use renewable and low carbon fuels for end-use application where direct heating or electrification is not feasible, inefficient, or have higher costs'.

[15] ibid 6–7.

[16] ibid.

[17] ibid.

[18] This concept of the circular economy has been endorsed by the Commission. See European Commission, 'Closing the loop – An EU action plan for the Circular Economy' COM (2015) 614, and European Commission, 'A new Circular Economy Action Plan. For a cleaner and more competitive Europe' COM (2020) 98. However, there are various existing definitions, classifications and taxonomies of the circular economy. Based on a comprehensive literature review, Pablo del Rio et al. conclude it is a two-sided concept: it is a vision of how an economic system can be based on closed cycles of physical resources and retained value. See, Pablo del Rio and others, 'Defining the Circular Economy: A Review of Definitions, Taxonomies and Classifications' in Pablo del Rio, Christopher P Kiefer, Javier Carrillo-Hermosilla

Already in 2017, the Communication on 'the role of waste-to-energy in the circular economy'[19] advocated for the application of the EU waste hierarchy to ensure higher levels of waste prevention, reuse and recycling among the waste-to-energy options, including the use of organic and wood waste to produce biogas. Similarly, the Renewable Energy Directive 2018/2001 (RED II) imposes an obligation on the Member States (MSs) to consider the sustainable supply of biomass and the move towards a CE when developing support schemes for renewable energy sources.[20] However, neither of these documents created a legal framework that could create a complete circular energy system, considering its complex multi-level legal landscape system and the many economic sectors involved.

The decarbonisation of the energy sector, in particular the gas and transportation sectors, imposes challenges but also opportunities for a circular energy system. Scenarios that forecast a rapid shift of the EU energy mix to hydrogen, direct heating or electrification are not feasible in the short term due to the need for a high-intensity investment in generation and transportation infrastructure adjustments.[21] By contrast, biogases upgraded to biomethane can use the existing natural gas grids,[22] while liquid biofuels are substitute fuels for all kinds of internal combustion engines that work with diesel, gasoline or kerosene for use in transport vehicles on land, air and sea. Efficient in all end-use applications, there is a heavy reliance on renewable and low-carbon fuels to reduce the con-

---

and Totti Könnölä (eds), *The Circular Economy: Economic, Managerial and Policy Implications* (Springer, Cham 2021). On the contrary, there are scholars that exclude renewable biological resources and their conversion into food, feed, bio-based products and bioenergy from the concept of the circular economy. For them, these are features of the bioeconomy which resemble linear economy production. See Walter R Stahel, *The Circular Economy: A User's Guide* (Routledge 2019), and Ken Webster and others, *A New Dynamic: Effective Business in a Circular Economy* (2nd edn, Ellen MacArthur Foundation Publishing 2014).

[19] European Commission, 'The role of waste-to-energy in the circular economy', COM (2017) 43.

[20] Directive 2018/2001 on the promotion of the use of energy from renewable sources [2018] OJ L328/82 ('RED II'), art 2(35) defines 'recycled carbon fuels' as 'liquid and gaseous fuels that are produced from liquid or solid waste streams of non-renewable origin which are not suitable for material recovery in accordance with Article 4 of Directive 2008/98/EC, or from waste processing gas and exhaust gas of non-renewable origin which are produced as an unavoidable and unintentional consequence of the production process in industrial installations'. Recycled carbon fuels, as derived from non-renewable waste streams such as fossil wastes like plastic, rubber, gaseous wastes, cannot be considered to contribute to overall renewable energy targets.

[21] Zachmann and others (n 6).

[22] Daan Peters and others, *Gas Decarbonization Pathways 2020–2050: Gas for Climate* (Guidehouse 2020) vi.

sumption of natural gas and other fossil fuels. Biofuels and biogases constitute a short-term sustainable solution.

At the moment, biofuels and biogas account for only 3.5% of all gas and fuel consumption in the EU and are based mainly on food and feed crops and woody biomass.[23] To fulfil the Commission's goals for decarbonising the gas and transportation sectors, these numbers will have to increase significantly. For instance, the decarbonisation pathways in the energy mix scenario of the Joint Research Centre (of the European Commission) in the Fit for 55 Communication predicted an increase in the demand for biofuels and biogases from 1.584 TWh to 3.580 TWh from 2019 to 2050, respectively.[24] However, increasing biofuel and biogas production based on food and feed crops is barred by the indirect land-use change (ILUC) measures introduced by RED II.[25] In the gas market, in particular, the rapid phase-out of natural gas imported from Russia will have to be achieved through the rapid deployment of sustainable biomethane – meaning, biogas upgrading to biomethane – based on the responsible use of waste and organic residues. The International Energy Agency (IEA) outlook for biogas and biomethane showed that more than 80% of European production potential relies on feedstock sources from animal manure, crop residues, woody biomass and municipal solid waste. A tiny portion lies in wastewater treatment plants.[26] This is expected to create unprecedented demand for these resources and requires a legal framework to match this demand, and more generally the changing markets for biowaste as raw material for biofuel and biogas.

However, the creation of such a circular energy system does not take place in a (legislative) vacuum: the EU's energy policies and law-setting production and consumption targets for renewable energy sources need to align with a plethora of other policies and legislative proposals regulating waste recycling and regulatory incentives derived from finance, carbon tax reforms and emission trade schemes.

Moreover, core concepts, such as 'renewable fuels' and 'biogases', are too often left undefined, creating confusion and critical omissions in policy and

---

23 Andrea Camia and others, *The Use of Woody Biomass for Energy Production in the EU* (Publication Office of the European Union 2020).

24 See European Commission, 'Energy Scenarios' (visitors-centre.jrc.ec.europa.eu n.d), available at https://visitors-centre.jrc.ec.europa.eu/tools/energy_scenarios/app.html#today:EU27/today:EU27.

25 RED II (n 20).

26 International Energy Agency (IEA), 'Outlook for Biogas and Biomethane: Prospects for organic growth' (IEA 2020) 7.

scholarly discussions on this topic.[27] In the context of this edited volume, the following definitions and distinctions are especially important: 'renewable fuels' refers collectively to biofuels, bioliquids, biomass fuels and renewable fuels of non-biological origin.[28] 'Renewable gases' refers more narrowly to biogas produced from biomass, including biogas upgrading to biomethane, or gases from non-biological origins such as green hydrogen and synthetic natural gas.[29] Biogases and biofuels are the main focus of this edited volume. These are both renewable energy sources produced from 'biomass', which must be distinguished from those renewables from non-biological origins or recycled carbon fuels.[30] Biomass is broadly defined as 'the biodegradable fraction of products, waste and residues of biological origin from agriculture, including vegetal and animal substances, from forestry and related industries, including fisheries and aquaculture, as well as the biodegradable fraction of waste, including industrial and municipal waste of biological origin'.[31] Biomass is, therefore, a broader category than biowaste. Within the EU's policy context,

---

[27] There are also alternative classification systems for liquid and gaseous biofuels which are used in the literature, as well as throughout the chapter of this edited volume. One well-known classification distinguishes biofuels in terms of first, second and third generations. First-generation biofuels are derived from sugar, starch or lipids extracted from crops; second-generation biofuels are derived from cellulose, hemicellulose or lignin (such as agricultural, food or forestry residues) and lignocellulosic crops; and third-generation biofuels are derived from aquatic autotrophic organism (e.g. algae). Another classification distinguishes biofuels into conventional and advanced types. Conventional biofuels are also called first-generation biofuels, while advanced biofuels would encompass both second- and third-generation biofuels.

[28] Definition proposed by the Commission in 'Proposal for a Directive amending Directive (EU) 2018/2001, Regulation (EU) 2018/1999 98/70/EC as regards the promotion of energy from renewable sources, and repealing Council Directive (EU) 2015/652' COM (2021) 557 ('Proposal for RED III'), art 2(22a).

[29] The definition of biogas already existed in RED II (n 20). The Commission proposed a new definition of renewable gases, which encompasses the prior definition of biogas and adds to it renewable gases of non-biological origins. See art 2(2) of the 'Proposal for a Directive of the European Parliament and of the Council on common rules for the internal markets in renewable and natural gases and in hydrogen' COM (2021) 803.

[30] RED II (n 20) art 2(35) defines 'recycled carbon fuels' as 'liquid and gaseous fuels that are produced from liquid or solid waste streams of non-renewable origin which are not suitable for material recovery in accordance with Article 4 of Directive 2008/98/EC, or from waste processing gas and exhaust gas of non-renewable origin which are produced as an unavoidable and unintentional consequence of the production process in industrial installations'. Recycled carbon fuels, as derived from non-renewable waste streams such as fossil wastes like plastic, rubber, gaseous wastes, cannot be considered to contribute to overall renewable energy targets.

[31] RED II (n 20) art 2(22).

however, the focus lies on biofuels and biogases produced from 'biowaste', such as those occurring in the agriculture, food and forestry sectors.[32]

The remainder of this chapter discusses the treatment of biofuel and biogas produced from biowaste in the policies and legislative proposals released within the framework of the European Green Deal (Section II). From this discussion, several areas of research are identified that are in particular need of clarification to create a law and policy framework that will facilitate the move from a linear to a circular energy system (Section III). These research areas form the basis for the contributions to this edited volume.

II. BIOFUEL, BIOGAS AND BIOWASTE IN THE EUROPEAN GREEN DEAL

The Green Deal is presented primarily as a forward-looking policy. Nevertheless, its execution is contextualised by, and largely dependent on, a large body of pre-existing EU legislation and policy. The full scope of the Green Deal's policy ambitions and legislative proposals can only be grasped by considering the plethora of communications, legislative proposals and other policy documents accompanying the Green Deal.[33]

The Green Deal's roadmap identifies eight areas in which further action plans must be created, many of which have crystallised in the Fit for 55 package.[34] Four of these areas are directly and indirectly related to the decarbonisation of the energy system: supplying clean, affordable and secure energy; mobilising industry for a clean CE; building and renovating in an energy- and resource-efficient way; and accelerating the shift to sustainable and smart mobility.[35]

The importance of biogas and biofuels produced from biowaste in the green transition, in particular, is not explicitly stated in the Commission's Green Deal Communication, which generically refers to the role of 'renewable fuels

---

[32] Directive 2008/98/EC (on waste and repealing certain Directives [2008] OJ L312/3 ('Waste Framework Directive', 'WFD')) art 3(4) defines 'biowaste' as 'biodegradable garden and park waste, food and kitchen waste from households, offices, restaurants, wholesale, canteens, caterers and retail premises and comparable waste from food processing plants'. For the purpose of this edited volume, biowaste also encompasses the residues from the agriculture and forestry sectors.

[33] For all documentation, see: https://commission.europa.eu/strategy-and-policy/priorities-2019-2024/european-green-deal_en#documents (last accessed 11 January 2022).

[34] European Commission, '"Fit for 55": delivering the EU's 2030 Climate Target on the way to climate neutrality', COM (2021) 550 ('Fit for 55').

[35] Green Deal (n 1) 3.

and gases' for the decarbonisation of the gas and heavy transportation sectors.[36] In order to explicate the topic of this edited volume, the current regulatory framework and legislative proposals must be analysed and mapped to put feasible energy mix scenarios into perspective.

Moreover, Russia's unjustified invasion of Ukrainian territory (February 2022), introduced additional urgency to the policy goals for decarbonising gas and transportation sectors.[37] The deployment of biomethane to substitute natural gas is central to the REPowerEU framework. The following subsections will underline the place of biofuel and biogas produced from biowaste in the Fit for 55 package (A) and the REPowerEU plan (B).

A. Fit for 55

In the words of the Commission, the Fit for 55 package is the 'most comprehensive set of proposals that has ever been presented on climate and energy'.[38] It aims to deliver transformational change across the economy, society and industries to reduce net emissions by at least 55% by 2030 – a starting point for the implementation of the Green Deal's goals. The package consists of several interconnected legislative proposals, which line up towards the common goal of ensuring a fair, competitive and green transition.[39] Those proposals covered a broad scope of issues, ranging from the new Social Climate Fund, which intends to support citizens most affected or at risk of energy or mobility poverty,[40] to the expansion of the EU Emission Trading System (ETS) to new sectors,[41] including transportation; a series of legislative proposals to promote cleaner mobility, such as the uptake of sustainable fuels in aviation, maritime and road transport;[42] parts of the energy sector's reform, including the Renewable Energy Directive and Energy Taxation Directive;[43] and biodiversity issues through the review of the land use, land-use change and forestry (LULUCF) Regulation.[44]

---

36 ibid 6, 11.

37 On 27 and 28 January 2022, the editors of this volume hosted an online workshop, where contributors presented and discussed the first draft of their chapters. The final chapters were reviewed and updated to reflect changes in law and policy motivated by the Russia-Ukraine war where relevant.

38 Fit for 55 (n 34) 2.

39 ibid 3.

40 ibid 4.

41 ibid 5.

42 ibid 8–9.

43 ibid 9.

44 ibid 10.

The Communication does not discuss the circular energy system directly. In order to find the foundations of a circular energy system, as discussed in this volume, we must look to the many interconnected legislative proposals the package proposes, especially those designed to enable and promote the production and consumption of renewable fuels.

Central to this discussion is the Renewable Energy Directive 2018/2001 (RED II), which is currently under review, despite its recent recast in 2018. RED II increased the share of renewable energy in the Union's gross energy consumption to at least 40% by 2030.[45] However, it does not prescribe the composition of the renewable energy mix, except for the transportation sector. In the latter, the share of advanced biofuels and biogas produced from feedstock must increase from 0.2% in 2022 to 2.2% in 2030, and the share of renewable fuels of non-biological origin should be at least 2.6% in the same year.[46] Considering advanced biofuels are, by definition, non-food-based feedstocks, MSs must fill those targets with renewable fuels aligned to the concept of a circular energy system. These targets are complemented by obligations on fuel suppliers in maritime and air transportation as proposed in two other legislative reforms of the Fit for 55: the ReFuelEU Aviation[47] and FuelEU Maritime.[48]

The RED II already recognised the need to align national policies for bioenergy with the waste hierarchy to avoid distortive effects on the raw material biomass market.[49] However, it does not clarify which biofuels and biogases could be considered disruptive to the waste hierarchy, except for banning support schemes for electricity produced from waste incineration.[50] The Fit for 55 package amends the recast of RED II provisions so as to add MS submission to other biomass use principles, such as the waste hierarchy and the cascading principle,[51] taking into consideration the principles of the CE and increased use of woody biomass.[52] However, the legislative proposal provides no guidance

---

[45] Proposal for RED III (n 28) art 1(2).

[46] ibid art 1(14).

[47] European Commission, 'Proposal for a Regulation on ensuring a level playing field for sustainable air transport' COM (2021) 561.

[48] European Commission, 'Proposal for a Regulation on the use of renewable and low-carbon fuels in maritime transport and amending Directive 2009/16/EC' COM (2021) 562.

[49] RED II (n 20) art 3(3).

[50] ibid.

[51] Proposal for RED III (n 28) art 1(2). It aims to amend Article 3(3), RED II. See also Proposal for RED III (n 28) rec 4.

[52] The cascading principle aims to achieve resource efficiency of biomass use through prioritising biomass material use to energy use wherever possible, increasing thus the amount of biomass available within the system. In line with the cascading prin-

on the application of the principle of the CE to bioenergy. Importantly, it does bar the expansion of conventional biofuels through the strengthening of sustainability criteria in the revision of RED II, by limiting the use of conventional biofuels produced from food and feed crops. Also, the recast aims to prohibit support schemes for energy produced from logs, stumps and roots,[53] which is a legislative response to climate change litigations arising before the Court of Justice of the European Union (CJEU) against the classification of wood biomass as renewable energy.[54] Besides the recast of RED II, the reform of the LULUCF Regulation will record and account for the emission of woody biomass used in energy, increasing the incentives for the deployment of biofuels and biogas produced by waste products without biodiversity loss. On the other hand, there are also measures that could undermine the place of biogas and biomethane, such as the new regulation on methane emission reduction, which counts the methane losses in the production and use of natural gas and biomethane indistinctly.[55]

The Fit for 55 legislative proposals do not impose harmonised targets on the MSs regarding the share of biofuels and biogas produced from biowaste in the renewable energy mix. Rather, MSs must continue to ensure the implementation of their National Energy and Climate Plans (NECPs), submitted by

---

ciple, woody biomass should be used according to its highest economic and environmental added value in the following order of priorities: (1) wood-based products; (2) extending their service life; (3) reuse; (4) recycling; (5) bioenergy; and (6) disposal. See O Olsson, 'Cascading of Woody Biomass: The Tricky Path from Principle to Policy to Practice' (2017) SEI discussion brief.

[53] Proposal for RED III (n 28) art 1(2)(a)(i).

[54] See Case T-141/19 *Sabo and Others v Parliament and Council* [2020] ECR I-179. Plaintiffs from six countries filed suit to challenge the treatment of forest biomass as renewable in RED II, claiming it is incompatible with the environmental objectives of the TFEU and ECHR. On 6 May 2020, the Court dismissed the case on standing grounds, reasoning that an EU directive is an act of general application, the applicants are not in a situation different from an indeterminate and indeterminable body of EU citizens, and therefore the directive is not of individual concern to them. Plaintiffs appealed to the Court of Justice of the EU (ECJ). On 14 January 2021, the ECJ rejected the appeal, upholding the lower court decision dismissing the case on standing grounds. The ECJ reasoned that the lower court made no error in law in concluding that the plaintiffs had not demonstrated that the directive was of individual concern to them. Other climate change litigations are about to be brought to the CJEU against the approved EU taxonomy that labels investments in wood biomass as sustainable finance.

[55] European Commission, 'Proposal for a Regulation on methane emissions reduction in the energy sector and amending Regulation (EU) 2019/942' COM (2021) 805, 3–4.

31 December 2019,[56] and release progress reports every two years, through which the Commission monitors compliance. Some of these NECPs do intend to replace a large proportion of natural gas and fossil fuels in heating and heavy transportation sectors with biomethane and other biofuels.[57] At the same time, these NECPs tend to stress the limits of increasing the production of conventional biofuels due to the negative externalities on biodiversity and the food system.[58]

The Fit for 55 also heralds the development of a new EU framework aimed at decarbonising the gas market through the reform of Directive 2009/7 on the internal market in natural gas, and Regulation 715/2009 on conditions for access to the natural gas transmission networks.[59] The Commission's proposals for the new Directive and Regulation aim at removing barriers to access of renewable and low-carbon gases into the gas infrastructure, including, for instance, grant discounts of entry tariffs and the elimination of cross-border tariffs, and equal access to the wholesale markets.

B. REPowerEU

Shortly after the Russian invasion of Ukraine, the EU embraced the decarbonisation of the energy sector not only as a tool to fight the climate crisis, but also as a tool to fight an imminent (energy) security crisis. The EU imports 90% of its gas, with Russia providing more than 40% of the total gas consumption (as well as 27% of oil imports). The Russian threats to cut off the gas supply as a means to pressure the EU and its MSs to lift their embargos – imposed

---

56 As imposed by Regulation (EU) 2018/1999 (on the Governance of the Energy Union and Climate Action, amending Regulations (EC) 663/2009 and (EC) 715/2009, Directives 94/22/EC, 98/70/EC, 2009/31/EC, 2009/73/EC, 2010/31/EU, 2012/27/EU and 2013/30/EU, Directives 2009/119/EC and (EU) 2015/652 and repealing Regulation (EU) 525/2013 [2018] OJ L328/1) art 3(1).

57 See, for instance, NECPs submitted by Germany, Austria, Italy, France and Portugal (available at https://energy.ec.europa.eu/topics/energy-strategy/national-energy-and-climate-plans-necps_en#final-necps). On the other hand, there is a criticism of the NECPs, which plan to significantly increase their reliance on bioenergy over the same period without explaining how and where they will source this biomass, or what impact it will have on climate or biodiversity. See Matthew Smith, Anna Kralli and Peter Lemoine, *Analysis on Biomass in National Energy and Climate Plans* (Trinomics 2021) https://www.fern.org/fileadmin/uploads/fern/Documents/2021/Fern_-_Biomass_in_NECPs_-_Final_report.pdf.

58 ibid.

59 Proposal for a Directive on common rules for the internal markets for renewable and natural gases and in hydrogen (n 29); European Commission, 'Proposal for a Regulation on internal markets for renewable and natural gases and in hydrogen (recast)' COM (2021) 804.

as countermeasures in response to Russian human rights violations against Ukrainians – underscored the EU's vulnerabilities linked to its continued fossil fuel dependence.

On 8 March 2022, the European Commission released a short Communication launching the so-called REPowerEU programme,[60] which was soon developed more fully.[61] REPowerEU aims to accelerate the green transition started in the Green Deal by increasing the targets for renewable energy to 45% of the Union's energy gross consumption by 2030.[62] Moreover, while the Fit for 55 package left MSs free to decide on the composition of their renewable energy mixes, REPowerEU sets quantitative targets for scaling up the production of biomethane and hydrogen by 2030, which should be matched by the phasing out of natural gas imported from Russia.[63] The EU political choice of relying on sustainable biomethane in this transition revives the ESIS's original proposals for a more circular energy system.

The REPowerEU stresses the feasibility of lowering gas use by at least 155 billion cubic metres (bcm) – equivalent to the amount of gas imported from Russia in 2021. To reach these targets, the Commission aims to boost sustainable biomethane production to 35 bcm by 2030. Until 2021, the EU produced 17 bcm of biogas, of which part was upgraded and transformed into 3 bcm of biomethane. Therefore, the new target would mean increasing biomethane production tenfold.[64] Moreover, the Commission emphasises that this 'biomethane should be waste-based, avoiding the use of food and feed stocks that would lead to a land change problems',[65] and 'ensuring produc[tion] from organic waste and forest and agricultural residues'.[66] In parallel, the Biomethane Action Plan lists a series of other actions to ensure fulfilment, including mobilising residues as raw material for the production of biomethane '(e.g. agricultural and agro-industry waste and residues, forest and forest-industry waste and residues, food industry waste, energy and chemical

---

60 European Commission, 'REPowerEU: Joint European Action for more affordable, secure and sustainable energy' COM (2022) 108.

61 European Commission, 'REPowerEU Plan' COM (2022) 230 ('REPowerEU').

62 ibid 6.

63 ibid 5–6.

64 Sacha Alberici, Wouter Grimme and Gemma Toop, *Biomethane Production Potentials in the EU: Feasibility of REPowerEU 2030 Targets, Production Potentials in the Member States and Outlook to 2050* (Gas for Climate 2022) https://gasforclimate2050.eu/news-item/new-study-on-biomethane-production-potentials-in-the-eu/.

65 European Commission, 'Implementing the REPower EU Action Plan: investment needs, hydrogen accelerator and achieving the bio-methane targets' SWD (2022) 230 ('Biomethane Action Plan'), 34.

66 REPowerEU (n 61) 8.

industry biogenic CO_2 effluents and waste, industrial wastewater, domestic organic waste)',[67] and infrastructure adjustment to ensure access to the gas grid by biomethane producers.[68]

The REPowerEU represents an unprecedented acceleration of the green transition towards a more circular energy system based on biogas and biomethane production. The estimated required investment for this acceleration is EUR 37 billion between 2022 and 2030.[69] This would require the mobilisation of EU funding under, *inter alia*, the Connecting Europe Facility, Cohesion Policy, Recovery and Resilience Facility and the Common Agriculture Policy,[70] as well private co-funding.

III. EDITED VOLUME STRUCTURE

The development of the EU's circular energy system takes place in an already complex legal landscape, made up of multiple jurisdiction systems and many layers of governance, and affects many economic sectors, from production to consumption. These legal complexities need to be mapped and addressed holistically in order to make good on the promises of a circular energy system – using resources that are currently discarded – with a view to addressing the urgent climate and energy crises that the EU faces; improving human, animal and plant life; and allowing for a more sustainable society while maintaining quality of life.

The regulatory reforms to create a new EU energy market, including a circular energy system, are mostly aimed at amending energy sector regulation. The reforms fail to consider the need for legal and policy coherence with other crucial sectors, such as waste, agriculture, food and forestry, and with non-sectoral legal-economic instruments that are also crucial to the failure or success of redesigning markets, such as financing, state aid, and carbon trade schemes. In order to better equip scholars and practitioners in the field for this task, this edited volume is structured around three topics, each with overlapping and interacting challenges.

Part I of the volume – *From Waste to Biofuels and Biogas* – considers the interactions, intended and unintended, between EU waste, agricultural, food and forestry law and policy (Chapters 2, 3, 4 and 5 respectively). Waste-to-energy (W2E) implicates at least three areas of EU policies: energy union, environmental policy (especially air quality regulation and climate

---

67 Biomethane Action Plan (n 65) 35.
68 ibid 40.
69 REPowerEU (n 63) 8.
70 ibid.

change law), and waste regulation.[71] The key sectors to this transition – agriculture, food and forestry – all deal with waste in different ways. The current environmental and sectoral regulations applying to these industries do not envisage, and often actively discourage, circularity within the production process. Moreover, an effective circular energy system depends on strengthening cooperation between supranational, national, regional and local authorities to enable the reuse of biowaste, biofuel and biogas production and consumption. For instance, while the management of organic waste usually is a concern for local authorities, the definition of biowaste falls under national authorities' competence, and the classification of biofuels and biogas that counts towards the MSs' renewable energy targets is established at the supranational level. The compatibility of these legal frameworks is fundamental to our ability to 'fuel' the transition to a circular energy system.

Part II of the volume – *The Use of Biofuel and Biogas in the Circular Energy System* – focuses on how, when and by whom the energy sources created from biowaste can become part of the EU's energy mix. Differences between the needs and capabilities of the heating, power and transportation sectors are discussed (Chapters 6 and 7). It also reflects on the impact of greenhouse gas (GHG) emission monitoring schemes, in particular regarding methane emissions, to discourage the use of natural gas and other fuels and encourage their replacement by renewable energy sources (Chapter 8).

Part III of the volume – *Cross-Sectoral Issues* – considers a range of legal instruments issues that impact, directly and indirectly, the financing of the circular energy system through taxation (Chapter 9), EU financing (Chapter 10) and state aid (Chapter 11). It also considers the role of support schemes and Guarantees of Origin with respect to these renewable energy sources (Chapter 12).

The final chapter (Chapter 13) concludes by reflecting on the areas of conflict or incompatibility that result from these discussions of specific law and policy areas related to the circular energy system.

LEGISLATION

Directive 2018/2001 on the promotion of the use of energy from renewable sources [2018] OJ L328/82 ('RED II')

Directive 2008/98/EC on waste and repealing certain Directives [2008] OJ L312/3 ('Waste Framework Directive', 'WFD')

Regulation (EU) 2018/1999 on the Governance of the Energy Union and Climate Action, amending Regulations (EC) 663/2009 and (EC) 715/2009, Directives 94/22/EC,

---

71 J Malinauskaite and H Jouhar, 'The Trilemma of Waste-to-Energy: A Multi-Purpose Solution' 129 Energy Policy 636.

98/70/EC, 2009/31/EC, 2009/73/EC, 2010/31/EU, 2012/27/EU and 2013/30/EU, Directives 2009/119/EC and (EU) 2015/652 and repealing Regulation (EU) 525/2013 [2018] OJ L328/1.

CASES

Sabo and Others v Parliament and Council (Case T-141/19) ECLI:EU:T:2020:179 [2020] ECR I-179

PART I

From Waste to Biofuels and Biogas

2. Waste in the circular energy system

Geert van Calster

I. INTRODUCTION: WASTE, WASTE RECOVERY AND THE CIRCULAR ECONOMY

Waste management operations currently play an important role in renewable energy generation. Energy recovery was an early by-product of European Union (EU) waste law, and in more modern engineering environments the creation of energy from biodegradable waste is seen as an advanced way of killing the two birds of waste management and renewable energy creation with one stone. This chapter generally introduces the most important features of the waste management market, and its regulation, with a particular focus on those elements which have an impact on energy policy.

This chapter therefore firstly summarily recalls the overall historic economic rationale that underlies waste management operations (Section II). It then looks at the impact of the EU's waste hierarchy on circularity (Section III); and discusses the impact of waste streams and their regulation under the EU's Waste Shipment Regulation and the International 'Basel' Convention (Section IV). It does not as such discuss the impact of EU energy law 'principles' on waste policies.[1]

'One man's waste is another man's treasure' is an old proverb. That the incineration of waste in particular may yield energy from the produced heat is an old insight. One of the first documented installations recovering such heat in the US goes back to 1898,[2] and in Denmark (in the EU traditionally a Member State (MS) with a high proportion of waste to energy ('W2E') systems) the municipality of Frederiksberg installed its first district heating system fuelled by W2E in 1903.[3] Biodegrading waste as a source of energy is a more recent

---

[1] See Kathleen Garnett and Geert van Calster, 'On Principles of and in EU Energy Law and Policy', 2023.

[2] Lisa Gibson, 'Witnessing a Waste-to-Energy Revival' (n.d.) *Biomass Magazine* https://bit.ly/3vVk2St accessed 10 May 2022.

[3] Heron Kleis and Søren Dalager, *100 Years of Waste Incineration in Denmark* (Babcock Wilcox & Ramboll 2007) https://bit.ly/3kWB3Fy accessed 10 May 2022.

addition to the tools of energy recovery. Biodegradable wastes are then transformed into biogas, the basic ingredient of which is methane (a very potent greenhouse gas). Most often, biogas is then burned in a cogeneration process, and/or after purification it can be injected into the high-methane gas network or converted into hydrogen in a steam reforming process.[4]

If all the waste produced by mankind could be recovered circularly, waste prevention would be less urgent and the circular economy (CE) would be helped enormously. In reality of course this is not currently and probably never can be the case.

Not currently, because many waste streams escape the CE cycle, particularly when this cycle is looked at on a global scale. To take but one problematic waste, macro plastics, these are facing high hurdles for recoverability, even in the EU,[5] and are an urgent environmental, biodiversity and public health problem in many parts of the world.

Not ever, for two main reasons. Firstly, because energy consumed in recycling and recovery associated with CE approaches counts towards the circularity (or not) of the approach. A 'full circle' of design, production, consumption, recovery and/or recycling is almost impossible to achieve given that the CE process will invariably require energy consumption that is 'lost' in the circularity calculation. That is a result of the Second Law of Thermodynamics, essentially leading to regression of the purity of materials, and therefore the infinite repetition of recycling processes is impossible without substantial input from outside the system, for example in the form of energy and/or new materials.[6] Every transition through a material cycle demands energy and creates material losses.[7] Further, the renewable character of the energy resources used in the CE is a precondition for the CE to be truly 'sustainable'. This suggests that while mere energy reduction in the circular cycle would contribute to circularity, only the use of renewable energy can attribute to CE's sustainability. This aspect of the CE has not received much attention.

---

[4] Marta Szyba and Jerzy Mikulik, 'Energy Production from Biodegradable Waste as an Example of the Circular Economy' (2022) 15(4) Energies 1269 https://www.mdpi.com/1996-1073/15/4/1269.

[5] Thomas J. de Römph and Geert van Calster, 'REACH in a Circular Economy: The Obstacles for Plastics Recyclers and Regulators' (2018) 27 RECIEL – Review of European, Comparative and International Environmental Law 267.

[6] Karel Van Acker and others, 'Circular Economy' (2016) Position Paper working group Metaforum, KU Leuven https://bit.ly/3hWlhcg 10.

[7] ibid 30.

II. THE HISTORIC RATIONALE OF EU (AND INTERNATIONAL) WASTE LAW AND ITS DEVELOPMENT IN CONTEXT

EU law on waste management is prolific, has an important business impact and ranks historically among the earlier pieces of EU environmental law.[8] A common thread running through it is recognising waste as a commodity and as an important source of energy. Core EU waste law and policy aims at creating a more competitive EU market for recycling and recovery, using waste as a resource to relieve the pressure on finite raw materials. Waste prevention, too, ranks high in waste policy priorities.

Historically, the EU's waste management approach was inspired to a considerable degree by the Organisation for Economic Co-operation and Development (OECD). The bottom line of EU waste law as well as of OECD interest is to combine a healthy business interest in the sector with the need to ensure proper environmental protection. The EU is very much of the view that were business to lose interest in waste management, local authorities in particular would be overwhelmed by the logistic and financial strains involved.[9]

This approach has led to a visible, if gradual, change in the economic operators active in the sector. In particular, most MSs have gradually moved away from a first-tier role of public authorities in waste processing – these typically retain responsibility for waste collection. Moreover, while in most MSs up until the 1990s, a wide variety of companies operated in the waste sector, this has now been substantially reduced to a more limited number of, inevitably larger, operators. This has made the sector on the whole more professional than was previously the case, with large upfront capital investment required for many waste processing facilities.[10]

The 2005 Thematic Strategy for the prevention and recycling of waste[11] crucially influenced current Commission thinking on waste management strategy. Of note are first of all its suggested emphasis on materials, rather than on specific streams of waste. For instance, the Commission argued that the EU's

---

8 For more detail and references see Geert van Calster, *EU Waste Law* (2nd edn, Oxford University Press 2015).

9 Geert van Calster and Leonie Reins, *EU Environmental Law* (Edward Elgar 2017) 264 (second edition forthcoming 2023).

10 See *inter alia* Geert de Clercq, 'Suez Eyes Consolidation in the EU Waste Industry', *Reuters* (31 July 2013).

11 European Commission, 'Taking Sustainable Use of Resources Forward – A Thematic Strategy on the Prevention and Recycling of Waste' COM (2005) 666. Some might suggest its numbering was a bad omen for its future success in tackling the challenges of waste management.

Packaging and Packaging Waste Directive[12] applied to at the time about 5 per cent of all waste in the EU, and the End-of-Life Vehicles Directive[13] just 1 per cent. Yet a disproportionate amount of time went into the negotiation and subsequent amendments of each of these, and of other 'sectoral' Directives. Focusing on the waste *materials* (PVC, say, or glass, regardless of whether it ends up in a building, a notebook, a solar panel or a beer bottle) would therefore seem to be of some value. Conversely, however, the Commission itself indicated that a shift of focus towards materials rather than types of waste would endanger the concept of producer responsibility. Producer responsibility acts as a strong signal in the marketplace, by focusing on an identifiable group within the waste stream. Moreover, a waste streams approach is attractive from the point of view of 'knowing who to talk to' when designing waste regulation. It is fair to say that despite the waste materials suggestions made, the focus of the regulatory effort has remained on waste streams.

A further point to note is the Commission's taste for identifying recycling targets per material to be set not at the national level but at the EU level. This should enable the recycling industry to operate flexibly in a pan-European recycling area. Commentators however feared that should the approach entail the EU as a whole reaching certain targets, rather than each MS individually, this may tempt the environmentally weaker MSs to withdraw from the stricter obligations without fear of backlash. Moreover, it is argued by some that the approach would also lead to increased trade in waste, in particular to MSs with weaker standards for the recycling of waste. The EU continues to struggle with this issue. On waste trade, too, signals have been mixed since 2005. The most recent emphasis in that area, as I also recall below, is on making waste trade within the EU on the whole more flexible.[14]

The Commission also expressed a strong preference for economic instruments to reach the targets put forward. The European Commission was thinking, for example, of tradable waste rights. An undisputed, inevitable consequence of the focus on economic instruments is higher charges for the landfill of waste. This continuous presentation of a focus on economic instruments as being 'new', in 2005 but much beyond that date, is a clear illustration that the EU struggles to adopt the kind of measures that truly internalise the environmental costs of waste management processing. The option of tradable waste rights, however, was generally received as being too radical in 2005 and the idea has not been heard of since.

---

[12] Directive 94/62/EC on packaging and packaging waste [1994] OJ L365/10, as amended.

[13] Directive 2000/53/EC on end-of life vehicles [2000] OJ L269/34, as amended.

[14] European Commission, 'Proposal on Shipments of Waste and Amending Regulations (EU) 1257/2013 and (EU) 2020/1056' COM (2021) 709.

In the 2003 Communication the Commission also announced that it wanted to investigate how the then IPPC Directive[15] may have been employed to facilitate more harmonised recycling techniques throughout the EU, and that Directive's successor, the Industrial Emissions Directive 2010/75,[16] includes stricter standards on emissions for waste processing, however it does not as such address stricter recycling requirements.

Of high relevance in this field are the Best Available Techniques Reference (BREF) Guides, which are completed by the European IPPC Bureau. The general assumption is that BREF help create a 'level playing field' in the European recycling market, and avoid a 'race to the bottom' in which environmentally less ambitious MSs would employ weak EU standards to attract recycling industries. Comments on this approach have been supportive overall, and the IPPC Bureau has indeed resorted to issuing a number of BREFs in the waste management area.[17] The IPPC process as such is not without its problems. Civil society is almost invariably underrepresented in the development process, and there is a serious risk of 'locking in' existing, incumbent technology, to the detriment of new approaches, for example in recycling.

Any substantial EU role in the prevention of waste has always been optimistic. MSs have always been very reluctant to accept much of an EU role on waste prevention, and to this day it is a hurdle which the Commission finds very difficult to overcome.

Progress towards the objectives set out in the strategy was reviewed in 2011 when the Commission adopted a 'Report on the Thematic Strategy'[18] and a staff working document.[19] The Commission concluded that the main objectives of the strategy remained valid. It underlined that it has played an important role in guiding policy development and that significant progress has been achieved in the improvement and simplification of legislation and the establishment and diffusion of key concepts such as the waste hierarchy and life-cycle thinking, alongside the shifting of focus onto waste prevention, the coordination of efforts to improve knowledge, and setting new European collection and recycling targets.

---

15 In the meantime replaced with the industrial emissions Directive (Directive 2010/75/EU on Industrial Emissions (integrated pollution prevention and control), [2010] OJ L334/159 ('IED').

16 ibid.

17 They may be consulted via http://eippcb.jrc.ec.europa.eu/reference/.

18 European Commission, 'Report on the Thematic Strategy on the Prevention and Recycling of Waste' COM (2011) 13.

19 European Commission, 'Commission staff working document accompanying the Communication on the Thematic Strategy on the Prevention and Recycling of Waste' SEC (2011) 70 http://goo.gl/keF4Bl/ accessed 26 July 2022.

Looking ahead, the targets and goals of the EU in terms of resource efficiency and waste strategy are captured by a variety of high-profile policy documents. These include the 7th Environmental Action Plan ('Living well, within the limits of our planet');[20] the Europe 2020 Strategy;[21] the Roadmap for Resource Efficiency;[22] and the June 2014 Communication 'Towards a Circular Economy: A Zero Waste Programme for Europe',[23] which was followed up by a 2015 CE Action Plan that included 54 action points of which four were legislative proposals.[24]

The General Union Environment Action Programme to 2020[25] highlights a second priority objective, the shift towards an economy that is resource efficient. That package implied the amendment of a wide range of secondary legislation, in particular the Waste Framework Directive; the Packaging Waste and Landfill Directives; and the Waste from Electrical and Electronic Equipment (WEEE) Directive.

III. IMPACT OF THE EU'S WASTE HIERARCHY ON CIRCULARITY

Under the initial 'waste hierarchy',[26] that is the preferred sequence of waste management approaches, MSs were to take measures to encourage:

- First, the prevention or reduction of waste production and its harmfulness (mainly through R&D);
- Second, the recovery of waste by means of recycling, reuse or reclamation of any other process with a view to extracting secondary raw materials; and
- Third, the use of waste as a source of energy.

The currently applicable hierarchy in the Waste Framework Directive (WFD)[27] has a slightly different emphasis, as shown in Article 4:

---

[20] Decision 1386/2013/EU on a General Union Environment Action Programme to 2020 – 'Living well, within the limits of our planet' [2013] OJ L354/171.

[21] European Commission 'Europe 2020: A Strategy for Smart, Sustainable and Inclusive Growth' COM (2010) 2020.

[22] European Commission, 'Roadmap to a Resource Efficient Europe' COM (2011) 571.

[23] European Commission, 'Towards a Circular Economy: A Zero Waste Programme for Europe' COM (2014) 398.

[24] European Commission 'First Circular Economy Action Plan' (environment.ec.europa.eu, n.d.) https://bit.ly/3wfvp84 accessed 12 May 2022.

[25] Decision 1386/2013 (n 20).

[26] Directive 91/156/EEC amending Directive 75/442/EEC on waste [1991] OJ L78/32.

[27] Directive 2008/98/EC on waste and repealing certain Directives [2008] OJ L312/3 ('Waste Framework Directive', 'WFD').

1. The following waste hierarchy shall apply as a priority order in waste prevention and management legislation and policy:
   (a) prevention;
   (b) preparing for re-use;
   (c) recycling;
   (d) other recovery, e.g. energy recovery; and
   (e) disposal.
2. When applying the waste hierarchy referred to in paragraph 1, Member States shall take measures to encourage the options that deliver the best overall environmental outcome. This may require specific waste streams departing from the hierarchy where this is justified by life-cycle thinking on the overall impacts of the generation and management of such waste.

   Member States shall ensure that the development of waste legislation and policy is a fully transparent process, observing existing national rules about the consultation and involvement of citizens and stakeholders.

   Member States shall take into account the general environmental protection principles of precaution and sustainability, technical feasibility and economic viability, protection of resources as well as the overall environmental, human health, economic and social impacts, in accordance with Articles 1 and 13.

Waste prevention is a long-running European Commission ambition and has been emphasised again in the CE package. MSs however are likely to continue to resist EU initiatives in this area which are too forceful. At a more fundamental level, and given the aforementioned Second Law of Thermodynamics which entails no economy is ever truly circular, the most far-reaching waste prevention method is production and consumption prevention. Putting it colloquially, stuff not produced is stuff not wasted. At first sight there seems little the EU can do to encourage this systemic shift to simply less production, however in practice of course it can, and does, interfere at this level. EU initiatives to prevent food waste,[28] for instance, as well as the EU's drive towards a right to repair[29] (meaning purchased items will last longer) and, at a more radical level, current plans to restrict the marketing of hazardous chemicals to those with an 'essential use' … each attempt to turn the Club of Rome's 'limits to growth' analysis into practical reality.[30]

Article 3(15) of the WFD defines *waste recovery* operations as 'any operation the principal result of which is waste serving a useful purpose by replacing other materials which would otherwise have been used to fulfil

---

[28] European Commission, 'Food Waste' (food.ec.europa.eu, n.d.) https://ec.europa.eu/food/safety/food-waste_en/ accessed 17 May 2022. Note the EU does not have any dedicated 'food waste' law, rather anchors to addressing the issues in a variety of action points.

[29] The European Commission has committed to putting forward specific legislation on the right to repair in the course of 2022.

[30] Club of Rome, *Limits to Growth* (1972) https://bit.ly/3yIMBnU/ accessed 13 May 2022.

a particular function, or waste being prepared to fulfil that function, in the plant or in the wider economy'. This definition is based on the Court's case-law (notably *Abfall*[31] and *Commission v Germany*[32]). According to the European Commission's Waste Directive Guidelines,[33] the new recovery definition was also aimed at facilitating the classification of waste incinerators with efficient energy generation as a recovery operation, since the substitution can take place not just in the plant where waste is being treated, but also in the 'wider economy'. The currently applicable definition therefore arguably has been developed in direct support of W2E, seeing as most W2E plants use, as their main resource, waste that originates elsewhere.

Waste *disposal* is defined negatively only, namely as not being recovery: Article 3(19) of the WFD: disposal 'means any operation which is not recovery even where the operation has as a secondary consequence the reclamation of substances or energy. Annex I sets out a non-exhaustive list of disposal operations;'. A noteworthy inclusion in the list of other recovery operations are highly energy efficient municipal waste incineration facilities dedicated to the processing of such waste only. This, too, is the result of the Court of Justice of the European Union (CJEU) case-law which wanted to discourage the inclusion, in recovery targets, of installations purely built to process waste, even if they also recovered the released heat by way of energy recovery.[34]

The waste hierarchy is not merely a policy gismo. It is a relevant factor in local planning decisions, usually following the national waste management plans. The hierarchy is also used in the roll-out of national tax measures, again with reference to national plans: waste disposal tends to be taxed more highly than waste recovery. Finally, the hierarchy is also very relevant in assessing applications for waste trade, as I discuss briefly below.

IV. THE IMPACT OF WASTE TRADE[35]

Common to many waste regimes is some form of restriction on the movement of waste, particularly hazardous waste. Trade in waste, particularly from developed countries to developing countries, became an issue in the

---

31 Case C-6/00 *Abfall Service* [2002] ECR I-1961.

32 Case C-228/00 *Commission v Germany* [2003] ECR I-1439.

33 European Commission – Directorate-General Environment, 'Guidance on the Interpretation of Key Provisions of Directive 2008/98/EC on Waste' (2012) https://bit.ly/3PRU75m/ accessed 26 July 2022, heading 1.4.5.

34 In particular Case C-116/01 *SITA Eco Service*, ECLI:EU:C:2003:193 [2003].

35 Adapted from Natalie Jones and Geert van Calster, 'Waste Regulation' in Jorge E. Viñuales and Emma Lees (eds), *Oxford Handbook of Comparative Environmental Law* (Oxford University Press 2019) 607–625.

1980s.[36] Following the 1989 adoption of the Convention on the Control of Transboundary Movements of Hazardous Wastes and Their Disposal (Basel Convention),[37] many states introduced export and import restrictions. In addition, there are regional conventions which prohibit, rather than merely restrict, hazardous waste exports and imports. Furthermore, some systems have controls on the internal movement of waste, not merely movement across borders.

Prior to the Basel Convention's adoption, early impetus was provided by the United States, the EU and the OECD. In the United States, the Resource Conservation and Recovery Act was amended in 1984 to provide that exports of hazardous waste were prohibited, unless the United States provided notification in advance of shipment to the receiving country, which in turn consented to accept the hazardous waste.[38] The OECD adopted this 'notification and consent' approach to govern trade in hazardous waste between OECD countries, and later extended it to cover hazardous waste trade between OECD and non-OECD countries.[39] It also prohibited the movement of hazardous waste to a non-OECD country unless the waste was 'directed to an adequate disposal facility in that country'. Similarly, the EU adopted the notification and consent approach in 1984.[40]

The Basel Convention takes the approach of regulating, rather than prohibiting, the movement of hazardous waste across borders.[41] Following the approach adopted by the United States, the EU, and the OECD, there must be full and informed consent by the importing country to each shipment of hazardous waste.[42] The exporting and importing countries must take all appropriate measures to ensure the waste is disposed of in an environmentally

---

36 Alexander Gillespie, *Waste Policy – International Regulation Comparative and Contextual Perspectives* (Edward Elgar 2015) 19.

37 Convention on the Control of Transboundary Movements of Hazardous Wastes and Their Disposal (Basel Convention) (adopted 22 March 1989, entered into force 5 May 1992) 1673 UNTS 126.

38 The Hazardous and Solid Waste Amendments of 1984 [1984] PL 98-616, 98 Stat. 3221.

39 OECD, Decision-Recommendation on Transfrontier Movements of Hazardous Wastes (1 February 1984) C(83)180/FINAL; Resolution on International Co-Operation Concerning Transfrontier Movements of Hazardous Waste (20 June 1985) C(85)100; Decision-Recommendation on Exports of Hazardous Wastes from the OECD Area (5 June 1986) C(86)64/FINAL.

40 Directive 84/631/EEC on Transfrontier Shipment of Hazardous Waste [1984] OJ L 326/31; Now Regulation (EC) 1013/2006 on Shipment of Hazardous Waste [2006] OJ L190/1.

41 Except the general prohibition on the export of hazardous waste to Antarctica: Reg 1013/2006 (n 40), art 4(6).

42 ibid art 4(1).

sound manner.[43] In addition, there are requirements around packing, labelling, tracking, monitoring and insurance coverage.[44] If the terms of the consent are not followed, the waste must be re-imported by the exporting country.[45] The implementation of the Basel Convention can be seen in many domestic systems. In the EU, for instance, Articles 17 to 20 of the WFD require MSs to take action to ensure the traceability of hazardous waste from production to final destination, and of course the EU has a comprehensive Waste Shipments Regulation that covers many aspects of transfrontier waste trade.[46]

In general, movements of waste within states tend to be less regulated. For example, in the EU, shipments within an MS are only required to be subject to a monitoring system,[47] although some of the Union's federal MSs (including Belgium and Germany) have provisions restricting the intra-MS movement of waste. In its most recent initiative to review the Waste Shipments Regulation, the Commission proposes to relax the obstacles to intra-EU waste trade, while at the same time tightening the procedures for extra-EU trade, the latter with a view both to better protect the environment and workers in developing countries in particular, and to ensure that critical materials which can be extracted from waste streams do not leave the EU.[48]

V. CONCLUSION

The encouraging by the EU and other states of W2E systems as an alternative for waste disposal raises specific legal issues with respect to specific types of waste so 'recovered',[49] and has provoked both case-law and regulatory developments, as I outline above. However, in line with the EU's waste hierarchy, the bonus of recovering energy from managing the waste society produces must not distract us from the more fundamental task at hand, which is to prevent the very generation of waste.

---

43 ibid art 4(2)(f), (8).

44 See eg ibid art 4(7)(b).

45 ibid, arts 4(3) and 9(1)–(4).

46 Reg 1013/2006 (n 40).

47 ibid arts 1(5) and 33.

48 Proposal for a Regulation on shipments of waste and amending Regulations (EU) 1257/2013 and (EU) 2020/1056 (n 14).

49 See eg Topi Turunen and Geert van Calster, 'Burning Construction and Dem-olition Waste: An Assessment of the European Waste Hierarchy and Recycling Targets' (2016) 14 Oil, Gas and Energy Law Intelligence 1; and Geert van Calster, 'Waste Management and Climate Change in the EU', in Geert Van Calster and Wim Vandenberghe and Leonie Reins (eds), *Research Handbook on Climate Mitigation Law* (Edward Elgar 2015) 361–372.

EU LEGISLATION

Directive 2000/53/EC on end-of life vehicles [2000] OJ L269/34
Directive 2010/75/EU on industrial emissions (integrated pollution prevention and control) [2010] OJ L334/159 ('IED')
Directive 94/62/EC on packaging and packaging waste [1994] OJ L365/10
Directive 84/631 on Transfrontier Shipment of Hazardous Waste [1984] OJ L 326/31
Directive 91/156/EEC amending Directive 75/442/EEC on waste [1991] OJ L78/32
Regulation (EC) 1013/2006 on shipments of waste [2006] OJ L190/1
Decision 1386/2013/EU on a General Union Environment Action Programme to 2020 – 'Living well, within the limits of our planet' [2013] OJ L354/171
Directive 2008/98/EC on waste and repealing certain Directives [2008] OJ L312/3 ('Waste Framework Directive', 'WFD')

LEGISLATION IN OTHER JURISDICTIONS

OECD, Resolution on International Co-Operation Concerning Transfrontier Movements of Hazardous Waste (20 June 1985) C(85)100
OECD, Decision-Recommendation on Exports of Hazardous Wastes from the OECD Area (5 June 1986) C(86)64/FINAL
OECD, Decision-Recommendation on Transfrontier Movements of Hazardous Wastes (1 February 1984) C(83)180/FINAL
United Nations, Convention on the Control of Transboundary Movements of Hazardous Wastes and Their Disposal (Basel Convention) (adopted 22 March 1989, entered into force 5 May 1992) 1673 UNTS 126
United States, The Hazardous and Solid Waste Amendments of 1984 [1984] PL 98–616, 98 Stat. 3221

CASES

Abfall Service (Case C-6/00) [2002] ECR I-1961.
Commission v Germany (Case C-228/00) [2003] ECR I-1439.
SITA Eco Service (Case C-116/01) ECLI:EU:C:2003:193 [2003]

3. Agricultural waste to biofuel and biogas: law and policy

Mirta Alessandrini, Edwin Alblas, and Lin Batten

I. INTRODUCTION

The European Union (EU) is at the onset of tackling one of the most acute issues in the light of climate change, namely the just and equitable transition from a fossil fuel economy to a low or zero carbon economy.[1] In this endeavour, EU energy policy has set out to favour renewable energy resources not only in its consumption but also its production.[2] Currently, the EU has, in line with the EU Green Deal, set to achieve 32% of its renewable energy target by 2030.[3]

The EU's transition towards a decentralized energy system and the push towards renewable energy has gained an additional impetus through the invasion of Ukraine by Russian forces in early 2022, causing the already steadily increasing fuel prices to soar.[4] These geopolitical developments, together with the consequences of climate change, accentuate the endemic inefficiencies and vulnerabilities of the EU's energy economy, as over 55% of its fuel is imported.[5] The ongoing transition has so far resulted in 22.8% of the EU's

---

1 Thijs Etty and others, 'Energy Transition in a Transnational World – Transnational Environmental Law' (2021) 10 TEL 197.

2 Jon Birger Skjærseth, 'Towards a European Green Deal: The Evolution of EU Climate and Energy Policy Mixes' (2021) 21 IEA: Politics, Law and Economics 25.

3 Eurostat, 'Archive: Agri-environmental indicator – renewable energy produ-ction' (2018) https://ec.europa.eu/eurostat/statistics-explained/index.php?title=Archive:Agri-environmental_indicator_-_renewable_energy_production/ accessed 10 August 2022.

4 Douglas Fraser, 'The Effect of War on Food Prices' (*BBC News* 7 March 2022) https://www.bbc.com/news/uk-scotland-60644376/ accessed 10 August 2022.

5 Eurostat, 'Energy Statistics – an overview' (2023) https://ec.europa.eu/eurostat/statistics-explained/index.php?title=Energy_statistics_-_an_overview accessed 5 September 2023.

energy consumption being derived from renewable sources in 2021, with varying degrees of commitment from the EU's Member States (MSs).[6] Of this percentage, 8% is derived from solid biofuels, and an additional 8% from other renewable energy resources such as liquid and gaseous biofuels.

The latter percentage indicates the central role of the agricultural sector in biofuel production, or growing energy crops used for ethanol and biodiesel. A recent Eurostat report, for instance, found that crop-based biofuels including renewable ethanol made up no less than 60% of the renewables used in the transport sector.[7] Through the ripple effect of the increasing demand for biofuels, however, land traditionally used for food production increasingly competes with the production of energy crops used to generate biofuels, resulting in an 'indirect land-use change' (ILUC). ILUC is a contentious and nearly immeasurable concept which is at the core of a political and societal debate on the importance of yield for food production versus using land and resources to meet the energy demand.[8] This is also reflected in the EU's political agenda, as the new Energy Directive has set the target to eliminate the consumption of energy-derived food and feed crops in the EU by 2030.[9]

This debate is largely fuelled by the fact that agriculture, as the most dominant mode of land use in Europe, has significant influence on the environment through its use of natural resources, fuel, and chemicals.[10] The importance of engaging sustainable land use practices by farmers for attaining climate

---

[6] Eurostat, 'Renewable Energy Statistics' (2023) https://ec.europa.eu/eurostat/statistics-explained/index.php?title=Renewable_energy_statistics accessed 5 September 2023; Eurostat, 'SHARES Summary Results (2021 data)' (2021) https://ec.europa.eu/eurostat/web/energy/database/additional-data#Short%20assessment%20of%20renewable%20energy%20sources%20(SHARES) accessed 5 September 2023.

[7] See Epure, 'Crop-based Biofuels Still Make Up the Majority of Renewables in EU Transport' (2022) https://www.epure.org/news/crop-based-biofuels-still-make-up-the-majority-of-renewables-in-eu-transport/ accessed 5 September 2023. It is important to note here, however, that fossil fuels constitute the energy source of 92.5% of transport with a reduction of a mere 3.1% since 2020. This means that the majority of MSs have not yet met their legal obligations to ensure at least 10% of renewables in transport. See Biofuels International, 'Crops-based Biofuels Made Up Majority of Renewables in EU Transport, Report Reveals' (2022) https://biofuels-news.com/news/crop-based-biofuels-made-up-majority-of-renewables-in-eu-transport-report-reveals/ accessed 10 August 2022.

[8] Ane Katharina Paarup Meyer and others, 'Future European Biogas: Animal Manure, Straw and Grass Potentials for a Sustainable European Biogas Production' (2018) 111 Biomass and Bioenergy 154.

[9] Directive 2018/2001 on the promotion of the use of energy from renewable sources [2018] OJ L328/82 ('RED II') art 29(2).

[10] Guy Pe'er and others, 'A Greener Path for the EU Common Agricultural Policy' (2019) 365 Science 449.

objectives has been widely recognized in the literature, focusing on increasing carbon sequestration in soils and forests as well as promoting bioenergy as a substitute for fossil fuels.[11] In addition, there is increasing attention in the literature on the shift in focus from the use of energy crops for fuel to the use of waste streams for the generation of energy. In this context, it is argued, biofuel derived from agricultural waste such as crop residues and manure can be a potential resource for biofuel.[12]

Despite the increasing importance of agricultural waste for the generation of biofuel, thus far the role and potential of the EU's circular energy and agricultural law and policy in steering this move have received little attention in the literature.[13] This in both in terms of their overlap and synergies, but also in their disconnect and perhaps contesting provisions. This brings us to the research question of this chapter: what are the convergences and divergences of the Common Agricultural Policy (CAP) and the Renewable Energy Directive (RED II) in relation to using agricultural waste and manure for bioenergy production? Answering this research question will contribute to the understanding of the role of agricultural waste for biofuel within the two frameworks, and on how to jointly leverage these frameworks to improve the use of the agricultural waste streams towards a more circular energy economy.

This chapter is outlined as follows: firstly, Section II will further discuss the development and current situation of the role of the agricultural sector towards the production of biofuels, including the use of agricultural waste. Thereafter, Section III will outline the legal framework related to the production of biofuels, in particular RED II and the CAP. Both legislations will be extrapolated in relation to the role of the agricultural sector in biofuel production, how it has developed over time, and what its prospects are in terms of capitalizing agricultural waste streams in the future. Then Section IV will contrast the frameworks using legal comparative analysis. Finally, Section V will conclude and summarize the findings of the previous sections.

---

11 Alan Matthews, 'How to Move from our Current Land Use Structure to One that is Compatible with our Climate Targets' (*Irish Independent* 2018) https://www.independent.ie/business/farming/comment/alan-matthews-how-to-move-from-our-current-land-use-structure-to-one-that-is-compatible-with-our-climate-targets-37567086.html/ accessed 10 August 2022.

12 Meyer and others (n 8).

13 For an exception see Davide Viaggi, 'Bioeconomy and the Common Agricultural Policy: Will a Strategy in Search of Policies Meet a Policy in Search of Strategies?' (2018) 7 Biobased and Applied Economics Journal 179.

II. BIOFUEL AND BIOGAS FROM AGRICULTURAL WASTE

The use of biofuels for energy started in the early 1980s and was thereafter stimulated by the policy and regulatory agricultural frameworks of the EU, which will be elaborated upon in Section III of this chapter. The development of biofuels is most commonly referred to as the 'three generations' of biofuel. The first generation of biofuels is derived from food crops to produce bioethanol, biodiesel, and oil. The main food crops used for this purpose are cereals, maize, sugar beet and cane, rapeseed, and sunflowers as these stabilize the digestion process. The second generation of biofuels focuses on feedstock, lignocellulosic biomass, agricultural waste, forest waste, and municipal solid wastes. The third and last generation of biofuels focuses on the use of algae and microbes for the generation of energy.[14]

In particular, the first generation of biofuels sparked a political debate on the priorities of our land and other natural resources such as water or soil, as the demand for energy crops is drastically increasing.[15] Arable land for food and feed is scarce and is subject to various environmental pressures such as soil erosion, contamination, decline in soil fertility, and climate change, further reducing the amount of arable land available for cultivation. An increase in the demand for food and decrease in available land has been associated with rising food prices, putting European food systems at risk.[16]

Substituting areas of arable land to produce energy crops has not only increased the pressure on agricultural land by replacing land used for food and feed to land used for biofuels. It has also resulted in the expansion of cultivated land into protected natural areas, encroaching on natural habitats in Europe, threatening precious ecosystems such as permanent grassland, wetlands and peatlands, and areas of high biodiversity and carbon stock.[17] The eradication through cultivation of these natural habitats, in particular peatland – a carbon sink – and the deforestation of our natural woodlands, has emitted greenhouse

---

[14] Rajkamal Kesharwania and others, 'Moving Second Generation Biofuel Manufacturing Forward: Investigating Economic Viability and Environmental Sust-ainability Considering Two Strategies for Supply Chain Restructuring' (2019) 242 Applied Energy 1467.

[15] Elena Tamburini and others, 'Is Bioenergy Truly Sustainable When Land-Use-Change (LUC) Emissions Are Accounted for? The Case-Study of Biogas from Agricultural Biomass in Emilia-Romagna Region, Italy' (2020) 12 Sustainability 1.

[16] Jennifer Clapp, Peter Newell, and Zoe W Brent, 'The Global Political Economy of Climate Change, Agriculture and Food Systems' (2018) 45 The Journal of Peasant Studies 80.

[17] Meyer and others (n 8).

gases and caused a significant decline in biodiversity.[18] In this, most, if not all, the benefits from the reduction of fossil fuel use is offset.[19] Both the food-to-fuel debate as well as the expansion of agricultural land into natural habitats is referred to as 'indirect land-use change' (ILUC).

The metrics to accurately measure ILUC are limited due to the complex influence from economic and political factors involved, though it should be dealt with accordingly to reduce greenhouse gas (GHG) emissions.[20] Alternatives are emerging, however, including gearing agriculture-based bioenergy production towards agricultural waste, rather than crops – especially regarding crop residue and manure.

Agricultural waste is a major component of lignocellulose biomass – a more sustainable alternative to conventional energy sources – and can be used as a source for the generation of biofuels, especially for bioethanol, biobutanol, biogas, biohydrogen, and biodiesel.[21] Agricultural waste does not only consist of residues from cultivation but also those originating from the processing of agri-products, and managing livestock. Lignocellulosic waste includes grasses, sawdust, wood chips, rice, wheat, corn straw, and sugarcane bagasse, amongst others.[22] Some academics have estimated the total crop residues in Europe as amounting to 94.4 million tonnes of dry mass across the 27 MSs, which has the potential of being used towards bioenergy production.[23]

In addition to the use of crop residues, the use of animal manure for the production of bioenergy is also gathering momentum. While the excess of environmental pollution within the livestock sector, e.g. methane and other GHG emissions, and nitrogen contamination amongst others, is significant, this could be mitigated by leveraging animal manure for bioenergy produc-

---

18 Yasar Dahman and others, 'Biofuels: Their Characteristics and Analysis' in Verma Deepak and others (eds), *Biomass, Biopolymer-Based Materials, and Bioenergy* (Woodhead Publishing 2019).

19 Tamburini and others (n 15).

20 Meyer and others (n 8); Nicolae Scarlatt and others, 'Future Role of Bioenergy' (2019) 15 Environmental Development 3.

21 Deepak Panpatte and Yogeshvari Jhala, 'Agricultural Waste: A Suitable Source for Biofuel Production' in Ali Asghar Rastegari, Ajar Nath Yadav, and Arti Gupta (eds), *Prospects of Renewable Bioprocessing in Future Energy Systems* (Springer International Publishing 2019).

22 ibid.

23 Stephanie Searle and Christopher Malins, 'Waste and Residue Availability for Advanced Biofuel Production in EU Member States' (2016) 89 Biomass and Bioenergy 2.

tion.[24] Meyer, Ehimen, and Nielsen estimated that the EU produces 83–122 Mt per year – all suitable for biofuel production.[25]

Another possibility explored in practice and literature is the use of phytoremediation by energy crops. In short, phytoremediation is a holistic approach which can remediate contaminated soil by taking up heavy metals and other pollutants from the ground and storing them in certain plants which are cultivated on this land. In 2011, the European Environment Agency identified 342,000 contaminated sites across Europe, while estimating an additional 2.2 million potentially contaminated sites in 2011.[26] Managing this contaminated land has cost Europe €6.5 billion per year. Additionally, any crop produced on this land would not be suitable for human nor animal consumption due to its contamination, but would be able to be used for biofuel production.[27] Pandey, Bajpai, and Singh have identified four types of energy crops adept at filtering the soil, thereby reclaiming arable land while creating biomass for biofuel production, and also acting as a potential carbon sink.[28] Experimental sites are already in place to create the infrastructure necessary to make such production feasible.[29] This technology and its generation of biofuels could also use the technique of pyrolysis – the incineration of biomass from which energy is not only generated but its product is biochar, a fertilizer and carbon stock for agricultural soils.[30] The capitalization of these alternatives can only be scaled by leveraging law and regulatory frameworks more broadly for a positive change in energy transition. The following section will outline the relevant legal framework set to regulate the production and consumption of bioenergy in the EU.

III. THE LEGAL FRAMEWORK

This section sets out the legal framework that connects the EU's circular energy system with the agriculture sector. Specifically, it considers the convergences

---

24 Andrew Green, 'Agricultural Waste and Pollution' in Daniel A Vallero and Valerie Schulman (eds), *Waste: A Handbook for Management* (Academic Press 2019).

25 Scarlatt and others (n 20).

26 European Environment Agency (EEA), 'Progress in Management of Contaminated Sites' (2022) https://www.eea.europa.eu/data-and-maps/indicators/progress-in-management-of-contaminated-sites-3/assessment accessed 10 August 2022.

27 ibid.

28 Vimal C Pandey and others, 'Energy Crops in Sustainable Phytoremediation' (2016) 54 Renewable and Sustainable Energy Reviews 58.

29 Phy2Climate (n.d.) https://www.phy2climate.eu/ accessed 10 August 2021.

30 Jechan Lee and others, 'Pyrolysis Process of Agricultural Waste Using CO2 for Waste Management, Energy Recovery, and Biochar Fabrication' (2017) 185 Applied Energy 214.

and divergences of the measures in the Renewable Energy Directive (RED II) and the Common Agriculture Policy (CAP). In line with the overarching research question, the focus is on the use of agricultural waste and manure for biofuel production, as contrasted with the production of crops for biofuel generation. As a final point of notice, one potentially relevant candidate in this legal analysis, namely the Waste Framework Directive (WFD), has been left outside of the consideration here. This is because Article 2(f) of this Directive states that agricultural materials used for the production of energy are excluded from the scope of the Directive. This includes not only crops intended for biofuel production, but also crop residues and animal manure.[31] This exclusion means the agricultural waste usage for biofuel production does not have to adhere to the rules laid out by the WFD – such as the 'waste hierarchy' – and could therefore have more freedom in its priority of use.[32]

A. The 2018 Renewable Energy Directive (RED II) and Bioenergy

The ratification of the Paris Agreement,[33] and the EU policy framework for climate and energy for the period 2020 to 2030 have influenced the directionality and composition of the European Commission's approach towards the use of renewable energy. In this context, RED II[34] – as part of the Clean Energy for All Europeans package[35] – aims at decarbonizing the EU's energy system and ensuring the positioning of the EU as a global leader in renewables. As aforementioned, The EU is set to achieve 32% of its renewable energy target by 2030 with a clause for a possible upwards revision by 2023, up to 45%.[36]

The shift from the original legal framework on renewable fuels for transport, governed by Directive 2003/30 on the promotion of the use of biofuels or

[31] Directive 2008/98/EC on waste and repealing certain Directives [2008] OJ L3/12 ('Waste Framework Directive', 'WFD'), art 2(f).

[32] Madhura Rao, Aalt Bast, and Alie de Boer, 'Food Waste to Biogas and Biofuel: Law and Policy' in this volume.

[33] Council Decision (EU) 2016/1841 on the conclusion, on behalf of the European Union, of the Paris Agreement adopted under the United Nations Framework Convention on Climate Change [2016] OJ L282/1.

[34] RED II (n 9).

[35] European Commission – Directorate-General for Energy, 'Clean energy for all Europeans' (Publications Office of the European Union 2019) https://energy.ec.europa.eu/topics/energy-strategy/clean-energy-all-europeans-package_en.

[36] European Commission, '"Fit for 55": delivering the EU's 2030 Climate Target on the way to climate neutrality' COM (2021) 550 final.

other renewable fuels for transport,[37] to 2009/28 (RED I)[38] has determined the increase of the 5.75% target of renewables used for transport[39] to at least 10% by the end of 2020.[40] A pivotal change in the EU policy on circular energy relating to biofuel was carried out by Directive 2018/2001 (RED II) in 2018. The ambitious environmental goals set at European level to achieve zero net carbon emissions by 2050 have been further translated into a set of measures gathered under this Directive.[41] Entered into force in January 2021 and repealing the previous legislation on the matter (RED I), RED II sets up a new legal framework aimed at enhancing the development of renewable energy across all sectors of the EU economy.[42] Below, it will be further examined if and how RED II advocates the use of agricultural waste and animal manure as a source of renewable energy over the production of energy crops. Moreover, this section will examine the effectiveness of the sustainability criteria and the ILUC impact embedded in RED II.

1. Biofuel in the Renewable Energy Directive

In the past decades in the EU, due to the steady decrease of income from food crops, several investments made by farmers have shifted to massive conversion of grasslands and prime agricultural land into land for energy crops.[43] With respect to biofuel production in the agricultural domain, one of the objectives of RED II is to support the development and trade of high-tech alternative fuels and, in doing so, redesign the space taken up by biofuel crops in this sector.[44] RED II increased the overall binding EU target for renewable energy sources consumption from 27% to 32% by 2030,[45] involving the electricity, heating

---

37 Directive 2003/30/EC on the promotion of the use of biofuels or other renewable fuels for transport [2003] OJ L123/42.

38 Directive 2009/28/EC on the promotion of the use of energy from renewable sources and amending and subsequently repealing Directives 2001/77/EC and 2003/30/EC [2009] OJ L140/16 ('RED I').

39 Dir 2003/30 (n 37) art 3(1).

40 RED I (n 38) art 3(4).

41 RED II (n 9).

42 RED I (n 38); Directive (EU) 2015/1513 amending Directive 98/70/EC relating to the quality of petrol and diesel fuels and amending Directive 2009/28/EC on the promotion of the use of energy from renewable sources [2015] OJ L239/1 and Council Directive 2013/18/EU on the promotion of the use of energy from renewable sources [2013] OJ L158/230.

43 Tamburini and others (n 15).

44 International Council on Clean Transportation, 'The European Commission's Renewable Energy Proposal for 2030' (2017) https://theicct.org/sites/default/files/publications/RED%20II_ICCT_Policy-Update_vF_jan2017.pdf accessed 10 August 2022.

45 RED II (n 9) art 3(1).

and cooling, and transportation sectors. The Directive also promotes a pivotal role for MSs in this energy transition; as part of their integrated national energy and climate plans,[46] countries are required to establish national contributions aiming at achieving that target.[47] MSs can rely on EU funds and targeted financial aid, as well as on policy measures meant to support regional cooperation among them, and between MSs and third countries.[48]

To streamline the just transition towards a climate-neutral Europe, sustainability and GHG emission criteria for bioenergy have been reinforced in RED II. This was done by extending the scope to cover all fuels produced from agricultural biomass regardless of their final energy use. As such, Article 29 of RED II limits the production of biofuels on land that had high biodiversity status or high carbon content in or after 2008. Therefore, biofuels derived from agricultural land should not be obtained from highly biodiverse land, land with high carbon stock, and peatland.[49] It is important to note that a number of these criteria were already included in the previous RED I legislation. RED I did not define sustainability criteria for solid and gaseous biomass in electricity, heating, and cooling, however. Additional requirements have been introduced for this purpose in RED II, as in the case of biomass produced from forestry feedstocks, others addressing land use, land use change, and minimum GHG emissions savings.[50] RED II further allows MSs to establish stricter and/or additional sustainability criteria for solid biomass.[51]

RED II also provides a classification of raw materials in different categories, such as wastes, residues, co-products, and a few primary products. On the one hand, this provides MSs with a clearer overview of the specific sustainability criteria and the traceability requirements applicable to any specific case. On the other hand, it gives rise to a system with different levels of expectations in terms of productivity and sustainability and different certification requirements. Only biofuels produced from food and feed crops certified to be low ILUC risk can be considered in the target for the overall share of energy from renewable sources in the Union's gross final consumption of energy. The criteria for certification of ILUC-risk biofuels, bioliquids, and biomass fuels are laid down in the Commission Delegated Regulation 2019/807.[52] According to

---

46 ibid art 3(2).
47 ibid.
48 ibid art 3(5).
49 ibid art 29(3), (4) and (5).
50 Elisa Cavallin, 'Forestry Waste to Biofuel and Biogas: Law and Policy' in this volume.
51 RED II (n 9) art 29(14).
52 Commission Delegated Regulation (EU) 2019/807 supplementing Directive (EU) 2018/2001 as regards the determination of high indirect land-use change-risk

Article 4, the following requirements must be simultaneously met: the bioenergy sources must comply with the sustainability and GHG emissions saving criteria; they have been produced from additional feedstock where the latter either becomes financially attractive or does not hinder the achievement of the mandatory target for renewable energy, or they allow for cultivation of food and feed crops on degraded land, or, finally, are put into place by smallholders;[53] and additional feedstock is identified by duly collected and thoroughly documented evidence.

For what concerns biofuels produced from agricultural waste, MSs must comply with sustainability criteria related to impacts on soil quality and soil carbon and meet the GHG emissions saving requirements. However, it is not compulsory to trace them as far as the upstream part of the process.[54] A set of sustainability criteria have been laid down by RED II to confine the production of bioenergy from agricultural waste, however, requiring that national authorities should put into place monitoring or management plans to identify the repercussions on soil quality and soil carbon. The information must be collected and verified by an adequate standard of independent auditing arranged by national economic operators. The auditing also verifies the accuracy, reliability, and ability to protect against fraud of the systems used by economic operators.[55]

2. Renewable Energy Directive: diverting land from food to energy production

After the initial RED of 2009 was widely criticized for its regulatory uncertainty on the ILUC issue and its inability to include ILUC emissions under the GHG emissions accounting, RED II finally called for a new approach on the matter.[56] The reformed RED II Directive set a new challenging target: from December 2023 until December 2030, MSs' gross final consumption of energy from renewable sources produced from food and feed crops should gradually decrease to 0%.[57] To achieve this goal, the Directive limits the use of biofuels and biomass fuels produced from food and feed crops consumed in transport,

feedstock for which a significant expansion of the production area into land with high carbon stock is observed and the certification of low indirect land-use change-risk biofuels, bioliquids and biomass fuels [2019] OJ L133/1.

53 ibid art 5.

54 Transport and Environment, 'Red II and Advanced Biofuels' (2020) https://www.transportenvironment.org/wp-content/uploads/2021/06/2020_05_REDII_and_advanced_biofuels_briefing.pdf accessed 10 August 2022.

55 RED II (n 9) art 30(3).

56 International Council on Clean Transportation (n 44).

57 RED II (n 9) art 29(2).

and introduces domestic limits for the total contribution of fuels of this nature. The EU legislator has clearly stated its position on the matter, declaring that land should not be converted to accommodate the production of agricultural raw material for biofuels[58] and even that degraded land should be remediated.[59] On the one hand, the Directive sets national limits, according to which the total amount of biofuels, bioliquids and biomass fuels produced from food or feed crops consumed in the transport sector should be 'no more than one percentage point higher than the share of such fuels in the final consumption of energy in the road and rail transport sectors in 2020 in that Member State, with a maximum of 7 % of final consumption of energy'.[60] On the other, the Directive sets national limits at MSs' 2019 level for the period 2021–2023, impacting the amount of alternative fuels that can be considered when calculating the overall national share of renewable energy.[61]

Nevertheless, as specified in Annex VIII of RED II, bioliquids and biomass fuels derived from feedstock other than cereals and other starch-rich crops, sugars and oil crops, and for which the estimated ILUC emissions are considered to be zero, are exempted from that limit. Regulation 2019/807 also set specific standards for both identifying high ILUC-risk feedstock for which a significant expansion of the production area into land with high carbon stock is observed[62] and certifying bioenergy with a low ILUC risk.[63] Non-certified biofuels can be still imported from third countries but they will not count towards the renewable energy target. To further assist MSs in carrying out these tasks, a supporting document on the status of production expansion for relevant biofuel crops worldwide has been adopted by the Commission.[64] For these reasons, though the causality between ILUC and GHG emissions cannot be accurately determined, this Directive has capped the production of food and feed-crops-based biofuels, bioliquids, and biomass fuels.[65]

3. The way forward: RED III

The European Commission is presently seeking to amend the RED II with the aim of setting a more ambitious target, by proposing to rise the current binding EU-level target of 'at least 32%' of renewable energy sources in the global

---

58 ibid rec (98).
59 ibid rec (121).
60 ibid art 26(1).
61 ibid art 26(2).
62 Commission Delegated Regulation (EU) 2019/807 (n 52) art 3.
63 ibid art 4.
64 European Commission, 'Report on the status of production expansion of relevant food and feed crops worldwide', COM (2019) 142.
65 RED II (n 9) rec (81).

energy mix to at least 40% by 2030. It must be noted that, a few months after the Russian invasion of Ukraine, the Commission presented the REPowerEU Plan,[66] where it proposed to increase the target in the Renewable Energy Directive to 45% by 2030, up from the 40% of the initial proposal. To pursue this goal, the Commission launched a public consultation in 2020, after which a proposal for RED III was presented in July 2021.[67] Overall, the proposal does not set out a complete disruption of the current legal framework, but seeks tailored intervention in critical areas, allowing the EU energy systems to become more flexible, accessible, and efficient. In particular, a two-step approach is pursued: a short-term targeted revision, limited in scope, and a subsequent longer-term revision that would eventually lead to a RED III. Sustainability criteria for forest biomass are reinforced, administrative procedures to obtain permissions are simplified, and the use of renewable hydrogen for hard-to-decarbonize sectors is favoured. Nevertheless, no substantial changes have been announced for the production of bioenergy originating from either agricultural waste or for biofuel crops in the RED III proposal.

B. The Common Agricultural Policy and Bioenergy

Established in the aftermath of the Second World War, the EU's Common Agricultural Policy (CAP) has traditionally focused on using economic instruments such as subsidies to increase food production, secure farm incomes, and secure employment after demobilization.[68] Over the years, various iterations of the CAP have sought to shift the policy's focus from 'quantity to quality', *inter alia* through including specific policies on climate and environment.[69] According to the CAP's two-pillar structure, both 'direct payments' for all farmers subject to certain conditions (pillar one) as well specific measures for rural development and other socio-environmental considerations (pillar two) are provided. One of the explicit goals of the CAP now is that it should contribute to climate change mitigation and adaptation, not only by reducing

66 European Commission,'REPowerEU Plan' COM (2022) 230 final.

67 European Commission, 'Proposal for a Directive amending Directive (EU) 2018/2001, Regulation (EU) 2018/1999 and Directive 98/70/EC as regards the promotion of energy from renewable sources, and repealing Council Directive (EU) 2015/652', COM (2021) 557 ('Proposal for RED III'). Hereinafter also referred to as 'Proposal'.

68 David Harvey, 'What Does the History of the CAP Tell Us?' in Joseph A McMahon and Michael N Cardwell (eds), *Research Handbook on EU Agriculture Law* (Edward Elgar 2015), 7.

69 Joseph A McMahon, 'The Common Agricultural Policy: From Quantity to Quality' (2002) 53 Northern Ireland Legal Quarterly 9.

GHG emissions and enhancing carbon sequestration,[70] but also by promoting sustainable energy.[71] This latter objective is particularly interesting for our purposes here, as it points towards the potential role of agriculture in energy production. Below, this role will be further explored, focusing on both the current iterations of the CAP as well as the plans for the new CAP which entered into force in 2023.

1. The place of bioenergy within agricultural policy

This chapter focuses first and foremost on the production of biofuel from biowaste. To understand the interconnection between the CAP and biofuel production, it is important to also consider the production of biofuel from energy crops. In particular, the CAP has played a very instrumental role in the development of first-generation biofuels, which, as stated previously, are biofuels derived from food crops to produce bioethanol, biodiesel, and oil.[72] The socio-political context of this development is that the use of internal pricing supports for farmers through the CAP from the late 1960s increasingly led to very significant production surpluses, also referred to as '[m]ountains of butter and grain and lakes of wine', which had no prospect of being sold in or outside of the EU's common market.[73] At the time when biofuels came on the EU political agenda around 1980 with the introduction of the Biofuels Directive, there was large political momentum for diverting this surplus agricultural production towards the generation of bioenergy.[74]

---

[70] This aim is also reflected in the CAP's financial spending: between 2014 and 2020, about a quarter of the total CAP budget was attributed to the objective of mitigating and adapting to climate change. This comes down to no less than €100 billion in total. As the European Court of Auditors recently concluded, however, these subsidies have had 'little impact on agricultural emissions, which have not changed significantly since 2010'. This is mainly because the CAP does not provide significant incentives to reduce livestock numbers, nor does it effectively finance other measures with a high climate mitigation potential.

See European Court of Auditors, *Special Report 16/2021: Common Agricultural Policy and Climate: Half of EU Climate Spending but Farm Emissions Are Not Decreasing* (Publication Office of the European Union 2021) 3–4.

[71] Regulation (EU) 2021/2115 establishing rules on support for strategic plans to be drawn up by Member States under the common agricultural policy (CAP Strategic Plans) and financed by the European Agricultural Guarantee Fund (EAGF) and by the European Agricultural Fund for Rural Development (EAFRD) and repealing Regulations (EU) 1305/2013 and (EU) 1307/2013 [2021] OJ L435/1, art 6.

[72] See Ausilio Bauen and others, 'Bioenergy: A Sustainable and Reliable Energy Source. A Review of Status and Prospects' (IEA Bioenergy 2009).

[73] Harvey (n 68).

[74] Stelios Rozakis and Robert Borek, 'Evaluation of Agricultural Reactivation on Abandoned Lands in Poland' (2018) 21 AgBioForum 2.

While various subsequent CAP reforms, including the 1992 MacSharry reforms, sought to first of all reduce the incentives for farmers to increase production, including by linking agricultural subsidies to farm sizes as opposed to agricultural production, they also opened the way for farmers to use agricultural land for energy crop production specifically.[75] In particular, the 1992 reform introduced a mandatory set-aside scheme through which farmers would be required to set aside 10% of their land on which no agricultural production would be allowed, to address overproduction. Farmers *could* however use this land to produce non-food crops earmarked for biofuel, which for farmers became an important way to stabilize their farm incomes.[76] The set-aside requirements were relaxed over the years to help mitigate shortages in wheat production, and were subsequently abolished after the Commission's Health Check of 2008.[77] As already detailed above, biofuel production now takes place on farmland that could alternatively be used for the production of food or feed.

Beyond the MacSharry reform, the 2000 CAP reform made energy crops eligible for the area-based subsidies that cereals also fall under, independent of whether the energy crops are produced on land that falls under the 'set-aside' heading.[78] The 2003 CAP reform further introduced an 'energy crop support scheme', a hectare-based subsidy payment scheme for farmers.[79] This subsidy came down to a total of 45 euros per hectare per year for farmers cultivating energy crops on land that is *not* part of set-aside land, and for which they have a contract with a buyer.[80] The subsidy would be guaranteed in the first place for a maximum of 1.5 million hectares, which was later increased to 2 million hectares.

While the CAP has traditionally focused first and foremost on the production of energy crops, an increasing role seems to be foreseen for the use of biowaste for biofuel in the newest agricultural policies and plans. Consider

---

75 Council Regulation (EEC) 1765/92 establishing a support system for producers of certain arable crops [1992] OJ L181/12.

76 Rozakis and Borek (n 74).

77 See Carsten Daugbjerg and Alan Swinbank, 'Explaining the "Health Check" of the Common Agricultural Policy: Budgetary Politics, Globalisation and Paradigm Change Revisited' (2011) 32 Policy Studies 127.

78 Karin Ericsson, Håkan Rosenqvist and Lars J Nilsson, 'Energy Crop Production Costs in the EU' (2009) 33 Biomass and Bioenergy 1577.

79 Giovanni Sorda, Martin Banse, and Claudia Kemfert, 'An Overview of Biofuel Policies Across the World' (2010) 38 Energy Policy 6977.

80 Ericsson, Rosenqvist, and Nilsson (n 78). See also: Council Regulation (EC) 1782/2003 establishing common rules for direct support schemes under the common agricultural policy and establishing certain support schemes for farmers [2003] OJ L270/1.

for instance the EU's Farm to Fork Strategy,[81] as part of the EU's new Green Deal. This Strategy explicitly mentions the 'untapped potential' of the circular bio-based economy, in which bioenergy can play an important role in moving towards a climate-neutral European economy, as well as creating new jobs in primary production.[82] The Strategy notes the potential of producing biogas from agricultural waste and residues, such as manure.[83] The Strategy emphasizes that any type of energy solution and accompanying investments have to be carried out in 'a sustainable manner and without compromising food security or biodiversity, under the clean energy initiatives and programmes'.[84]

The European Commission's Communication on the new CAP entitled 'The future of food and farming' is another key source for understanding what the EU foresees as the future role of bioenergy within agricultural policy. In this Communication, bioenergy and circular energy are described as '[e]merging sustainable rural value chains' which can provide opportunities for farmers 'to diversity their business, hedge risks and provide additional income'.[85] The Communication proceeds to describe that *by-products* from agri-food could find new value as inputs for bioenergy, and manure as biogas and fertilizer, as ways in which the energy transition can be supported.[86] As such, the Communication emphasizes, the CAP should 'increasingly focus on supporting such efforts'.[87]

In discussing how this could practically be given shape, the Communication first of all foresees a strong role for the bio-economy within the 2023 CAP National Strategic Plans, as discussed in more detail below. These plans stipulate how CAP measures under both the first and second pillar can promote clean and efficient energy production in the form of bioenergy as key ways in which CAP measures can support the EU circular economy strategy, the EU and the EU Industrial Policy.[88] It is further put forward that the European Structural and Investment Funds be used to 'leverage additional support from Rural Development Programs' in order to boost bioenergy investments in rural areas – thus noting the potential ways in which other investment programmes and the CAP can reinforce each other.[89] Below, it will be further examined

---

[81] European Commission, 'A Farm to Fork Strategy for a fair, healthy and environmentally-friendly food system', COM (2020) 381.

[82] ibid 8.

[83] ibid.

[84] ibid.

[85] European Commission 'The Future of Food and Farming' COM (2017) 0713 final, para 3.2.2.

[86] ibid para 3.4.1.

[87] ibid.

[88] ibid para 3.4.1.

[89] ibid para 3.4.1.

how the 2023 CAP and specifically the National Strategic Plan requirements engage the production of biofuel.

2. National Strategic Plans: connecting CAP instruments and bioenergy

In their National Strategic Plans, MSs thus laid down the types of interventions they will implement at the national level, presenting quantitative targets and milestones to achieve the CAP's specific objectives.[90] Through these national plans, the 2023 CAP shifts the focus from an emphasis on uniform rules and assessment of compliance, towards a focus on results monitored by the Commission. For this purpose, Annex I of the Regulation lists various impact indicators linked to the CAP's objectives, as well as performance reviews.[91] In relation to the climate objectives, impact indicator 12 reads: 'Increasing sustainable energy in agriculture: Sustainable production of renewable energy from agriculture and forestry'.[92] Following results numbers R.15 and R.16, the Commission monitors advancement in relation to both the production of (bio-based) renewable energy from agriculture, as well as the share of farms benefitting from CAP investment support contributing to climate change mitigation and adaptation, and to the production of renewable energy or biomaterials.[93]

As the Commission states, MSs have various possibilities under the CAP strategic plans that they may use to 'increase sustainable domestic generation of renewable energy, including biogas'.[94] The Commission does not elaborate whether this generation should come from energy crops or rather from agricultural waste. It is clear however that, when the Commission refers to 'sustainable biogas production', as it emphasizes in its observations, this means biogas

---

[90] As laid out in art 6(1)–(2) of Reg 2021/2115 (n 71).

[91] ibid annex 1.

[92] ibid.

[93] Note: the methods of data collection for the impact indicators and results differ. Data for the impact indicators, thus for instance 'increasing sustainable energy in agriculture' are collected via various channels such as European statistics, the Commission's Joint Research Centre, the European Environment Agency, and more. Data for the results indicators are submitted annually by the MSs and are subsequently used by the Commission to monitor progress towards the targets the MSs themselves have established in their National Strategic Plans. For more details on monitoring, see: European Commission 'Common Monitoring and Evaluation Framework' (agriculture.ec.europa.eu, n.d.) https://ec.europa.eu/info/food-farming-fisheries/key-policies/common-agricultural-policy/cmef_en / accessed 14 February 2022.

[94] European Commission – Directorate-General for Agriculture and Rural Development, 'Observations on the proposal by Ireland for a CAP Strategic Plan 2023–2027 – CCI: 2023IE06AFSP001' Ref. Ares (2022) 2416190, 4.

that respects the sustainability and GHG-emission-saving criteria laid out in Article 29 of RED II.[95]

The only instrument presented by MSs in their strategic plans to promote biofuel, specifically biogas, is that of support for investments that target environmental and climate-related objectives, as part of the rural development pillar. These investments can be 'productive', meaning they also bring economic gain, or 'non-productive', meaning they are geared primarily towards environmental and climate-related benefits.[96]

In the Nation Strategic Plans, 18 MSs have included investment interventions for the promotion of biogas and some, such as Latvia, specifically included the use of agricultural waste streams (both crop residue and manure) for energy production.[97] Other countries did not include any interventions on biofuel production. The Dutch NSP, for instance, mentions that there are various national and regional policies in place in relation to the production of renewable energy in agricultural contexts (mainly wind and solar), as a result of which it has been decided not to use the CAP for this purpose.[98] The Irish National Strategic Plan mentions that it will seek to link its strategic plan with other national policies on, *inter alia*, energy, but emphasises the large-scale availability of feedstock and agricultural residues for bioenergy production.[99] An in-depth comparative analysis of the National Strategic Plans would shed more light on the national implementation the use of agricultural waste for bioenergy production. However, this is beyond the scope of this Chapter.

---

[95] European Commission – Directorate-General for Agriculture and Rural Development, 'Observations on the proposal by Poland for a CAP Strategic Plan 2023–2027 – CCI: 2023PL06AFSP001' Ref. Ares (2022) 2418100.

[96] ibid.

[97] These include Austria, Estonia, Finland, Greece, Ireland, Italy, Latvia, Lithuania, Poland, Portugal, Cyprus, Romania, Slovakia, Slovenia, Spain, Bulgaria, Croatia, and France. One example is Latvia, who will invest in manure management systems to produce energy. See European Commission, 'CAP Strategic Plans' https://agriculture.ec.europa.eu/cap-my-country/cap-strategic-plans_en#:~:text=CAP%20Strategic%20Plans%20encourage%20the,ensuring%20long%2Dterm%20food%20security. Accessed 5 October 2023.

[98] It also mentions that the share of agricultural inputs (including forestry) for bioenergy production is relatively marginal, namely 4.3% of the total national production of renewable energy in 2016. Ministerie van Landbouw, Natuur en Visserij, 'Nederlands Nationaal Strategisch Plan GLB 2023-2027' (2022) 68-69.

[99] Government of Ireland - Department of Agriculture, Food and the Marine, 'Ireland's Summary of the CAP Strategic Plan 2023-2027' (2022), 30.

IV. DISCUSSION: EXPLORING LEGAL CONVERGENCES AND DIVERGENCES

The EU legal and policy approach towards bioenergy has seen an overall shift from food-to-biofuels to waste-to-energy in the past years. After years spent on incentivizing EU farmers to introduce, maintain, or increase the cultivation of energy crops through CAP subsidies, the EU's approach appears to increasingly promote the use of agricultural waste as opposed to energy crops. Nevertheless, a comprehensive and harmonized system for discouraging biofuel crops, and in turn encouraging biofuels from agricultural waste, is not in place yet. For this reason, both the legal convergences and divergences of the strategies adopted by the RED II and the CAP deserve further attention.

As a first observation, RED II imposes a gradual capping of the share of biofuel from food crops until a drastic reduction is reached, and then a complete phasing out by the end of 2030. At the same time, it promotes certain types of biofuels generated from a list of materials included in Annex IX and encourages MSs to also rely on agricultural waste as a potential renewable source of energy, such as biofuels, bioliquids, and biomass fuels. Even though agricultural waste, as said, falls outside of the scope of the WFD,[100] if the same hierarchical approach were to be applied to agricultural residues, the energy recovery of such waste could be one of the priority options. This is important because, from a social perspective, the sustainability criteria under Article 29 of RED II takes only the geography, the environmental effects, and the impact on the land into account, while neglecting any interest in safeguarding the needs of the affected rural communities. Incentivizing the use of agricultural waste will decrease the creation of additional demand for land.

A strong legal convergence between the RED II and CAP is found in that where the Commission pushes MSs to increase the sustainable production of biogas, it points to the provisions of Article 29 of the RED II as detailing what sustainability entails. Even though in its observations on MSs' strategic plans under the CAP the Commission does not elaborate a preference for the production of energy crops or the use of agricultural waste, this clear link with the RED II signals a move towards the latter. For future policy elaborations, it would be useful to make these preferences more explicit and align the CAP and RED II to prevent the misdirection of subsidies away from set goals.

Another convergence between the two legal frameworks is that farmers can use the requirements under Article 29 of RED II to signal compliance with their basic requirements for agricultural production ('cross-compliance'), necessary for receiving direct subsidy payments under the CAP. This was not

---

[100] Dir 2008/98 (n 31) art 2.

the case before; the 2009 RED I required that agricultural raw materials used for the production of biofuels and bioliquids should be produced in accordance with the requirements for cross-compliance prescribed by the first pillar of the CAP, laying down minimum requirements for farmers to maintain good agricultural and environmental conditions to obtain access to subsidies.[101] With RED II, the decision has been made to streamline these requirements, noting that including CAP requirements in '[…] the sustainability scheme is not appropriate as the sustainability criteria for bioenergy should set out rules that are objective and apply globally. Verification of compliance under this Directive would also risk causing an unnecessary administrative burden'.[102] The idea here is thus to prevent subjecting farmers to a dual level of stringent requirements. It is important to note that the provisions of Article 29 of RED II are much more geared towards bioenergy compared to the conditionality provisions of the CAP, laying down rules prohibiting for instance the production of bioenergy from raw materials obtained from land with a high biodiversity value.[103] Regrettably, RED II lacks a mandatory criteria on how to sustainably harvest agricultural waste and residues, as well as a clear control mechanism, which exacerbates legal uncertainty that could have been prevented by streamlining the CAP and RED II further.

An important divergence between the two legislations is that, where RED II has set the binding target to eliminate the consumption of energy derived from food and feed crops in the EU by 2030, the 2023 CAP has not put in place concrete instruments to meet this objective. In fact, both with regard to the prevention of ILUC as well as the meeting of overall bioenergy targets, the CAP leaves the elaboration fully to the MSs in their National Strategic Plans. While the Commission has emphasized to MSs the importance of using CAP instruments for the promotion of sustainable bioenergy, in particular biogas, the CAP lacks a specific set of binding rules to support this transition towards using agricultural waste in particular for bioenergy production. To meet the RED II objectives, it seems crucial to strengthen the way in which the two legal instruments jointly leverage the energy transition.

---

[101] RED I (n 38) art 17(6); Regulation (EU) 1306/2013 on the financing, management and monitoring of the common agricultural policy and repealing Council Regulations (EEC) No 352/78, (EC) No 165/94, (EC) No 2799/98, (EC) No 814/2000, (EC) No 1290/2005 and (EC) No 485/2008 [2013] OJ L347/549.

[102] RED II (n 9) rec (99).

[103] RED II (n 9) art 29.

V. CONCLUSION

This chapter examined the role and potential of EU's renewable energy and agricultural law and policy in steering the use of agricultural waste for the generation of biofuel. In doing so, it sought to provide new insights on whether and how the EU's energy and agricultural policies can jointly be leveraged to improve the use of the agricultural waste streams towards a more circular energy economy.

As was found, the use of arable land for the production of biofuels and biogas is contested as it can drive scarce fertile land away from food production towards energy production, also referred to as indirect land-use change (ILUC). Within the EU, Renewable Energy Directive 2018/2001 (RED II) has recently regulated ILUC, focusing on crop residues and animal manure as the primary alternative for biofuel and biogas production, and thereby responding to the increasing demand for low-carbon bioenergy in the renewable energy sector. Similarly, it has set binding targets for bioenergy production. While the Commission has highlighted the importance of MSs employing the CAP for the sustainable production of bioenergy, the CAP presently leaves MSs with wide discretion in this domain, signalling a divergence between the RED II and the CAP.

As such, this chapter concludes that while both RED II and the CAP convey political intent on promoting the use of bioenergy, the EU lacks a specific set of (binding) rules to support this transition towards using agricultural waste in both the upcoming RED Reform (RED III) as well as the National Strategic Plans in the CAP. For future research, it will be important to further examine ways to jointly exploit these frameworks to improve the use of the agricultural waste streams towards a more circular energy economy and address the issue of ILUC. For the latter, producing energy crops strictly on contaminated lands could be a promising approach, the capitalization of which can however only be realized by leveraging law and regulatory frameworks more broadly for achieving positive changes in the energy transition.

LEGISLATION

Directive 2003/30/EC on the promotion of the use of biofuels or other renewable fuels for transport [2003] OJ L123/42

Directive 2009/28/EC on the promotion of the use of energy from renewable sources and amending and subsequently repealing Directives 2001/77/EC and 2003/30/EC [2009] OJ L140/16 ('RED I')

Directive (EU) 2018/2001 on the promotion of the use of energy from renewable sources [2018] OJ L328/82 ('RED II')

Directive 2008/98/EC on waste and repealing certain Directives [2008] OJ L3/12 ('Waste Framework Directive', 'WFD')

Regulation (EC) 1782/2003 establishing common rules for direct support schemes under the common agricultural policy and establishing certain support schemes for farmers [2003] OJ L270/1
Regulation (EU) 2021/2115 establishing rules on support for strategic plans to be drawn up by Member States under the common agricultural policy (CAP Strategic Plans) and financed by the European Agricultural Guarantee Fund (EAGF) and by the European Agricultural Fund for Rural Development (EAFRD) and repealing Regulations (EU) 1305/2013 and (EU) 1307/2013 [2021] OJ L435/1
Regulation (EEC) 1765/92 establishing a support system for producers of certain arable crops [1992] OJ L181/12
Regulation (EU) 1306/2013 on the financing, management and monitoring of the common agricultural policy and repealing Council Regulations (EEC) No 352/78, (EC) No 165/94, (EC) No 2799/98, (EC) No 814/2000, (EC) No 1290/2005 and (EC) No 485/2008 [2013] OJ L347/549
Delegated Regulation (EU) 2019/807 supplementing Directive (EU) 2018/2001 as regards the determination of high indirect land-use change-risk feedstock for which a significant expansion of the production area into land with high carbon stock is observed and the certification of low indirect land-use change-risk biofuels, bioliquids and biomass fuels [2019] OJ L133/1
Council Decision (EU) 2016/1841 on the conclusion, on behalf of the European Union, of the Paris Agreement adopted under the United Nations Framework Convention on Climate Change [2016] OJ L282/1

4. Food waste to biogas and biofuel: law and policy

Madhura Rao, Aalt Bast, and Alie de Boer

I. INTRODUCTION

Globally, one in three people do not have access to sufficient quantities of safe food. At the same time, one-third of the food produced for human consumption ends up as waste every year. The co-existence of these extremes suggests a need to recalibrate our food system if it is to meet the nutritional needs of the growing population while operating within planetary boundaries. Transitioning towards a circular way of operating, where resources are utilised to their utmost potential, is one way to address both issues. In the context of food waste, circularity would imply developing novel ways of utilising food that becomes unfit for human consumption. Dependent on the field of study and geographic location, many definitions of food waste exist in current literature.[1] In this chapter we define food waste as proposed by FUSIONS (2012–2016), a European Commission-funded project which is focused on the harmonisation of food waste monitoring: 'Food waste is any food, and inedible parts of food, removed from the food supply chain to be recovered or disposed'.[2] By including biomass from all stages of the supply chain, whether edible or not, this definition provides the possibility of discussing food waste valorisation in the broadest possible way.

---

1 Of the various definitions of food waste that are currently in use, many make the distinction between food loss and waste. For instance, the FAO (2011) defines food waste as 'decrease in the quantity or quality of food resulting from decisions and actions by retailers, food service providers and consumers'. Decrease in quantity and quality of food in earlier stages of the supply chain such as agriculture is termed as food loss (https://www.fao.org/3/mb060e/mb060e00.htm). However, in this chapter we will work with the definition proposed by EU FUSIONS which does not distinguish between loss and waste; Jenny Gustavsson, Christel Cederberg, and Ulf Sonesson, 'Global Food Losses and Food Waste' (2011) accessed 30 July 2022.

2 Jenny Gustavsson and others, 'FUSIONS Definitional Framework for Food Waste' (2014) https://hal.inrae.fr/hal-02800861 accessed 10 November 2021.

Using food waste as feedstock for bioenergy is widely accepted as a way to create value out of surplus or waste food material. The chemical composition of food waste allows for conversion to energy in several ways. Some methods currently employed for this purpose include the transesterification of fats for biodiesel production, the fermentation of carbohydrates for bioethanol or biobutanol production, anaerobic digestion for biogas production, and incineration.[3] For the bioenergy industry, recovering energy from food waste presents a lucrative opportunity because waste is considered a zero cost material and its composition allows for the development of cost-effective and commercially viable methods to produce biofuel and biogas.[4] Bioenergy created from food, which would have otherwise ended up expanding landfills, is lauded for its two-fold contribution towards sustainability. First, it offers partial replacement for conventional energy resources that face the threat of dissipation. Second, using food waste, a biomass that is at the end of its life cycle, instead of food crops for generating bioenergy circumvents the food versus fuel debate.[5] Therefore, from the perspective of energy policy, biofuel and biogas that use food waste as feedstock merit an elevated status. In line with this, policy and legislation surrounding the topic have incentivised the redirection of food waste towards energy recovery in recent years. As a result, businesses in the European Union (EU) have been increasingly investing in infrastructure that enables this kind of valorisation. However, from a food policy perspective, using food material for generating bioenergy may not be seen as an ideal valorisation route; it robs this biomass of the opportunity to be utilised for some of its unique characteristics such as nutritionally or biologically valuable compounds. This chapter will address both food and energy policies and compare their considerations of food waste as feedstock for bioenergy. Section II provides an overview of current laws and policies that govern food waste valorisation in the EU. Section III elaborates on the end-of-waste status in the context of food waste valorisation. Section IV sets out how waste-to-bioenergy is perceived in comparison to other valorisation options by relevant stakeholders and whether its low position in the food waste hierarchy is justified. Section

---

3 Thi Phuong Thuy Pham and others, 'Food Waste-to-Energy Conversion Technologies: Current Status and Future Directions' (2015) 38 Waste Management 399; Francesca Girotto, Luca Alibardi, and Raffaello Cossu, 'Food Waste Generation and Industrial Uses: A Review' (2015) 45 Waste Management 32.

4 Sanjib Kumar Karmee and Carol Sze Ki Lin, 'Valorisation of Food Waste to Biofuel: Current Trends and Technological Challenges' (2014) 2 Sustainable Chemical Processes 22.

5 See Julia Tomei and Richard Helliwell, 'Food Versus Fuel? Going Beyond Biofuels' (2016) 56 Land Use Policy 320; Eden Tafesework Geletu and Margherita Paola Poto, 'Balancing Agro-Fuels and Food Security on the Tightrope Towards Sustainability' (2019) 14 European Food and Feed Law Review 261.

V explores whether better cooperation between food, feed, and energy private standards could aid food business operators (FBOs) in making the right decision when valorising food biomass. Section VI present concluding remarks.

II. CURRENT STATE OF FOOD WASTE VALORISATION IN THE EU

The 2011 'Roadmap to a Resource Efficient Europe' was the first EU policy document to explicitly mention a food waste reduction goal.[6] The roadmap recommended a 20% reduction in the food chain's resource input by 2020. It suggested that this should be achieved by halving the disposal of edible food, but did not provide further guidance. Since then, several discussions have been had at EU as well as Member State (MS)-levels regarding reducing food waste, first through preventative actions and then via the valorisation of any remaining food materials.[7]

Although relatively new on the policy agenda, food waste has rapidly become an environmental issue requiring urgent attention. In 2017, the Commission adopted the 'Resource Efficiency: Reducing Food Waste, Improving Food Safety' resolution which reiterates previous EU-level discussions on the subject.[8] It invited MSs to measure food waste levels using a common methodology, officially adopt a food waste hierarchy based on Article 4 of the Waste Framework Directive 2008/98 (WFD) and provide clarification regarding the implications of various pieces of domestic legislation on food waste.[9] Most notably, the resolution called on MSs to examine the possibility of setting up binding, Union-wide food waste reduction targets by December 2020.[10] This is the first ever mention of legally binding targets with regard to food waste.

In May 2020, the Farm to Fork Strategy indicated that the Commission would propose legally binding targets for food waste reduction based on data

---

6 European Commission, 'Communication from the Commission to the European Parliament, the Council, the European Economic and Social Committee and the Committee of the Regions: Roadmap to a Resource Efficient Europe' COM (2011) 571 final.

7 Some notable discussions and documents that focused on food waste to varying degrees include the 2012 Resolution on How to Avoid Food Wastage, the 2013 Consultation on Communication on Sustainable Food, the 2013 (7th) Environmental Action Programme, the 2014 Circular Economy Package, and the 2015 Closing the Loop Action Plan.

8 European Parliament, 'Resolution on Initiative on Resource Efficiency: Reducing Food Waste, Improving Food Safety' (2017) 2016/2223 (INI).

9 Directive 2008/98/EC on waste and repealing certain Directives [2008] OJ L3 12/3 ('Waste Framework Directive', 'WFD').

10 ibid.

expected from MSs in 2022.[11] While the intention to set up legally binding targets shows political will to reduce and better utilise food waste, tangible actions in the direction are yet to be seen across all MSs. Currently, no legislation or policy document at the EU level provides concrete guidance regarding food waste valorisation.[12] However, the Commission's Sustainable Food System Framework Initiative,[13] which at the time of writing is pending public consultation, has the potential to change this. The impact assessment for this proposed regulation mentions improved food loss and waste management as well as better recovery and redistribution of surplus food as one of its likely impacts.[14] When adopted in 2023, it is probable that it will be among the first food-focused regulations to address the reduction and valorisation of food waste.[15]

Of the numerous legal and policy areas that affect food waste valorisation, waste law is perhaps the most significant. Food law comes a close second but excludes food that is no longer considered fit for human consumption.[16] Instead, it focuses on consumer interest, human health, and effective functioning of the internal market.[17] It is therefore the WFD that regulates food waste and its valorisation. It lays down definitions and best practices related to waste management and includes environmental protection, human health, and resource efficiency in its scope. The current version of the WFD was adopted in November 2008.

In May 2018, the WFD was amended through the adoption of Directive 2018/851.[18] With this amending directive, food waste was recognised as a special category within biodegradable waste. This is a noteworthy change because the 2008 Directive simply considered food waste as part of bio-waste,

---

[11] European Commission, 'A Farm to Fork Strategy for a Fair, Healthy and Environmentally-Friendly Food System' COM (2020) 381.

[12] ibid.

[13] European Commission, 'Sustainable EU Food System – New Initiative' https://ec.europa.eu/info/law/better-regulation/have-your-say/initiatives/13174-Sustainable-EU-food-system-new-initiative_en accessed 14 February 2022.

[14] European Commission, 'Inception Impact Assessment for the Sustainable Food System Framework Initiative' (2021) Ref. Ares (2021) 5902055 https://ec.europa.eu/info/law/better-regulation/ accessed 14 February 2022.

[15] ibid.

[16] Regulation (EC) 178/2002 laying down the general principles and requirements of food law, establishing the European Food Safety Authority and laying down procedures in matters of food safety [2002] OJ L31/1 ('GFL').

[17] It is, however, important to note that the EU General Food Law does demarcate the line between 'edible' and 'inedible'. Thus, it decides when certain material will no longer be classified as food but as waste.

[18] Directive (EU) 2018/851 of the European Parliament and of the Council of 30 May 2018 amending Directive 2008/98/EC on waste [2018] OJ L 150/109.

detaching it from its value as a basic human need and natural resource different from other biomass.[19] By contrast, the amending directive includes a separate definition for food waste, derived from the EU General Food Law's (GFL) definition of food.[20] For the first time since 1975, when the first WFD was adopted, a link between legislation on food and waste has been established. However, it is interesting to note that the GFL defines food as 'any substance or product, whether processed, partially processed or unprocessed, intended to be, or reasonably expected to be ingested by humans'.[21] Therefore, the WFD's definition only considers the wastage of food that humans can be reasonably expected to ingest as food waste. In contrast to this, the EU FUSIONS definition considers wasted inedible parts of food to be food waste as well. By excluding inedible parts such as pits, peels, and trimmings from the definition, the current WFD deprives a significant volume of food waste from being considered as such. Therefore, despite the WFD adopting a definition for food waste, food processing by-products may end up being categorised as bio-waste instead of food waste.

Article 9 of Directive 2018/851 guides MSs to take measures to reduce food waste at all stages of the supply chain in line with the (non-binding) United Nations' Sustainable Development Goal 12. Article 9(h) also states that donation and redistribution should be prioritised over use in animal feed or reprocessing into non-food products. This change is highly relevant with regard to food waste valorisation because never before in the history of EU waste law has the waste hierarchy been modified to accommodate the unique characteristics of food waste. Additionally, in May 2019, a Commission delegated decision (2019/1597) supplementing the WFD was adopted. This decision establishes a common methodology and minimum quality requirements for the uniform measurement of levels of food waste in MS.[22] Considering that data on the measurement of food waste is an important step towards its valorisation, the delegated decision is a step in the right direction if binding targets are to be set in the coming years.

In the context of valorising food waste as feedstock for bioenergy, legislation on renewable energy is relevant as well. In December 2018, Directive 2018/2001 (RED II) replaced the existing Directive 2009/28 on the promotion of the use of energy from renewable sources (RED I). When considering

---

[19] Carrie Bradshaw, 'Waste Law and the Value of Food' (2018) 30 Journal of Environmental Law 311.

[20] GFL (n 16).

[21] ibid art 2.

[22] Delegated Decision (EU) 2019/1597 supplementing Directive 2008/98/EC as regards a common methodology and minimum quality requirements for the uniform measurement of levels of food waste [2019] OJ L248/77.

bioenergy that uses waste as feedstock, RED II relies on the principles of the WFD by referring to 2008/98 wherever relevant. In comparison, RED I considered waste biomass independently, without referring to legislation on waste management. This connection between legislation on renewable energy and waste management has the potential to improve the way in which MSs valorise their food waste. RED II directs MSs to consider the principles of the circular economy and the waste hierarchy when developing support schemes for renewable energy.[23] Additionally, with regard to meeting renewable energy targets for the transportation sector, RED I (art 21(2)) considered the contribution made by biofuels produced from waste to be twice that of other biofuels. RED II introduces an important nuance to this. Annex IX (part A(d)) of RED II listing feedstocks for the production of biofuels that can be considered twice for their energy content specifies that only biomass which is 'not fit for use in the food or feed chain' can be counted as such.[24] This is a significant addition with the potential to prevent material fit for higher levels of valorisation from being redirected for energy production. Another salient feature of RED II is that it explicitly states that waste prevention and recycling should be given priority over being used as feedstock for biofuel and that MSs should avoid creating support schemes leading to the inefficient use of waste that is recyclable.[25] The transposition to RED II was to be achieved by MSs by June 2021 and therefore, at the time of writing,[26] there is no data available to indicate whether RED II has made a significant difference to the way in which food waste is utilised as feedstock for bioenergy.

In line with the rapid developments in this area, a proposal to amend RED II was published by the Commission in July 2021.[27] When addressing food as feedstock for biofuel, the proposal focuses on food and feed crops. Changes likely to impact how food waste is used for energy recovery are numbered. One among these is a proposal to remove biomass from the list of renewable

---

[23] Directive (EU) 2018/2001 on the promotion of the use of energy from renewable sources [2018] OJ L328/82 ('RED II') para 21.

[24] An exception is applicable in the case of used cooking oil and animal fats classified as categories 1 and 2 in accordance with Regulation (EC) 1069/2009 laying down health rules as regards animal by-products and derived products not intended for human consumption and repealing Regulation (EC) 1774/2002 ('Animal by-products Regulation'). Section III will discuss this further.

[25] RED II (n 23) para. 21.

[26] Chapter written in November 2021.

[27] European Commission, 'Proposal for a Directive Amending Directive (EU) 2018/2001 of the European Parliament and of the Council, Regulation (EU) 2018/1999 of the European Parliament and of the Council and Directive 98/70/EC of the European Parliament and of the Council as Regards the Promotion of Energy from Renewable Sources and Repealing Council Directive (EU) 2015/652' COM (2021) 557.

resources. Ninety-nine per cent of the 38,786 participants involved in the creation of the proposal voted to limit the use of biomass for energy recovery to locally available waste and residues.[28] If approved, this change would make waste streams exceedingly important as feedstock for biofuels while allowing biomass such as food and feed crops, along with the land required for their production, to be available for their primary purpose of ensuring food security.

Overall, recent changes to waste and renewable energy law have improved the interconnectedness between the two areas and recognised food waste biomass as different from other biomass. Contingent on the interpretation and implementation by MSs, these changes have the potential to make sure that food waste is used as feedstock for bioenergy only if higher priority valorisation options such as donation, use in animal feed, or extraction of valuable biological compounds, are not feasible. In addition, both legislations prioritise other valorisation routes for food waste over being utilised as bioenergy feedstock. This is likely to reduce the incidence of competing policy goals at MS level.

III. END-OF-WASTE CRITERIA AND FOOD WASTE

To transition to a circular economy, materials that are classified as waste at the end of their life cycle must be transformed in a way that enables their reintroduction into the economy. In the 2008 update of the WFD, legal provisions for conferring end-of-waste (EoW) status to such transformed material were introduced.[29] The directive states *inter alia* that waste materials that had undergone specific recycling or recovery processes could be classified as EoW if market demand for them existed and if their use would have no adverse environmental or health impacts.[30] Despite the EU Joint Research Centre developing EoW criteria for several materials, currently EU-level criteria exist only for three kinds of waste; iron scrap, copper scrap, and glass cullet.[31] For most other materials, MSs are responsible for deciding when a certain waste material ceases to be waste.[32] Discussions on EoW do not often overlap those concerning the valorisation of food waste. However, a 2019 decision of the European Court of Justice (ECJ) had a significant impact on the valorisation of waste vegetable oil as biofuel.

---

28 ibid.

29 WFD (n 9).

30 ibid art 6.

31 N Johansson and C Forsgren, 'Is This the End of End-of-Waste? Uncovering the Space between Waste and Products' (2020) 155 Resources, Conservation and Recycling 104656.

32 ibid.

In 2016, Prato Nevoso Termo Energy Srl ('Prato Nevoso'), an Italian power plant operator, wished to replace methane that was used in its operations with a bioliquid obtained by chemically treating used cooking oil and its residues. The producer of this product had the permit to market it as an EoW product within the ambit of the relevant Italian law. The EoW status was granted in relation to its use for biodiesel production. Since used vegetable oil was not part of a national list indicating the categories of biomass fuels that could be used in operations producing atmospheric emissions, a provincial court denied Prato Nevoso the authorisation to use it as an EoW product. This decision was challenged by Prato Nevoso on the basis of its violation of Article 6 of the WFD setting rules on EoW as well as Article 13 of the RED I that obliges MSs to streamline administrative procedures concerning the use of renewable energy. The ECJ was therefore asked by the involved parties for a preliminary ruling.

The ECJ referred to its decision in the *Tallinna Vesi* case wherein it was found that Article 6 of the WFD does not, in principle, allow the waste holder to demand the recognition of EoW status by a competent authority or court of the MS.[33] Furthermore, the ECJ confirmed that MSs have a wide margin of discretion with regard to establishing appropriate procedural arrangements as well as the substantive examination of compliance with the conditions for EoW status.[34] The Court's judgement established that since the used vegetable oil was not included in the list of authorised fuels, the bioliquid in question must be regarded as waste and not as a fuel.[35]

This decision of the ECJ highlights that in the EU food waste valorisation by way of energy recovery is dependent on MSs' interpretation and application of relevant legislation. Despite waste material such as used vegetable oil, husks, cobs, nut shells, and residues from processing, such as crude glycerine and bagasse, having low greenhouse gas emission values as per RED II, whether they can be used as EoW products is, in many cases, left to the discretion of competent authorities and courts of individual MSs.[36]

---

[33] Case C-212/18 *Prato Nevoso Termo Energy Srl v Provincia di Cuneo and ARPA Piemonte* EU:C:2019:898 [2019], para 31; Case C-60/18 *AS Tallinna Vesi v Keskkonnaamet* EU:C:2019:264 [2019].

[34] ibid para 36.

[35] ibid para 41.

[36] These materials, among others, are listed as having low emissions in Annex V of Directive (EU) 2018/2001 (RED II) which lays down the rules for calculating the greenhouse gas impact of biofuels, bioliquids, and their fossil fuel comparators.

IV. COMPETING VALORISATION OPTIONS

In recent years, the waste hierarchy has been adapted by various institutions and scholars to address food waste.[37] In all versions of the adapted hierarchy, prevention is the topmost priority. The least preferred option is disposal without obtaining any value from the biomass. All options listed between the most and least preferred ones are valorisation routes because they seek to derive value out of material that would have otherwise gone unexploited. Figure 4.1 presents a version of the waste hierarchy adapted by REFRESH (2015–2019), a European Commission-funded project focused on food waste reduction.[38] This model places the option of recovering energy from food waste at the bottom of the hierarchy, making it the least preferred valorisation option. However, in practice, the waste-to energy route might be preferred by FBOs over other options. This section will explore if energy recovery competes with higher priority options and whether the low priority designated to it is justified.

The most preferred valorisation option as per the hierarchy is redistribution and reprocessing of safe and edible surplus food for human consumption. Redistribution is traditionally carried out by hunger relief organisations and social enterprises that collect surplus food from retailers and redistribute it to those in need. However, taxation and food-safety-related liability are two critical bottlenecks in this kind of valorisation. Under normal circumstances, value-added tax (VAT) is paid by consumers when they purchase the food product. However, if food is donated, the retailer must pay VAT unless MS-level legislation allows otherwise.[39] Next to this, food safety is an important concern. When retailers or suppliers choose to donate food, they

---

[37] Some examples of the adapted hierarchy include Jochen Moerman, 'Rechtsvergelijkende studie over de investeringssteun met betrekking tot de afv-alstoffen- en recyclageproblematiek: Europa vs. VS' (Universiteit Ghent 2009) https://libstore.ugent.be/fulltxt/RUG01/001/391/554/RUG01-001391554_2010_0001_AC.pdf accessed 14 February 2022; Effie Papargyropoulou and others, 'The Food Waste Hierarchy as a Framework for the Management of Food Surplus and Food Waste' (2014) 76 Journal of Cleaner Production 106; US EPA, 'Food Recovery Hierarchy' (12 August 2015) https://www.epa.gov/sustainable-management-food/food-recovery-hierarchy accessed 14 February 2022; Stephanie Wunder and others, 'REFRESH Deliverable D3.3 – EU Policy Review for Food Waste Prevention and Valorisation' (REFRESH 2018) https://eu-refresh.org/sites/default/files/REFRESH_D3.3_EU%20policy%20screening_18052018_25072018.pdf accessed 14 February 2022. We consider the version developed by Wunder and colleagues since it was created as part of the REFRESH project which is relevant to various sections of the chapter.

[38] Wunder and others (n 37).

[39] Mattias Eriksson, Simone Giovannini, and Ranjan Kumar Ghosh, 'Is There a Need for Greater Integration and Shift in Policy to Tackle Food Waste? Insights from a Review of European Union Legislations' (2020) 2 SN Applied Sciences 1347.

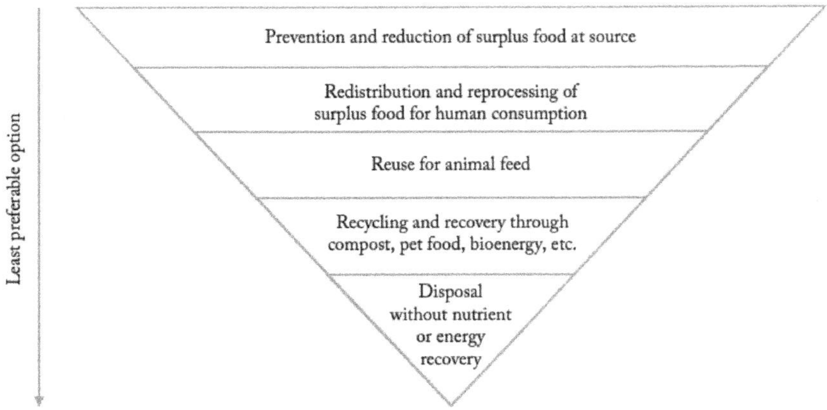

Source: Stephanie Wunder et al., 'REFRESH Deliverable D3.3 – EU Policy Review for Food Waste Prevention and Valorisation' (2018), https://eu-refresh.org/sites/default/files/REFRESH_D3.3_EU%20policy%20screening_18052018_25072018.pdf.

Figure 4.1 The food use hierarchy

often have little or no control over its handling and storage, but the GFL holds FBOs liable if any food safety issues arise. This can have serious legal and reputational consequences for businesses. As a result, discarding surplus food or removing it from the food supply chain becomes cheaper and easier than donating it.[40]

Food or its by-products that are fit for human consumption may also be retained in the food supply chain through reprocessing. Such surplus is usually generated at the manufacturing or processing stage and is easier to valorise compared to surplus from other stages due to its homogeneous nature. Trimmings from fresh produce, whey from the dairy industry, oilseed cakes, and spent grains are examples of by-products that can be valorised in this manner through the extraction of valuable biological components.[41] However, FBOs must deal with food safety risks such as higher pesticide concentration and biological deterioration during storage or transportation.[42] Reprocessing by-products also often requires investment in new technologies and legal accommodations.[43]

---

[40] ibid.

[41] Madhura Rao, Aalt Bast, and Alie de Boer, 'Valorized Food Processing By-Products in the EU: Finding the Balance between Safety, Nutrition, and Sustainability' (2021) 13 Sustainability 4428.

[42] ibid.

[43] ibid.

Against this background, if FBOs are offered fiscal incentives to send their waste to energy recovery, it is likely that they will consider it a more inviting choice.[44] For instance, Bowman and colleagues (2020) point out that 19,898 tonnes of food fit for human consumption was redirected to anaerobic digestion by UK's largest food retailer in 2017–18.[45] Some MSs even prioritise waste-to-energy valorisation over redistribution of surplus to improve food security. Sweden, for example, frames food waste as an environmental and economic issue and therefore does not consider the social dimension of food security while making policies that tackle food waste.[46] In 2017, the Commission published guidelines on food donation with the aim of clarifying relevant provisions in EU legislation and promoting a common interpretation of rules across MS and regulatory authorities.[47] Given the non-binding nature of these guidelines, it is up to MSs to amend relevant pieces of legislation and to ensure that donating or reprocessing surplus food for human consumption becomes the most favoured valorisation option.

Reusing food waste for animal feed is the next level of the hierarchy. This practice can address two pressing environmental issues simultaneously: reducing the negative impacts of meat production and reducing food waste. Several food processing by-products such as spent grains, fresh produce trimmings, and oilseed meals are currently successfully valorised as animal feed in the EU.[48] Next to this, surplus food from various stages of the food supply chain, known as former food products, are also redirected to animal feed.[49] By using food waste and surplus to feed livestock, the biomass partially fulfils its original purpose by remaining within the food supply chain. However, not all food surplus and by-products can be valorised in this manner. EU feed regulation heavily restricts the use of animal products in animal feed to prevent the spread of prion diseases. These restrictions are informed by the 1986 bovine

---

44 Clementine O'Connor, Manuela Gheoldus, and Olivier Jan, 'Comparative Study on EU Member States' Legislation and Practices on Food Donation: Final Report' (European Economic and Social Committee 2014) https://www.eesc.europa.eu/sites/default/files/resources/docs/qe-02-13-506-en-c.pdf accessed 9 December 2021.

45 Martin Bowman, Karen Luyckx, and Christina O'Sullivan, 'Keeping Unavoidable Food Waste in the Food Chain as Animal Feed' in Christian Reynolds and others (eds), *Routledge Handbook of Food Waste* (Routledge 2020).

46 Nils Johansson, 'Why Is Biogas Production and Not Food Donation the Swedish Political Priority for Food Waste Management?' (2021) 126 Environmental Science & Policy 60.

47 European Commission, 'Commission Notice – EU Guidelines on Food Donations' (2017) 6872.

48 Rao, Bast, and de Boer (n 41).

49 Alice Luciano and others, 'Potentials and Challenges of Former Food Products (Food Leftover) as Alternative Feed Ingredients' (2020) 10 Animals 125.

spongiform encephalopathy (BSE) outbreak which was caused largely by the mismanagement of animal feeding. As a result, animal by-products are often excluded from higher valorisation routes.[50] This not only includes products from meat processing operations but also domestic food waste and leftovers from catering operations that may contain traces of meat or where the absence of meat cannot be verified.

EU regulations in this area are known to be among the most stringent in the world and only a small volume of products that may contain meat and animal by-products are currently used for the purpose of animal feeding despite the high nutritional value they offer.[51] According to results from REFRESH, these restrictions cannot be scientifically justified in the case of non-ruminant livestock that are not susceptible to prion diseases.[52] REFRESH underlined that changes in legislation could allow over 14 million tonnes of surplus food to be safely valorised as non-ruminant feed.[53] Results from the project indicated the need to adjust Regulation 999/2001, which prohibited the feeding of meat to all herbivorous and omnivorous farmed animals.[54] Excluded from animal feeding, conversion to bioenergy becomes the most feasible valorisation route for animal by-products and food waste that has come in contact with animal products.[55] In doing this, animal products are insupportably removed from the food supply chain. However, a recent amendment to Regulation 999/2001 has the potential to change this. In August 2021, Regulation 2021/1372 was adopted.[56] Subject to various hygiene, safety, and traceability conditions, the new

---

50 Rao, Bast, and de Boer (n 41).

51 D Jędrejek and others, 'Animal By-Products for Feed: Characteristics, European Regulatory Framework, and Potential Impacts on Human and Animal Health and the Environment' (2016) 25 Journal of Animal and Feed Sciences 189.

52 Jan Broeze and Karen Luyckx, 'REFRESH Deliverable D6.11 – Identification of Food Waste Conversion Barriers' (REFRESH 2019) https://www.eu-refresh.org/sites/default/files/D6.11%20Identification%20of%20food%20waste%20conversion%20barriers_Final.pdf accessed 9 December 2021.

53 Karen Luyckx and others, 'REFRESH Deliverable D6.7 – Technical Guidelines Animal Feed' (REFRESH 2019) https://eu-refresh.org/sites/default/files/REFRESH%20D6.7%20Technical%20Guidelines%20Animal%20Feed%20Final.pdf accessed 9 December 2021.

54 Broeze and Luyckx (n 52); Regulation (EU) 2021/1372 amending Annex IV to Regulation (EC) 999/2001 of the European Parliament and of the Council as regards the prohibition to feed non-ruminant farmed animals, other than fur animals, with protein derived from animals [2021] OJ L295/1.

55 Within this valorisation route as well, many animal products end up being incinerated as opposed to be being sent to anaerobic digestion plants. Regulation 1069/2009 allows only certain kinds of animal products (categories 2 and 3) to be sent to anaerobic digestion plants.

56 Reg 2021/1372 (n 54).

regulation re-authorises the use of processed animal proteins derived from pigs and insects in poultry feed, processed animal proteins derived from poultry and insect in pig feed, and gelatine and collagen of ruminant origin in the feed of non-ruminant farmed animals.[57] Combined with appropriate market incentives and strict enforcement, this amendment could be a game changer for valorising food waste as animal feed.

When comparing the position of various valorisation options, Marie Mourad's work on competing hierarchies of food waste solutions is especially noteworthy.[58] As illustrated by Figure 4.2, her research indicates that different valorisation routes may be seen as the best fit depending on which lens the issue is viewed through. In the environmental sustainability context, waste-to-energy is seen as more desirable than other options such as food donation or the sale of food products for lower prices. This is due to the success of different valorisation options being evaluated using different criteria. For instance, environmental impact is measured by parameters such as carbon dioxide emissions and effect on soil and water, whereas social impact is measured by the number and kind of calories, and economic impact by savings or profits.[59]

Results from Mourad's work indicate that despite being at the bottom of the hierarchy, companies and municipalities show a strong preference for the waste-to-energy route.[60] A notable advantage of this kind of valorisation is that its positive impact can be easily measured by quantifying waste diverted from landfills.[61] The legislative push to use waste, food or otherwise, to fulfil renewable energy targets has also led to MSs undertaking fiscal measures such as tax incentives to reward businesses that send their waste to energy recovery.[62] Mourad concludes that in terms of social, environmental, and economic values, various valorisation routes constitute competing categories when positioned in a hierarchical manner.[63]

This brings us to the question of whether the ranking of valorisation options through a hierarchy can be justified in the first place. When considered on its own, converting food waste to bioenergy presents much promise in the circular bioeconomy. It allows for biomass to be valorised without the health and safety

---

57 ibid.

58 M Mourad, 'Recycling, Recovering and Preventing "Food Waste": Competing Solutions for Food Systems Sustainability in the United States and France' (2016) 126 Journal of Cleaner Production 461.

59 ibid.

60 ibid.

61 ibid.

62 ibid; Wunder and others (n 37).

63 Mourad (n 58).

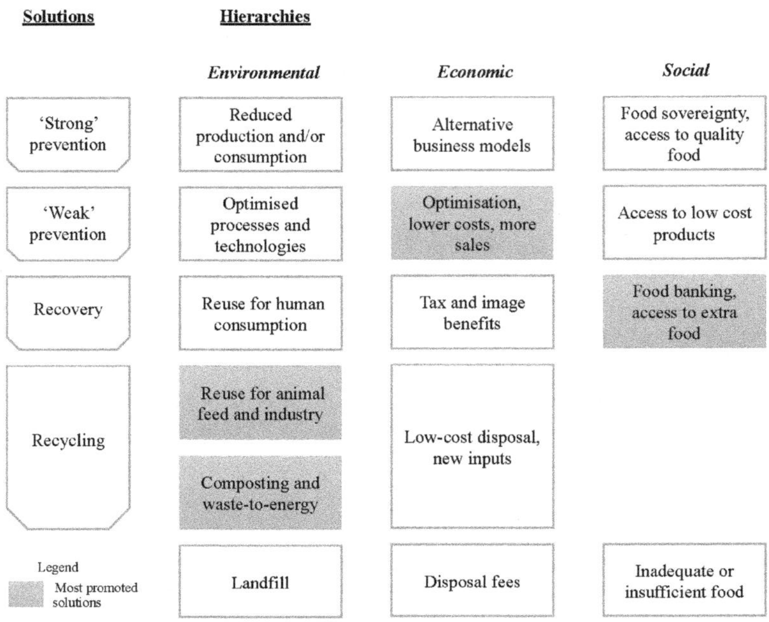

Source: M Mourad, 'Recycling, Recovering and Preventing "Food Waste": Competing Solutions for Food Systems Sustainability in the United States and France' (2016) 126 Journal of Cleaner Production 461.

Figure 4.2 Competing hierarchies of solutions to food waste

risks associated with higher priority valorisation options, while at the same time reducing dependence on fossil fuels and first-generation biofuels. Nadine Arnold, in her work on competition in the food waste hierarchy, discusses this from the perspective of organisation theory.[64] Unique to the situation of food waste valorisation is the likelihood that actors involved in lower-ranking valorisation operations do not have any interest in achieving a 'better' position in the hierarchy.[65] Arnold elaborates that bioenergy producers (Swiss biogas plants in the case of her study) dissociate themselves from the broader field of food waste by creating their own sub-field centred on food waste recovery.[66]

[64] Nadine Arnold, 'Avoiding Competition: The Effects of Rankings in the Food Waste Field' in Stefan Arora-Jonsson and others (eds), *Competition: What It Is and Why It Happens* (Oxford University Press 2021).

[65] ibid.

[66] ibid.

By exercising linguistic nuances, these actors shape the discourse in their sub-field to their advantage.[67] In the Swiss case, terms that signal 'food waste' (*Verschwendung* in German and *gaspillage* in French) are rarely used. Instead, terms like *Abfall* (German) and *déchets* (French), meaning unwanted material, are used. This way, the biogas plants convey the message that they transform unwanted and worthless materials into something of value. Despite bioenergy created from food waste ranking low in the food waste hierarchy, it is viewed favourably when compared to other sources of energy. It can therefore be argued that it is not the actors involved in these various valorisation operations that compete with one another. It is, instead, FBOs that feel the pressure to choose the most sustainable option and justify this choice. In doing this, their social (people), environmental (planet) and economic (profit) priorities may come into conflict with one another.

It is worthwhile at this point to discuss whether the people-planet-profit approach to sustainability, also known as the triple bottom line, is effective when designing policies aimed at optimising food waste valorisation. The concept of the triple bottom line is rooted in the field of management science and was proposed by John Elkington to operationalise corporate social responsibility.[68] Kuhlman and Farrington propose that separating the environmental aspect from the social and economic ones might be a more sensible approach when it comes to assessing the impacts of sustainability policies.[69] They suggest that because the social and economic dimensions of sustainability consider the needs of the present while the environmental dimension considers the needs of the future, they must be viewed separately.[70] Kuhlman and Farrington propose to call the former 'well-being' and the latter 'sustainability'.[71]

Applying this reasoning to food waste, we suggest setting different priorities for the different stages of food biomass. When food is a commodity that is saleable to consumers for its nutritional value, it is of greater consequence for meeting the needs of today. This kind of food must be prevented from turning into waste. At this stage, both strong (systemic change)[72] and weak (process optimisation)[73] prevention strategies must be applied. If prevention fails, the redistribution and donation of such food must be considered and supported by

---

67 ibid.

68 John Elkington, 'Towards the Sustainable Corporation: Win-Win-Win Business Strategies for Sustainable Development' (1994) 36 California Management Review 90.

69 Tom Kuhlman and John Farrington, 'What Is Sustainability?' (2010) 2 Sustainability 3436.

70 ibid.

71 ibid.

72 Mourad (n 58).

73 ibid.

relevant legislation. If food processing by-products can be safely reprocessed into new food products, this must be considered after or alongside donation and redistribution. In doing this, however, once food is no longer safe for human consumption, environmental sustainability must become a priority. This is because the way in which this biomass is dealt with will impact the future. Whenever feasible from a safety and nutrition perspective, such food must be reused as animal feed because it offers more environmental benefits as compared to valorisation in the form of energy recovery.[74] If the biomass is unfit for use in animal feed, it must be considered for energy recovery, first through anaerobic digestion and then incineration.[75] Figure 4.3 presents this bifurcated hierarchy.

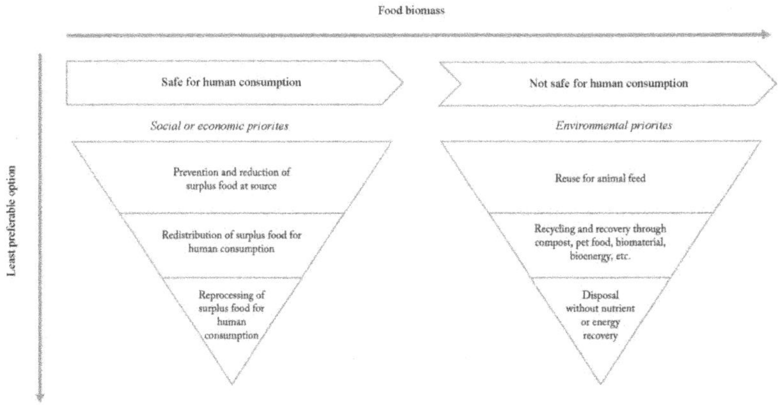

Figure 4.3 The bifurcated food use hierarchy

For this approach to be practicable, FBOs must be provided with pragmatic guidelines. While public law plays an important role in facilitating this, co-regulation by private actors may be able to help businesses deal with the liability and risks that come with food waste valorisation. FBOs have utilised private standards, a means of private co-regulation, as a tool to cope with regulatory uncertainty for over two decades now. In the following section, we

[74] Ramy Salemdeeb and others, 'Environmental and Health Impacts of Using Food Waste as Animal Feed: A Comparative Analysis of Food Waste Management Options' (2017) 140 Journal of Cleaner Production 871.

[75] Papargyropoulou and others (n 37).

will deliberate on whether such standards can help facilitate better food waste valorisation.

V. PRIVATE STANDARDS AND FOOD WASTE

As described above, safety for human consumption is key when choosing the most fitting valorisation option for food surplus and waste. In the EU, food safety is overseen by the GFL.[76] Since its introduction, the GFL has developed around the idea of food safety being the combined responsibility of the State and private actors.[77] Paragraph 30 of the preamble to the GFL explicitly places responsibility on FBOs by stating that they have the primary legal responsibility for ensuring food safety.[78] Regarding the responsibility of businesses, Article 17 states: 'Food and feed business operators at all stages of production, processing and distribution within the businesses under their control shall ensure that foods or feeds satisfy the requirements of food law which are relevant to their activities and shall verify that such requirements are met'.[79]

Given that the exact means to fulfil this responsibility are not specified, FBOs are left in a state of regulatory uncertainty.[80] To cope with ambiguity, FBOs use contracts, hygiene guides, and food safety management systems to specify criteria such as contaminant levels, handling and storage requirements, and quality specifications.[81] Influential actors like supermarket chains, trade organisations, and multinational corporations develop and enforce their own food safety management systems.[82] In addition to compliance with GFL and international law, these systems also cover consumer expectations.[83] Although technically voluntary in nature, food safety management systems (also known

---

[76] GFL (n 16).

[77] Madhura Rao, Aalt Bast and Alie de Boer, 'European Private Food Safety Standards in Global Agri-Food Supply Chains: A Systematic Review' (2021) 24 International Food and Agribusiness Management Review 1.

[78] GFL (n 16) para 30.

[79] ibid.

[80] Christophe Charlier and Egizio Valceschini, 'Food Safety, Market Power and Private Standards: An Analysis of the Emerging Strategies of Food Operators' (2010) 1 International Journal on Food System Dynamics 103.

[81] Theo Appelhof and Ronald van den Heuvel, 'Inventory of Private Food Law' in Bernd van der Meulen (ed) *Private Food Law: Governing Food Chains through Contract Law, Self-regulation, Private Standards, Audits and Certification Schemes* (Wageningen Academic Publishers 2011); Bernd van der Meulen, 'The Anatomy of Private Food Law' in Bernd van der Meulen (ed), *Private Food Law: Governing Food Chains through Contract Law, Self-regulation, Private Standards, Audits and Certification Schemes* (Wageningen Academic Publishers 2011).

[82] Rao, Bast and de Boer (n 77); Appelhof and van den Heuvel (n 81).

[83] Appelhof and van den Heuvel (n 81).

as standards or schemes) that are created or favoured by influential actors have become *de facto* mandatory in agri-food supply chains.[84] Standards that were once established with the aim of regulating food safety have expanded their scope to include several contemporary issues such as labour conditions, animal welfare, and environmental impacts of food production.[85] This is often done by adding plug-ins to existing standards or through collaborations between two private standards specialising in different aspects of food production and trade. We posit that food waste prevention and valorisation could also be incorporated into private food safety standards in a similar manner.

It is expected that private standards already influence the state of food loss and waste. On the one hand, through prescriptive and often unduly strict product specifications, private standards can cause perfectly safe food products to be classified as unwanted or unsalable.[86] On the other hand, they can help prevent food waste by improving traceability, aiding in the early identification of food safety issues, and reducing product failure.[87] By taking cognisance of these impacts, standards can be optimised to prevent food waste. Where prevention is not possible, they can help FBOs decide on the most suitable valorisation option. In the case of reuse as animal feed, private standards are already instrumental in helping FBOs adhere to feed safety requirements.[88] This cooperation can be replicated in food-to-energy or feed-to-energy valorisation.

Similar to the food sector, the European bioenergy sector is no stranger to private standards. RED II encourages co-regulation by directing actors to demonstrate compliance with sustainability criteria through Commission-recognised voluntary schemes.[89] In fact, this model of compliance checking has inspired several other sectors of the bioeconomy to develop similar certification schemes.[90] As a result, actors in the bioenergy supply chain, like those in the

---

[84] Rao, Bast and de Boer (n 77).

[85] Spencer Henson and John Humphrey, 'Understanding the Complexities of Private Standards in Global Agri-Food Chains as They Impact Developing Countries' (2010) 46 Journal of Development Studies 1628; Rao, Bast and de Boer (n 77).

[86] Rao, Bast and de Boer (n 77).

[87] ibid.

[88] See for example standards such as GMP+, Qualimat, and FAMI-QS that work with several food producers to set requirements regarding food products which can be valorised through reuse in animal feed.

[89] Stefan Majer and others, 'Gaps and Research Demand for Sustainability Certification and Standardisation in a Sustainable Bio-Based Economy in the EU' (2018) 10 Sustainability 2455.

[90] Kirsten Selbmann and Lydia Pforte, 'Evaluation of Ecological Criteria of Biofuel Certification in Germany' (2016) 8 Sustainability 936.

food and feed supply chains, work according to the chain of custody principle.[91] Connecting food and feed safety standards with bioenergy standards could aid FBOs in directing biomass that can no longer be used for food and feed purposes to energy recovery. In line with public legislation on waste, renewable energy, and food moving towards improved interconnectedness, private standards must follow suit to allow for these changes to be practicable for market actors. For the circular bioeconomy model to succeed, it is critical that the traceability of biomass is ensured in not only individual supply chains but also when biomass is transferred from one supply chain to another. Majer and colleagues propose the development of meta-standards based on the mutual recognition of different certification frameworks that play a role in the bioeconomy.[92] They also point out that most standards, whether food, feed, or energy, do not consider the end-of-life (EoL) scenario for biomass.[93] It is likely that standards, even those focused on sustainability-related issues, are designed for linear, cradle-to-grave or cradle-to-gate operations. Therefore, EoL scenarios are either not given much importance or included as an afterthought. Instead, if standards are designed keeping in mind that many supply chains, especially those dealing with biomass, are likely to move to a circular, cradle-to-cradle way of operating in the future, EoL scenarios would become significantly more important.

Private regulation, especially in the United States, seems to already be moving in this direction. Cradle to Cradle Certified® is a US-based scheme that certifies the 'circularity' of materials, products, and systems. The Upcycled Certified Program, which is also US-based, certifies the environmental credentials of food products made from by-products. It is, however, important that such standards develop in tandem with other standards that regulate this area. Like it is in the case of public policy, cooperation instead of competition is the need of the hour in the private regulation space if biomass is to be utilised in a manner that is fair and environmentally sustainable.

This brings us back to Mourad's distinction between strong and weak measures to prevent food waste. As defined in her work, a weak food waste prevention strategy is one that 'relies on the belief that improved processes and technologies without a fundamental change in business models are enough to significantly prevent and almost eradicate waste'.[94] This approach is criticised because it relies primarily on companies' voluntary commitment

---

[91] Seita Romppanen, 'The EU's Biofuels: Certified as Sustainable' (2012) 3 Renewable Energy Law and Policy Review 173.

[92] Majer and others (n 89).

[93] ibid.

[94] Mourad (n 58).

to reducing waste.[95] However, considering the urgent need to address the issue of food waste, the role of private actors can no longer be seen as voluntary or optional. In contrast to weak prevention is strong prevention, which proposes reducing food waste through comprehensive, systemic changes such as the implementation of short food supply chain models and avoiding overproduction.[96] Modifying private standards, without changing the way in which businesses that implement them operate, would be classified as weak prevention. However, even weak prevention strategies have the potential to drive systemic change in the long run. Increased cooperation among food, feed, and bioenergy private standards can help drive this change by translating the new interconnectedness in public law on these topics into a language that businesses are well versed in.

VI. CONCLUSION

This chapter discusses the valorisation of food as energy in the EU. It is evident that the pressure to meet global and regional sustainability goals is driving EU legislators to consider food waste as a multidimensional issue that is impacted by a broad range of policy areas. The legal patchwork that oversaw food waste valorisation is gradually being replaced by pieces of legislation that are better aligned with one another. However, the food waste hierarchy model that forms the backbone of all legislative changes concerning food waste might cause various valorisation options to compete with one another. Despite energy recovery being ranked the lowest among valorisation options, it may end up being seen more favourably by FBOs since it helps keep food out of landfills while avoiding the safety risks and costs associated with reuse as food or feed.

To prevent such competition, we propose that valorisation options for food be based on its safety for human consumption. By prioritising economic and social well-being when food is fit for human consumption and environmental sustainability when it is not, conflicts between FBOs' economic, social, and environmental priorities may be largely avoided. At the same time, businesses are likely to require additional support in their decision-making process when it comes to choosing the most suitable option for their food surplus or waste. In both the food and energy sector, public law affords private actors the opportunity to self-regulate some aspects of decision-making and compliance. Private regulation measures such as voluntary standards may offer a bridge that allows the sustainable and fair valorisation of food waste. In line with the legislation on these subjects, private standards on food, feed, and energy must cooperate

[95] ibid.
[96] ibid.

better to enable transitioning to a future where biomass at the end of its life in one supply chain is safely utilised in another.

LEGISLATION

Directive (EU) 2018/2001 on the promotion of the use of energy from renewable sources [2018] OJ L328/82 ('RED II')

Directive 2008/98/EC on waste and repealing certain Directives [2008] OJ L312/3 ('Waste Framework Directive', 'WFD')

Directive (EU) 2018/851 amending Directive 2008/98/EC on waste [2018] OJ L150/109 ('GFL')

Regulation (EU) 2021/1372 amending Annex IV to Regulation (EC) 999/2001 as regards the prohibition to feed non-ruminant farmed animals, other than fur animals, with protein derived from animals [2021] OJ L295/1

Regulation (EC) 999/2001 laying down rules for the prevention, control and eradication of certain transmissible spongiform encephalopathies [2001] OJ L147/1

Delegated Decision (EU) 2019/1597 supplementing Directive 2008/98/EC as regards a common methodology and minimum quality requirements for the uniform measurement of levels of food waste [2019] OJ L248/77

CASES

AS Tallinna Vesi v Keskkonnaamet (Case C-60/18) EU:C:2019:264 [2019]

Prato Nevoso Termo Energy Srl v Provincia di Cuneo and ARPA Piemonte (Case C-212/18) EU:C:2019:898 [2019]

5. Forestry waste to biofuel and biogas: law and policy

Elisa Cavallin

I. INTRODUCTION

A. Challenges and Trade-offs in Forestry Biomass Generation

Bioenergy is believed to have a role in meeting the international and European Union's (EU) climate targets;[1] global estimates suggest that bioenergy will make up for 30% of the growth in renewable consumption from 2018 to 2023[2] and that its use will quadruple in the next 20 years.[3] Global demand for biofuels is expected to grow as well, by 28% over the period 2021–2026.[4] More specifically, biomass is seen as one of the few alternatives to fossil fuel feedstock, especially in specific sectors, such as the chemical industry and the heavy road transport and marine and aviation sectors.[5] In addition, contrary to

---

[1] Joeri Rogelj and others 'Mitigation Pathways Compatible with 1.5 C in the Context of Sustainable Development' in Valérie Masson-Delmotte and others (eds), *Global Warming of 1.5°C. – An IPCC Special Report on the Impacts of Global Warming of 1.5°C above Pre-industrial Levels and Related Global Greenhouse Gas Emission Pathways, in the Context of Strengthening the Global Response to the Threat of Climate Change, Sustainable Development, and Efforts to Eradicate Poverty* (Intergovernmental Panel on Climate Change (IPCC) 2018).

[2] The growth is expected to come from the use of solid, liquid and gaseous fuels, because of their considerable use in heating and increasing consumption in the transport sector. See: International Energy Agency (IEA), *Renewables 2018. Analysis and Forecasts to 2023* (IEA 2018).

[3] Emily Webster, 'Transnational Legal Processes, the EU and RED II: Strengthening the Global Governance of Bioenergy' (2020) 29 Review of European, Comparative & International Environmental Law 1.

[4] International Energy Agency (IEA), *Renewables 2021. Analysis and Forecasts to 2026* (IEA 2021) 89.

[5] Paul Stegmann, Marc Londo and Martin Junginger, 'The Circular Bioeconomy: Its Elements and Role in European Bioeconomy Clusters' (2020) 6 Resources, Conservation & Recycling: X 100029, 1.

fossil fuels, biomass as a source of energy can be considered renewable, and its use emits carbon that is already a part of the biogenic carbon cycle.[6]

A large amount of forestry biomass is used, along with other types of biomass, to produce bioenergy. Data on wood products from 2015 shows that 63% of all the wood used in the EU was exploited for bioenergy production: around 37% of the total wood used for energy was primary wood (wood purposefully harvested to produce energy), and 49% of it was considered to be secondary wood biomass, comprising, for example, by-products and residues from the wood processing industry, but also post-consumer recovered wood. Data also highlights a problematic 14% of uncategorised woody biomass used for energy, the origin of which is not known but likely to be also primary wood.[7] In addition, considering trends over the years, data highlights that the overall use of woody biomass in the EU for the past two decades has been increasing – roughly a 20% increase since 2000.[8] While this data is useful to give an impression of forestry-related operations and bioenergy, some studies have found that this data tends to underestimate actual removals and felling.[9]

From a biodiversity and ecosystem preservation perspective, forestry biomass generation presents several challenges. First, not all biomass from tree harvesting is, or should be, removed from the site during operations. Within the EU, between 2004 and 2013, biomass removal accounted for about 80%,[10] and the remaining 20% was left behind as residues.[11] This process of leaving some logging residues or by-products behind provides ecological benefits: nutrient cycling, maintenance of carbon content in the soil, provision of habitats and effects on habitat structure (and, therefore, on biodiversity),

---

6 Michael T Ter-Mikaelian, Stephen J Colombo and Jiaxin Chen, 'The Burning Question: Does Forest Bioenergy Reduce Carbon Emissions? A Review of Common Misconceptions about Forest Carbon Accounting' (2015) 113 Journal of Forestry 1.

7 Andrea Camia and others, *The Use of Woody Biomass for Energy Production in the EU* (Publication Office of the European Union 2020) 7, 41.

8 European Commission, 'New EU Forest Strategy for 2030' COM (2021) 651, 7.

9 See, for example, Dominik Jochem and others, 'Estimation of Wood Removals and Fellings in Germany: A Calculation Approach Based on the Amount of Used Roundwood' (2015) 134 European Journal of Forest Research 5.

10 Camia and others (n 7). Estimate also based on: Roberto Pilli and others, 'The European Forest Sector: Past and Future Carbon Budget and Fluxes under Different Management Scenarios' (2017) 14 Biogeosciences 9.

11 Camia and others (n 7). Estimate also based on: Pilli and others (n 10). It is not easy to ascertain whether the aforementioned 80% vs 20% when it comes to biomass removal from a site is a good balance: the effects relating to biomass removal are highly variable and depend on the site, meaning that the possibility of making generalised determinations about impacts is limited. It should also be noted that it might not always be possible to leave residues on sites; see, for example, the case of forestry clearance for certain development projects.

all of which ultimately have an impact on ecosystem services. Different types of residues have different ecological roles, and their removal is, accordingly, associated with different impacts.[12] Therefore, and given that the effects of biomass removal from a site are highly variable and site-dependent, ideally the determination of what may be removed and what should be left behind ought to be based on careful scientific considerations and (impact) assessments.

Second, afforestation, reforestation and conversion to plantations, which could be considered solutions to (re)establish forest areas in the EU and/or to increase the biomass pool, are also not necessarily suitable or desirable operations. The impacts on ecosystems and their severity[13] depend on several factors: historic land use, previous land use (if, for example, expansion of tree plantations takes place at the expense of forests with higher environmental value), the establishing method (e.g. natural regeneration or planting and seeding), the features of the planted forests (e.g. the type of species, the species mixture, density), and post-planting management (e.g. site tending, harvesting method). Depending on these variables, different consequences ensue. In other words, while possibly increasing climate mitigation efforts in the short or medium-term (and not even in every scenario), afforestation, reforestation and conversion to plantation might have unwanted consequences[14] on ecosystems and on biodiversity, with different trade-off rates depending on the variables mentioned above.[15] Once again, this would indicate that every activity needs to be carefully considered. Generally speaking, the circular use of wood and wood products and prioritisation of the use of residues within certain parameters are key aspects in the pursuit of solutions in terms of the energy transition that are genuinely sustainable and future-oriented.

Third, concepts of the sustainable use of forests or sustainable forest management (i.e. and simply put, the finding of a balance between exploitation and nature conservation) are particularly in need of attention. Their development is influenced by policy and law, and private schemes or voluntary initiatives and standards, which should all be guided by the realisation of the prevention and precautionary principles in forestry. At the same time and possibly overlapping with some of the above, there exist also so-called 'zero-deforestation approaches' (that range from 'zero net deforestation' to 'zero gross deforest-

---

[12] Camia and others (n 7) 108–122.

[13] Social impacts, while of paramount importance, are beyond the scope of this chapter.

[14] In particular: impact on community composition, impact on species populations, impact on carbon stocks, impacts on water cycle (for afforestation), impact on soil quality (for conversion to plantations). See: Camia and others (n 7) 125–142.

[15] ibid 123–142.

ation' and generally rely on the determination of the concept of 'acceptable deforestation').[16]

Additionally, the potential role of forestry products and waste in the EU's circular energy system needs to take into consideration the state of EU forests. Forested areas – forests and wooded land[17] – cover about 45% of the EU's land area.[18] The forested area in Europe has been generally stable over the last couple of decades. The slight and slow expansion (6% between 1990 and 2020)[19] is only the result of afforestation programmes and spontaneous regeneration on abandoned agricultural land, and the changes in forest land cover are now generally localised in a few European states.[20] However, despite this overall stable status, forest ecosystems are still subjected to pressures and changes in their conditions, leading to increasing concerns over their long-term

---

16 See, for more information: Till Neeff and Thaís Linhares-Juvenal, 'Zero Deforestation Initiatives and their Impacts on Commodity Supply Chains' (Discussion paper prepared for the 57th Session of the FAO Advisory Committee on Sustainable Forest-based Industries) (2016) https://www.fao.org/3/i6857e/i6857e.pdf/.

17 The Food and Agriculture Organization (FAO) defines 'forests' as lands of more than 0.5 hectares and having trees higher than 5 metres and a canopy cover of more than 10% and it does not include land that is predominantly under agricultural or urban land use. The concept of 'other wooded land' includes other afforested lands that do not amount to forests as described above but do meet, however, certain criteria: coverage of more than 0.5 hectares, a canopy cover of 5 to 10% of trees with a height of 5 metres *in situ* or a canopy cover of more than 10% when other types of flora, such as shrubs and bushes, are also included. Peter Holmgren and Robert Davis, 'FRA 2000. On Definitions of Forest and Forest Change' (2000) Food and Agriculture Organization (FAO) Forestry Department, Working Paper 33. While this goes beyond the scope of the chapter, it is worth mentioning that the definition of what constitutes a forest from a legal standpoint is a matter of paramount importance and that, in the EU, we will have a definition of 'forest' (mirroring the FAO definition) with the adoption of the new so-called "Deforestation-free Product Regulation". Yet, forest management remains primarily a matter of national competence. See European Parliament, 'Fact Sheets on the European Union. The European Union and Forests' (n.d.) https://www.europarl.europa.eu/factsheets/en/sheet/105/the-european-union-and-forests#:~:text=Nevertheless%2C%20for%20the%20purposes%20of,more%20than%2010%25%20and%20an/. The FAO definition itself has been subjected to criticism as it is broad enough to include certain tree plantations or monocultures. See: Rainforest Movement and others, 'Open letter from various NGOs to FAO on the Occasion of the International Day of Forests 2014' (2014) https://www.wrm.org.uy/all-campaigns/open-letter-to-fao-on-the-occasion-of-the-international-day-of-forests-2014.

18 New EU Forest Strategy for 2030 (n 8).

19 Edward Cook, *Agriculture, Forestry and Fishery Statistics: 2020 Edition* (Publications Office of the European Union 2020) 87.

20 European Environment Agency (EEA), *The European Environment: State and Outlook 2020: Knowledge for Transition to a Sustainable Europe* (Publications Office of the European Union 2019) 122.

health and stability.[21] Biodiversity decline is also a prominent issue in forested areas: forest management and agricultural intensification being drivers of habitat loss, fragmentation, and degradation.[22] This biodiversity loss also takes place in protected forests; assessments of habitats protected under the Habitats Directive at the EU level show that several protected forest habitats exhibit an unfavourable conservation status and a deteriorating trend.[23] While the designation of forest habitats as protected areas surely helps and encourages the sustainable management of the sites, the fate of forests does not solely depend on this aspect, as the network can still suffer from several pressures such as climate change, the mitigation of which – as in a twisted loop – also lies in the proper management and protection of the natural carbon stocks and sinks, such as forests. What is more, forests are crucial environmental assets, as they represent a hub of ecosystem services: flood regulation, resource provision, cultural and recreational services, and climate change mitigation and adaptation, among others. Accordingly, their existence and their good management should be at the forefront of all the relevant policies and measures.

Against this backdrop, one of the most promising routes in the area of sustainable use of forestry products is, as already implied, the idea of a circular bioeconomy, where waste plays a substantial role. Accordingly, (certain) biological waste, including forestry waste, should be seen as a resource, and sustainable material flows and pathways should be designed according to both the so-called waste hierarchy and the cascading use principle to fully exploit and prolong the use of these materials in the economic cycle. In particular, the waste hierarchy is regarded as the foundation of EU waste management; a five-step hierarchy, formally introduced in the Waste Framework Directive

---

21 Annemarie Bastrup-Birk, Johnny Reker and Nihat Zal, *European Forest Ecosystems: State and Trends* – EEA Report No 5 (Publication Office of the European Union 2016) 30; European Environment Agency (EEA), 'Forest Dynamics in Europe and their Ecological Consequences' (eea.europa.eu, 27 November 2018) https://www.eea.europa.eu/themes/biodiversity/forests/forest-dynamics-in-europe-and/. Accessed 9 August 2022.

22 See, for example, Raimo Virkkala, 'Long-term Decline of Southern Boreal Forest Birds: Consequence of Habitat Alteration or Climate Change?' (2016) 25 Biodiversity and Conservation 1; Sara Fraixedas, Andreas Lindén and Aleksi Lehikoinen, 'Population Trends of Common Breeding Forest Birds in Southern Finland Are Consistent with Trends in Forest Management and Climate Change' (2015) 92 Ornis Fennica 4.

23 EEA (n 20), 81. Original source: European Environment Agency (EEA), 'Habitats of European Interest – Indicator Assessment' (2016) https://www.eea.europa.eu/data-and-maps/indicators/habitats-of-european-interest-1/assessment/. The data is based on the conservation status of habitat types and species reporting as per art 17 of Directive 92/43/EEC (on the Conservation of Natural Habitats and of Wild Fauna and Flora [1992] OJ L206/7 ('Habitat Directive')).

(WFD), which establishes an order of preference for managing and disposing of waste (in order, from most preferred to least preferred or last resort: prevention, preparing for re-use, recycling, other recovery, and disposal).[24]

The cascading use principle then refers to the resource-efficient and circular use of any biomass (or other material): one use would follow another (use and re-use), which would be followed by recycling and recovery. Often, the cascading use principle also features a 'decreasing value' component with each step downwards, with energy use as the final step: in essence, most valuable uses (e.g., with decreasing value, food, feed, material products) would be preferred over less valuable ones (e.g. energy use). While this seems a linear concept (and it was mostly regarded as such in the past), the more recent circularity aspect of the principle also covers the numerous interlinked pathways that reflect developments in technology and other aspects, such as the emergence of new products and markets and industrial and organisational changes (e.g. industrial symbiosis). In short, the cascading use principle has as underlying principles those of sustainability, resource efficiency, circularity in every stream and at every step, the stimulation of those uses of biomass with high added value (and relevance of new products and new markets), and subsidiarity and the importance of national, regional and local contexts.[25] It is also described as 'a complex interaction of material flows and their utilisation in different products and sectors', as 'a strategy to increase resource efficiency by using wood as often and as efficiently as possible in product applications before it is finally used for energy recovery' and as 'the efficient utilisation of resources by using residues and recycled materials for material use to extend total biomass availability within a given system'.[26]

In conclusion, in a world with a growing demand for goods and, thus, for raw materials, increased energy demands and related paucity of non-renewable resources, in the context of a changing climate and increased pressure on nature due to human activities, true sustainable management (which considers ecological impacts of every action undertaken and is based on the precautionary principle and the principle of prevention), the cascading use principle and the waste hierarchy are to be considered key strategic elements to pursue.

---

[24] Directive 2008/98/EC on Waste and Repealing Certain Directives [2008] OJ L312/3 ('Waste Framework Directive', 'WFD') art 4. See also: European Commission 'Waste Framework Directive' (environment.ec.europa.eu, n.d.) https://ec.europa.eu/environment/topics/waste-and-recycling/waste-framework-directive_en/.

[25] European Commission, 'Guidance on Cascading Use of Biomass with Selected Good Practice Examples on Woody Biomass' (2018) 7, 11–22.

[26] Martijn Vis, Udo Mantau and Ben Allen, *CASCADES: Study on the Optimised Cascading Use of Wood* – No 394/PP/ENT/RCH/14/7689 (Publications Office of the European Union 2016) i, 8.

B. The EU Policy and Legal Panorama Regarding Forestry and Forestry Waste: A Changing and Complex Web

Forest policy and waste management find themselves at the intersection of the EU's climate and energy policies, circular economy and environmental protection.[27] Of particular policy importance are the EU Bioeconomy Action Plan;[28] the Communication on the Role of Waste-to-Energy in the Circular Economy;[29] the Green Deal;[30] the Circular Economy Action Plan;[31] the Farm to Fork Strategy;[32] the Biodiversity Strategy;[33] the New Soil Strategy;[34] and, naturally, the Forest Strategy.[35]

As for legislative texts or revisions thereof that are in the pipeline, the legislative proposals in the so-called 'Fit for 55' package play an important role.[36] Several (legal) initiatives under these documents show some promise for a more balanced management of natural resources, for nature protection, and for climate change mitigation and adaptation. Among these, especially interesting are the proposals to amend the 2018 Renewable Energy Directive (RED II)[37] and the Land Use, Land Use Change and Forestry Regulation.[38] The

---

[27] For an overview of the broader legal landscape, see Asha Singh, Thomas Christensen and Calliope Panoutsou, 'Policy Review for Biomass Value Chains in the European Bioeconomy' (2021) 3 Global Transitions, 13–42.

[28] European Commission, 'A Sustainable Bioeconomy for Europe: Strengthening the Connection between Economy, Society and the Environment' COM (2018) 673.

[29] European Commission, 'The Role of Waste-to-Energy in the Circular Economy' COM (2017) 34.

[30] European Commission, 'The European Green Deal' COM (2019) 640.

[31] European Commission, 'A New Circular Economy Action Plan. For a Cleaner and More Competitive Europe' COM (2020) 98, 11.

[32] European Commission, 'A Farm to Fork Strategy for a Fair, Healthy and Environmentally-Friendly Food System' COM (2020) 381.

[33] European Commission, 'EU Biodiversity Strategy for 2030. Bringing Nature Back into our Lives' COM (2020) 380.

[34] European Commission, 'EU Soil Strategy for 2030. Reaping the Benefits of Healthy Soils for People, Food, Nature and Climate' COM (2021) 699.

[35] New EU Forest Strategy for 2030 (n 8).

[36] European Commission, 'European Green Deal: Commission Proposes Transformation of EU Economy and Society to Meet Climate Ambitions' (14 July 2021) https://ec.europa.eu/commission/presscorner/detail/en/IP_21_3541/.

[37] European Commission, 'Proposal for a Directive Amending Directive (EU) 2018/2001, Regulation (EU) 2018/1999 and Directive 98/70/EC as Regards the Promotion of Energy from Renewable Sources, and Repealing Council Directive (EU) 2015/652' COM (2021) 557 ('Proposal for RED III').

[38] European Commission, 'Proposal for a Regulation Amending Regulations (EU) 2018/841 as Regards the Scope, Simplifying the Compliance Rules, Setting Out the Targets of the Member States for 2030 and Committing to the Collective Achievement

RED II[39] and its revision (the Proposal for the RED III) are, in particular, at the centre of the bioenergy debate and some of their provisions will be further explored in this chapter.

Another very relevant document, whose revision is also planned (for 2023), is the already mentioned WFD, which is the EU document of reference for basic concepts, definitions and rules related to waste and waste management. A specific part of this document related to forestry waste will also be the object of a deeper analysis in this chapter. It should, however, be mentioned in this context that the Commission is working on a targeted revision of the WFD, aiming at improving the outcome of waste management in line with the waste hierarchy and the realisation and implementation of the polluter pays principle, as well as focusing on policy areas related to prevention and the separate collection of waste, among others.[40]

In addition, other interesting ongoing normative initiatives are the new proposal for a Regulation on nature restoration setting legally binding EU nature restoration targets (including for forest ecosystems)[41] and the future Regulation on deforestation-free products,[42] which will repeal, if adopted, the so-called EU Timber Regulation.[43, 44]

---

of Climate Neutrality by 2035 in the Land Use, Forestry and Agriculture Sector, and (EU) 2018/1999 as Regards Improvement in Monitoring, Reporting, Tracking of Progress and Review' COM (2021) 554.

39 Directive (EU) 2018/2001 on the Promotion of the Use of Energy from Renewable Sources [2018] OJ L328/82 ('RED II').

40 Waste Framework Directive (n 24). See also The European Green Deal (n 30) and The New Circular Economy Action Plan (n 31).

41 European Commission, 'Proposal for a Regulation on Nature Restoration' COM (2022) 304. See, in particular, art 10. See also EU Biodiversity Strategy for 2030 (n 33).

42 European Commission, 'Proposal for a Regulation on the Making Available on the Union Market as well as Export from the Union of Certain Commodities and Products Associated with Deforestation and Forest Degradation and Repealing Regulation (EU) 995/2010' COM (2021) 706. It should be noted that environmental NGOs have expressed some concern over the fact that the proposal falls short on some actions and presents some loopholes. See, for example: Client Earth, 'The Proposed EU Law on Deforestation-Free Products. What is In the European Commission's Proposal and What is Left Out?' (2021) https://www.clientearth.org/media/sbjhtw3c/eu-deforestation-proposal_main-elements-and-omissions_dec21.pdf.

43 Regulation (EU) 995/2010 Laying Down the Obligations of Operators Who Place Timber and Timber Products on the Market [2010] OJ L295/23 ('Timber Regulation').

44 The EU Timber Regulation prohibits the placing of illegally harvested timber and timber products on the market of the EU, and it foresees due diligence obligations for operators who place timber on the market for the first time and obligations for traders regarding the keeping of traceable records of suppliers and customers. In addition, the so-called FLEGT Regulation (Regulation (EC) 2173/2005 on the establishment of

Other legislative texts with forestry relevance which need to be mentioned in this context are the newly adopted Common Agricultural Policy,[45] with its green architecture and the introduction of Eco-schemes,[46] and, naturally, the long-established EU Nature Directives (the so-called Birds[47] and Habitats[48] Directives), which are the backbone of EU biodiversity protection and nature conservation policies.

Apart from the actual strength and ambitiousness of the texts, the implementation of and coherence and synergy across different legal texts and policies are crucial to the success of these legal instruments.

---

a FLEGT licensing scheme for imports of timber into the European Community [2005] OJ L347/1 'FLEGT Regulation'), establishes a Forest Law Enforcement, Governance and Trade licensing scheme for imports of timber into the European Community, and it lays down the EU procedure for the implementation of this FLEGT scheme via bilateral Voluntary Partnership Agreements. Both Regulations were the object of a Fitness Check: the assessment determined that this legislation has had a positive impact on forest governance but, at the same time, highlighted that the objectives of these instruments have not been met. The Regulation on deforestation-free products, if adopted, would render redundant the EU Timber Regulation (which would be repealed, art 35 of the Proposal). It would also include a provision that would regard wood and wood-based products covered by a valid FLEGT licence as fulfilling the *legality requirement* under the deforestation-free products Regulation (art 10(3) of the Proposal). This addition was included to respect bilateral agreements and to preserve the progress achieved with partner countries; however, it should be noted that timber products would also have to fulfil other requirements, for example the deforestation-free requirement. See recs 23, 56 and 57 of the Proposal. See also European Commission, 'Fitness Check on Regulation (EU) 995/2010 Laying Down the Obligations of Operators who Place Timber and Timber Products on the Market (the EU Timber Regulation) and on Regulation (EC) 2173/2005 on the Establishment of a FLEGT Licensing Scheme for Imports of Timber into the European Community (FLEGT Regulation)' SWD (2021) 328.

45 Regulation (EU) 2021/2115 Establishing Rules on Support for Strategic Plans to be Drawn up by Member States under the Common Agricultural Policy (CAP Strategic Plans) and Financed by the European Agricultural Guarantee Fund (EAGF) and by the European Agricultural Fund for Rural Development (EAFRD) and Repealing Regulations (EU) 1305/2013 and (EU) 1307/2013 [2021] OJ L435/1.

46 The new CAP (2023–2027) has also been the object of some criticism and concern. See, for example: Birdlife International, European Environmental Bureau (EEB) and Greenpeace, 'Does the New CAP Measure Up? NGOs Assessment against 10 Tests for a Green Deal-Compatible EU Farming Policy' (2021) https://eeb.org/wp-content/uploads/2021/06/Copy-of-10-tests-for-a-Green-Deal-compatible-farm-policy.pdf. For a broader view, see: Alan Matthews, 'Can the New CAP Help EU Agriculture to Meet the Targets in the European Green Deal?' (2021) ECA Journal 2.

47 Directive 2009/147/EC on the Conservation of Wild Birds [2009] OJ L20/7 ('Birds Directive').

48 Habitat Directive (n 23).

In this regard, a fundamental role is played by cross-cutting pieces of legislation, such as the new Taxonomy Regulation[49] and its Delegated Acts (DAs)[50] in the area of sustainable finance. The EU Taxonomy, adopted in 2020, is a classification system for sustainable activities: it includes criteria for environmentally sustainable activities as well as a list of environmental objectives the economic activity would need to contribute to in order to be considered sustainable[51] and, interestingly, lays down broad criteria for economic activities that significantly harm said environmental objectives. While the Regulation is fundamental as it establishes the general framework for determining whether an economic activity qualifies as environmentally sustainable, the technical screening criteria on the sustainable activities themselves are laid down in the DAs. For forestry activities, especially interesting is the Climate DA, where, in Annexes I and II, the technical screening criteria for determining the conditions under which an activity qualifies as contributing substantially to climate change mitigation (Annex I) and adaptation (Annex II) and that do not cause significant harm to the other environmental objectives are listed.[52] In particular, the criteria pertaining to bioenergy broadly rely *inter alia* on the criteria of the RED, which will be discussed in Section III of this chapter, and on requirements laid down in other EU legislation, such as the Industrial Emissions Directive (IED),[53] which will not be explored here. While the forestry and bioenergy criteria in this DA are extremely important for the sustainability of forestry operations, they will also not be further explored: it will suffice to mention on this occasion that the Climate DA has sparked a negative reaction from environmental NGOs, who claimed, throughout the

---

49 Regulation (EU) 2020/852 on the Establishment of a Framework to Facilitate Sustainable Investment, and Amending Regulation (EU) 2019/2088 [2020] OJ L198/13.

50 European Commission, 'Sustainable Finance Taxonomy – Regulation (EU) 2020/852, Implementing and Delegated Acts' (n.d.) https://ec.europa.eu/info/law/sustainable-finance-taxonomy-regulation-eu-2020-852/amending-and-supplementary-acts/implementing-and-delegated-acts_en.

51 Climate change mitigation, climate change adaptation, the sustainable use and protection of water and marine resources, the transition to a circular economy, pollution prevention and control, the protection and restoration of biodiversity and ecosystems.

52 Delegated Regulation (EU) 2021/2139 Supplementing Regulation (EU) 2020/852 by Establishing the Technical Screening Criteria for Determining the Conditions under which an Economic Activity Qualifies as Contributing Substantially to Climate Change Mitigation or Climate Change Adaptation and for Determining whether that Economic Activity Causes no Significant Harm to Any of the Other Environmental Objectives [2021] OJ L442/1. Annexes I and II, no. 1 (forestry) and nos. 4.8, 4.20 and 4.24 (bioenergy).

53 Directive 2010/75/EU on Industrial Emissions (Integrated Pollution Prevention and Control) [2010] OJ L334/17 ('IED').

adoption process and afterwards, that the criteria are not sufficiently strict and are not based on science.[54]

In light of all of the above and of the role of forestry waste in EU bioenergy, this chapter will consider two legal frameworks in more detail, the WFD and the RED II (and the new Commission proposal to amend the RED II, i.e. the Proposal for the RED III), as these are at the core of the issue of forestry and forestry waste management. In particular, the analysis intends to shed some light on the application of the WFD with regard to forestry waste and on the suitability of the current renewable energy support framework for forestry (waste) materials laid down in the RED II. It also aims at identifying issues in these texts vis-à-vis the waste hierarchy, cascading principle and wider sustainability concerns, and offers a different perspective and possible remedies.

Against this background, first, the EU's waste legislation, specifically Directive 2008/98 on waste (the WFD), and its application to forestry materials will be discussed (Section II).[55] The most debated issues[56] in the subject matter of waste transcend the topic of this chapter (forestry materials), and should be analysed from a systemic 'biogenic waste' perspective rather than from a forestry biomass standpoint. For this reason, this contribution will focus on another feature of said legislation that pertains explicitly to forestry waste (and agricultural waste): the non-application of the WFD to certain materials, a decision that can interfere with the waste hierarchy, the proper management of waste and the establishment of a suitable cascading pathway of waste materials.

Second, EU forest management and forest exploitation are an important aspect of social, policy and legal debates on sustainable development and climate change.[57] Decarbonisation policy in particular has had an important knock-on effect on forest management: for example, renewable energy support to bioenergy in the EU generally results in an increased demand for wood

---

[54] See Client Earth, 'Environmental Lawyers Take First Step to Challenge EU Taxonomy in Court' (2022) https://www.clientearth.org/latest/press-office/press/environmental-lawyers-take-first-step-to-challenge-eu-taxonomy-in-court. See also: European Environmental Bureau (EEB), 'Open Letter to the Commission Asking for Removal of Forestry and Bioenergy from the Current Climate Taxonomy Delegated Act – NGO letter' (2021) https://eeb.org/library/remove-forestry-and-bioenergy-from-the-climate-taxonomy-delegated-act-ngo-letter/.

[55] WFD (n 24).

[56] For example: the discrimination between waste and non-waste materials, the concepts of by-product and end-of-waste status, and their take-up and harmonisation across the EU.

[57] See, for example, Case T-141/19 *Sabo and Others v Parliament and Council* ECLI:EU:T:2020:179 [2020] ECR I-179; Case C-297/20 P *Sabo and Others v Parliament and Council* ECLI:EU:C:2021:24 [2021].

products and for biomass for bioenergy.[58] This situation potentially leads to more intensive forest management and shifts in the import of biomass,[59] and to increased pressure on nature and biodiversity,[60] in the EU and elsewhere. Particularly important in this respect is Directive 2018/2001 on the promotion of the use of energy from renewable sources (RED II)[61] and the new Proposal for the RED III.[62] This helps to understand which measures and, specifically, operations concerning forestry materials to produce biogas and biofuels are being promoted and if adjustments should be made to the legal framework concerning *inter alia* the cascading principle and the preferential use of forestry residues and waste (when suitable) for energy production rather than primary woody products, and keeping in mind the far-reaching consequences of these measures also beyond the EU territory.[63] In the current framework, the criteria that are relevant for primary forestry products are also generally relevant for forestry residues and waste, as per the inclusive definition of biomass and forestry biomass in the RED II. These and other aspects will be dealt with under Section III. Given the importance of private initiatives, Section IV sheds some light on the role of private standards and schemes in ensuring sustainable forestry. Finally, Section V concludes.

II. FORESTRY WASTE AND RESIDUES AND THE WASTE LEGISLATION

The WFD aims to establish a legal framework for the treatment of waste in the EU, a framework designed to protect human health and the environment by, for example, implementing proper waste management and applying the waste hierarchy with the ultimate objective of improving circularity and reducing pressure on – and making more efficient use of – natural resources.

The WFD revolves around the concept of waste as the Directive applies only to waste materials: everything that is not considered waste is outside the Directive's scope. On the definition of the concept of waste, besides the letter of the law which defines 'waste' as 'any substance or object which the holder

58 See, for example: PricewaterhouseCoopers EU and Services EESV's consortium, 'Sustainable and Optimal Use of Biomass for Energy in the EU Beyond 2020' (2017).

59 EEA (n 20).

60 See, for example, Ernst-Detlef Schulze and others, 'Large-scale Bioenergy from Additional Harvest of Forest Biomass Is Neither Sustainable nor Greenhouse Gas Neutral' (2012) 4 GCB Bioenergy 6.

61 RED II (n 39).

62 Proposal for RED III (n 37).

63 See Webster (n 3).

discards or intends or is required to discard',[64] elaborations and explanations can be found both in the European Commission's guidance document on the interpretation of key provisions of the WFD,[65] and in the extensive case-law of the European Court of Justice on the matter. For the purpose of this contribution, it should suffice to mention that the concept of waste is purposefully broad and includes both the recovery and the disposal of waste (both comprising waste treatment).[66, 67]

In view of these concepts and by applying them to the case at hand, it would be logical to consider forestry by-products and residues or, more generally, forestry waste as waste within the meaning of the WFD. However, Article 2, which defines the scope of the Directive, provides a list of certain materials to which the Directive does not apply. Among these are certain types of forestry and agricultural materials: 'non-hazardous agricultural or forestry material used in farming, forestry or for the production of energy through processes or methods that do not harm the environment or endanger human health' are excluded from the scope of the Directive.[68] What the Directive means by 'forestry material' is not further defined; however, it is implausible that the Article means to refer to purposefully harvested biomass (which, being considered a raw or virgin material, would not fit the definition of waste in the first place and would be out of the scope of the Directive *tout court*) and in all probability intends to cover those instances where forestry operations take place and generate the production of materials that, if not used in the manner indicated by the Article, would be otherwise discarded. In short, so worded, the Article is compatible with an interpretation covering certain materials that are not the main or intended product of traditional or less traditional forestry operations. Examples that come to mind could be, for instance, the residues of the felling of trees to obtain wood as a raw material – wood to be then used in production and manufacturing processes or as biomass in energy production

---

64 WFD (n 24), art 3(1).

65 European Commission – Directorate-General Environment, 'Guidance on the Interpretation of Key Provisions of Directive 2008/98/EC on Waste' (2012).

66 It has been considered the case since before the new Directive was adopted on account of the provisions of the old Directive (Council Directive 75/442/EEC on Waste [1975] OJ L194/39) covering both options of disposal and recovery. See for example: Case C-129/96 *Inter-Environnement Wallonie ASBL* [1997], para 27. In this sense: Guidance on the Interpretation of Key Provisions of Directive 2008/98/EC on Waste (n 65) 10–11.

67 It should be noted that the fact that a substance undergoes recovery or disposal does not automatically mean that said substance is waste; these operations can, however, be regarded as evidence of a substance being waste. Case C-9/00 *Palin Granit Oy* ECLI:EU:C:2002:232 [2002], paras 27–30.

68 WFD (n 24) art 2(1)(f).

(traditional forestry operations) – or the felling of trees as part of preparatory work for development operations, as these activities would generate forestry by-products, residues or waste.

It is also not required for the 'use' to be an *in situ* use, which confirms that the Article would apply to a broader array of situations, including that of the material being also used outside the place of production or being transferred to third parties. On the matter of use, the only requirement the Directive lays down is that these materials be used through processes or methods which do not harm the environment or human health. This criterion is based on compliance with the standards of EU environmental legislation,[69] the Directive, thus, providing a potential link with other legislative documents, such as, for example, the IED.

It is essential, however – for these materials to be excluded from the scope of the WFD – that they are indeed *used*, the Article likely suggesting that, in practice, the further use of these materials should be identified in a timely manner (possibly prior to the carrying out of these forestry operations), and certainly includes the case where this further use concerns the production of energy (as the Article explicitly specifies). If this is not the case, then the material should be regarded as waste. In short, with this provision, the Directive seems to want to ensure that these materials fall outside of the scope of the Directive only when further use according to Article 2(1)(f) is assured, providing a fast and less burdensome track for these materials, at least from the operators' point of view. In addition, for this provision to apply, it is also required that these materials be non-hazardous, an appraisal that needs to be carried out based on the definition of hazardous waste according to Article 3(2), read in conjunction with Annex III of the WFD.

It is worth mentioning that the exclusion according to Article 2(1)(f) concerns certain woody materials as the Article clearly refers to 'forestry material', which leads to considering the broader category of woody waste, if not identified in the subset of materials listed in Article 2(1)(f), as potentially falling within the definition of waste and, thus, falling within the scope of the Directive, as a consequence.

Finally, it should also be noted *en passant* that these materials also cannot be considered to fall under the umbrella of 'bio-waste', whose definition lists, and is limited to, biodegradable garden and park waste, food and kitchen waste from households, offices, restaurants, wholesale, canteens, caterers and retail premises and comparable waste from food processing plants.[70]

---

[69] Guidance on the Interpretation of Key Provisions of Directive 2008/98/EC on Waste (n 65).

[70] WFD (n 24) art 3(4).

As already mentioned, when the above circumstances apply, these materials are not covered by the WFD.[71] Whether these forestry materials are excluded from the scope of the Directive or not is not just a theoretical question because on that determination depends the application of the provisions of WFD and, more to the point, of the waste hierarchy. In other words, this exemption causes certain materials to fall outside the scope of the Directive and, potentially, pushes certain materials towards uses that might be less suitable from a circularity and use hierarchy point of view: for example, they could be burned to produce (*in situ*) energy with no energy efficiency requirement, while they could serve other uses or be recycled. This provision also seems in contrast with the principle of the cascading use of biomass, as uses for these materials – those indicated by the Article – might not be selected according to a cascading principle, potentially resulting in said biomass being employed for less valuable uses instead of more valuable ones: while it is true that the Article explicitly mentions farming and forestry uses, thereby likely including *in situ* soil use (arguably a very important one), no hierarchy is foreseen among the uses and 'farming' and 'forestry uses' are likely to encompass a wide range of activities, well beyond the use of these materials on soil for ecological purposes. For these reasons, this exemption should be revisited or at least reformulated to include an order of preference for the uses (e.g. *in situ* use to be preferred when possible and advisable) and require the application of the cascading use principle as one of the criteria regarding the use of the material.

III. RAW OR VIRGIN FORESTRY MATERIALS, FORESTRY WASTE AND RESIDUES IN RED II

Another crucial point concerning forestry biomass that warrants some consideration regards certain provisions under the RED II for biomass materials used for renewable energy production.

In particular, the RED II foresees an EU binding target towards 2030 of at least 32% of energy from renewable sources, but it also sets the renewable energy shares of Member States (MSs) and, in addition, it lays down other renewable energy obligations; for example, under Article 25, MSs must impose an obligation on fuel suppliers to ensure that the share of renewable

---

[71] It should also be pointed out that, while these materials may fall outside the scope of WFD, they might nonetheless be considered as waste materials in other legislation. These materials do fit the definition of waste in the WFD; they are simply excluded from its scope, meaning that if another legislative document mentions forestry waste and refers to the definition of waste as indicated in the WFD, these materials should be considered waste according to this second legislative act, and, as a consequence, different regimes for the treatment of these materials might apply.

energy within the final consumption of energy in the transport sector is at least 14% by 2030. What is interesting for this contribution is that the Directive also attaches some conditions in the accounting mechanism for these targets, meaning that not all energy from renewable sources can be counted as contributing towards those targets.

In order to count energy from biofuels, bioliquids and biomass fuels for the purpose of contributing to the renewable targets mentioned above – and to be eligible for financial support for the consumption of biofuels, bioliquids and biomass fuels – biofuels, bioliquids and biomass fuels are required to fulfil certain criteria: the sustainability criteria (for certain waste, agricultural biomass and for forest biomass); the greenhouse gas (GHG) emission savings criteria for biofuels, bioliquids and biomass fuels; and the efficiency criteria for biomass fuels. All these, except for the efficiency criteria, will be explored in the paragraphs below, as their content is relevant for both waste and residues and virgin or raw materials.

Before delving into these matters, it is interesting to spend a few words on the consideration of the waste hierarchy and the cascading principle in the RED II. In its current version, the RED II does not dedicate ample space to the waste hierarchy. There are a few references that concern the obligation to duly consider the principles of the circular economy and the waste hierarchy, as established in the WFD, in the national policies and in the development of support schemes for renewable sources of energy by MSs, both in the recitals and in Article 3(3). Additional references to the waste hierarchy are limited to the provisions regarding advanced biofuels, as will be explained in subsection III.C of this chapter.

While a limited reference to the waste hierarchy might be somewhat justifiable as waste to energy remains at the bottom of the waste hierarchy before waste disposal, the lack of explicit consideration for the cascading principle of biomass sticks out quite prominently, especially in a legislative document on renewable energy; in this light, a mere reference to the principles of the circular economy might not suffice. The cascading principle was mentioned in the previous version of the RED II, i.e. the RED I,[72] but such mentions were limited to reporting obligations by MSs and to monitoring and reporting by the Commission, in Articles 22 and 23. In particular, in their reports the MSs and the European Commission (EC) had to detail (MSs) and analyse (EC) the development and share (MSs) and the availability and sustainability (EC) of biofuels from waste feedstocks (i.e. advanced biofuels), taking due account

---

[72] Directive 2009/28/EC on the Promotion of the Use of Energy from Renewable Sources and Amending and Subsequently Repealing Directives 2001/77/EC and 2003/30/EC [2009] OJ L140/16.

of the principles of the waste hierarchy and the biomass cascading principle.[73] Being merely confined to reporting obligations, such a reference to the cascading principle was only marginally effective and useful. In the RED II, the cascading principle was omitted altogether. The new Proposal for the RED III does reintroduce the cascading principle, and seemingly to a larger extent than in the first version of the RED: not only is it mentioned in the recitals (Recital 4), but an amendment is proposed to Article 3 according to which the cascading principle is to be taken into account and implemented by MSs, also by way of prohibiting the granting of support for the use of certain raw materials for the production of energy.[74] More on this aspect will be described in subsection III.C below.

A. Sustainability and the LULUCF Criteria

Article 29 of the RED II establishes two sets of criteria depending on the origin of the material: criteria for agricultural biomass,[75] which will not be discussed in this chapter, and criteria for forestry biomass. Forestry waste and residues – constituting forest biomass[76] – have to comply with the criteria pertaining to forest biomass. While being applicable also to waste and residues, these criteria are *especially* relevant for raw materials because they are aimed at ensuring the sustainable provenance of the biomass. However, the effect of these criteria on the use of waste materials should not be underestimated as laxer or more stringent requirements especially dedicated to raw or virgin materials could affect the use, in practice, of waste or residue biomass streams. More on the prospect of a differentiation being made between the use of waste and residue materials and raw materials for the production of energy, and thus on a support mechanism for a preferential use of waste materials over raw materials for the generation of energy and energy products, will be discussed under subsection III.C, where the double-counting mechanism currently in place for the use of waste and residue materials for advanced biofuel production and more on the cascading principle and its implementation will be presented.

Article 29 of the RED II sets criteria for biomass used for fuel production; the scope of these criteria has, with the 2018 revision, been extended to all

---

[73] ibid, arts 22 and 23

[74] Proposal for RED III (n 37) point (2)(b).

[75] It should be noted that these criteria also help prevent impact to forests, as carbon-rich and biodiverse lands.

[76] Which is defined as biomass produced from forestry, where biomass comprises products, waste and residues. See RED II (n 39) arts 2(26) and 2(24).

fuels produced from biomass irrespective of the energy use.[77] As with all criteria laid down in Article 29, these requirements are also established to ascertain which energy sources from biofuels, bioliquids and biomass fuels can be counted for the renewable targets expressed in the RED II and as eligible for financial support.

With regards to *forest biomass*, there are two sets of criteria. The *first* set of criteria is represented by the so-called 'sustainability criteria', indicated in Article 29(6) of the RED II.[78] Additionally, MSs may establish additional sustainability criteria for biomass fuels,[79] meaning that, irrespectively of the kind of biomass used (waste, raw agricultural or raw forest biomass), and only when biomass is used for the production of biomass fuels, MSs may add sus-

---

[77] EUR-Lex, 'Summaries of EU Legislation – Renewable Energy' (eurlex.europa.eu, last update 21.04.2022) https://eur-lex.europa.eu/legal-content/EN/TXT/?uri=legissum%3A4372645.

[78] Biofuels, bioliquids and biomass fuels produced from forest biomass taken into account for the purposes referred to in points (a), (b) and (c) of the first subparagraph of paragraph 1 shall meet the following criteria to minimise the risk of using forest biomass derived from unsustainable production:

(a) the country in which forest biomass was harvested has national or sub-national laws applicable in the area of harvest as well as monitoring and enforcement systems in place ensuring:
   (i) the legality of harvesting operations;
   (ii) forest regeneration of harvested areas;
   (iii) that areas designated by international or national law or by the relevant competent authority for nature protection purposes, including in wetlands and peatlands, are protected;
   (v) that harvesting maintains or improves the long-term production capacity of the forest;

(b) when evidence referred to in point (a) of this paragraph is not available, the biofuels, bioliquids and biomass fuels produced from forest biomass shall be taken into account for the purposes referred to in points (a), (b) and (c) of the first subparagraph of paragraph 1 if management systems are in place at forest sourcing area level ensuring:
   (i) the legality of harvesting operations;
   (ii) forest regeneration of harvested areas;
   (iii) that areas designated by international or national law or by the relevant competent authority for nature protection purposes, including in wetlands and peatlands, are protected unless evidence is provided that the harvesting of that raw material does not interfere with those nature protection purposes;
   (iv) that harvesting is carried out considering the maintenance of soil quality and biodiversity with the aim of minimising negative impacts; and
   (v) that harvesting maintains or improves the long-term production capacity of the forest.

RED II (n 39) art 29(6).

[79] ibid art 29(14).

tainability criteria for the purpose of reaching the renewable targets mentioned above and for financial support eligibility. This is, however, not the case for bioliquids and biofuels[80] and is an aspect of the current legislation that could be addressed. Extending the possibility for the MSs to be more ambitious and affording them the possibility to add sustainability criteria also for the production of bioliquids and biofuels might serve to extend the effectiveness of the criteria themselves and reach a higher level of sustainability, even if from a voluntary initiative and even if it might cause situations of leakage. Moreover, *biomass fuels* have to meet the sustainability criteria if they are used in installations (installations producing electricity, heating and cooling or fuels) with a total rated thermal input equal to or exceeding 20 MW in the case of solid biomass fuels, and with a total rated thermal input equal to or exceeding 2 MW in the case of gaseous biomass fuels. However, MSs may decide to apply these criteria also to installations with lower total rated thermal input.[81] This provision limits the application of the (forest) sustainability criteria to facilities of a certain size, thus affecting their effectiveness. This aspect has been addressed in the Proposal for the RED III, where, were the proposal to be adopted as is, biomass fuels would have to fulfil the sustainability (and GHG emission savings criteria) in installations with a total rated thermal input equal to or exceeding 5 MW and in installations producing gaseous biomass fuels with a specific average biomethane flow rate.[82] The *second* set of criteria pertaining to forest biomass is indicated in Article 26(7), which lays down the so-called LULUCF criteria (land use, land-use change and forestry criteria).[83]

---

80 ibid art 29(14). Art 29(14) only mentions biomass fuels and not also other kinds of fuel. In addition, art 29(12) specifies that, without prejudice to arts 25 and 26 on renewable energy in the transport sector, MSs may not refuse to take into account, on other sustainability grounds, biofuels and bioliquids meeting the requirements laid down in art 29 for the purposes of reaching the renewable targets and for financial support eligibility.

81 ibid art 29(1) para 4.

82 Proposal for RED III (n 37) point (18)(a).

83 Biofuels, bioliquids and biomass fuels produced from forest biomass taken into account for the purposes referred to in points (a), (b) and (c) of the first subparagraph of paragraph 1 shall meet the following land-use, land-use change and forestry (LULUCF) criteria:

(a) the country or regional economic integration organisation of origin of the forest biomass
   (i) is a Party to the Paris Agreement;
   (ii) has submitted a nationally determined contribution (NDC) to the United Nations Framework Convention on Climate Change (UNFCCC), covering emissions and removals from agriculture, forestry and land use which ensures that changes in carbon stock associated with biomass

These sets of criteria (both sustainability and LULUCF criteria) have been deemed insufficient and/or weak, especially if assessed against the criteria relevant for agriculture.[84] More specifically, if one compares the criteria laid down for agricultural biomass with the criteria foreseen for forest biomass, it is noticeable that the criteria laid down for forests do not offer the same level of safeguards in terms of carbon stocks and protection of key areas and environmental features. The forest criteria simply require the existence of laws and monitoring and enforcement systems or management systems at forest sourcing area level, ensuring that certain aspects are considered (sustainability criteria), and being a Party to the Paris Agreement, having submitted the Nationally Determined Contribution or having laws or management systems in place ensuring that certain aspects are considered (LULUCF criteria). In other words, the provisions are clearly focused on the formal legality of harvesting and on the legal framework in place, rather than focusing on actual sustainability standards. This assessment also seems relevant for the new draft RED II implementing act on sustainability criteria concerning forest biomass, a regulation supposed to establish operational guidance on the evidence to demonstrate compliance with the sustainability criteria for forest biomass indicated in Article 29.[85]

---

harvest are accounted towards the country's commitment to reduce or limit greenhouse gas emissions as specified in the NDC; or

(iii) has national or sub-national laws in place, in accordance with Article 5 of the Paris Agreement, applicable in the area of harvest, to conserve and enhance carbon stocks and sinks, and provides evidence that reported LULUCF-sector emissions do not exceed removals;

(b) where evidence referred to in point (a) of this paragraph is not available, the biofuels, bioliquids and biomass fuels produced from forest biomass shall be taken into account for the purposes referred to in points (a), (b) and (c) of the first subparagraph of paragraph 1 if management systems are in place at forest sourcing area level to ensure that carbon stocks and sinks levels in the forest are maintained, or strengthened over the long term.

RED II (n 39) art 29(7).

[84] Proposal for RED III (n 37), explanatory memorandum 7; European Commission, 'Impact Assessment Accompanying the Proposal for a Directive Amending Directive (EU) 2018/2001, Regulation (EU) 2018/1999 and Directive 98/70/EC as Regards the Promotion of Energy from Renewable Sources, and Repealing Council Directive (EU) 2015/652 – 1/2' SWD (2021) 621, 17 ff. See also Timothy D Searchinger and others, 'Europe's Renewable Energy Directive Poised to Harm Global Forests' (2018) 9 Nature Communications 1, 1–4; Mary S Booth and Ben Mitchell, 'Why the EU's RED II Biomass Sustainability Criteria Fail Forests and the Climate' (2020) http://eubiomasscase.org/wp-content/uploads/2020/07/RED-II-biomass-Paper-Tiger-July-6-2020.pdf.

[85] European Commission, 'Draft Commission Implementing Regulation on Establishing Operational Guidance on the Evidence for Demonstrating Compliance

The new Proposal for the RED III addresses some of the concerns mentioned above, for example by (partially) extending the sustainability criteria for agricultural biomass indicated in Article 29(3),[86] 29(4)[87] and 29(5)[88] to forest biomass and by strengthening the forest biomass criteria of Article 29(6) (better consideration of soil quality, biodiversity and, in particular, primary forests).[89] Here, however, stronger wording could be used.

Another issue that could be addressed going forward is the limited application of Article 29(2). According to Article 29(2) of the RED II, biofuels, bioliquids and biomass fuels produced from *waste and residues* derived *not from forestry but from agricultural land* can be taken into account only when operators and national authorities have monitoring or management plans in place to address the impact on soil quality and soil carbon. Where no such monitoring or management plans are in place, biofuels, bioliquids and biomass fuels produced from waste and residues derived *from agricultural land* cannot be taken into account for accounting and financial support purposes.[90, 91] With regard to a similar criterion for forest biomass in the current version of the RED, there exists in Article 26(6) a mere – and very vague – reference to soil quality and biodiversity being ensured by the laws or the management systems of the country; there is, however, nothing that mentions, in particular, residues and wastes, highlighting another (possibly unwarranted?) difference between biomass from agricultural land and biomass from forestry. Accordingly, amendments to the Article could extend the application of Article 29(2) to forestry residues and waste as well, given the crucial ecological role they might serve when left *in situ*. In this light, the new Proposal for the RED III does address the issue and adds to Article 26(6) by expanding the requirements regarding soil quality and biodiversity and by introducing a reference to deadwood extraction.

Finally, biofuels, bioliquids and biomass fuels produced from agricultural and forest biomass are required to fulfil also the GHG emission savings criteria. These will be explored in the following section.

---

with the Sustainability Criteria for Forest Biomass laid down in Article 29 of Directive (EU) 2018/2001' Ref. Ares (2021) 2233415.

86 Proposal for RED III (n 37) point (18)(b).

87 ibid point (18)(c).

88 ibid point (18)(d).

89 ibid point (18)(e) and (f).

90 It should be noted that, additionally, agricultural waste and residues – constituting agricultural biomass as this is defined as biomass produced from agriculture, where biomass comprises products, waste and residues as per Art 2(25) and 2(24) – will also have to fulfil criteria pertaining to agricultural biomass.

91 RED II (n 39) art 29(2).

B. GHG Emission Savings Requirements in the RED II

The GHG emission savings criteria are not specific to the kind of biomass used (whether waste biomass, raw forest biomass, raw agricultural biomass) but on the type of fuel produced or used. The criteria are specified under Article 29(10), the provision requiring GHG emission savings from the use of these fuels to be of a certain amount for certain installations. These criteria are calculated according to the rules laid down in Article 31,[92] with the calculations indicated in Annex V for biofuels and bioliquids,[93] and in Annex VI for biomass fuels.[94] For such calculations, it is also rather important to note that one of the values in the formula for the calculation of the GHG impact – the value corresponding to the emissions from the fuel in use – is set to zero as the default for biofuels and bioliquids, as is the number corresponding to the emissions of CO_2 from fuel in use for the calculation of the GHG impact for biomass fuels, whereas non-CO_2 emissions (CH_4 and N_2O) from the fuel in use are counted in the value for bioliquids and biomass fuels.[95]

The implication of such provisions is a partial emissions lifecycle accounting in the RED II and a general implicit position of carbon neutrality for biomass in the energy legislation, meaning that emissions are generally counted for the harvesting, processing and transporting, and distribution of the biomass, but not during the actual use of the fuel.[96] This decision is accompanied by the counting of the biomass emissions in the land sector, which has been adduced as the reason for the partial lifecycle accounting in the RED II, meant, hence, to avoid double counting; however, a 2016 impact assessment on bioenergy sustainability has offered some criticism of this approach and presented arguments for introducing a full GHG accounting in order to have a full picture of the climate impacts from forest feedstocks, given that, for example, the current system does not seem to take into consideration the time lag between emissions and regrowth of the biomass,[97] the so-called 'carbon debt'.[98] However, the impact assessment posited that introducing biogenic carbon emissions in

---

[92] ibid art 31, 'Calculation of the greenhouse gas impact of biofuels, bioliquids and biomass fuels'.

[93] ibid annex V, 'Rules for calculating the greenhouse gas impact of biofuels, bioliquids and their fossil fuel comparators', specifically Part C 'Methodology'.

[94] ibid annex VI, 'Rules for calculating the greenhouse gas impact of biomass fuels and their fossil fuel comparators', specifically Part B 'Methodology'.

[95] ibid annex V, part C, point 13 and annex VI, Part B, point 13.

[96] See Booth and Mitchell (n 84) 31–32; Searchinger and others (n 84).

[97] European Commission, 'Impact Assessment – Sustainability of Bioenergy – 4/4' SWD (2016) 418.

[98] On the 'carbon debt' issue see, for example, Ter-Mikaelian, Colombo and Chen (n 6).

the methodology on lifecycle emissions from solid biomass is extremely difficult, which is why this option was discarded for the new RED.[99] In any event, finding a way to have a clear GHG accounting mechanism that gives a precise and full, and perhaps more realistic, picture regarding emissions might also represent a way to incentivise the use of other materials, namely, residues and waste materials for the production of energy products, which are likely to have a better GHG emission profile than raw, virgin biomass. In this regard, displacement effects should also be considered, as explained in subsection III.C.

Finally, *biomass fuels* have to meet the GHG emission savings criteria (and the sustainability criteria indicated above) if they are used in installations (installations producing electricity, heating and cooling or fuels) with a total rated thermal input equal to or exceeding 20 MW in the case of solid biomass fuels, and with a total rated thermal input equal to or exceeding 2 MW in the case of gaseous biomass fuels. However, MSs may decide to apply these criteria also to installations with lower total rated thermal input.[100] On this point, the same reflections already made in the context of the sustainability criteria can be extended to the GHG emission savings criteria, including the novelties of the Proposal for the RED III related to the application of the GHG emission savings criteria to biomass fuels used in installations with a total rated thermal input equal or exceeding 5 MW and in installations producing gaseous biomass fuels with a specific average biomethane flow rate.[101]

C. Waste- and Residues-sourced Fuels and Raw or Virgin Materials-sourced Fuels: How is a Distinction Made?

Among the several targets laid down in the Directive, in Article 25 the RED II also sets binding targets for transportation (14% in 2030) and for advanced biofuels (3.5% in 2030).

Advanced biofuels are defined in the RED II as biofuels (liquid fuel for transport produced from biomass) that are produced from the feedstock listed in Part A of Annex IX.[102] Annex IX Part A enumerates, therefore, specific kinds of feedstock, and, among these, letter (o) refers to 'Biomass fraction of wastes and residues from forestry and forest-based industries, namely, bark, branches, pre-commercial thinning, leaves, needles, tree tops, saw dust, cutter shavings, black liquor, brown liquor, fibre sludge, lignin and tall oil'. Article 2(34), read in combination with Article 27(2)(a) and Annex IX Part A, thus

99 Impact Assessment – Sustainability of Bioenergy (n 97).
100 RED II (n 39) art 29(1) para 4.
101 RED III (n 37) point (18)(a).
102 RED II (n 39) art 2(34).

means that biofuels that are made from forestry waste biomass there indicated (among others) are to be considered as 'advanced biofuels' and, as a direct consequence, their contribution towards the minimum shares referred to in the first and fourth subparagraphs of Article 25(1) may be considered to be twice their energy content. This accounting method was designed to foster the use of specific (waste) materials: to increase the attractiveness of the use of these waste and residue materials for the production of biofuels and the use of these advanced biofuels.

The Annex IX feedstock list is not static as the Commission periodically has to review it and is empowered to modify it with a view to adding (but not removing) feedstocks through DAs. It is essential to mention that the DAs must be based on an analysis of the materials, taking into account certain aspects: the principle of the circular economy and the waste hierarchy; the sustainability criteria indicated in Article 29(2) to (7); the need to avoid substantial distortions in the markets for (by-)products, wastes or residues; the GHG emission savings profile; and the need to avoid negative impacts on the environment and biodiversity and to create additional demand for land.[103] The list does not consider the cascading principle and, while referring to the circular economy and the waste hierarchy (which are kindred concepts), an express reference to it in this context would have probably represented an added value.

This solution of double counting the energy content indeed represents a way in which waste and residues *might* be valorised over raw or virgin materials, but it is not the only way and might not be the best way. On this particular point, the Proposal for the RED III modifies the targets on transport by setting a 13% *greenhouse gas intensity reduction target*[104] and a sub-target for advanced biofuels (2.2% compared to the current 3.5%, but single-counted), and intends to slash this double-counting mechanism (defining a '1.2 times' account mechanism for advanced biofuels used in aviation and maritime sectors, by slightly modifying the current provision).[105] A new advanced biofuels mandate would not necessarily represent a more ambitious pathway, however, as one needs to be mindful of unwelcome displacement effects.[106]

---

[103] ibid art 28(6).

[104] Expressing the target as such is meant to stimulate an increasing use of the most cost-effective and performing fuels in terms of greenhouse gas savings in the transport sector and to avoid the use of multipliers.

[105] Proposal for RED III (n 37) points (14) and (16)(c).

[106] On displacement effects from waste, residue, and by-product biofuel feedstocks, see for example: Nikita Pavlenko and Stephanie Searle, 'A Comparison of Methodologies for Estimating Displacement Emissions from Waste, Residue, and By-Product Biofuel Feedstocks' (2020) International Council on Clean Transportation Working Paper 2020-22.

On the matter of promoting the use of residues and waste rather than the use of primary wood for energy production, the new proposal seems to mainly rely on the obligation for the MSs to consider the cascading principle when designing their support schemes for bioenergy and on prohibiting them from granting support for the production of energy from sawlogs, veneer logs, stumps and roots[107] and for the production of energy from waste incineration when rules on the separate collection have not been complied with, or for practices that are not compatible with the cascading principle (as defined by a future new DA).[108]

In addition to setting an obligation for the MSs to take the cascading principle (and the waste hierarchy, as it already is) into account in relation to woody biomass (which, admittedly, could be more strongly worded), the proposal also gives an indication as to what the cascading principle would look like: woody biomass should be used according to the highest economic and environmental added value with a priority order for its use (wood-based products in the first place, followed by extension of their service life, re-use, recycle, bioenergy and, finally, disposal as the last use).[109] The proposal also indicates that the Commission will adopt a DA on how to apply the cascading principle for biomass and, in particular, on how to minimise the use of quality roundwood for energy production, focusing on support schemes and with special attention given to national specificities.[110]

To further promote the use of forestry residues and waste for energy production, however, a differentiation (starting from the definitions in Article 2) between primary and secondary wood biomass should be introduced; the more trenchant option of not granting support for the use of primary wood for the production of energy should be considered; and a reference to the cascading principle and the waste hierarchy should be included in Article 29.

In any event, whatever the solution might be to set a preferential use of waste and residues over raw materials, in order to establish the right pathways for the right materials, lifecycle assessments and impact assessments are of utmost importance so that displacement effects that might lead to indirect GHG emissions due to diverting resources to the production of biofuels and biogas (and energy) are avoided. In the case of forestry residues and forestry waste, for example, composting or *in situ* use or use as animal bedding might result in a better GHG emission profile. This would mean that fostering the use of residues and waste for biofuels and biogas, which can generate displacement

---

[107] Stumps and roots are possible waste and residue materials which are potentially better left *in situ*.

[108] Pavlenko and Searle (n 106) point (2)(b).

[109] ibid rec (4).

[110] ibid point (2)(b).

effects for other uses, might not be the most ecologically and environmentally sound solution.[111]

It should also be kept in mind that making use of the cascading principle should not be considered a hindrance to the development and use of these fuels, as it does not necessarily prevent the use of certain materials as feedstock for the production of energy products. After all, energy recovery is amongst the 'bottom' uses and might be preferred in some cases to other uses for environmental reasons. Another possible pathway potentially compatible with both the waste hierarchy and the cascading principle might be the production of biofuels and biogas with the co-production (or recovery) of other materials with specific characteristics that are not used for energy purposes, for example biochar, enabling at the same time the recovery of materials and energy recovery, and entailing a possible upward graduation in the waste hierarchy.

In order for these pathways to be workable, however, a better use of the instruments and concepts given by the WFD (especially those of by-product and end-of-waste status) and better coordination with the IED are needed.

IV. THE ROLE OF PRIVATE SCHEMES IN ENSURING SUSTAINABLE FORESTRY

While much is achieved through public instruments and measures, the importance of private standards and voluntary schemes in ensuring sustainability in the forestry sector should not be downplayed.

The RED II itself requires economic operators to demonstrate that the sustainability and GHG emission savings criteria have been met,[112] which can also be achieved through voluntary national or international schemes setting standards for the production of biofuels, bioliquids or biomass fuels.[113] The Commission may facilitate this process by assessing schemes that seek European Commission recognition under Article 30(4) of the RED II against reliability, transparency, and independent auditing standards.[114] So far, as far

[111] See, for example, Institute for European Environmental Policy (IEEP), 'Sustainability Criteria for Biofuels made from Land and Non-Land Based Feedstocks' (2016), 19–23.

[112] RED II (n 39) art 30(1).

[113] ibid art 30(4).

[114] European Commission, 'Voluntary Schemes – Voluntary Schemes and National Schemes of EU Countries Certify whether Biofuels Comply with the EU's Sustainability Criteria' (energy.ec.europa.eu, n.d.) https://energy.ec.europa.eu/topics/renewable-energy/biofuels/voluntary-schemes_en. In this sense, see also the call for interest: European Commission – Directorate-General for Energy, 'Call for Interest: Recognition of voluntary schemes under Article 30(4) of the revised Renewable Energy Directive' Ref. Ares (2020) 4044182 https://energy.ec.europa.eu/system/files/2020-08/

as the RED II is concerned, the European Commission has recognised some voluntary schemes or national certification schemes, after having received the necessary applications;[115] in addition, the European Commission has received applications for recognition from additional voluntary schemes and national certification schemes, and the draft decision regarding some of these will be soon subject to a vote of the RED II committee on the sustainability of biofuels, bioliquids and biomass fuels.[116]

Furthermore, the Commission is also working on an Implementing Act on rules to verify sustainability and GHG emission savings criteria and indirect land-use change-risk criteria,[117] an initiative meant to lay down rules to encourage the development of voluntary schemes that set standards for – and certify the sustainable production of – biofuels, bioliquids and biomass fuels, including standards on reliability, transparency and independent auditing.[118]

It is crucial to note that standards and voluntary schemes may go beyond the sustainability and GHG emissions saving criteria established at the EU level. In particular, it has been noted that some of the existing schemes define stricter criteria than those indicated in the RED II with regards to legal sourcing, maintenance of forest productivity and ecosystems, and nature and biodiversity conservation.[119] For instance, some schemes introduce encompassing sustainable forest management criteria that are stronger than the sustainability criteria of the RED II; one scheme has been found to require anti-corruption measures; another addresses the long-term conservation of nature with its ecosystem services and cultural values; another requires that a producer is able

---

recognition_of_voluntary_schemes_revised_renewable_energy_directive_0.pdf. This document is also accessible from the following webpage: https://energy.ec.europa.eu/topics/renewable-energy/biofuels/voluntary-schemes_en.

[115] Voluntary Schemes and National Schemes of EU Countries Certify whether Biofuels Comply with the EU's Sustainability Criteria (n 114). The Commission's decisions on the recognition of these voluntary schemes were published on 12 April 2022 in the Official Journal: OJ, L 114, 12 April 2022.

[116] Voluntary Schemes and National Schemes of EU Countries Certify whether Biofuels Comply with the EU's Sustainability Criteria (n 114).

[117] European Commission – Directorate-General for Energy 'Draft Commission Implementing Regulation on Rules to Verify Sustainability and Greenhouse Gas Emissions Saving Criteria and Low Indirect Land-use Change-risk Criteria' Ref. Ares (2021) 4234307.

[118] European Commission, 'Sustainable Biofuels, Bioliquids and Biomass Fuels – Voluntary Schemes (Implementing Rules)' (n.d.) https://ec.europa.eu/info/law/better-regulation/have-your-say/initiatives/12723-Sustainable-biofuels-bioliquids-and-biomass-fuels-voluntary-schemes-implementing-rules-_en.

[119] Thuy Mai-Moulin and others, 'Effective Sustainability Criteria for Bioenergy: Towards the Implementation of the European Renewable Directive II' (2021) 138 Renewable and Sustainable Energy Reviews.

to prove good management practices and continuous improvement; and a few include air, soil and water protection by indicating dedicated comprehensive sustainability requirements. Schemes may also go beyond the classic notion of environmental sustainability and include socio-economic criteria, such as requiring that biomass production is in line with national or international labour laws and standards and worker rights, and that basic working conditions are met,[120] which might be of particular importance for imported biomass and is an aspect generally considered relevant in a sustainability discourse.[121] In addition, schemes and standards may also include criteria regarding the cascading use of biomass to ensure that bioenergy feedstocks are raw-material efficient.[122] Nevertheless, voluntary standards and schemes established in addition and next to legislative requirements remain an appealing option for organisations, especially if the schemes are included as environmental criteria in public procurement procedures or if countries or, more generally, public institutions decide to rely on these private instruments for their own policy and legislation or to encourage certifications.[123]

V. CONCLUSIONS

As it can be understood from what has been noted so far, forest protection and forestry are not mutually exclusive, provided that the decisions taken are science-based, sensible and, more generally, do not drive unsustainable behaviour.

It is true that forest and energy policies and legislation can be a heavily political subject matter, especially in these times and for countries that rely on forests and bioenergy to meet their renewables targets and goals, and that, for this reason, pressures from stakeholders can be intense. However, it is essential to approach certain decisions, especially those that will affect the energy transition path, future investments and future generations, with equanimity and objectivity. The risk goes beyond meeting or not meeting the climate and

[120] ibid.

[121] Parisa Rafiaani and others, 'Social Sustainability Assessments in the Biobased Economy: Towards a Systemic Approach' (2018) 82 Renewable and Sustainable Energy Reviews.

[122] ibid. See also Nederlands Normalisatie-Instituut (NEN), 'Standard NTA 8080-1:2015 (en) – Sustainably Produced Biomass for Bioenergy and Bio-Based Products – Part 1: Sustainability Requirements' (2015).

[123] On the deep and mutual dependence between public and private under the framework of the RED I and on the hybridity of this governance system based on both public and private measures, see the analysis made by: Stefano Ponte and Carsten Daugbjerg, 'Biofuel Sustainability and the Formation of Transnational Hybrid Governance' (2015) 24 Environmental Politics 1.

environmental objectives the EU has set for itself and at the international level; much more than this is at stake.

It is also crucial to point out that, for results to be achieved and steps forward to be made, synergies and coherence in and between policy and legal instruments are of the utmost importance, especially for those profoundly cross-cutting matters; that flexibilities and exceptions or derogations granted to operators or, more in general, relevant industries, are heavily scrutinised and checked against environmental and climate trade-offs; and that situations of leakage are avoided. This is nothing new, but, nonetheless, it bears repeating.

Increased climate targets and increased environmental protection goals have now prompted a revision of a number of key texts, and the putting forward of proposals and initiatives. Some of these have a clear circularity aim, such as those expressed in the new Circular Economy Action Plan on the valorisation of secondary raw materials[124] and those reflected in the new Forest Strategy to extend the life of woody products,[125] which will likely have an impact on the implementation of the waste hierarchy and of the cascading principle.

The new Proposal for the RED III is also one of these measures. While being a keystone of the energy policy of the EU, the RED II and its implementation equally affect natural resources where biomass is considered a renewable source of energy. The proposed new text seems to have considered (some of) the issues and glitches of the current framework, and it seems to somewhat better align with the climate, environmental and circularity objectives of the EU.

The current 32% EU-level renewable target becomes, in the proposal, a slightly increased 40% target by 2030 (which could be, however, more ambitious in view of a faster deployment of renewables), and the proposal sets up a framework for the deployment of renewables across the different sectors of the economy, focusing, in particular, on transport, buildings and industry. As already mentioned, the proposal also seeks to strengthen the sustainability and GHG emission savings criteria for forest biomass and their application to a broader array of installations using biomass fuels while maintaining, however, support for bioenergy. A way in which waste and residues are valorised in the new proposal is through strengthened sustainability and GHG emission savings criteria, and the reference to and alignment with the waste hierarchy and the cascading principle, with the concomitant exclusion of certain feedstocks from support schemes. Whether this will be enough in terms of climate action and whether this will 'pass muster' throughout the legislative

---

[124] A new Circular Economy Action Plan. For a Cleaner and More Competitive Europe (n 31).

[125] New EU Forest Strategy for 2030 (n 8).

procedure and all the way through adoption, without being undercut in the Council and European Parliament or during the trialogues, remains to be seen.

In general terms, the more evident measures should be considered, such as adopting a prevention-based and precautionary approach and disincentivising or possibly excluding altogether (or, at least, not incentivising) the use of primary wood for energy, and incentivising circular, cascading and sustainable pathways, fostering good management practices and supporting carbon sequestration schemes that would leave nature (and forests in particular) undisturbed as much as possible. Besides this, however, achieving less strain on natural resources and possibly a better valorisation of waste materials can also occur via ambitious private schemes and standards.

With regard to the waste legislation, in particular, it ought to be stressed that the legal framework should not create flexibilities with problematic implications for the cascading principle and the waste hierarchy that are not justified by lifecycle thinking and environmental reasons. Waste legislation should also be centred on the idea that waste, at least certain streams, should be considered a resource and not necessarily something to be excessively wary of: secondary raw materials are vital to achieving a higher degree of circularity and, consequently, their use should be enabled and supported by possibly leaving behind ad hoc approaches, whenever these are not warranted for environmental or health protection purposes.

Another essential element to consider in these rather turbulent times is that amelioration of the efficiency of the processes and energy efficiency (i.e. the energy efficiency first principle)[126] is crucial not only to curb energy needs

---

[126] The energy efficiency first principle is one of the key principles of the energy policy of the EU and it aims at ensuring, *inter alia*, sustainable, secure and affordable energy supply in the European Union territory. It was included in the so-called Governance Regulation (Regulation (EU) 2018/1999 on the Governance of the Energy Union and Climate Action, amending Regulations (EC) 663/2009 and (EC) 715/2009, Directives 94/22/EC, 98/70/EC, 2009/31/EC, 2009/73/EC, 2010/31/EU, 2012/27/EU and 2013/30/EU, Council Directives 2009/119/EC and (EU) 2015/652 and repealing Regulation (EU) No 525/2013 [2018] OJ L328/1) and in the Energy Efficiency Directive (Directive (EU) 2018/2002 Amending Directive 2012/27/EU on Energy Efficiency [2002] OJ L/328/210), and has been, since then, further expanded in the Proposal for recasting the Energy Efficiency Directive, where the proposed Article 3 provides a stronger and wider legal basis for the application of the principle. It is defined as follows in the Governance Regulation: '"energy efficiency first" means taking utmost account in energy planning, and in policy and investment decisions, of alternative cost-efficient energy efficiency measures to make energy demand and energy supply more efficient, in particular by means of cost-effective end-use energy savings, demand response initiatives and more efficient conversion, transmission and distribution of energy, whilst still achieving the objectives of those decisions'. For more information, see: European Commission, 'Energy Efficiency First Principle'

but also to lessen energy dependence and strengthen self-sufficiency. For these same reasons, support of renewable sources where fewer trade-offs are needed (such as solar and wind in the proper circumstances) should also be incentivised. Accordingly, going forward, sustainable finance will be pivotal in directing investments towards the most (?) suitable activities.

In addition, as mentioned multiple times throughout this contribution, intelligent biomass pathways are also created and nurtured through synergetic legislation and their coherent and harmonised implementation and application in the EU: this would concern, in particular, the legislation on waste, industrial emissions, land use, energy (e.g. RED II(I), IED, ETS (Emissions Trading System)), the agricultural policy and the nature protection legislation.

As a final, perhaps slightly candid, remark, it should be highlighted that the key guiding overarching principles behind future developments in law and policy should be, not surprisingly, those of planetary boundaries, social justice, and the rights of future generations. We – the collective snapshot of humanity in this moment in time – are 'simple' stewards of this planet for a brief instance in its considerable existence. In other words, we have a responsibility and our behaviour should be tailored accordingly.

LEGISLATION

Directive 92/43/EEC on the Conservation of Natural Habitats and of Wild Fauna and Flora [1992] OJ L206/7 ('Habitat Directive')

Directive 2009/147/EC on the Conservation of Wild Birds [2009] OJ L20/7 ('Birds Directive')

Directive (EU) 2018/2002 Amending Directive 2012/27/EU on Energy Efficiency [2002] OJ L/328/

Directive 2010/75/EU on Industrial Emissions (Integrated Pollution Prevention and Control) [2010] OJ L334/17 ('IED')

Directive 2009/28 on the Promotion of the Use of Energy from Renewable Sources and Amending and Subsequently Repealing Directives 2001/77/EC and 2003/30/EC [2009] OJ L140/16

Directive (EU) 2018/2001 on the Promotion of the Use of Energy from Renewable Sources [2018] OJ L328/82 ('RED II')

Directive 75/442/EEC on Waste [1975] OJ L194/39

Directive 2008/98 on Waste and Repealing Certain Directives [2008] OJ L312/3 ('Waste Framework Directive, WFD')

Regulation (EU) 2020/852 on the Establishment of a Framework to Facilitate Sustainable Investment, and Amending Regulation (EU) 2019/2088 [2020] OJ L198/13

(energy.ec.europa.eu, n.d.) https://energy.ec.europa.eu/topics/energy-efficiency/energy-efficiency-targets-directive-and-rules/energy-efficiency-first-principle_en#:~:text=The%20%E2%80%9Cenergy%20efficiency%20first%20principle,and%20making%20relevant%20investment%20decisions.

Regulation (EC) 2173/2005 on the Establishment of a FLEGT Licensing Scheme for Imports of Timber into the European Community [2005] OJ L347/1 'FLEGT Regulation'
Regulation (EU) 2021/2115 Establishing Rules on Support for Strategic Plans to be Drawn up by Member States under the Common Agricultural Policy (CAP Strategic Plans) and Financed by the European Agricultural Guarantee Fund (EAGF) and by the European Agricultural Fund for Rural Development (EAFRD) and Repealing Regulations (EU) 1305/2013 and (EU) 1307/2013 [2021] OJ L435/1
Regulation (EU) 2018/1999 on the Governance of the Energy Union and Climate Action, Amending Regulations (EC) 663/2009 and (EC) 715/2009, Directives 94/22/EC, 98/70/EC, 2009/31/EC, 2009/73/EC, 2010/31/EU, 2012/27/EU and 2013/30/EU, Council Directives 2009/119/EC and (EU) 2015/652 and Repealing Regulation (EU) 525/2013 [2018] OJ L328/1
Regulation (EU) 995/2010 Laying Down the Obligations of Operators Who Place Timber and Timber Products on the Market [2010] OJ L295/23 ('Timber Regulation')
Commission Decision of 18 December 2014 Amending Decision 2000/532/EC on the List of Waste Pursuant to Directive 2008/98/EC [2014] OJ L370/44
Delegated Regulation (EU) 2021/2139 Supplementing Regulation (EU) 2020/852 by Establishing the Technical Screening Criteria for Determining the Conditions under which an Economic Activity Qualifies as Contributing Substantially to Climate Change Mitigation or Climate Change Adaptation and for Determining whether that Economic Activity Causes no Significant Harm to Any of the Other Environmental Objectives [2021] OJ L442/1

CASES

Inter-Environnement Wallonie ASBL (Case C-129/96) [1997]
Palin Granit Oy (Case C-9/00) ECLI:EU:C:2002:232 [2002]
Sabo and Others v Parliament and Council (Case C-297/20 P) ECLI:EU:C:2021:24 [2021]
Sabo and Others v Parliament and Council (Case T-141/19) ECLI:EU:T:2020:179 [2020] ECR I-179

PART II

The Use of Biofuel and Biogas in the Circular Energy System

6. From gas to biogas from biowaste: heating, power generation, and cogeneration

Maciej M Sokołowski

I. INTRODUCTION

Biogas is a renewable energy resource with many advantages. First and foremost, it can be used to generate heat and power in place of traditional fuels. Biogas may be utilised to produce electricity as well as satisfy heating needs, by offering an alternative way to meet local energy demands, particularly when connectivity to national grids is more difficult or if there is a significant need for heat.[1] In developing countries, biogas lessens dependency on solid biomass as a cooking fuel, enhancing economic and health effects; however, its usage and competitiveness depend on local conditions.[2] Its contribution to the energy transition toward carbon neutrality based on the circular economy (CE) is important, but it is not the only one. To improve energy security and reduce reliance on fossil fuels, which are frequently exploited as political weapons,[3] biogas produced locally from waste and residues can play a significant role.[4] In this regard, biogas has the potential to be a key component of a robust and sustainable future energy system.

[1] International Energy Agency (IEA), 'Outlook for Biogas and Biomethane: Prospects for Organic Growth' (IEA, 2020) 8.

[2] ibid.

[3] See Maciej M Sokołowski, 'Energy as a Conflict Trigger: Comparative Analysis of International Disputes in the Middle East with Energy Relations in the Background' in Anita Garnuszek, Aleksandra Surma, and Laura Mazur (eds), *International Disputes – a Challenge for the Contemporary World* (Faculty of Law and Administration, the University of Warsaw 2012).

[4] See Spyridon Achinas, Vasileios Achinas, and Gerrit Jan Willem Euverink, 'A Technological Overview of Biogas Production from Biowaste' (2017) 3 Engineering 299, 299.

Prior to moving on to the main portion of the analysis, the distinction between biogas and biomethane should be emphasised. Biogas is a combination of methane (CH_4), carbon dioxide (CO_2), and trace amounts of other gases created by the anaerobic digestion of organic matter in an oxygen-free environment, whereas biomethane (also referred to as 'renewable natural gas') is a near-pure source of methane produced either by 'upgrading' biogas (a process that eliminates any CO_2 and other contaminants found in the biogas) or by the gasification of solid biomass followed by methanation.[5] Without underestimating the role of biomethane in the energy transition, this chapter focuses on biogas from waste.

Agricultural waste, manure, municipal waste, sewage sludge, green waste, or food waste are some examples of the raw materials from which biogas is often produced through anaerobic digestion – although it can also be obtained by capturing landfill gas.[6] Due to its fast rate of degradation and the cost-effectiveness of methane mitigation, food waste is a good substrate for anaerobic digestion.[7] Biogas production can thus provide farmers with alternative revenue streams as well as opportunities for development and investment in rural areas.[8] Wheat, maize, rice, other coarse grains, sugar beet, sugar cane, soybeans, and other oilseeds remaining from harvest,[9] and generally, any type of organic waste can be used to produce biogas; however, the sustainability of the processes prompts consideration of extensive dewatering and disposal of digested biosolids.[10] Moreover, the problems with land use brought on by low-cost and low-maintenance energy crops grown solely for energy production are avoided when waste and residues are used as resources for the needs of biogas production.[11] It should also be noted that biogas obtained from food or feed crops increases methane emissions, which might call into question biogas's mitigation benefits, whereas biogas derived from agricultural waste

---

[5] IEA (n 1) 13.

[6] IEA Bioenergy ExCo, 'IEA Bioenergy Countries' Report – Update 2021: Implementation of Bioenergy in the IEA Bioenergy Member Countries' (IEA Bioenergy 2021) 13.

[7] Godwin Glivin and others, 'Conversion of Biowaste to Biogas: A Review of Current Status on Techno-Economic Challenges, Policies, Technologies and Mitigation to Environmental Impacts' (2021) 302 Fuel 121153.

[8] See European Commission, 'Communication from the Commission to the European Parliament, the Council, the European Economic and Social Committee and the Committee of the Regions on an EU Strategy to Reduce Methane Emissions' COM (2020) 663, 7.

[9] IEA (n 1) 15.

[10] Glivin and others (n 7).

[11] IEA (n 1) 15.

or residues can also cost-effectively mitigate methane emissions in the agriculture and waste sectors.[12]

Regarding the current usage of biogas, its conversion into power and/or heat has been the most popular use thus far.[13] Around two-thirds of the biogas produced globally in 2018 was used to generate electricity and heat, with cogeneration installations and facilities using it approximately equally.[14] Most production came from crops and animal manure, followed by municipal solid waste and municipal wastewater.[15] With respect to installed biogas-powered power generation capacity, the International Energy Agency (IEA) estimates that there were roughly 18 GW in 2018 (between 2010 and 2018, capacity rose by an average of 4% each year), with most of these installations located in Germany, the United States, and the United Kingdom.[16] More than 17,000 biogas installations and about 450 biomethane facilities were located in the European Union (EU) in 2015, together accounting for more than 8 GW of power installed.[17] Still, there is significant potential for biogas and/or biomethane production in every region of the world, and the availability of sustainable feedstocks for these purposes is expected to increase by 40% by the year 2040.[18]

These processes are also recognised in the EU, where the use of natural gas is projected to decline substantially in the residential and service sectors. Power generation and heat pumps, as well as biomethane supplied through the existing gas networks, are anticipated to take the place of natural gas in these areas.[19] According to projections under the European Long-Term Strategic Vision, biogas utilisation in the European power system will reach consumption levels of between 22 and 45 Mtoe in 2050, almost matching natural gas in the decarbonisation scenarios.[20] Various scenarios predict that by 2050 the total consumption of biogas produced exclusively in the EU will vary between

---

12 On an EU Strategy to Reduce Methane Emissions (n 8) 8.

13 IEA Bioenergy ExCo (n 6).

14 Approximately 30% was consumed in buildings, primarily in the residential sector for cooking and heating, with the remaining converted to biomethane and blended into gas networks or used as a transportation fuel, IEA (n 1) 19.

15 IEA (n 1) 16.

16 ibid 20.

17 European Commission, 'In-Depth Analysis in Support of the Commission Communication COM (2018) 773 – A Clean Planet for All – A European Strategic Long-Term Vision for a Prosperous, Modern, Competitive and Climate Neutral Economy' (2018), 59.

18 IEA (n 1) 7.

19 European Commission, 'Implementing the Repower EU Action Plan: Investment Needs, Hydrogen Accelerator and Achieving the Bio-Methane Targets – Accompanying the Document Communication REPowerEU Plan' SWD (2022) 230, 13.

20 In-Depth Analysis in Support of the Commission Communication COM (2018) 773 (n 17) 75.

45 Mtoe and 79 Mtoe, up from 16 Mtoe in 2015.[21] Moreover, the recent analysis by the Commission indicates that the higher energy prices and the measures announced in the March 2022 Communication will alter the energy system and its Fit for 55 transition in the following ways: natural gas use in the EU will decline more quickly than in the Fit for 55 proposals, and over the long term, the analysis, in addition to more renewables and energy savings, shows a larger space for direct natural gas substitutes like biomethane and hydrogen than in the Fit for 55.[22]

Against this backdrop, the purpose of this chapter is to investigate whether the complex regulatory framework of EU policies and laws promotes or hinders the increase in the consumption of biogas produced from biowastes in heating and power generation, and the cogeneration of heat and power. Section II looks at the most recent development in the EU policies issued by the Commission through official Communications. Section III examines the current regulatory framework, as well as relevant proposed amendments by the Commission, to what concerns, specifically, the regulation of heat, electricity, and cogeneration. Section IV compares National Energy and Climate Plans (NECPs) to picture how the MSs have so far promised to implement EU law and their reliance on biogas for the decarbonisation of the above-mentioned services. Section V concludes.

II. EU POLICIES PROMOTING BIOGAS

1. From the European Green Deal to the REPowerEU

Interestingly, biogas is not directly addressed in one of the European key energy transition documents presented in 2019 – the Communication on the European Green Deal.[23] However, one can find there a declaration on facilitating the decarbonisation of the gas sector conducted, *inter alia*, 'via enhancing support for the development of decarbonised gases, via a forward-looking design for a competitive decarbonised gas market'.[24] Moreover, as presented in the European Green Deal, the long-term vision for rural regions will reflect how European funds, especially those for rural development, can assist rural communities in using their potential in the circular and bio-economy.[25] Regarding the latter, as announced in the Communication on a new Circular Economy Action Plan, increasing the synergies between circularity and greenhouse gas

---

21 ibid 81–82.
22 Implementing the Repower EU Action Plan (n 19) 13.
23 European Commission, 'The European Green Deal' COM (2019) 640.
24 ibid 6.
25 'The European Green Deal' (n 23), 6.

(GHG) emission reduction is necessary to attain climate neutrality by the EU.[26] As a result, the Commission declared it will advocate for a stronger role for circularity, also in upcoming revisions of the NECPs.[27]

Biogas is also addressed in the European Green Deal's follow-up documents from 2020. For instance, the EU Strategy for Energy System Integration presents its cornerstones of an integrated energy system with a 'more "circular" energy system' that prioritises the least energy-intensive options, reuses unavoidable waste streams into energy, and takes advantage of synergies between different sectors.[28] As noted in the Strategy, this is already taking place in cogeneration or through the use of particular types of waste and residues; however, in order to fully utilise the circularity potential of waste heat from industrial processes, data centres, or energy produced from biowaste or in wastewater treatment plants, additional steps must be taken.[29]

Opportunities in biogas production are also addressed in the EU Methane Strategy.[30] This relates to non-recyclable human and agricultural waste that together with residue streams can be effectively used in anaerobic digesters to produce biogas and lower methane emissions.[31] The biogas produced from such feedstocks is a highly sustainable and useful renewable energy resource with multiple applications, while digestate (i.e. the material remaining after anaerobic digestion) can be used as a soil improver after further processing, which is consistent with the waste hierarchy because waste-derived biodegradable input into biorefineries and biogas plants can contribute to the municipal waste recycling targets outlined in Directive 2018/98.[32] The EU Methane Strategy calls for further incentivising of the collection and use of high methane emitting organic wastes or residues from farming as biogas substrates, with actions including identifying best practices for collection and/or harvesting of sustainable wastes and residues, promoting the use of digestate as a sustainable soil improver in lieu of mined fertilisers, or incentivising sequential cropping used in combination with manure as feedstock for sustainable biogas production.[33] However, as underlined in the Strategy, any measures to encourage biogas production must be carefully considered in order to avoid creating perverse

---

26 European Commission, 'A New Circular Economy Action Plan for a Cleaner and More Competitive Europe' COM (2020) 98, 16.

27 ibid.

28 European Commission, 'Powering a Climate-Neutral Economy: An EU Strategy for Energy System Integration' COM (2020) 299, 2.

29 See ibid.

30 On an EU Strategy to Reduce Methane Emissions (n 8).

31 ibid 7.

32 ibid.

33 ibid 8.

incentives that could lead to an increase in overall emissions from the waste, land, and agricultural sectors, as well as an increase in the landfilling of unutilised digestate as soil improvers.[34] In this context, the Commission declared it would provide targeted support to accelerate the development of the market for biogas from sustainable sources such as manure or organic waste and residues through upcoming policy initiatives[35] such as the aforementioned future gas market regulatory framework and the revision of the Renewable Energy Directive (RED).[36] The European plans include a pilot project to engage rural areas and farming communities in developing installations and obtaining finance for agricultural waste biogas production.[37]

In May 2022, major steps to cut dependency on Russian gas and to unleash the full biogas and biomethane potential that exists across all EU Member States (MSs) were presented. The announced actions are intended to make it easier for biomethane to be included in the EU internal gas market by tackling existing barriers and to enhance biogas production while adhering to the environmental standards established by the RED II.[38] This necessitates improved coordination of EU, national, and regional biogas and biomethane assistance while also addressing issues with infrastructure deployment, financial access, research and development, and innovation.[39] In terms of timing, medium-term arrangements on biomethane are taken into consideration (until 2027).[40] This relates to expanding biomethane infrastructure and production as well as converting the current gas networks to biomethane.[41]

With respect to the scale of the investments, sustainable biomethane developments account for only EUR 37 billion of the EUR 300 billion in investment needed between 2022 and 2030. This results in 17 bcm utilised in households, industry, and agriculture.[42] Additionally, under the REPowerEU, biogas use in power plants is expected to total 12.3 Mtoe, while biogas use as a transformation input in industry and district heating is anticipated to reach 6.9 ktoe.[43] The REPowerEU calls for an increase compared to Fit for 55, with growth account-

---

[34] ibid.

[35] See Maciej M Sokołowski, *Regulation in the European Electricity Sector* (Routledge 2016) 208.

[36] 'Communication from the Commission to the European Parliament, the Council, the European Economic and Social Committee and the Committee of the Regions on an EU Strategy to Reduce Methane Emissions' (n 8) 9. Also known as the RED II.

[37] ibid.

[38] Implementing the Repower EU Action Plan (n 19) 3.

[39] See ibid.

[40] See ibid 7.

[41] See ibid 4–5.

[42] ibid 7.

[43] ibid 16.

ing for 0.5 Mtoe in power generation and 3.6 ktoe in industrial and district heating.[44] One should note the former is only slightly higher, while the latter is twice as high; although their scale is different (Mtoe compared to ktoe).[45]

2. The 2022 Action Plan

To meet the REPowerEU Communication's target of 35 bcm annual biomethane production by 2030, the Commission listed steps targeted at both boosting production to a sustainable maximum potential volume of biogas with the goal of further upgrading it to biomethane, as well as direct biomethane production from waste and residues.[46] All together, these measures constitute a Biomethane Action Plan, setting the preconditions for sustainable upgrading and the safe injection of biomethane into the gas network.[47] One should take note of the waste-based nature of biomethane production driven by the avoidance of using food and feedstocks that would cause problems with land use change, and the scaling up of sustainable biogas and biomethane production, offering opportunities for farmers and foresters.[48]

Although biomethane is a focus of the 2022 Action Plan, waste-based biogas is a significant component, and a Biomethane Action Plan includes concrete steps to promote biogas in order to meet the 35 bcm 2030 target. These are actions related to areas such as: (i) promotion of the sustainable production and use of biogas and biomethane at EU and national/regional level and the injection of biomethane into the gas grid; (ii) providing incentives for biogas upgrading into biomethane; (iii) promoting the adaptation and adjustment of existing, and the deployment of new, infrastructure for the transport of increased shares of biomethane through the EU gas grid; (iv) addressing research, development, and innovation gaps; and (v) providing access to finance for projects on the production and use of biomethane and biogas.[49] Within these areas specific activities are considered. They range from creating a biogas and biomethane industrial partnership/forum and developing national strategies on sustainable biogas and biomethane to assessing challenges and bottlenecks related to the utilisation of biogas and biomethane.[50] The following part discusses some of them in detail.

---

44 See ibid.
45 Accordingly, 10^6 and 10^3.
46 See Implementing the Repower EU Action Plan (n 19) 34–46.
47 ibid 34.
48 ibid.
49 See ibid 34–46.
50 See ibid.

The proposed establishment of national strategies on sustainable biogas and biomethane production, as well as the use or integration of a biogas and biomethane component in NECPs, would require examining each MS's national potential for biogas and biomethane production, as well as their integration into the gas network, together with a path to realising the identified potentials by 2030 and 2050.[51] Aside from national plans, the Commission may consider developing an EU strategy for rural energy transition to assist the implementation of such integrated energy solutions in rural areas, benefiting from the decentralised small biogas plants in the EU and integrating them into the overall renewable energy mix, while also addressing related environmental and social aspects.[52] Agricultural cooperatives and other multi-stakeholder local organisations, such as energy communities, might be utilised to satisfy these demands, in conjunction with rural development funds from the Common Agricultural Policy or structural and cohesion policy (Community Led Local Development).[53]

III. EU REGULATORY FRAMEWORK

When examining the European legal framework for energy, biogas is already covered in the first legal directive on renewable sources, Directive 2001/77,[54] albeit being regulated in a very general manner. Among definitions included in Article 2, 'landfill gas, sewage treatment plant gas and biogases' are categorised as 'renewable energy sources'. Directive 2009/28,[55] another directive on renewables, similarly gives biogas little consideration. Apart from qualifying as 'energy from renewable sources', as its predecessor did, the preamble to Directive 2009/28 (Renewable Energy Directive I, RED I) made only a broad reference to biogas's potential and practical applications.[56] Additionally, the Directive's annexes addressed biogas in terms of the energy content of

---

51 ibid 35.

52 ibid 38.

53 Implementing the Repower EU Action Plan (n 19) 38.

54 ibid 38. Directive 2001/77/EC on the promotion of electricity produced from renewable energy sources in the internal electricity market [2001] OJ L283/33.

55 Directive 2009/28/EC on the promotion of the use of energy from renewable sources and amending and subsequently repealing Directives 2001/77/EC and 2003/30/EC [2009] OJ L140/16 ('RED I').

56 As stated in rec 12, '[t]he use of agricultural material such as manure, slurry and other animal and organic waste for biogas production has, in view of the high greenhouse gas emission saving potential, significant environmental advantages in terms of heat and power production and its use as biofuel. Biogas installations can, as a result of their decentralised nature and the regional investment structure, contribute significantly to sustainable development in rural areas and offer farmers new income opportunities'.

transport fuels[57] and rules for calculating the GHG gas impact of biofuels, bioliquids and their fossil fuel comparators.[58]

The introduction of Directive 2018/2001[59] (Renewable Energy Directive, RED II) established a more specific approach to this sort of renewable energy. Nevertheless, the RED II introduces a definition of biogas as 'gaseous fuels produced from biomass'.[60] It should also be noted that when the RED II refers to biogas, it is referring to biogas used for transportation.[61] Together with solid fuels produced from biomass, biogas constitutes a category of 'biomass fuels'.[62] The core of both definitions is 'biomass'. In RED II it means 'the biodegradable fraction of products, waste and residues from biological origin from agriculture, including vegetal and animal substances, from forestry and related industries, including fisheries and aquaculture, as well as the biodegradable fraction of waste, including industrial and municipal waste of biological origin'. In this context, it is worth noticing the reference to biowaste as defined in Directive 2008/98 (Waste Framework Directive, WFD),[63] namely, 'biodegradable garden and park waste, food and kitchen waste from households, restaurants, caterers and retail premises and comparable waste from food processing plants'.[64] Moreover, one cannot ignore the issue of the waste hierarchy provided by the WFD. This includes energy recovery, which comes after prevention, preparation for re-use, and recycling, and is then followed by disposal.[65]

The principles of waste hierarchy, together with the EU's sustainability criteria and a need to ensure no additional demand for land created (while promoting the use of wastes and residues), apply to the list of feedstock to produce biogas, as set out in an annex to the RED II.[66] The sustainability criteria, together with the GHG emissions saving criteria provided in the RED II, have an impact on the possibility of integrating the biomass fuels that meet them into the share of energy from renewable sources.[67] Here one should also

---

57 RED I (n 55) annex III.

58 ibid annex V.

59 Directive 2018/2001 on the promotion of the use of energy from renewable sources [2018] OJ L328/82 ('RED II').

60 ibid art 2(28).

61 See ibid recs 85, 91, 106, and 126 of the preamble and arts 2(36), 25(1), 27(1)–(2), or 28(5)–(7).

62 See ibid 2(27).

63 Directive 2008/98/EC on waste and repealing certain Directives [2008] OJ L312/3 ('Waste Framework Directive', 'WFD').

64 ibid art 3(4).

65 ibid art 4.

66 See RED II (n 59) rec 37 of the preamble.

67 See ibid art 7(1).

note the specific rules for biomass fuels (but also for biofuels and bioliquids) produced from food and feed crops that apply to the calculation of an MS's gross final consumption of energy from renewable sources. The percentage of high indirect land-use change risk biomass fuels produced from food and feed crops for which a significant expansion of the production area into land with high-carbon stock is seen shall not surpass the level of consumption of such fuels in a given MS in 2019, unless they are certified to be low indirect land-use change risk.[68] Moreover, this limit shall progressively decline to 0% beginning on December 31, 2023, and ending on December 31, 2030, at the latest.[69]

Nevertheless, the general rules on sustainability and GHG emissions saving criteria for biogas are laid down in Article 29 of the RED II. However, RED II contains important exemptions concerning biogas, as follows. First, biogas (qualified as biomass fuels) produced from waste and residues, other than agricultural, aquaculture, fisheries, and forestry residues, is required to fulfil only the GHG emissions saving criteria laid down in Article 29(10) of the RED II in order to be taken into account for the three groups of targeted purposes related to contributing towards the EU target[70] and the MSs' renewable energy shares, compliance with renewable energy obligations, and eligibility for financial support.[71] Second, electricity, heating and cooling produced from municipal solid waste are exempt from the GHG emissions saving criteria outlined in Article 29(10) of the RED II.[72] Third, smaller units are also exempted from these criteria – this concerns installations producing electricity, heating and cooling or fuels with a total rated thermal input less than 2 MW. Member States may apply the sustainability and GHG emissions saving criteria to installations with lower total rated thermal input.[73] Additionally, biogas produced from waste and residues sourced not from forestry but from agricultural land qualifies for the needs of the targeted objectives only where operators or national authorities have monitoring or management plans in place to address the consequences on soil quality and soil carbon.[74]

To be considered for the above-mentioned targeted purposes (contribution to the EU target and national renewable energy shares, compliance with renewable energy obligations, and eligibility for financial support), for electricity, heating, and cooling production from biomass fuels, the GHG emission

---

[68] ibid art 26(2).
[69] ibid art 26(2).
[70] See ibid art 3(1).
[71] ibid art 29(1).
[72] ibid.
[73] ibid.
[74] ibid.

savings must reach at least 70% or 80%.[75] The lower cap applies to facilities that began operation between 1 January 2021 and 31 December 2025, while the latter applies to installations started after 1 January 2026.[76] Furthermore, electricity generated from biomass fuels shall be considered for the aforementioned targeted purposes only if it meets one or more of the four requirements.[77] First, it is generated in facilities with a total rated thermal input of less than 50 MW. Second, for installations with a total rated thermal input ranging from 50 to 100 MW, for combined heat and power (CHP) units, it is produced applying high-efficiency cogeneration technology,[78] or, for electricity-only units, it satisfies an energy efficiency level associated with the best available techniques (BAT-AEELs).[79] Third, the same condition related to applying high-efficiency cogeneration technology concerns installations with a total rated thermal input above 100 MW, while for electricity-only installations, achieving a net-electrical efficiency of at least 36% is required. Fourth, it is produced applying biomass CO_2 capture and storage. Moreover, for the needs of the first, second, and third requirements, electricity-only-installations shall be taken into account only if they do not use fossil fuels as a main fuel and only if there is no cost-effective potential for the application of high-efficiency cogeneration technology according to the assessment in accordance with Directive 2012/27/EU.[80]

The RED II offers some other exemptions from this regime. The first and second requirement paragraph apply only to installations starting operation or converted to the use of biomass fuels after 25 December 2021, while the third requirement applies without prejudice to support granted under support schemes approved by 25 December 2021.[81] With respect to the third, MSs may

---

75 ibid art 29(10)(d).

76 According to RED II (n 59) art 29(10)(d) '[a]n installation shall be considered to be in operation once the physical production of biofuels, biogas consumed in the transport sector and bioliquids, and the physical production of heating and cooling and electricity from biomass fuels has started'.

77 RED II (n 59), art 29(11)(a)–(d).

78 See Maciej M Sokołowski, 'Energy Efficiency at Energy Production Level: Promoting Combined Heat and Power' in Martha M Roggenkamp, Kars J de Graaf, and Ruven C Fleming (eds), *Energy Law, Climate Change and the Environment* (Edward Elgar Publishing 2021).

79 See Commission Implementing Decision (EU) 2017/1442 establishing best available techniques (BAT) conclusions, under Directive 2010/75/EU for large combustion plants [2017] OJ L212/1; see Maciej M Sokołowski, *European Law on Combined Heat and Power* (Routledge 2020) 106–107.

80 See Directive 2012/27/EU on energy efficiency, amending Directives 2009/125/EC and 2010/30/EU and repealing Directives 2004/8/EC and 2006/32/EC [2012] OJ L315/1, art 14.

81 RED II (n 59) art 29(11).

derogate, for a limited period of time, from the criteria laid down in the RED II (*inter alia*, those related to addressing impacts on soil quality and soil carbon, GHG emission savings, or energy efficiency)[82] by adopting different criteria for two types of installations, subject to a notification to the Commission. First, to the extent that such facilities generate electricity or provide heating or cooling using biomass fuels, this applies to installations situated in an outermost region as specified in Article 349 of the Treaty on the Functioning of the European Union (TFEU).[83] The second relates to biomass fuels used in these installations, regardless of where the biomass was produced, provided that such criteria are objectively justified on the grounds that they aim to ensure a smooth phase-in of the exempted criteria for that outermost region and thereby encourage the switch from fossil fuels to sustainable biomass fuels.[84] Naturally, the MSs can also establish additional sustainability criteria for biomass fuels.[85] This also concerns the higher energy efficiency requirement for installations with lower rated thermal input.[86]

IV. NECPS

Developing national strategies for sustainable biogas and biomethane production, as well as using or integrating biogas and biomethane, is a proposed component of the NECPs. The national production potentials for biogas and biomethane in each MS, as well as their integration into the gas network, will be examined using these strategies, along with a plan for attaining their potential by 2030 and 2050.[87] These plans will concentrate on the most sustainable options, based on such production as agricultural and agro-industry waste and residues, forest and forest-industry waste and residues, food industry waste, energy and chemical industry biogenic CO_2 effluents and waste, industrial wastewater, and residential organic waste, as well as the evaluation of the preconditions to further boost the potential of sustainable biomass.[88]

This evaluation should take the cascade concept of Article 3(3) of the proposal for a revised RED II into consideration.[89] Furthermore, national strategies should assess any hurdles to biomethane production or injection

---

[82] See ibid art 29(2)–(7) and (10)–(11).

[83] ibid art 29(13)(a); Consolidated version of the Treaty on the Functioning of the European Union [2012] OJ C 326/47.

[84] RED II (n 59) art 29(13)(b).

[85] ibid art 29(14).

[86] ibid art 29(11).

[87] Implementing the Repower EU Action Plan (n 19) 35.

[88] ibid.

[89] ibid 36.

into the network in the national or regional context and incorporate efforts to overcome these barriers.[90] The strategies should continue to assess the need for standardisation and market regulatory harmonisation with other MSs.[91] Furthermore, the national biogas and biomethane strategies should be reflected in the national Recovery and Resilience Plans, in coordination with support envisaged in other strategic planning documents like the Common Agriculture Policy National Strategic Plans or the national programming documents for EU structural funds.[92]

Still, this is a matter for the future, when national strategies for sustainable biogas and biomethane production become part of the NECPs. Before that happens and the various NECPs are altered, let us examine their existing versions and how they relate to biogas use in the energy sector.

1. Austria

Austria has an objective of increasing the percentage of domestic agricultural waste fermented in biogas facilities from 1% to 30%.[93] A range of options are taken into consideration to accomplish this goal in addition to those under the Renewable Energy Expansion Act. This relates to finding locations for biogas plants (including suitable livestock or raw material supply, short distances, the possibility of feeding into the gas grid); offering appropriate incentives in energy price regulations (like a slurry bonus) and for raw materials management of agricultural residues; incentives for cooperation between farms, raising awareness, and research.[94] Moreover, Austria offers biogas-favourable tax treatment, together with a tax exemption for sustainable biogas.[95] Regarding biogas plants, the system established by the 2017 amendment to the Green Electricity Act 2012 will be systematically developed, especially in accordance with the 'Greening the gas' initiative.[96]

2. Belgium

In Belgium both the Walloon Region and the Flemish Region include biogas in their plans. Support will be given to the biogas industry in the Walloon Region so that it can deliver an increasing proportion of gas based on short

---

[90] ibid.
[91] ibid.
[92] ibid 37.
[93] Austria, 'Integrated National Energy and Climate Plan for Austria' (2019) 134.
[94] ibid.
[95] ibid 159.
[96] ibid 152.

supply chains (5% biogas in 2025 and 15% in 2030).[97] A number of actions are required to create a framework for the implementation of renewable heating and cooling, such as the introduction of a renewable heat transition plan with a list of technological options for various applications, especially with a view to switching from oil products to cleaner alternatives like biogas.[98] In the Flemish Region, as at the end of 2019, the production of biogas has been somewhat increased due to the establishment of 10 new plants for the anaerobic digestion of vegetable, fruit, and garden waste, as well as additional small-scale anaerobic digesters in the agricultural sector.[99] Nevertheless, the use of available domestic flows should be encouraged to ensure the required transfer to green heat, and a biogas utilisation framework is being established to maximise the energy potential of biogas, notably through injection into the natural gas system.[100]

3. Bulgaria

In Bulgaria, the volume of biogas produced through the anaerobic fermentation of biomass and sewage sludge is still very small.[101] In order to improve this situation, it is proposed to implement low-emission methods of processing livestock waste, such as composting and anaerobic conversion of livestock manure into biogas.[102] Furthermore, biogas capture and burning are planned for all new and current regional landfills, as well as old municipal landfills scheduled for closure.[103] Plans also cover an introduction of anaerobic sludge stabilisation by biogas capture and incineration in new installations and those undergoing reconstruction in agglomerations of more than 20,000 residents equivalent.[104]

[97] Belgium, 'Belgian Integrated National Energy and Climate Plan 2021–2030. Section A – Context, Objectives, Policies and Measures' (2019) 55.
[98] ibid 183.
[99] ibid 67.
[100] ibid.
[101] Bulgaria, 'Integrated Energy and Climate Plan of the Republic of Bulgaria 2021–2030' (2019) 15.
[102] ibid 96.
[103] ibid.
[104] ibid 95.

4. Croatia

In Croatia, biogas technologies for the production of energy and heat are ranked among the fields with the greatest potential for both business and research.[105] The incentive of pricing (tariffs) based on the installed power of the plant is the key mechanism for stimulating the use of biogas for electricity generation and the building of cogeneration biogas plants.[106] However, for small farmers, this is an expensive investment, thus their cooperation might enable lowering the plant's installation cost.[107] In this context, Croatia plans to design and implement new business models for the realisation of anaerobic digestion plants for the production and use of biogas and biomass cogeneration.[108]

5. Cyprus

In Cyprus, a set of policy initiatives aimed at lowering the volume of biodegradable waste in solid waste treatment facilities was proposed.[109] This includes actions to encourage biowaste segregation, recycling, and anaerobic digestion energy recovery.[110] These steps are largely intended to decrease the amount of biodegradable waste in facilities that handle solid waste, including those that generate electricity and thermal energy from the production of biogas.[111] A support scheme for the installation of cogeneration systems using biomass or biogas to produce electricity for self-consumption was developed in 2017 to meet these needs.[112] Moreover, the aforementioned actions, which were already started as part of the National Municipal Waste Management Strategy, will be strengthened between 2021 and 2030.[113]

6. Czech Republic

The processing of agricultural waste in biogas plants is recognised in the Czech Republic as an important way of utilising methane and preventing its spontaneous formation.[114] Feed-in tariffs and green bonuses according to

---

105 Croatia, 'Integrated National Energy and Climate Plan for the Republic of Croatia for the Period 2021–2030' (2019) 78–79.
106 ibid 97.
107 ibid.
108 ibid 112.
109 Cyprus, 'Cyprus' Integrated National Energy and Climate Plan' (2020) 28.
110 ibid.
111 ibid.
112 ibid 36.
113 ibid 28.
114 Czechia, 'National Energy and Climate Plan of the Czech Republic' (2019) 77.

the volume of power produced have been the major tools used to encourage biogas utilisation.[115] Operational programmes have supported the development of biogas stations, and this assistance continues today: agricultural biogas stations were built with aid from the Rural Development Programme, while the operational programme Enterprise and Innovation for Competitiveness supports the output of heat from the existing biogas stations for its effective use, and the operational programme Environment supports the development of biogas stations using biowaste.[116] Further support for biogas sources will be provided to the maximum possible efficiency CHP facilities.[117] One option could be to convert existing biogas power plants to biomethane plants and to use biomethane for CHP units.[118]

7. Denmark

Since the 1980s, Denmark has encouraged the production and use of biogas through several financial incentives.[119] The production of biogas slowed down because of changes made to the support scheme in the late 1990s and in 2004, when it was decided that electricity generated from biogas would receive a fixed feed-in tariff for the first 10 years, followed by a reduced tariff for the next 10 years.[120] In 2008, a different option was presented to improve biogas production by making it more commercially viable: either a higher tariff or a price premium for power production (for all and existing biogas facilities).[121] Although it was anticipated that the increase in direct support would enhance biogas output, actual production only increased by about 4–5 PJ.[122] As a result, the incentive was once again modified in 2012, and two additional price premiums were established.[123] According to the June 2018 Energy Agreement, the biogas support programmes were to be phased out by 2020, and after 1 January 2020 existing installations continue to receive support[124] for a predetermined amount of depreciation time; however, no new installations are eligible for the subsidy programmes.[125]

---

115 ibid.
116 ibid.
117 ibid 89–90.
118 See ibid 93, 210.
119 Denmark, 'Denmark's Integrated National Energy and Climate Plan' (2019) 37.
120 ibid.
121 ibid.
122 ibid.
123 ibid.
124 See ibid 173–174.
125 ibid 90.

8. Estonia

Estonia is considering establishing measures to support the production of heat and electricity from biogas (investments to improve farm efficiency) and to increase biomethane production on farms, with the goal of producing biogas from manure, including slurry, that could replace the use of fossil fuels in energy production.[126] Smaller investments would be prioritised in this regard.[127] In terms of existing measures, biogas and biomethane are exempted from the excise duty.[128]

9. Finland

Finland offers a financial incentive for investments in energy-efficient and environmentally friendly energy sources, such as biogas facilities, as well as for the treatment and use of manure.[129] Consultations on energy efficiency and matters relating to climate change adaptation and mitigation are also provided as part of the programme's advisory services.[130] Finland implemented a sliding feed-in tariff scheme in March 2011 for the generation of electricity from renewable energy sources, including biogas.[131] The subsidy programme has been phased out, and as of January 2019 it was no longer available for new biogas-fired power plants, although the scheme's plants will receive support for up to 12 years after they begin production.[132] However, the government made the decision to establish a national biogas programme in order to utilise the potential of biogas.[133]

10. France

France intends to implement a variety of measures applicable across all sectors to increase the generation of renewable heat,[134] including making it obligatory to recover energy from biogas captured in waste storage facilities (where applicable).[135] Furthermore, plans include biogas support measures such as combin-

---

[126] Estonia, 'Estonia's 2030 National Energy and Climate Plan' (2019) 80.
[127] ibid.
[128] ibid 87.
[129] Finland, 'Finland's Integrated Energy and Climate Plan' (2019) 90.
[130] ibid.
[131] ibid 93.
[132] ibid.
[133] ibid 99.
[134] See France, 'Integrated National Energy and Climate Plan for France' (2020) 92–95.
[135] ibid 95.

ing the requirement to buy biogas at a regulated tariff and launching auctions that allow for the achievement of generating targets at a reasonable cost due to cost reductions.[136] French bioenergy resources are limited, so biomethane injection for biogas must be prioritised, and cogeneration must only be used in certain circumstances.[137] According to the priorities outlined in the National Biomass Mobilisation Strategy, the value in energy terms is to direct resources towards the pathways presenting the highest yields, particularly recovery in the form of heat, and so generation of electricity from biogas will be reserved for anaerobic digestion sites far from the gas network, where there is no potential for direct recovery as bioNGV or fuel.[138] The output of an anaerobic digestion plant is rather steady throughout the year, with the exception of concerns related to input supply, and cogeneration operations can be changed during the day thanks to the flexibility provided by biogas buffer storage.[139]

11. Germany

Germany intends to provide financial assistance for the fermentation of farmyard fertilisers originating from animals and agricultural wastes – with plans related to the use of farm manure of animal origin and agricultural waste materials for energy in biogas plants.[140] Increased use of agricultural manure in biogas plants and gas-tight digestate storage will be pushed, utilising existing and new tools.[141] Aside from the support scheme, it is planned to examine and remove barriers to farm manure fermentation, create options for follow-up use through the development of new funding and implementation models, and fund farm manure fermentation on farms with up to two livestock units per hectare (owned and leased land).[142]

12. Greece

Greece sees biogas projects as part of a larger effort to develop clean energy, funded by initiatives carried out by energy communities with public participation, local governments, and/or legal entities subject to both public and private law, with the goal of advancing renewable energy sources and reduc-

136 ibid 96.
137 ibid 256.
138 ibid 198.
139 See ibid 198, 244.
140 Germany, 'Integrated National Energy and Climate Plan of Germany' (2019) 64.
141 ibid.
142 ibid.

ing energy poverty.[143] These projects could be built with the help of regional livestock cooperatives, often as autoproduction projects with the potential to make use of existing energy infrastructure.[144] Regarding the policy measures, Greece intends to improve and optimise the licencing framework and technical requirements for renewable district heating networks and injection of biogas into the natural gas system.[145]

13. Hungary

The Green District Heating Programme, as well as increased consumption of energy recovered from wastewater treatment, landfill gas, and agricultural biogas, play a critical role in substituting natural gas and increasing the use of renewable energy on the Hungarian heat market (greening district heating).[146] Based on an examination of local features, incentives to employ these resources will be designed for each major district heating zone.[147] To put the concept into action, present district heating price regulations will be reviewed.[148] Following the evaluation of price regulations, competitive conditions on the district heat market will be established.[149] In this regard, Hungary will stimulate the development of biogas facilities that process agricultural waste to meet local heat demand while also feeding purified biomethane into the natural gas network.[150] Furthermore, in municipalities without a natural gas network, it may be feasible to create a biogas power plant that would offer electricity to the municipality, for instance, as a member of an energy community.[151]

14. Ireland

The Irish support scheme for renewable heat's main goal is to boost its use in heating to enable the country to fulfil its 2020 renewable energy targets while simultaneously lowering GHG emissions.[152] The government-funded programme encourages non-domestic heat users not covered by the emissions trading system (such as commercial, industrial, agricultural, district heating,

---

143 Greece, 'National Energy and Climate Plan of Greece' (2019) 116.
144 ibid.
145 ibid 150.
146 Hungary, 'National Energy and Climate Plan of Hungary' (2020) 77.
147 ibid.
148 ibid.
149 ibid.
150 ibid.
151 ibid 96.
152 Ireland 'National Energy & Climate Plan 2021–2030 of Ireland' (2019) 220.

the public sector, and other non-residential heat users) to use renewable heating systems.[153] The programme intends to close the cost gap between installing and maintaining renewable heating systems and their traditional fossil fuel-based counterparts, as well as to encourage the production and delivery of renewable heat.[154] Support for biogas (anaerobic digestion) is part of the scheme's operational support component, which debuted in June 2019.[155]

15. Italy

Cogeneration from waste and agricultural residues is of interest in Italy, particularly through plants that are part of a production cycle, because these allow waste to be optimised, with lower shares of raw materials in secondary collection, in accordance with CE principles; and in the case of biogas plants, advantages may also be realised in terms of the utilisation of digestate.[156] For a well-functioning CE, biogas facilities must also be able to make efficient use of livestock manure, and they have the right to utilise an incentive on electricity produced with that aim.[157] This applies to existing biogas-powered facilities that began operations before the end of 2017 and were established by agricultural entrepreneurs acting alone or in groups who do not qualify for other governmental incentives for power generation. The incentive must meet the criteria for sustainability outlined in the RED II.[158] To qualify for the incentive, plants must employ at least 40% manure by weight and reconvert daily produce using a programmable system in compliance with the standards stated annually.[159] Moreover, Italy is considering the reconversion of biogas plants to biomethane, already provided for in the existing legal framework.[160]

16. Latvia

Despite the fact that the volume of electricity produced at biogas cogeneration stations has increased in recent years, Latvia has no plans to expand its biogas capacity for power production.[161] The country is concentrating on enhancing

---

[153] ibid.
[154] ibid.
[155] ibid.
[156] Italy, 'Integrated National Energy and Climate Plan of Italy' (2019) 142.
[157] ibid 149.
[158] ibid.
[159] ibid.
[160] See ibid 141, 149.
[161] See Latvia, 'Latvia's National Energy and Climate Plan 2021–2030' (2020) 34, 82.

the infrastructure for biomethane and promoting its use in commercial and public transportation.[162]

17. Lithuania

The first biogas facilities in Lithuania began operations in 2003.[163] Since 2014, the number of biogas installations that process farm waste to biogas has increased.[164] To lead this growth between 2021 and 2030, investment support for the implementation of climate-friendly agricultural technologies in animal farms was projected.[165] As of 2019, Lithuania only had biogas production facilities for electricity and heat generation, and in order to maximise the potential of biogas, a shift from biogas usage for electricity and heat production to biogas treatment and delivery to the natural gas networks was planned.[166] A measure of this nature would allow for the quickest possible deployment of existing infrastructure and the anticipated arrival of biomethane gas on the Lithuanian market in 2022.[167] The measure would include financial assistance for the building and installation of treatment units in existing biogas plants.[168]

18. Luxembourg

Luxembourg intends to promote biogas as an energy source further in the interests of the CE.[169] This relates to the use of organic manure of animal origin as a priority in biogas facilities to reduce methane emissions.[170] Biogas will still be used for electricity and heat, but the framework conditions must be updated to effectively encourage biogas and take into consideration the substantial environmental and water protection challenges (methane, ammonia emissions, nitrate, phosphorus).[171] Therefore, Luxembourg set the main directions for its development, including those related to the CE, slurry, manure, biowaste, and other residues.[172] As a result, the biogas strategy is also part of the methane

---

[162] See ibid 12, 130, 159.

[163] Lithuania, 'National Energy and Climate Action Plan of the Republic of Lithuania for 2021–2030' (2019) 30.

[164] ibid 75.

[165] See ibid 76, 78.

[166] ibid 120.

[167] ibid.

[168] ibid.

[169] Luxembourg, 'Luxembourg's Integrated National Energy and Climate Plan for 2021–2030' (2018) 74–75.

[170] ibid.

[171] ibid 86.

[172] ibid.

reduction strategy, with the biogas produced being fed into the gas network as a priority.[173]

19. Malta

In Malta, given the current installed stock of heating and cooling technologies, which is already quite efficient, and the low share of heating demand, heating and cooling networks and CHP technology are expected to play only a minor role in the next decade.[174] This is exacerbated by the fact that Malta has virtually no indigenous biomass or biogas resources, and there is currently no natural gas distribution network to make fuel supply cheaper than the current options.[175] Consequently, it is anticipated that the power and heat generated from biogas in the existing CHP waste-to-energy facilities will not change.[176]

20. The Netherlands

The Netherlands has a varied system of taxes and levies that affect energy consumption, with no energy tax required for self-generated electricity utilising renewable energy sources or CHP units, self-extracted landfill gas, sewage treatment gas, or biogas.[177] Nonetheless, biogas is only mentioned in the context of solutions considered to absorb demand for natural gas in the Dutch integrated climate-energy plan.[178]

21. Poland

Along with the development of the agricultural biogas production sector in Poland, the importance of using agricultural by-products and agri-food industry residual products has grown, with the energy potential of the agri-food processing industry in terms of agricultural biogas production estimated to exceed 7.8 billion m^3 annually.[179] With respect to energy from biogas, Poland intends to utilise biogas mostly in cogeneration.[180] One advantage is the ability to store

---

173 ibid.

174 Malta, 'Malta's 2030 National Energy and Climate Plan' (2019) 151.

175 ibid.

176 ibid 189.

177 The Netherlands, 'Integrated National Energy and Climate Plan 2021–2030 of the Netherlands' (2019) 140.

178 ibid 116.

179 Poland, 'National Energy and Climate Plan for 2021–2030 of Poland: Objectives and Targets, and Policies and Measures' (2019) 28.

180 ibid 68.

energy in biogas, which may then be used for system regulation.[181] The expensive investment outlays, on the other hand, are the primary reason determining the moderate increase in installed capacity of biogas facilities.[182] Regarding promotion, new technology development should include the needs of many industries, both in terms of energy supply and the utilisation of various forms of biomass produced as a by-product of the agri-food industry while taking sustainability criteria into consideration (preserving soil fertility – humus level, water resources management, etc.).[183] Furthermore, Poland will identify local barriers to the development of renewables, particularly those resulting from a lack of social acceptance for certain investments (including agricultural biogas plants) due to concerns such as noise, odours, or other nuisance factors associated with power facilities, in order to encourage local communities to change their negative attitude towards investment projects.[184]

22. Portugal

Portugal intends to promote and support the installation of equipment that allows the recovery of landfill gases and biogas from anaerobic digestion facilities in order to convert them into biomethane, while also re-evaluating the process for remunerating electricity generated from urban waste.[185] This aligns with sector goals for the CE, with the promotion of the use of compost arising from biowaste processing and the use of biogas to produce energy.[186]

23. Romania

As of 2020, in Romania, no official statistics on the real potential of biogas and biomass resources were accessible at the national level, which was hampered further by the existence of an ambiguous legislative framework in this field that prevents a clear classification of some natural resources.[187] Nonetheless, the country anticipates raising energy production from less exploited renewable resources such as biogas, adding the measure of the development of R&D and technology for biogas production in Romanian territory.[188]

---

181 ibid.
182 ibid.
183 ibid 71.
184 ibid 101.
185 Portugal, 'National Energy and Climate Plan 2021–2030 of Portugal' (2019) 57.
186 ibid 59.
187 Romania, 'The 2021–2030 Integrated National Energy and Climate Plan of Romania' (2020) 52.
188 See ibid 34, 44.

24. Slovakia

In Slovakia, renewable energy sources funding was related to electricity production in 2019, while the heating sector only had access to it for cogeneration technologies, as well as biomass and biogas technologies.[189] To meet renewable objectives by 2030, it will be required to explore operational aid that will allow separate operating aid for the generation of heat in facilities using, *inter alia*, biogas or biomethane,[190] generated mostly from plant and animal waste, biodegradable municipal waste, biodegradable kitchen and restaurant waste, and waste from wastewater treatment facilities.[191] Heat generated by biogas is an essential component of the energy balance of wastewater treatment facilities in the Slovak climate.[192]

25. Slovenia

Because of Slovenia's relatively well-developed livestock breeding, animal excrement has a high potential for biogas production.[193] The present capacity is extended to a lesser extent in the scenarios examined for the expansion of power production from all forms of biogas – these might be biogas production sites or biogas purification, injection, and production at another place, with an emphasis on utilising existing heat wherever and to the greatest degree feasible.[194] To facilitate this development, Slovenia anticipates providing additional incentives for the construction of small and micro biogas plants for the production of biogas from livestock manure, and incentives for the collection of agricultural biomass (crop residues, slurry, etc.) at the locations of major biogas plants.

26. Spain

Spain announced a plan in 2015 to encourage the collection and treatment of organic waste, as well as the capture and use of biogas.[195] However, the

---

[189] Slovakia, 'Integrated National Energy and Climate Plan for 2021 to 2030 of Slovakia' (2019) 99.
[190] See ibid.
[191] See ibid 9.
[192] See ibid 171.
[193] Slovenia, 'Integrated National Energy and Climate Plan of the Republic of Slovenia' (2020) 148.
[194] ibid.
[195] Spain, 'Integrated National Energy and Climate Plan 2021–2030 of Spain' (2020) 329.

systems put in place to remunerate energy generation at biogas facilities have not produced the desired outcomes, with utilisation in Spain falling considerably short of the existing potential.[196] Nonetheless, the target scenario indicates a larger percentage of renewable energy in heating and cooling, with the promotion of end-use renewable energy (including biogas) driving a substantial influence on this percentage rise.[197]

27. Sweden

Up to the end of 2020, Sweden had state aid approval for tax relief on biogas.[198] There has been a support system for the production of biogas from anaerobic manure digestion since 2015.[199] The support is intended to increase biogas production from manure, resulting in twice the environmental and climate benefits by reducing methane emissions from manure and replacing fossil fuel energy.[200] The biogas produced can be utilised to generate electricity or heat, as well as a vehicle fuel.[201] Moreover, new biogas facilities can be financed from the Rural Development Programme.[202]

V. CONCLUSION

The use of biogas has various advantages, one of which is the cogeneration of green heat and green power, as they come from renewable resources not conventional fuels. Biogas generated locally from waste and residues can play an important role in improving energy security and reducing dependency on fossil fuels, being an option in energy transition towards carbon neutrality based on the CE. Consequently, by 2050, a large rise in the consumption of biogas is anticipated.

However, this process will necessitate several changes and adjustments, particularly those linked to the legal environment. This is the case of the EU, and as underlined in one of the recent EU's legal acts, i.e. Regulation (EU) 2022/869 on guidelines for trans-European energy infrastructure: 'a new infrastructure category should be created for smart gas grids to support investments which integrate a plurality of low-carbon and particularly renewable gases such as biogas, biomethane, and hydrogen, in the gas network and help

---

[196] ibid 95.
[197] ibid 234.
[198] Sweden, 'Sweden's Integrated National Energy and Climate Plan' (2020) 42.
[199] ibid 55.
[200] ibid.
[201] ibid.
[202] ibid.

manage a resulting more complex system, building on innovative digital technologies'.[203] Biogas therefore fits in with the transition of energy sector. However, in order for it to be produced and used in the most ecologically and climate-friendly way possible, its future development necessitates a focus on sustainable development. In this regard, high-efficiency cogeneration based on waste biogas appears to be an appealing solution. This, however, requires conditions including regulatory mechanisms to ensure its optimal use in the process of energy transformation.

LEGISLATION

Directive 2012/27/EU on energy efficiency, amending Directives 2009/125/EC and 2010/30/EU and repealing Directives 2004/8/EC and 2006/32/EC [2012] OJ L315/1

Directive 2001/77/EC on the promotion of electricity produced from renewable energy sources in the internal electricity market [2001] OJ L283/33

Directive 2009/28/EC on the promotion of the use of energy from renewable sources and amending and subsequently repealing Directives 2001/77/EC and 2003/30/EC [2009] OJ L140/16 ('RED I')

Directive 2018/2001 on the promotion of the use of energy from renewable sources [2018] OJ L328/82 ('RED II')

Directive 2008/98/EC on waste and repealing certain Directives [2008] OJ L312/3 ('Waste Framework Directive', 'WFD')

Regulation (EU) 2022/869 on guidelines for trans-European energy infrastructure, amending Regulations (EC) 715/2009, (EU) 2019/942 and (EU) 2019/943 and Directives 2009/73/EC and (EU) 2019/944, and repealing Regulation (EU) 347/201 [2022] OJ L152/45

Commission Implementing Decision (EU) 2017/1442 establishing best available techniques (BAT) conclusions, under Directive 2010/75/EU for large combustion plants [2017] OJ L212/1

[203] Regulation (EU) 2022/869 on guidelines for trans-European energy infrastructure, amending Regulations (EC) 715/2009, (EU) 2019/942 and (EU) 2019/943 and Directives 2009/73/EC and (EU) 2019/944, and repealing Regulation (EU) 347/201 [2022] OJ L152/45.

7. Sustainable biofuels and gaseous biomass fuels from biowaste in the EU transport sector

Piero Carlo dos Reis,[1] Phillip Lugmayr, and Benjamin Gomado

I. INTRODUCTION AND DEFINITIONS

The long-term project of the European Union (EU) to achieve climate neutrality and the shorter-term project of phasing out imports of Russian fossil fuels – in line with the political ambitions of the EU Green Deal[2] and the REPowerEU[3] – will require guiding the uptake of sustainable biofuels and gaseous biomass fuels from biowaste in the transport sector, among other solutions. This is also reflected in policy provisions in the recent EU legislative acts.

Although projections by 2030 exclusive to sustainable biofuels and gaseous biomass fuels from biowaste are not defined in the latest REPowerEU scenario[4] of the European Commission, it is foreseen that the total renewable energy sources (RES) share in final energy consumption in the transport sector

[1] Neither the European Commission, nor any person acting on behalf of the European Commission, is responsible for any use that might be made of the following information. The information and views set out in this work are those of the authors and do not necessarily reflect those of the European Commission. The authors are responsible for any possible content errors.

[2] In particular, the political ambitions of 55% reduction in net emissions of GHG by 2030 and of no net emissions of GHG by 2050 under the European Green Deal.

[3] In particular, the political ambition of phasing out 150 bcm of Russian natural gas imports by 2030.

[4] European Commission, 'REPowerEU Plan' SWD (2022) 230.

should increase from 6.9% by 2020[5] to 32% by 2030[6] – whereas the overall greenhouse gas (GHG) intensity in the transport sector should reduce by 16% up to 2030.

Indeed, although the COVID-19 pandemic has demonstrated that mobility demand could structurally decrease, 'we will not be able to deliver on the goals of the Paris Agreement if society is unable to develop sustainable transport with much lower emissions of greenhouse gases'.[7] Indeed, in line with the European Climate law[8] and the 'Sustainable and Smart Mobility Strategy – putting European transport on track for the future' communication,[9] the European transport sector should deliver a 90% reduction in emissions by 2050. One way of accomplishing this goal is by guiding the uptake of renewable energy in the transport sector which remains crucial. In particular, this chapter will refer to the uptake of one type of renewable energy: 'sustainable biofuels and gaseous biomass fuels produced from biowaste'. To better understand this choice of wording, this chapter will refer to the following definitions by relevant EU legislation:[10]

- The definitions for biofuels and (gaseous) biomass fuels under the RED II;[11]

---

5 Data extracted from the Eurostat Energy balance flow for EU27_2020 (2020) available at https://ec.europa.eu/eurostat/cache/sankey/energy/sankey.html?geos=EU27_2020&year=2020&unit=GJ&fuels=TOTAL&highlight=_&nodeDisagg=0101110000000&flowDisagg=true&translateX=-405&translateY=57&scale=1&language=EN (6.3% renewable energies share in the final energy consumption in the transport sector, plus 0.341 * 1.8%). The number 0.341 refers to the average share of electricity from renewable energy sources in the EU by 2020, and is taken from ESTAT SHARES 2020 available at https://ec.europa.eu/eurostat/documents/38154/4956088/The+average+share+of+electricity+from+renewable+energy+sources+in+the+EU_2004-2020.pdf/ea191211-676a-b8e8-7659-e26835bc0ca7?t=1664794632512.

6 REPowerEU Plan (n 4) Table 9.

7 Damien Meadows, Alex Paquot and Peter Vis 'Transport Emissions from Road, Aviation and Shipping' in Jos Delbeke and Peter Vis (eds), *Towards a Climate-neutral Europe: Curbing the Trend* (1st edn, Routledge 2019).

8 Regulation (EU) 2021/1119 establishing the framework for achieving climate neutrality and amending Regulations (EC) No 401/2009 and (EU) 2018/1999 ('European Climate Law') [2021] OJ L243/1.

9 European Commission, 'Sustainable and Smart Mobility Strategy – putting European transport on track for the future' COM (2020) 789.

10 See also Chapter 1 of this volume.

11 '"biofuels" means liquid fuel for transport produced from biomass' (art 2(33)); '"biomass fuels" means gaseous and solid fuels produced from biomass' (art 2(27)) in Directive (EU) 2018/2001 on the promotion of the use of energy from renewable sources [2018] OJ L328/82 ('RED II').

- The adjective 'sustainable' next to 'biofuels and gaseous biomass fuels' implies compliance with the sustainability and greenhouse gas emissions saving criteria under Article 29 of RED II, and with the respective verification under Article 30 of RED II;
- The definition of biowaste under point 4 of Article 3 of the 2008 Waste Framework Directive (WFD),[12] later referred to in the RED II,[13] in addition to other residues derived from agriculture and forest and to other feedstock from bio-related waste streams listed under Part A of Annex IX of RED II.[14]

Secondly, this chapter will refer to three main transport modes:[15] air[16] (which can be further differentiated into 'intra-EU air transport' and 'international air transport'[17]), maritime (which can similarly be further differentiated into 'intra-EU maritime' and 'international maritime'[18] and road transport[19]). Road transport accounted for the majority of GHG emissions in the overall EU transport sector up to 2019 (72% of all domestic and international transport GHG).[20] The road transport also accounted for the highest volume of final energy consumption in 2020 (9,972.8 EJ/year[21]), followed by international maritime

---

12 Directive 2008/98/EC on waste and repealing certain Directives [2008] OJ L312/3 ('Waste Framework Directive', 'WFD').

13 '"bio-waste" means biodegradable garden and park waste, food and kitchen waste from households, restaurants, caterers and retail premises and comparable waste from food processing plants'.

14 It is important to notice that the definition of 'advanced biofuels' under the RED II includes 'biogas for transport and biofuels' stemming not only from biowaste. Indeed, biogas for transport and biofuels stemming from other feedstock – listed in Part A of Annex IX of RED II (n 11) – are also included under 'advanced biofuels'.

15 Eurostat, 'Glossary: Transport mode' https://ec.europa.eu/eurostat/statistics-explained/index.php?title=Glossary:Transport_mode.

16 In this chapter we will also refer to 'air transport' simply as 'aviation'.

17 This chapter refers to 'international maritime' transport and to 'international air' transport as two categories of trips: those arriving in the EU from a third country and those departing from the EU to a third country.

18 This chapter refers to 'international maritime' transport and to 'international air' transport as two categories of trips: those arriving in the EU from a third country and those departing from the EU to a third country.

19 This chapter will not refer to rail transport, as the 'Sustainable and Smart Mobility Strategy – putting European transport on track for the future' (n 9) communication sees there a larger role for electrification and for hydrogen whenever electrification is not viable.

20 European Environmental Agency (EEA), 'Greenhouse gas emissions from transport in Europe' (eea.europe.eu 2021) https://www.eea.europa.eu/ims/greenhouse-gas-emissions-from-transport/.

21 Eurostat, 'Energy balance flow for EU27_2020' (ec.europa.eu 2020) https://ec.europa.eu/eurostat/cache/sankey/energy/sankey.html?geos=EU27_2020&year=2020

transport (estimated 1,633 EJ/year[22]), international air transport (753 EJ/year), intra-EU maritime transport (153 EJ/year) and domestic air transport (129 EJ/year). Although the decarbonisation of road transport plays a key role in terms of CO_2 emissions reduction, both the maritime and air transport modes are commonly known as 'hard-to-abate' sectors[23] and 'must have priority access to additional renewable and low-carbon liquid and gaseous fuels, since there is a lack of suitable alternative powertrains in the short term'.[24]

Thirdly, after examining the energy vectors underlying the final energy consumption of the domestic EU27 transport sector by 2020,[25] 'gas, oil and petroleum products' resulted as holding the highest amount at circa 9,690 EJ/year (circa 92%), whereas electricity and renewable energies amounted to respectively 192.5 EJ/year (2%)[26] and 669.2 EJ/year (6%). This latter category ('renewable energies') consists mainly of liquid biofuels (661.8 EJ/year) and only in a small amount of biogases (7.5 EJ/year). The final energy consumption of international maritime transport and international air transport were almost uniquely composed of 'oil and petroleum products'. No information is made available by Eurostat or by the 'ETC CM report 2022/02: Greenhouse gas intensities of transport fuels in the EU in 2020 – Monitoring under the Fuel Quality Directive'[27] on the specific share of sustainable biofuels and biogases from biowaste within 'renewable energies' in the transport sector.

In terms of scope, this chapter reviews the policy provisions identified as relevant for guiding the uptake of sustainable biofuels and gaseous biomass fuels from biowaste into the transport sector, and included in three blocks of recent EU legislative acts (EU energy legislative acts in Section II, EU transport legislative acts in Section III, and EU climate legislative acts in

&unit=TJ&fuels=TOTAL&highlight=_&nodeDisagg=0111110011001&flowDisagg=true&translateX=-1769&translateY=146&scale=1&language=EN/.

22 This chapter estimates the final energy consumption of international maritime transport through the final energy consumption of the 'marine bunker' Eurostat category. The estimates of intra-EU maritime transport do not include the final energy consumption of the 'marine bunker'.

23 European Commission proposals: 'Proposal for a Regulation on the use of renewable and low-carbon fuels in maritime transport and amending Directive 2009/16/EC' COM (2021) 562 ('FuelEU Maritime proposal') and 'Proposal for a Regulation on ensuring a level playing field for sustainable air transport' COM (2021) 561 ('ReFuelEU Aviation Initiative').

24 'Sustainable and Smart Mobility Strategy – putting European transport on track for the future' (n 9).

25 Eurostat (n 21).

26 Out of which, circa 26% of electricity stemmed from renewable energy sources.

27 EEA, 'Greenhouse gas intensities of transport fuels in the EU in 2020 – Monitoring under the Fuel Quality Directive' (2022) https://www.eionet.europa.eu/etcs/etc-cm/products/etc-cm-report-2022-02/.

Section IV).[28] In particular, this involves looking at relevant EU legislative acts proposed as part of the 'Clean Energy Package' (2018–2019) and which have already entered into force, at EU legislative acts proposed as part of the 'Fit for 55' package (2021) and still under discussion with the co-legislators, and at EU legislative acts more recently proposed as part of the 'REPowerEU' plan (2022). These three blocks and the respective EU legislative acts identified as relevant are reported in Table 7.1.
Overall, the rationale for these three blocks is the following:

- 'Block 1: EU energy legislative acts' focuses on relevant policy provisions included in legislative acts guiding the overall energy system, the underlying sectors (e.g., transport) and the uptake of renewable energy vectors – among which are sustainable biofuels and gaseous biomass fuels from biowaste – while reducing the penetration of fossil fuels.
- 'Block 2: EU transport legislative acts' focuses on relevant policy provisions included in legislative acts guiding the decarbonisation pathway for specific transport modes through provisions on the supply of sustainable fuels and on the uptake of more sustainable vehicles and of additional fuel infrastructure.
- 'Block 3: EU climate legislative acts' focuses on relevant policy provisions included in legislative acts whose scope is that of internalising the costs due to CO_2 emissions in the case of fossil fuel-driven vehicles and of establishing limits to such emissions.

In Section V this chapter will conclude.

II. RELEVANT PROVISIONS IN BLOCK 1: EU ENERGY LEGISLATIVE ACTS

The legislative acts considered in this block, given the relevant policy provisions included in them towards the analysis of this chapter, are reported in Table 7.2 – together with the year of adoption of the proposal and the relative status in August 2022:[29]

---

[28] Relevant provisions in the recent EU policy framework concerning the uptake of sustainable biofuels and gaseous biomass fuels from biowaste in other sectors – apart from the transport sector – will be examined in other chapters, as will the relevant provisions concerning the production of the needed volumes of sustainable biofuels and gaseous biomass fuels from biowaste.

[29] This chapter will also not examine the Energy Governance Regulation 2018/1999 as it focuses on the framework underlying the National Energy and Climate Plans (NECPs) and on the planning, reporting and monitoring obligations by MSs, but it does not include provisions which directly promote the deployment of sustainable biofuels

Table 7.1 *Schematic presenting the three blocks of EU policy framework analysed and the underlying policy files with the associated status*

	Block 1: EU energy legislative acts (Section II)	Block 2: EU transport legislative acts (Section III)	Block 3: EU climate legislative acts (Section IV)
Examined policy files	• RED II • Proposal for RED III • Increased RES targets and biomethane strategy plan under the REPowerEU Plan	• Fuel quality directives • Proposal for FuelEU Maritime initiative ('proposal for a regulation on the use of renewable and low-carbon fuels in maritime transport and amending Directive 2009/16/EC') • Proposal for ReFuelEU Aviation Initiative ('proposal for a regulation on ensuring a level playing field for sustainable air transport')	• 2018 EU ETS Directive & Commission Implementing Regulation 2022/388 on monitoring and reporting of greenhouse gas emissions • 2018 EU Effort Sharing Regulation (ESR) & implementing decision 2020/2126 • Proposal for Revision of the existing EU ETS Directive • Proposal for Revision of the existing EU ETS Directive for aviation • Proposal for Revision of the EU Effort Sharing Regulation (ESR)

A. RED II

Directive 2018/2001,[30] better known as RED II, is the core legal framework regulating renewable energy in the EU. It obliges the EU to consume at least 32% of its energy from renewable sources by 2030 and sets out various measures to achieve that goal. One such measure is a target for the share of renewable energy in the transport sector (RES-T): namely, the first sub-paragraph of Article 25(1) requires that 'each Member State shall set an obligation on fuel suppliers to ensure that the share of renewable energy within the final consumption of energy in the transport sector is at least 14% by 2030'.[31] Renewable energy can include electrification, renewable fuels of

and gaseous biomass fuels from biowaste in the transport sector. Likewise, although provisions of the 'Gas Package' may concern the injection of biomethane into the natural gas grid, this chapter does not examine them as they are assumed to be not so significant to the core topic of this chapter (guiding the uptake of sustainable biofuels and gaseous biomass fuels from biowaste in the transport sector).

30 RED II (n 11).

31 Recycled carbon fuels (RCFs) may be counted towards such a target.

Table 7.2 EU energy policy files examined in this chapter[a]

Name of the legislative act	Year of adoption of the proposal	Status in August 2022
RED II[b]	2018 (Clean Energy Package)	Entered into force
Proposal for RED III[c]	2021 (Fit for 55 Package)	Not yet agreed in co-decision and not yet entered into force
Increased RES targets and Biomethane strategy plan under REPowerEU Plan[d]	2022 (REPowerEU)	

Notes: a. Readers who are interested in the relevant provisions within the Energy Taxation Directive can refer to Chapter 9 in this volume; b. RED II (n 11); c. European Commission, 'Proposal for a Directive amending Directive (EU) 2018/2001, Regulation (EU) 2018/1999 and Directive 98/70/EC as regards the promotion of energy from renewable sources, and repealing Council Directive (EU) 2015/652' COM (2021) 557 ('Proposal for RED III'); d. REPowerEU Plan SWD (n 4) and European Commission 'REPowerEU Plan' COM (2022) 230.

non-biological origin (RFNBOs), as well as biofuels. For some biofuels there are concerns (e.g., those produced from food and feed crops[32]), which is why RED II promotes some types while limiting others. For instance, biofuels coming from biowaste have, among other attributes, the least impact on the environment and are therefore promoted (i.e. Part A of Annex IX), unless certain industries like the chemical sector need the same feedstock such as used cooking oil (i.e. Part B of Annex IX). In both cases (Part A and Part B of Annex IX), their energy content may be counted twice towards the compliance with the abovementioned obligation. Biofuels based on food and feed crops are limited. For all three types of biofuels additional sustainability criteria apply. The overview below elaborates on all three types of biofuels and the sustainability criteria.

'Advanced biofuels' are one of the preferred types of renewable transport fuels. Part A of Annex IX defines the feedstocks of advanced biofuels, which includes, among others, different forms of biowaste such as the biomass fraction of mixed municipal waste or industrial waste not fit for use in the food or feed chain. These feedstocks 'can be processed only with advanced technologies'. In the fourth sub-paragraph of Article 25(1), RED II foresees minimum shares for advanced biofuels and stipulates that their contribution to the 'final consumption of energy in the transport sector shall be at least 0,2 %

32 Definition in RED II (n 11) art 2(40): '"food and feed crops" means starch-rich crops, sugar crops or oil crops produced on agricultural land as a main crop excluding residues, waste or ligno-cellulosic material and intermediate crops, such as catch crops and cover crops, provided that the use of such intermediate crops does not trigger demand for additional land'.

in 2022, at least 1 % in 2025 and at least 3,5 % in 2030'. Moreover, the energy content of the feedstock[33] used for the production of advanced biofuels can be counted twice, which, in turn, affects the calculation of minimum shares of RES-T, following the rules outlined in Article 27 ('Calculation rules with regard to the minimum shares of renewable energy in the transport sector').[34] In simple terms, this option enables fuel suppliers to reach the minimum shares more easily vis-à-vis other types of renewable transport fuels. It thus makes the production of advanced biofuels more attractive and provides an incentive.

In contrast to advanced biofuels based on feedstock listed in Part A of Annex IX, there are two types of renewable biofuels whose contribution towards the 14% RES-T target are limited by RED II. The first type are fuels based on feedstock listed in Part B of Annex IX, which means cooking oil and certain animal fats, which can be processed into biofuels or biogas for transport, with mature technologies. The limit specified for fuels based on such feedstocks is established in the second sub-paragraph of Article 27(1)(b), whereby 'for the calculation of the numerator the share of biofuels and biogas produced from the feedstock listed in Part B of Annex IX shall, except for in Cyprus and Malta, be limited to 1,7 % of the energy content of transport fuels supplied for consumption or use on the market'.

The second type are biofuels, bioliquids and biomass fuels produced from food and feed crops, also called conventional biofuels. While they could significantly contribute to the achievement of the 14% RES-T target, the limit imposed on these fuels is justified by sustainability concerns. For example, their cultivation may displace the traditional production of crops for food and feed purposes (i.e. direct land use change), which, in turn, can push agricultural land into non-cropland (i.e. indirect land-use change). This can include areas with high carbon stock, such as forests, wetlands and peatlands, and thus cause additional greenhouse gas emissions directly or indirectly. The term 'indirect land-use change' (ILUC) describes the latter developments.[35] Article 26(1)

---

[33] See Annex III of RED II for the energy content of fuels.

[34] Note that this refers to both minimum shares of advanced biofuels and the 14% target.

[35] Article 26(2) (of RED II) outlines an approach towards high and low ILUC-risk feedstock. The first sub-paragraph freezes the amount of high ILUC-risk feedstock at 2019 levels for the period 2021–2023, whereas the second sub-paragraph foresees a gradual decrease to 0% by 31 December 2030 at the latest. Low ILUC-risk feedstock can receive exemptions from these rules, provided it has an appropriate certificate. As required by the fourth sub-paragraph of Article 26(2), the Commission adopted the Delegated Regulation (EU) 2019/807 to set out the criteria for determining the high ILUC-risk feedstock and certifying low ILUC-risk biofuels, bioliquids and biomass fuels (Delegated Regulation 2019/807 supplementing Directive (EU) 2018/2001 as regards the determination of high indirect land-use change-risk feedstock for which

defines the extent to which Member States (MSs) can count the share of biofuels, bioliquids and biomass fuels produced from food and feed crops towards the 14% RES-T target. It stipulates that the share

> shall be no more than one percentage point higher than the share of such fuels in the final consumption of energy in the road and rail transport sectors in 2020 in that Member State, with a maximum of 7 % of final consumption of energy in the road and rail transport sectors in that Member State.

In addition to this limit, Article 26(1) explains that if such fuels are 'limited to a share lower than 7 % or a Member State decides to limit the share further, that Member State may reduce the minimum share referred to in the first subparagraph of Article 25(1)', i.e. the 14% target, 'by a maximum of 7 percentage points'.

Renewable transport fuels, regardless of being advanced or conventional biofuels, need to comply with additional sustainability and greenhouse gas emissions saving criteria in order to count towards the 14% RES-T target. Article 29 of RED II keeps many provisions of RED I, but also adds new ones, including, among others, sustainability criteria related to fuels produced from forest biomass. Paragraph 2 is of particular relevance for this chapter, as it stipulates that 'fuels produced from waste and residues derived … from agricultural land shall be taken into account … only where operators or national authorities have monitoring or management plans in place in order to address the impacts on soil quality and soil carbon'. Paragraph 10 defines the greenhouse gas emissions savings and requires 'at least 65 % for biofuels, biogas consumed in the transport sector, and bioliquids produced in installations starting operation from 1 January 2021'.[36]

B. Proposal for the RED III

Following the European Green Deal, the 2030 Climate Target Plan and the Climate Law, the Commission adopted the 'Fit for 55' package in July 2021. It consists of several proposals that will help the EU reach its more ambitious climate targets for 2030 and 2050. One of the proposals is the revision of

---

a significant expansion of the production area into land with high carbon stock is observed and the certification of low indirect land-use change-risk biofuels, bioliquids and biomass fuels [2019] OJ L133/1).

[36] Paragraphs 3, 4 and 5 place conditions on fuels that use agricultural biomass as a feedstock, which shall not be obtained from land with a high biodiversity value like primary forests or a high carbon stock such as wetlands as well as from peatland. Paragraphs 6 and 7 set out criteria for fuels produced from forest biomass, including the existence of national or sub-national law and monitoring and enforcement systems.

RED II, also known as RED III. Based on the Impact Assessment of the 2030 Climate Target Plan, the revision proposes a 40% binding renewable energy target for the EU for 2030 (up from the 32% target adopted under RED II). In addition, it adjusts sectoral ambitions according to this new target. The following overview presents the main proposed changes with regard to the transport sector[37], and, in particular, sustainable biofuels and gaseous biomass fuels from biowaste.

RED III keeps the provision requiring MSs to put an obligation on fuel suppliers. However, it changes the approach – instead of stipulating a minimum share of renewable energy in the transport sector, based on penetration, RED III defines a target based on GHG emissions reductions. Article 1(14) of the proposal replaces the 14% RES-T target with a 13% greenhouse gas emissions reduction in the transport sector from the use of renewable energy by 2030.[38] Although the new target is nominally lower, its level of ambition is actually significantly higher. Translated into RES-T, it constitutes a 28% share of renewable energy within the final consumption of energy in the transport sector.[39]

Another important change concerns the sub-targets relative to the contribution of advanced biofuels towards the minimum shares – as per Article 1(14). RED III keeps the sub-target of 0.2% in 2022, but changes the sub-targets for 2025 and 2030 to 0.5% and 2.2% respectively.

A third substantial change addresses multipliers towards minimum shares. Indeed, RED III deletes the option for the energy content of the feedstock used for the production of advanced biofuels to be double counted. This concerns both advanced biofuels and fuels based on feedstock listed in Part B of Annex IX. This modification is also justified by the target based on GHG emissions reductions.

C. Increased RES Targets under REPowerEU Plan

On 18 May 2022, the Commission presented its REPowerEU plan as a reaction to the economic hardships and the energy challenges caused by Russia's invasion of Ukraine. The plan aims at ending the EU's dependency on Russian fossil fuels while further advancing the fight against the climate crisis. It rests on three main pillars, namely energy savings, the diversification of energy

---

[37] Note that this section focuses on the main changes proposed by RED III and thus excludes the consequential adjustments to the relevant provisions.

[38] 'For biofuels, for the purposes of the calculation referred to in point 3 (transport), the fossil fuel comparator EF(t) shall be 94 g CO_2 eq/MJ.'

[39] As reported in the Commission Staff Working Document accompanying the REPowerEU Plan (n 4).

supplies, and the accelerated rollout of renewable energy. With regard to the latter, the plan proposes to increase the 2030 renewable energy target from 40% to 45% under the 'Fit for 55' package.

In the transport sector, this increased 2030 renewable energy target under the REPowerEU Plan would imply an increased greenhouse gas emissions reduction from the use of renewable energy from 13% to 16% by 2030, and an increased renewable energy share within the final energy consumption in the transport sector of 32% (up from the previously mentioned 28%).[40]

III. RELEVANT PROVISIONS IN BLOCK 2: EU TRANSPORT LEGISLATIVE ACTS

The legislative acts considered in this block, given the relevant policy provisions included in them towards the analysis of this chapter, are reported in Table 7.3 – together with the relative status and year of adoption or enforcement:

A. Fuel Quality Directives

With regard to 'fuel quality directives' this chapter refers to Directive 98/70 relating to the quality of petrol and diesel fuels,[41] including successive amendments,[42] and to Directive 2016/802 relating to a reduction in the sulphur content of certain liquid fuels.[43] However, only the former (Directive 98/70 and successive amending Directives) includes relevant provisions of interest to the analysis of this chapter. Indeed, Directive 2016/802 lists the use of biofuels, or of mixtures of biofuels and marine fuels, as a possible emission abatement method towards reducing sulphur dioxide emissions in Article 8 –

---

40 According to the Commission Staff Working Document SWD (2022) 230 final accompanying the REPowerEU Plan (n 4).

41 Directive (EC) 98/70 relating to the quality of petrol and diesel fuels and amending Council Directive 93/12/EEC [1998] OJ L350/58.

42 Directive (EU) 2011/63 amending, for the purpose of its adaptation to technical progress, Directive 98/70/EC relating to the quality of petrol and diesel fuels [2011] OJ L47/15, Directive (EU) 2014/77 amending Annexes I and II of Directive 98/70/EC relating to the quality of petrol and diesel fuels [2014] OJ L170/62; Directive (EU) 2015/1513 amending Directive 98/70/EC relating to the quality of petrol and diesel fuels and amending Directive 2009/28/EC on the promotion of the use of energy from renewable sources [2015] OJ C239/1.

43 Directive (EU) 2016/802 relating to a reduction in the sulphur content of certain liquid fuels [2016] OJ L132/58; building on the Directive 1999/32/EC relating to a reduction in the sulphur content of certain liquid fuels and amending Directive 93/12/EEC [1999] OJ L121/13.

Table 7.3 *EU transport policy files examined in this chapter*[a]

Name of the legislative act	Year of adoption of the proposal	Status in August 2022
Fuel quality directive[b]	2015 (Clean Energy Package)	Entered into force
Proposal for the FuelEU Maritime initiative ('proposal for a regulation on the use of renewable and low-carbon fuels in maritime transport and amending Directive 2009/16/EC')[c]	2021 (Fit for 55 package)	
Proposal for the ReFuelEU Aviation Initiative ('proposal for a regulation on ensuring a level playing field for sustainable air transport')[d]	2021 (Fit for 55 package)	

Notes: a. The Proposal for the Alternative Fuels Infrastructure Regulation (Proposal for a Regulation of the European Parliament and of the Council on the deployment of alternative fuels infrastructure, and repealing Directive 2014/94/EU of the European; COM (2021) 559) will not be examined in detail in this chapter as it does not contain provisions of relevance for guiding the uptake of sustainable biofuels and gaseous biomass fuels in the transport sector; b. Directive (EU) 2015/1513 amending Directive 98/70/EC relating to the quality of petrol and diesel fuels and amending Directive 2009/28/EC on the promotion of the use of energy from renewable sources [2015] OJ C239/1; c. FuelEU Maritime proposal (n 23); d. ReFuelEU Aviation Initiative (n 23) & European Parliament – Think Tank 'ReFuelEU Aviation Initiative: Sustainable aviation fuels and the fit for 55 package' (Briefing, 2022) https://www.europarl.europa.eu/thinktank/en/document/EPRS_BRI(2022)698900/.

but does not include provisions guiding the uptake of sustainable biofuels and gaseous biomass fuels.

The scope of Directive 98/70 and successive amending Directives is two-fold and specific to 'road transport and non-road mobile machinery (including inland waterway vessels), agricultural and forestry tractors, and recreational craft when not at sea':

(a) technical specifications on health and environmental grounds for fuels to be used with positive ignition and compression-ignition engines, taking account of the technical requirements of those engines; and
(b) a target for the reduction of life cycle greenhouse gas emissions

The relevant provisions this chapter identified related to the first scope (a) are within Article 3 'Petrol' and Article 4 'Diesel fuel', which respectively regulate – among others – the volumetric share of certain chemicals (typical of biofuels) in market fuel respectively for vehicles equipped with positive ignition engines and for vehicles equipped with compression ignition engines.[44] Whereas under Article 3 'Petrol' the limit set for ethanol within petrol fuels is 10% v/v, under Article 4 'Diesel' there is a provision allowing the limit set for fatty acid methyl ester (FAME) to exceed the level of 7% v/v.[45] Fuels complying with this directive can benefit – according to Article 5 – from the principle of free circulation across the Union.

The relevant provisions this chapter identifies related to the second scope (b) are within Article 7a 'greenhouse gas emission reductions', which sets an increasing ambition level up to 2020 of a reduction of at least 6% in the lifecycle GHG intensity of fuels used in the Union for the abovementioned vehicles. Beyond this year, this provision is supposed to be superseded by the proposed provision under RED III setting a mandatory reduction of at least 13% in the greenhouse gas emissions intensity of transportation fuels by 2030.[46]

B. Proposal for the FuelEU Maritime Initiative (Proposal for a Regulation on the Use of Renewable and Low-carbon Fuels in Maritime Transport and Amending Directive 2009/16)

The FuelEU Maritime initiative aims at reducing the GHG intensity of energy used by all ships above a gross tonnage of 5,000,[47] therefore increasing the use of renewable and low-carbon fuels towards the energy demand. This is done through two main mechanisms – from 1 January 2025 – as per Article 1:

- 'A (yearly) limit on GHG intensity of energy used by a ship arriving at, staying within or departing from ports under the jurisdiction of a Member State' – including the entirety of the energy used on voyages between two ports of call under the jurisdiction of a Member State, and half of the energy used on voyages between a port of call under the jurisdiction of a Member State and a port of call under the jurisdiction of a third country.

[44] Under Annex I – referred to by Article 3 – the maximum volumetric shares of oxygenates – in particular methanol (3% v/v), ethanol (10% v/v), iso-propyl alcohol (12% v/v), tert-butyl alcohol (15% v/v), iso-butyl alcohol (15% v/v), ethers containing five of more carbon atoms per molecule (22 % v/v) and other oxygenates (15 % v/v) – are of interest to this chapter. Under Annex II – referred to by Article 4 – the maximum volumetric share of FAME content (EN 14078) is regulated (7 % v/v).

[45] The regulation of other chemical and physical properties is outside the scope of this chapter.

[46] The reader can find more details regarding compliance with this provision in the EEA (n 27).

[47] Except for warships, naval auxiliaries, fish-catching or fish-processing ships, wooden ships of a primitive build, ships not propelled by mechanical means, or government ships used for non-commercial purposes.

Table 7.4 Reductions in GHG intensity of energy used on-board over different time periods compared to a fossil fuel comparator

Time period	Reductions in GHG intensity of energy used on-board
From 1 January 2025	–2%
From 1 January 2030	–6%
From 1 January 2035	–13%
From 1 January 2040	–26%
From 1 January 2045	–59%
From 1 January 2045	–75%

In particular, the 'well-to-wake' method is used, which 'means a method for calculating emissions that takes into account the greenhouse gas impact of energy production, transport, distribution and use on-board, including during combustion'.

In Table 7.4 the reductions in GHG intensity of energy used on-board over different time periods are specified compared to a fossil fuel comparator.[48] Ships whose compliance with the limit abovementioned is verified will receive a 'FuelEU certificate of compliance'. Additional flexibility provisions and penalties are foreseen.

A 'review clause' (Article 28) foresees the possibility of amendments to the (yearly) limits on GHG intensity by 1 January 2030.

- From 1 January 2030, an 'obligation to use on-shore power supply or zero-emission technology in ports under the jurisdiction of a Member State' is foreseen. However, this provision does not concern the use of sustainable biofuels and gaseous biomass fuels in ship engines – since it does not fulfil either the definition of 'on-shore power supply' or the requirements of Annex III for 'zero-emission technology'.[49]

Throughout this regulation, references are made to the possibility of using liquid biofuels, bio-liquid natural gas (LNG) and bio-compressed natural gas (CNG) – among other options – towards the decarbonisation of maritime sector.[50]

[48] 94 g CO_2/MJ, as indicated in the RED II (n 11).

[49] No release of carbon dioxide (CO_2), methane (CH_4), nitrous oxide (N_2O), sulphur oxides (SO^x), nitrogen oxides (NO^x) and particulate matter (PM) into the atmosphere by the ships.

[50] For example, in the Impact Assessment accompanying this proposal, it is mentioned that 'concerning 2030, biofuels are perceived as most promising for use in navigation, followed by batteries. Looking at 2050, the expectations are different …'.

C. Proposal for the ReFuelEU Aviation Initiative ('Regulation on Ensuring a Level Playing Field for Sustainable Air Transport')

Under this initiative (in particular, Article 4) fuel suppliers for airlines are obliged to ensure that sustainable aviation fuels (SAF)[51] – including sustainable biofuels and gaseous biomass fuels from biowaste – are made available to aircraft operators at each Union airport and with an increasing amount over the minimum (see Table 7.5).[52, 53]

Table 7.5 Share of mandated sustainable aviation fuels mandated from 1 January 2025 to 1 January 2050

Timeline	Share of SAF mandated
From 1 January 2025	at least 2% of aviation fuels
From 1 January 2030	at least 5% of aviation fuels (out of which 0.7% synthetic aviation fuels – and the rest potentially including eligible biofuels and gaseous biomass fuels)
From 1 January 2035	at least 20% of aviation fuels (out of which 5% synthetic aviation fuels – and the rest potentially including eligible biofuels and gaseous biomass fuels)
From 1 January 2040	at least 32% of aviation fuels (out of which 8% synthetic aviation fuels – and the rest potentially including eligible biofuels and gaseous biomass fuels)

[51] As per Article 3 ('Definitions'),'"sustainable aviation fuels" ("SAF") means drop-in aviation fuels that are either synthetic aviation fuels, advanced biofuels as defined in Article 2, second paragraph, point 34 of Directive (EU) 2018/2001, or biofuels produced from the feedstock listed in Part B of Annex IX to that Directive, which comply with the sustainability and greenhouse gas emissions criteria laid down in Article 29(2) to (7) of that Directive and are certified in accordance with Article 30 of this Directive'.

[52] However, please note that a derogation over the period from 1 January 2025 until 31 December 2029 is foreseen (Article 13), whereby an aviation fuel supplier may count the mandated minimum share of SAF as a weighted average over all the aviation fuel it supplied across Union airports, rather than applying it individually at each Union airport.

[53] European Commission, 'Annexes to Proposal for a Regulation on ensuring a level playing field for sustainable air transport' COM (2021) 561 Annexes 1 to 2.

Timeline	Share of SAF mandated
From 1 January 2045	at least 38% of aviation fuels (out of which 11% synthetic aviation fuels – and the rest potentially including eligible biofuels and gaseous biomass fuels)
From 1 January 2050	at least 63% of aviation fuels (out of which 28% synthetic aviation fuels – and the rest potentially including eligible biofuels and gaseous biomass fuels)

While promoting the decarbonisation of the aviation sector, this legislative act also accounts for the competing needs for sustainable biofuels and gaseous biomass fuels towards the decarbonisation of other transport modes, such as road sector.[54]

IV. RELEVANT PROVISIONS IN BLOCK 3: EU CLIMATE LEGISLATIVE ACTS

The legislative acts considered in this block, given the relevant policy provisions included in them contributing to the analysis of this chapter, are reported in Table 7.6 – together with the relative status and year of adoption or enforcement.[55]

This chapter will not examine in detail:

- The 'Proposal for Regulation amending Regulation 2019/631 as regards strengthening the CO_2 emission performance standards for new passenger

[54] For example, 'the non-inclusion of crop-based biofuels should also aim to avoid the risk of biofuel displacement from the road sector towards air transport, as this could slow down the decarbonisation of road transport, which currently remains by far the most polluting transport mode'. Additionally, '… at present, the large majority of liquid biofuels are produced for the road sector. Therefore, a shift of feedstock for production of biofuels in the road sector to production for the aviation sector may occur, but would be limited'. ReFuelEU Aviation Initiative (n 23).

[55] There is also an upcoming legislative initiative to establish an EU framework for harmonised measurement of transport and logistics emissions – foreseen by Q4 2022 (Source: Legislative Train Schedule (europa.eu)) in order to inform consumers and business with an estimate of the carbon footprint of their choices. 'Information on the carbon footprint of a specific journey could become a new passenger right and in this case should apply to all transport modes.' This initiative would be in support of the Revision of the EU ETS.

cars and new light commercial vehicles in line with the Union's increased climate ambition';[56]

- Regulation 2019/1242 setting CO_2 emission performance standards for new heavy-duty vehicles.[57]

The Proposal for Regulation amending Regulation 2019/631 foresees revised EU fleet-wide targets for average 'tailpipe' CO_2 emissions[58] [g CO_2/km] of passenger cars and new light commercial vehicles newly registered in the European Union from 1 January 2030 and from 1 January 2035, respectively, increasing the ambition level in line with the 2030 climate target of a 55% GHG emissions reduction and the 2050 climate neutrality target. To deliver on the proposed stricter targets, zero- and low-emission vehicles (vehicles with tailpipe emissions from zero to 50 g CO_2/km[59]) will need to be increasingly deployed over time. By 2035, all newly registered passenger cars and light commercial vehicles placed on the EU market will have to be zero-emission. These newly registered passenger cars and light commercial vehicles placed on the EU market would therefore not be eligible to use of sustainable biofuels and gaseous biomass fuels.

Regulation 2019/1242[60] setting CO_2 emission performance standards for new heavy-duty vehicles was adopted under the 'Clean Energy Package', and it is currently being reviewed in order to be in line with the updated 2030 climate target and with the 'Fit for 55 package'. Regulation 2019/1242 sets tailpipe CO_2 emission performance standards for new heavy-duty vehicles.

---

[56] European Commission, 'Proposal amending Regulation (EU) 2019/631 as regards strengthening the CO_2 emission performance standards for new passenger cars and new light commercial vehicles in line with the Union's increased climate ambition' COM (2021) 556.

[57] Regulation (EU) 2019/1242 setting CO_2 emission performance standards for new heavy-duty vehicles and amending Regulations (EC) No 595/2009 and (EU) 2018/956 and Directive [2019] OJ L 198/202.

[58] Definition of '*tailpipe*': 'an outlet by which engine exhaust gases are expelled from a vehicle (such as an automobile or jet aircraft)' (according to Merriam Webster, 'Tailpipe Definition & Meaning' https://www.merriam-webster.com/dictionary/tailpipe/.

[59] In accordance with Article 3(1)(m) of Regulation (EU) 2019/631 Setting CO_2 emission performance standards for new passenger cars and for new light commercial vehicles, and repealing Regulations (EC) No 443/2009 and (EU) No 510/2011 [2019] OJ L111/13.

[60] Reg 2019/1242 (n 57).

Table 7.6 EU climate policy files examined in this chapter

Name of the legislative act	Year of adoption of the proposal	Status in August 2022
2018 EU ETS Directive[a] & Commission Implementing Regulation 2022/388 on monitoring and reporting of greenhouse gas emissions[b]	2018 (Clean Energy Package); 2022 (Fit for 55; Commission Implementing Regulation 2022/388)	Entered into force
2018 EU Effort Sharing Regulation (ESR)[c] & Implementing Decision 2020/2126[d]	2018 (Clean Energy Package; regulation) 2020 (Clean Energy Package; Implementing Decision)	Entered into force
Proposal for the Revision of the EU ETS Directive[e] [Please note that the supporting Commission Implementing Regulations on monitoring, reporting and verification of greenhouse gas emissions for the sectors under the new emissions trading scheme will only be proposed after the entry into force of the revision of the EU ETS Directive.]	2021 (Fit for 55 package)	Not yet agreed in co-decision and not yet entered into force
Proposal for the Revision of the EU ETS Directive for aviation[f]	2021 (Fit for 55 package)	Not yet agreed in co-decision and not yet entered into force
Proposal for the Revision of the EU Effort Sharing Regulation (ESR)[g]	2021 (Fit for 55 package)	Not yet agreed in co-decision and not yet entered into force

Notes: a. Directive 2018/410 amending Directive 2003/87/EC to enhance cost-effective emission reductions and low-carbon investments, and Decision (EU) 2015/1814 [2018] OJ L76/3; b. Implementing Regulation (EU) 2020/2085 amending and correcting Implementing Regulation (EU) 2018/2066 on the monitoring and reporting of greenhouse gas emissions pursuant to Directive 2003/87/EC of the European Parliament and of the Council [2020] OJ C 423/37; c. Regulation (EU) 2018/842 on binding annual greenhouse gas emission reductions by Member States from 2021 to 2030 contributing to climate action to meet commitments under the Paris Agreement and amending Regulation (EU) No 525/2013 [2018] OJ L156/26; d. Commission Implementing Decision (EU) 2020/2126 on setting out the annual emission allocations of the Member States for the period from 2021 to 2030 pursuant to Regulation (EU) 2018/842 [2020] OJ L426/58; e. European Commission, 'Proposal for a Directive amending Directive 2003/87/EC establishing a system for greenhouse gas emission allowance trading within the Union, Decision (EU) 2015/1814 concerning the establishment and operation of a market stability reserve for the Union greenhouse gas emission trading scheme and Regulation (EU) 2015/757' COM (2021) 551 ('Revised ETS proposal'); f. European Commission, 'Proposal for Directive amending Directive 2003/87/EC as regards aviation's contribution to the Union's economy-wide emission reduction target and appropriately implementing a global market-based measure' COM (2021) 552.; g. European Commission, 'Proposal for a Regulation amending Regulation (EU) 2018/842 on binding annual greenhouse gas emission reductions by Member States from 2021 to 2030 contributing to climate action to meet commitments under the Paris Agreement' COM (2021) 555.

A. 2018 EU Emissions Trading System (ETS) Directive & Commission Implementing Regulation 2022/388 on Monitoring and Reporting of Greenhouse Gas Emissions

'The EU ETS is the most important (EU) instrument of carbon pricing in order to internalise the cost of CO_2 emissions.'[61] In particular, the 2018 EU ETS Directive sets a framework for the carbon market in EU until 2030, which will soon be revised by the 2021 revision of the EU ETS Directive once it enters into force (sub-sections C and D below). In order to understand the financial incentives in using sustainable biofuels and gaseous biomass fuels for operators of installations subject to carbon pricing under the 2018 EU ETS Directive, this chapter needs to take into account three factors:

- **No exclusive incentives for using sustainable biofuels and gaseous biomass fuels from biowaste:** From 1 January 2022 to 31 December 2022, for the purpose of the EU ETS, installations where emissions from the combustion of any type of biofuels and gaseous biomass fuels occur are not subject to carbon pricing ('zero-rated') as 'Member States, or competent authorities as appropriate, may consider as fulfilled the sustainability and greenhouse gas emissions saving criteria'. Indeed, these emissions are already counted in the land use, land use change and forestry (LULUCF) sector,[62] according to Regulation 2018/841 (LULUCF Regulation)[63] and to the Proposal for amending the LULUCF Regulation[64]). Afterwards, installations where emissions from the combustion of sustainable biofuels and gaseous biomass fuels contribute to more than 95% of the total GHG emissions will not subject to carbon pricing as long as these fuels comply with the sustainability and GHG emissions savings criteria under RED II.

---

[61] Meadows, Paquot and Vis (n 7).

[62] For what LULUCF means, and what are relevant provisions within the 'LULUCF Regulation' (Regulation (EU) 2018/841 (On the inclusion of greenhouse gas emissions and removals from land use, land use change and forestry in the 2030 climate and energy framework, and amending Regulation (EU) No 525/2013 and Decision No 529/2013/EU [2018] OJ L156/1 ('LULUCF Regulation')) and European Commission, 'Proposal amending Regulations (EU) 2018/841 as regards the scope, simplifying the compliance rules, setting out the targets of the Member States for 2030 and committing to the collective achievement of climate neutrality by 2035 in the land use, forestry and agriculture sector, and (EU) 2018/1999 as regards improvement in monitoring, reporting, tracking of progress and review' (2021) 554 'Proposal amending the LULUCF Regulation'), readers may refer to Chapter 5 in this volume. This chapter will not examine the climate legislative acts dealing with the Agriculture, Forestry and Other Land Use (AFOLU) sector.

[63] LULUCF Regulation (n 62).

[64] Proposal amending the LULUCF Regulation (n 62).

In case the sustainability and GHG emissions saving criteria under RED II are not complied with, 'its carbon content (of the biofuel) should be considered as fossil carbon'. These provisions imply an associated reduction of the number of ETS allowances the operator using sustainable biofuels and gaseous biomass fuels has to surrender.[65]

- **Coverage of CO_2 emissions priced from fossil fuels used in the transport sector:** The coverage of emissions from fossil fuels used in the transport sector by the EU ETS is dependent on the transport mode. Indeed, while the EU ETS covers emissions from electricity, direct CO_2 emissions by road transport, international air transport[66] and (EU or international) maritime transport[67] are currently not priced under the EU ETS phase III. Only the CO_2 emissions of intra-EEA flights, or of flights between the EU and Switzerland, or flights between the EU and UK, are covered by the EU ETS and will continue to be so until 31 December 2023. Instead, the CO_2 emissions of flights arriving to an airport in the EU, or departing from one, are subject to the provisions under the International Civil Aviation Organization (ICAO)'s Carbon Offsetting and Reduction Scheme for International Aviation (CORSIA) – which are outside the scope of this chapter.

[65] In particular, the Commission Delegated Regulation, supplementing Directive 2003/87/EC as regards measures adopted by the International Civil Aviation Organization for the monitoring, reporting and verification of aviation emissions for the purpose of implementing a global market-based measure C (2019) 1644 prescribes an emission factor of 3.15 ton CO_2 per ton of jet kerosene – which could also be classified potentially as a sustainable biofuel.

[66] 'Over-flight of EU territory is not regulated. ... The Court confirmed that the EU's provisions have no extra-territorial effect because no obligations are imposed in the territory of any other State. The requirement to report emissions and to surrender allowances under the EU ETS only arises when an aircraft lands or takes off from an airport in an EU Member State. This point, at which a liability arises, is entirely and exclusively within the EU. The amount of liability depends on the emissions of the flight, taking into account length of journey and specific emissions of the aircraft, but irrespective of whether the flight was to or from another Member State or a third country. This is why the European Court of Justice upheld the measure as not infringing the sovereignty of other States, and not being discriminatory.' Jos Delbeke and Peter Vis, *EU Climate Policy Explained* (Routledge 2015).

[67] Although the maritime sector is not currently covered by EU ETS, it has been subject to a Monitoring, Reporting and Verification (MRV) scheme since 1 July of 2015 (Regulation (EU) 2015/757 on the monitoring, reporting and verification of carbon dioxide emissions from maritime transport, and amending Directive 2009/16/EC [2015] OJ L123/55). Regarding biofuels, the scheme reports that 'appropriate emission factors shall be applied'.

These provisions apply equally to all aircraft operators active over these flight routes. However, at the same time, the flight operators liable[68] still largely benefit from free allocation of allowances, and therefore do not have as much of an incentive to use sustainable biofuels and gaseous biomass fuels.

- **Prices of EU ETS allowances:** Recent prices for EU ETS allowances were mostly in the range of 75–90 EUR/tCO_2 in the first half of 2022.[69] Investigating the underlying drivers and the impact of recent prices for EU ETS allowances on the cost competitiveness of sustainable biofuels vis-à-vis fossil fuels is outside the scope of this chapter.[70, 71]

B. 2018 EU Effort Sharing Regulation (ESR) & Implementing Decision 2020/2126

The EU Effort Sharing Regulation (ESR) adds an additional layer of annually binding emission limits for each MS and, between 2021 and 2030, to the binding EU-level target for reducing GHG emissions in the transport sector by 2030 – under the RED III file described above. These emission limits cover different sectors not included in the EU ETS, among which is the road transport sector.[72] These annual limits were legislated before the adoption of the EU

[68] Independently from this aspect, compliance with EU ETS remains significantly high: 'Throughout phase 3, and despite the difficult economic situation due to the COVID-19 crisis in the 2020 and 2021 compliance cycles, the level of compliance in the EU ETS remained consistently very high. Operators responsible for over 99% of emissions from both stationary installations and aviation in most years, had complied with their legal obligations.' (European Commission, 'Report on the Functioning of the European Carbon Market in 2020 pursuant to Articles 10(5) and 21(2) of Directive 2003/87/EC (as amended by Directive 2009/29/EC and Directive (EU) 2018/410)' COM (2021) 962 ('Report on the Functioning of the European Carbon Market in 2020')).

[69] Ember, 'EU Carbon Price tracker' (website) https://ember-climate.org/data/data-tools/carbon-price-viewer/.

[70] Other legislation further defines the framework for free allocation of EU ETS allowances to aircraft operators: Implementing Regulation (EU) 2019/1842 of 31 October 2019 laying down rules for the application of Directive 2003/87/EC as regards further arrangements for the adjustments to free allocation of emission allowances due to activity level changes [2019] OJ L282/20 and Delegated Regulation (EU) 2019/331 determining transitional Union-wide rules for harmonised free allocation of emission allowances pursuant to Article 10a of Directive 2003/87/EC of the European Parliament and of the Council [2019] OJ L59/8.

[71] Without accounting for incentives seen in other policy files (targets, financing, etc.).

[72] In addition to road transport, the other sectors covered are small-scale industries, heating of buildings, agriculture and waste.

Climate Law, and therefore required the proposal of a revision (sub-section E below) increasing the ambition of such limits in line with the –55% target by 2030.

Several flexibility mechanisms and a compliance check mechanism are also established in the relevant legislation.[73]

The CO_2 emissions from biomass fuels, bioliquids and gaseous biomass fuels coming from the EU – including those from sustainable biofuels and gaseous biomass fuels from biowaste – are zero-rated under the ESR sectors. The reason is that, similarly to what was mentioned regarding the 2018 ETS Directive, these emissions are already counted in the LULUCF sector according to the LULUCF Regulation and the proposal amending the LULUCF Regulation. Ultimately, there is no direct financial impact on private entities whether or not they use sustainable biofuels and gaseous biomass fuels within ESR sectors.

C. Proposal for the Revision of the EU ETS Directive

In the Commission proposal for the revision of the EU ETS Directive there are two main sets of provisions this chapter identifies as relevant: those concerning the extension of the existing EU ETS to maritime transport and those concerning the establishment of a 'separate but adjacent emissions trading' scheme covering the road transport sector. The first covers emissions from intra-EU trips and half of the emissions from extra-EU trips. The latter covers instead emissions from regulated entities, which 'shall mean any natural or legal person, except for any final consumer of the fuels, that engages in the activity referred to in Annex III ("release for consumption of fuels which are used for combustion in the sectors of buildings and road transport")'.[74]

---

[73] European Commission, 'Proposal for a Regulation on binding annual greenhouse gas emission reductions by Member States from 2021 to 2030 for a resilient Energy Union and to meet commitments under the Paris Agreement and amending Regulation No 525/2013 of the European Parliament and the Council on a mechanism for monitoring and reporting greenhouse gas emissions and other information relevant to climate change' COM (2016) 482.

[74] '(i) where the fuel passes through a tax warehouse as defined in Article 3(11) of Council Directive (EU) 2020/262(*), the authorised warehouse keeper as defined in Article 3(1) of that Directive, liable to pay the excise duty which has become chargeable pursuant to Article 7 of that Directive; (ii) if point (i) is not applicable, any other person liable to pay the excise duty which has become chargeable pursuant to Article 7 of Directive (EU) 2020/262 in respect of the fuels covered by this Chapter; (iii) if points (i) and (ii) are not applicable, any other person which has to be registered by the relevant competent authorities of the Member State for the purpose of being liable to pay the excise duty, including any person exempt from paying the excise duty, as referred

In order to understand the financial incentives for operators to use sustainable biofuels and gaseous biomass fuels from biowaste under this proposal for a revised EU ETS, this sub-section takes into account three factors – in a similar way to sub-section IV.A above (2018 Directive of the EU ETS): benefits from using sustainable biofuels and gaseous biomass fuels; coverage of CO_2 emissions in the transport sector priced under the EU ETS; and prices of EU ETS allowances. For each of these factors, this sub-section differentiates between the relevant provisions for the maritime sector and those for the road transport sector whenever there are clear differences.

- **No exclusive incentives from using sustainable biofuels and gaseous biomass fuels from biowaste:** The same rules described in sub-section IV.A exempting operators using biofuels and gaseous biomass fuels from surrendering an ETS allowance, as long as these fuels comply with the sustainability and greenhouse gas emissions saving criteria under RED II, apply both in the case of the extension of the existing EU ETS to maritime transport, and in the case of the establishment of a 'separate but adjacent emissions trading' scheme covering the road transport sector. Similarly to what was mentioned regarding the 2018 EU ETS Directive, these emissions are already counted in the LULUCF sector according to the LULUCF Regulation and to the proposal amending the LULUCF Regulation.
- **Coverage of CO_2 emissions priced from fossil fuels used in the transport sector:** The coverage of carbon pricing on emissions from fossil fuels used in the transport sector will be almost complete. As mentioned above, CO_2 emissions by both ships (except for half of the emissions from extra-EU trips[75]) and road transport users are going to be priced. In terms of

to in Article 21(5), fourth sub-paragraph, of Council Directive 2003/96/EC(**); (iv) if points (i), (ii) and (iii) are not applicable, or if several persons are jointly and severally liable for payment of the same excise duty, any other person designated by a Member State'.

[75] 'Considering that emissions from international aviation outside Europe should be capped from January 2021 by global market-based action while there is no action in place that caps or prices maritime transport emissions, it is appropriate that the EU ETS covers a share of the emissions from voyages between a port under the jurisdiction of a Member State and a port under the jurisdiction of a third country, with the third country being able to decide on appropriate action in respect of the other share of emissions. The extension of the EU ETS to the maritime transport sector should thus include half of the emissions from ships performing voyages arriving at a port under the jurisdiction of a Member State from a port outside the jurisdiction of a Member State, half of the emissions from ships performing voyages departing from a port under the jurisdiction of a Member State and arriving at a port outside the jurisdiction of a Member State, emissions from ships performing voyages arriving at a port under the jurisdiction of a Member State from a port under the jurisdiction of a Member State, and emissions

free allocations of allowances, the approaches for the maritime sector and for the road transport sector differ:

- The surrendering of allowances by shipping companies for emissions from maritime transport – to be covered in the existing emissions trading system – will see initially a phase-in period (where shipping companies would only have to surrender allowances for a portion of their verified emissions), gradually rising to 100% by 2026. In other words, no free allowances from 2026 onwards.
- No free allocations are foreseen for allowances auctioned under the new emissions trading scheme for the road transport sector (Article 30d). Indeed, both the road transport and the buildings sectors covered by this scheme are 'under relatively small or non-existent competitive pressure from outside the Union and are not exposed to a risk of carbon leakage'.

- **Prices of EU ETS allowances**: Whereas the trends on the prices of the EU ETS allowances for the maritime sector will be the same as those for the existing ETS, those for the road transport sector will be distinct. In both cases, the trends on the prices of these EU ETS allowances are outside the scope of this analysis.[76] The estimation of the equivalent carbon pricing needed for the switching from fossil fuels to sustainable biofuels in maritime and road transport sector – in addition to the incentives seen in other policy files (targets, financing …) – is also outside the scope of this analysis.

D. Proposal for the Revision of the EU ETS Directive for Aviation

The aims of this proposal for the revision of the EU ETS Directive for aviation are two-fold:

- to reflect 'the implementation for aviation of the Union's contributions under the Paris Agreement, and of the regulatory framework to achieve the

---

at berth in a port under the jurisdiction of a Member State. This approach has been noted as a practical way to solve the issue of Common but Differentiated Responsibilities and Capabilities, which has been a longstanding challenge in the UNFCCC context.'

[76] The proposed linear reduction factor for the existing emission trading system is 4.2% from the year following the entry into force of this Directive amending the ETS Directive. Instead, the linear reduction factor for the new emission trading system will be set from 2026 onwards 'based on data collected under the Effort Sharing Regulation and ambition level and decrease to reach emissions reduction of 43% in 2030 compared to 2005 for the sectors of buildings and road transport (Article 30c and Annex IIIa)'. Recital (48) refers however to a linear reduction factor of 5.15%/year over the period 2026–2028 and of 5.43% from 2028.

binding Union 2030 climate target of a domestic reduction of net greenhouse gas emissions by at least 55% compared to 1990 levels by 2030 set out in Regulation (EU) 2021/...'.[77]

- to ensure that the ICAO's CORSIA[78] is implemented in EU to extra-European flights through the ETS Directive. However, measures foreseen by ICAO's CORSIA to flights by any aircraft operator between the European Economic Area, the UK and Switzerland and third countries, or to flights by EU-based aircraft operators between two third countries, will not be treated in this chapter.

Therefore, this chapter will examine the provisions under this proposal concerning flights by any aircraft operators (EU-based or not) between two airports within the European Economic Area, Switzerland and the UK. In particular, the relevant main legal amendments (to the provisions concerning aviation in the existing ETS Directive) are:

(1) to consolidate the total quantity of aviation allowances at current levels, and apply the linear reduction factor in accordance with Article 9 of the ETS Directive;
(2) to increase auctioning of aviation allowances;
(3) to continue intra-European application of the EU ETS while applying CORSIA as appropriate to extra-European flights; and
(4) to ensure that airlines are treated equally on the same routes with regard to their obligations with economic impacts.

Concerning the three factors previously identified to understand the financial incentives from using sustainable biofuels and gaseous biomass fuels for aircraft operators subject to carbon pricing, the following can be noticed:

- **No exclusive incentives from using sustainable biofuels and gaseous biomass fuels from biowaste:** The provisions by the Commission

[77] 'Projections, which largely did not consider the full pandemic effects, show a further expected increase of emissions from international aviation of 42 % between projected 2020 and 2030 levels with additional measures.' (EEA, *Trends and Projections in Europe 2021* (Publications Office of the European Union 2021)).

[78] The CORSIA is a global market-based measure which entered into force from 2021 for civil aircraft flying between two states which volunteered for such measure, and from 2027 onwards it is meant to become mandatory for all flights between most countries. CORSIA should last until 2035 and may be extended. However, the only CO_2 emissions offset through CORSIA are those above the level of 2020 emissions by international civil flights – unlike the EU ETS.

Implementing Regulation 2020/2085[79] for all intra-European flights by any aircraft operator are similar to those under the ETS Directive. From 1 January 2022 to 31 December 2022 installations where emissions from the combustion of any type of biofuels and gaseous biomass fuels occur are not subject to carbon pricing ('zero-rated') as 'Member States, or competent authorities as appropriate, may consider as fulfilled the sustainability and greenhouse gas emissions saving criteria'. Additionally, these emissions are already counted in the LULUCF sector according to the LULUCF Regulation and to the proposal for amending the LULUCF Regulation. Afterwards, installations where emissions from the combustion of sustainable biofuels and gaseous biomass fuels contribute to more than 95% of the total greenhouse gas emissions will not be subject to carbon pricing ('zero-rated') as long as these fuels comply with the sustainability and greenhouse gas emissions savings criteria under RED II. In case the sustainability and greenhouse gas emissions saving criteria under RED II are not complied with, 'its carbon content (of the biofuel) should be considered as fossil carbon'.

- **Coverage of CO_2 emissions priced from fossil fuels used in the aviation transport sector:** The revision of the EU ETS Directive for aviation covers – similarly to the ETS Directive – the CO_2 emissions by intra-EEA flights and by flights departing to Switzerland or to the UK. Similarly, these provisions apply equally to all aircraft operators active over these flight routes. However, the free allocation of the EU ETS allowances to airlines is reduced by a quarter each year, starting in 2024, until by 1 January 2027 no more allowances are freely allocated ('full auctioning of allowances').
- **Prices of EU ETS allowances**: The trends on the prices of these EU ETS allowances are complex to estimate and outside the scope of this analysis. The estimation of the equivalent carbon pricing needed for the switching from fossil fuels to sustainable biofuels in the maritime and road transport sectors – in addition to the incentives seen in other policy files (targets, financing …) – is also outside the scope of this analysis.

[79] Commission Implementing Regulation (EU) 2022/388 amending Implementing Regulation (EU) 2018/2066 on the monitoring and reporting of greenhouse gas emissions pursuant to Directive 2003/87/EC [2022] OJ L79/1.

E. Proposal for the Revision of the EU Effort Sharing Regulation (ESR)

The revision of the EU Effort Sharing Regulation (ESR) aligns the annually binding emissions limit – previously set by the 2018 EU Effort Sharing Regulation – with the –55% emission reduction target legislated under the EU Climate Law.

Similarly to the 2018 ESR, the emissions from biomass fuels, bioliquids and gaseous biomass fuels coming from the EU – including those from sustainable biofuels and gaseous biomass fuels from biowaste – are zero-rated under the ESR, as they are already counted in the LULUCF sector according to the LULUCF Regulation and to the proposal amending the LULUCF Regulation. Ultimately, there is no direct financial impact on private entities whether or not they use sustainable biofuels and gaseous biomass fuels within ESR sectors.

V. CONCLUSION

In line with the descriptive methodology of this chapter, it can be concluded that there are no provisions exclusively promoting the uptake of biofuels and gaseous biomass fuels from biowaste in the transport sector. Rather, there are different layers of provisions which promote in a non-exclusive way the uptake of sustainable biofuels and gaseous biomass fuels in the transport sector – promoting instead sub-categories of renewable energy sources[80] or of renewable fuels, the energy content of which is derived from renewable sources (see Table 7.7).

[80] 'Renewable energy sources, also called renewables, are energy sources that replenish (or renew) themselves naturally' (Eurostat, 'Glossary: Renewable Energy Sources' https://ec.europa.eu/eurostat/statistics-explained/index.php?title=Glossary:Renewable_energy_sources/).

Table 7.7 Layers of provisions per sub-categories of renewable energy sources or of renewable fuels promoted

Sub-categories of renewable energy sources or of renewable fuels promoted	Layers of provisions
'Sustainable' biofuels and gaseous biomass fuels [Biofuels and gaseous biomass fuels complying with the sustainability and greenhouse gas emissions saving criteria under RED II]	After 31 December 2022, for the purpose of the EU ETS, installations where emissions from the combustion of sustainable biofuels and gaseous biomass fuels contribute to more than 95% of the total greenhouse gas emissions will not be subject to carbon pricing ('zero-rated') as long as these fuels comply with the sustainability and greenhouse gas emissions savings criteria under RED II. These provisions imply an associated reduction of the number of ETS allowances the operator using sustainable biofuels and gaseous biomass fuels has to surrender. Indeed, these emissions are already counted in the LULUCF sector according to the LULUCF Regulation and to the proposal amending the LULUCF Regulation
Advanced biofuels [Note that the definition of 'advanced biofuels' does not coincide with that of '"sustainable" biofuels and gaseous biomass fuels']	The minimum shares for replacing fossil fuels in the transport sector with advanced biofuels according to RED II and RED III
Sustainable aviation fuels[a] [Including 'advanced biofuels', but please note that the definition of 'sustainable aviation fuels' does not coincide with that of '"sustainable" biofuels and gaseous biomass fuels')]	The obligatory shares for the deployment of sustainable aviation fuels in the aviation transport mode.
Biofuels and gaseous biomass fuels [Including '"Sustainable" biofuels and gaseous biomass fuels' and 'advanced biofuels', but note that the definition of 'biofuels and gaseous biomass fuels' does not coincide with that of 'sustainable aviation fuels')]	From 1 January 2022 to the 31 December 2022, for the purpose of the EU ETS, installations where emissions from the combustion of any type of biofuels and gaseous biomass fuels occur are not subject to carbon pricing ('zero-rated') as 'Member States, or competent authorities as appropriate, may consider as fulfilled the sustainability and greenhouse gas emissions saving criteria'. Indeed, these emissions are already counted in the LULUCF sector according to the LULUCF Regulation and to the proposal amending the LULUCF Regulation.

Sub-categories of renewable energy sources or of renewable fuels promoted	Layers of provisions
Renewable fuels [Including 'biofuels and gaseous biomass fuels', but note that the definition of 'renewable fuels' does not coincide with that of 'sustainable aviation fuels']	The targets for reduction in GHG intensity of energy used in the transport sector according to RED III and to the FuelEU Maritime initiative.
Biomass fuels, bioliquids and gaseous biomass fuels [Including 'biofuels and gaseous biomass fuels', but note that the definition of 'biomass fuels, bioliquids and gaseous biomass fuels' does not coincide with that of 'renewable fuels' nor with that of 'sustainable aviation fuels']	The CO_2 emissions from bioenergy coming from the EU – including those from sustainable biofuels and gaseous biomass fuels from biowaste – are zero-rated under the ESR sectors. The reason is that, similarly to what was mentioned regarding the 2018 EU ETS Directive, these emissions are already counted in the LULUCF sector according to the LULUCF Regulation and to the proposal amending the LULUCF Regulation.
Renewable energy sources [Including 'biomass fuels, bioliquids and gaseous biomass fuels', but note that the definition of 'renewable energy sources' does not coincide with that of 'renewable fuels']	The targets for the penetration of renewable energy at energy-system level according to RED II and RED III, and for the penetration of renewable energy in transport sector under RED II

Note: a. According to the definition within the ReFuelEU Aviation Initiative (n 23).

LEGISLATION

Directive 2014/94/EU on the deployment of alternative fuels infrastructure [2014] OJ L 307/1

Directive (EU) 2018/2001 of the European Parliament and of the Council of 11 December 2018 on the promotion of the use of energy from renewable sources [2018] OJ L328/82 ('RED II')

Directive 98/70/EC relating to the quality of petrol and diesel fuels and amending Council Directive 93/12/EEC [1998] OJ L350/58.

Directive (EU) 2011/63 amending, for the purpose of its adaptation to technical progress, Directive 98/70/EC relating to the quality of petrol and diesel fuels [2011] OJ L47/15

Directive (EU) 2015/1513 amending Directive 98/70/EC relating to the quality of petrol and diesel fuels and amending Directive 2009/28/EC on the promotion of the use of energy from renewable sources [2015] OJ C239/1.

Directive 1999/32/EC relating to a reduction in the sulphur content of certain liquid fuels and amending Directive 93/12/EEC [1999] OJ L121.

Directive 2016/802 relating to a reduction in the sulphur content of certain liquid fuels [2016] OJ L132/58.

Regulation (EU) 2018/842 on binding annual greenhouse gas emission reductions by Member States from 2021 to 2030 contributing to climate action to meet commitments under the Paris Agreement and amending Regulation (EU) No 525/2013 [2018] OJ L156/26

Regulation (EU) 2021/1119 establishing the framework for achieving climate neutrality and amending Regulations (EC) No 401/2009 and (EU) 2018/1999 ('European Climate Law') [2021] OJ L243/1

Regulation (EU) 2017/2392 amending Directive 2003/87/EC to continue current limitations of scope for aviation activities and to prepare to implement a global market-based measure from 2021 [2021] OJ L 350/7

Regulation (EU) 2015/757 on the monitoring, reporting and verification of carbon dioxide emissions from maritime transport, and amending Directive 2009/16/EC [2015] OJ L123/55

Regulation (EU) 2019/631 setting CO_2 emission performance standards for new passenger cars and for new light commercial vehicles, and repealing Regulations (EC) No 443/2009 and (EU) No 510/2011 [2019] OJ L111/13.

Regulation (EU) 2019/1242 setting CO_2 emission performance standards for new heavy-duty vehicles and amending Regulations (EC) No 595/2009 and (EU) 2018/956 and Directive [2019] OJ L 198/202.

Regulation (EU) 2018/841 on the inclusion of greenhouse gas emissions and removals from land use, land use change and forestry in the 2030 climate and energy framework, and amending Regulation (EU) No 525/2013 and Decision No 529/2013/EU [2018] OJ L156/1 ('LULUCF Regulation').

Delegated Regulation 2019/807 supplementing Directive (EU) 2018/2001 as regards the determination of high indirect land-use change-risk feedstock for which a significant expansion of the production area into land with high carbon stock is observed and the certification of low indirect land-use change-risk biofuels, bioliquids and biomass fuels [2019] OJ L133/1.

Delegated Regulation (EU) 2019/331 determining transitional Union-wide rules for harmonised free allocation of emission allowances pursuant to Article 10a of

Directive 2003/87/EC of the European Parliament and of the Council [2019] OJ L59/8.

Implementing Regulation (EU) 2020/388 of 8 March 2022 amending Implementing Regulation (EU) 2018/2066 on the monitoring and reporting of greenhouse gas emissions pursuant to Directive 2003/87/EC of the European Parliament and of the Council [2022] OJ L 79/1

Implementing Regulation (EU) 2019/1842 of 31 October 2019 laying down rules for the application of Directive 2003/87/EC as regards further arrangements for the adjustments to free allocation of emission allowances due to activity level changes [2019] OJ L282/20

Commission Implementing Decision (EU) 2020/2126 on setting out the annual emission allocations of the Member States for the period from 2021 to 2030 pursuant to Regulation (EU) 2018/842 [2020] OJ L426/58

Implementing Regulation (EU) 2022/388 amending Implementing Regulation (EU) 2018/2066 on the monitoring and reporting of greenhouse gas emissions pursuant to Directive 2003/87/EC [2022] OJ L79/1.

8. Methane emission in a circular economy

Maria Olczak and Andris Piebalgs

I. INTRODUCTION

Methane is a potent but short-lived greenhouse gas (GHG), which in contrast to carbon dioxide (CO_2) has received little attention. The focus on 'decarbonisation' is understandable: CO_2 is the most abundant and persistent GHG, which makes it the key driver of climate change. Over the last 30 years, the EU has introduced a combination of climate policies: carbon pricing (EU Emissions Trading System), the promotion of renewables and other low-carbon technologies, regulatory standards, and information provision. Those instruments targeted mostly the energy sector and emissions related to the combustion of fossil fuels.

Yet, as the near-term warming becomes higher priority,[1] methane emissions (CH_4) reduction is becoming more important. Methane is over 80 times (84–86) more potent than CO_2 in a short-term perspective.[2] Although it stays in the atmosphere for about a decade, methane has contributed to about 25% of warming since pre-industrial times, which makes it the second most important GHG.[3] Curbing methane emissions offers an opportunity to slow down the pace of warming and to improve air quality. Methane contributes to the formation of tropospheric ozone, an air pollutant and GHG causing premature death

1 IPCC, 'Climate Change 2021: The Physical Science Basis. Contribution of Working Group I to the Sixth Assessment Report of the Intergovernmental Panel on Climate Change' (Cambridge University Press 2021).

2 Paul Balcombe and others, 'Methane Emissions: Choosing the Right Climate Metric and Time Horizon' (2018) 20 Environmental Science: Processes & Impacts 1323.

3 Marielle Saunois and others, 'The Global Methane Budget 2000–2017' (2020) 12 Earth System Science Data 1561.

and harming ecosystems and plants.[4] Methane concentrations in the atmosphere have more than doubled since 1750,[5] and surpassed 1900 ppb in 2021.[6]

Achieving the 2030 and 2050 climate targets requires the reduction of both CO_2 and methane emissions. In the EU, methane originates mainly from agriculture, waste and energy sectors. In 2021, the EU Commission proposed a regulation on energy-related methane emissions occurring during the extraction, transport and use of fossil fuels: coal, oil and gas. Further measures tackling two major sources of methane emissions in the EU – agriculture and waste – are expected in the mid-2020s.

The production of biogas from agricultural waste and residues has received increasing attention in EU climate policies. It offers a unique opportunity to alleviate methane emissions, contributing to the decarbonisation of the gas sector and to the EU circular economy objectives. However, this will not be an easy task. Our understanding of methane emissions is improving rapidly but national methane inventories rely mostly on lower tier methodologies, which are more uncertain. This uncertainty challenges the choice and the effectiveness of chosen policies. The Intergovernmental Panel on Climate Change (IPCC) Guidelines specify methods for estimating emissions in national GHG inventories categorised in three tiers in terms of emission factors (EFs) and activity data used in calculations.[7] Tier 1 (T1) contains simple methods frequently utilising IPCC-recommended default values; Tier 2 (T2) is similar but includes country-specific EFs and activity data; and Tier 3 (T3) is the most demanding in terms of methodological complexity and data requirements, for example direct emission measurements. T2 and T3 are more accurate as they are more representative of the sources and facilities being monitored.

Experience with regulating agriculture- and waste-related GHG emissions at the EU level is limited. Currently GHG emissions from these sectors are covered by the Effort Sharing Framework, where Member States (MSs) are primarily responsible for implementing climate policies. Also, the production of biogas from organic waste does not lead to the reduction of the main source of methane emissions in the EU – enteric fermentation. Cutting those

---

4 United Nations Environment Programme and Climate and Clean Air Coalition, 'Global Methane Assessment: Benefits and Costs of Mitigating Methane Emissions' (United Nations Environment Programme 2021).

5 EG Nisbet and others, 'Very Strong Atmospheric Methane Growth in the 4 Years 2014–2017: Implications for the Paris Agreement' (2019) 33 Global Biogeochemical Cycles 318.

6 Ed Dlugokencky, 'Trends in Atmospheric Methane: Global CH_4 Monthly Means' (2022) https://gml.noaa.gov/ccgg/trends_ch4/ accessed 14 January 2022.

7 IPCC, '2019 Refinement to the 2006 IPCC Guidelines for National Greenhouse Gas Inventories' (IPCC 2019) https://www.ipcc-nggip.iges.or.jp/public/2019rf/vol1.html accessed 9 November 2021.

emissions requires behavioural changes, such as dietary shifts, which may be politically difficult to implement.

Taking note of these challenges, this chapter is organised as follows. Section II looks into the sources which contribute to EU methane emissions from agriculture and waste and how these emissions have evolved over the last 30 years. Section III critically analyses the current EU policy framework addressing methane emissions in agriculture and waste. On the basis of these findings, Section IV discusses a set of policy options to fill the gaps. Section V draws conclusions and provides policy recommendations.

II. NON-ENERGY METHANE EMISSIONS: KEY TRENDS AND SOURCES

In the EU, methane emissions account for 11% of all GHGs and originate mostly from three sectors: agriculture, waste and energy. Agriculture is the main source of anthropogenic methane emissions in the EU, accounting for 53% of emissions, mostly from enteric fermentation and manure management.[8] The waste sector is the second biggest source and is responsible for 26% of emissions, mostly from anaerobic decomposition of organic waste in landfills and wastewater treatment. Emissions resulting from fossil fuel use are the third biggest source of methane emissions (19%) but are beyond the scope of this chapter. Figure 8.1. presents a breakdown of methane emission sources in the EU.

In the last 30 years (1990–2019), methane emissions decreased by 39% (from 729 to 443 Mt CO_2 equivalent) in the EU, mostly thanks to reductions in emissions from coal mining and anaerobic waste. The former was a result of mine closure; the latter of the introduction of the 1999 EU Landfill Directive.[9] The third biggest reductions were driven by the decrease in the cattle population (–27.9% between 1990 and 2019). Figure 8.2 presents a breakdown of reductions between 1990 and 2019 by key source categories. The next sections discuss the main contributors of methane emissions in agriculture and waste.

[8] European Environment Agency (EEA), 'Annual European Union Greenhouse Gas Inventory 1990–2019 and Inventory Report 2021. Submission to the UNFCCC Secretariat' (European Environment Agency 2021) https://www.eea.europa.eu/publications/annual-european-union-greenhouse-gas-inventory-2021/.

[9] Directive 1999/31/EC on the landfill of waste [1999] OJ L182/1 ('Landfill Directive').

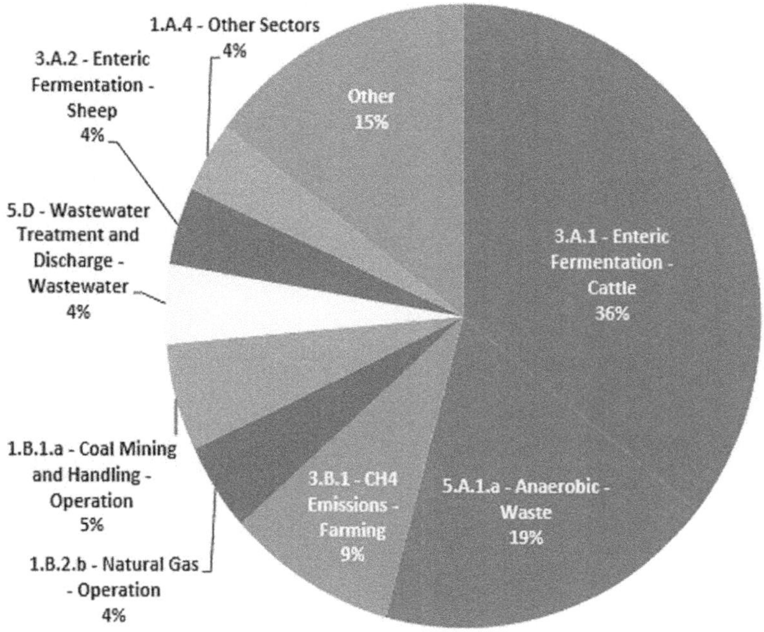

Source: Annual European Union Greenhouse Gas Inventory 1990 – 2019 and Inventory Report 2021.

Figure 8.1 *CH_4 emissions: shares of key source categories and all remaining categories in 2019*

A. Enteric Fermentation

Enteric fermentation refers to emissions occurring due to fermentation in the digestive system of animals, mostly ruminants (mostly non-dairy and dairy cattle). Despite a significant decrease in the last three decades (by 21% or 50.2 Mt CO_2-eq), enteric fermentation remains the largest source of methane emissions and is the key source of GHGs in agriculture. Since 2010, emissions from this category have remained stable. Between 2018 and 2019 they decreased by only 0.8%. The majority (21 of 27) of EU MSs use a combination of T1 and T2 methods to report emissions from this category. Only two countries – France and Spain – use a combination of T2 and T3 methods.

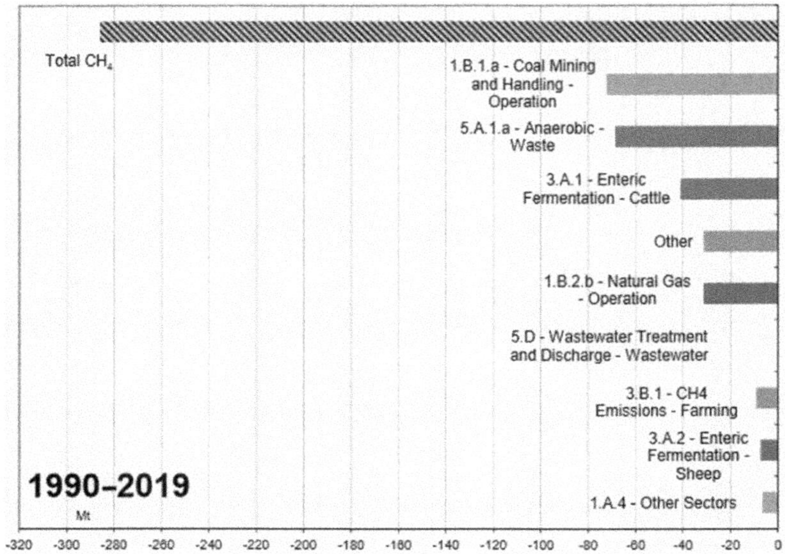

Source: Annual European Union Greenhouse Gas Inventory 1990 – 2019 and Inventory Report 2021.

Figure 8.2 *Absolute change in CH_4 emissions by large key source categories 1990 to 2019 in CO_2 equivalent (Mt) for EU-KP*

B. Anaerobic Waste

Methane from anaerobic digestion of organic matter in solid waste disposal sites is the second biggest source of methane emissions in the EU. Methane emissions account for 88% of emissions in the waste sector. These emissions are related to the amount of biodegradable waste and the volume of recovered and flared landfill gas. The former decreased by 40% in 1990–2019 and the latter increased by 35% in the same period, suggesting that management of landfill gas remains a challenge. Moreover, there is no information on the efficiency of flares used at landfills. On average, 39% of methane from solid waste disposal is recovered or flared, within significant differences between MSs, ranging from 59% in Ireland to 0% in Bulgaria and Cyprus. Detailed data are presented in Figure 8.3.

The majority of EU MSs (25) report methane emissions from managed waste disposal on land using the T2 reporting method. Only Czechia and Luxembourg use T1 methods.

Emissions from unmanaged waste disposal sites are decreasing due to a reduction in the municipal waste disposed of at unmanaged disposal sites.

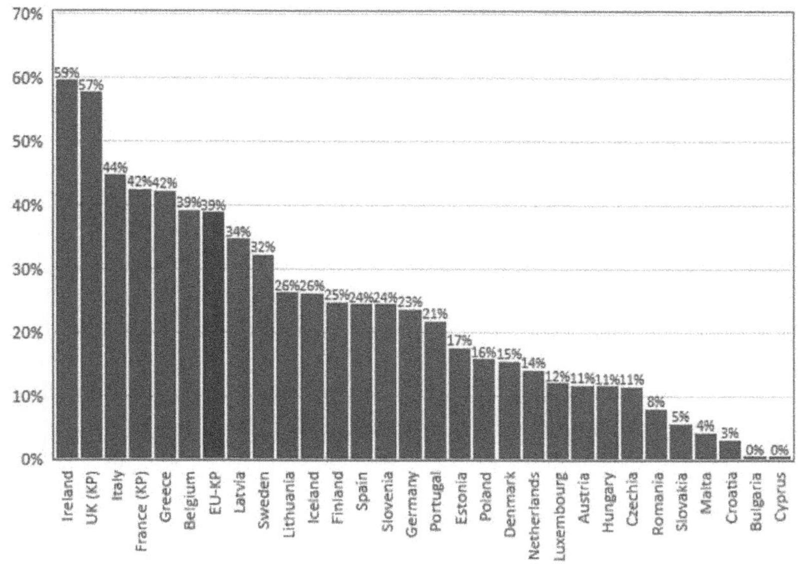

Source: Annual European Union Greenhouse Gas Inventory 1990–2019 and Inventory Report 2021.

Figure 8.3 *Managed solid waste disposal: methane recovery fraction (energy recovery and flaring) for 2019*

C. Manure Management

Manure management is the third main source of methane in the EU, accounting for 8.5% (40617.8 kt CO_2 equivalent) of total EU methane emissions. Swine is the key subcategory, accounting for 43% of emissions, followed by dairy cattle and non-dairy cattle, accounting for 29% and 21.1% of emissions respectively. Between 1990 and 2019 these emissions decreased by 18% or 9.2 Mt CO_2-eq, but have remained stable since 2010.

The majority of EU MSs (20) use a combination of T1 and T2 methods to report emissions from this category. Five countries (Croatia, Finland, France, Germany and Portugal) use T2 methods.

D. Wastewater Treatment and Discharge

Emissions from these sources decreased by 43.7% between 1990 and 2019. There was a 1.6% decrease between 2018 and 2019 due to the installation of centralised wastewater treatment plants, sludge removal and an increase in methane recovery and flaring (domestic wastewater treatment). While emissions from domestic wastewater are decreasing, industrial wastewater emissions have been largely stable since 2009, with yearly fluctuations related to the economic situation in individual countries.

This section has looked at where and how much non-energy methane is produced in the EU and how this trend has changed in the last 30 years. Non-energy methane emissions originate mostly from four categories: enteric fermentation and manure management in agriculture; and anaerobic waste and to a lesser extent wastewater treatment in the waste sector. These emissions decreased considerably between 1990 and 2019, with key reductions in the waste sector, but this trend has decelerated in recent years. This suggests that additional measures (new regulations/implementation) are necessary to further reduce emissions from these sources.

In agriculture, the main driving force of emissions is the animal population, mostly dairy and non-dairy cattle. Animal production is particularly concentrated in Europe – the top 10 countries account for over 80% of the population in Europe – with an uneven trend, as some EU MSs have had a decrease and other MSs an increase in the population. For instance, Denmark and Spain have had an increase in the swine population of 17.3 million heads, while the number of cattle in Ireland, Portugal and Spain has increased by 2.1 million heads.[10] In waste, the main driving force of emissions is the amount and type of waste disposed of in landfills, which is subject to EU environmental regulations.

III. THE CURRENT EU AGRICULTURE AND WASTE POLICY FRAMEWORK: WHAT IS MISSING?

This section presents the existing EU policy framework impacting methane emissions from agriculture and waste, even if in an unintended manner. The framework includes both secondary legislation and non-binding policy strategy documents and other initiatives. It focuses on current legislation and announced changes, instead of presenting how they evolved.

This section is divided into three parts. The first part presents key measures in agriculture: the Effort Sharing Framework[11] (which also applies to

10 EEA (n 8).

11 Regulation (EU) 2018/842 on binding annual greenhouse gas emission reductions by Member States from 2021 to 2030 contributing to climate action to meet commitments under the Paris Agreement and amending Regulation (EU) 525/2013 [2018] OJ L156/26 ('Effort Sharing Regulation'; 'ESR').

waste-related emissions), the Farm to Fork Strategy[12] and the new Common Agricultural Policy (CAP).[13] The second part focuses on the waste-relevant framework: the Waste Framework Directive,[14] the Landfill Directive[15] and the non-binding Guidance on Landfill Gas Control. The section concludes by presenting the changes and priorities alluded in the 2020 EU Methane Strategy: monitoring of methane emissions and mitigation via increased production of biogas and biomethane.

A. Agriculture

1. The Effort Sharing Decision and Regulation

Sectors not covered by the EU Emissions Trading System, such as buildings, road transport, agriculture and waste, come within the scope of the Effort Sharing Decision (2013–2020)[16] and the Effort Sharing Regulation (2021–2030). The Effort Sharing Regulation sets national reduction targets by 2030 for individual MSs, ranging between 0% and –40% compared to 2005 levels. The efforts undertaken by MSs are expected to contribute to an overall EU GHG reduction of 30% by 2030 compared to 2005 levels.

The Effort Sharing Regulation is currently under revision following the adoption of the 'Fit for 55' legislative package, in line with a new target to reduce net emissions by at least 55% by 2030 compared to 1990 levels. The proposal suggests increasing the EU-wide emission reduction target for the effort sharing sectors from 30% to 40% by 2030, compared to 2005, aligned with more ambitious national targets for MSs.[17] In addition, the proposal introduces two new flexibility mechanisms: the use of EU Emissions Trading System (ETS) allowances to offset emissions in the effort sharing sectors and the use of credits from the land use sector.

---

[12] European Commission, 'On an EU strategy to reduce methane emissions' COM (2020) 663.

[13] European Commission, 'New CAP: 2023–27' (2022) https://agriculture.ec.europa.eu/common-agricultural-policy/cap-overview/new-cap-2023-27_en accessed 25 August 2022.

[14] Directive 2008/98/EC on waste and repealing certain Directives [2008] OJ L312/3 ('Waste Framework Directive'; 'WFD').

[15] Landfill Directive (n 9).

[16] Decision 406/2009/EC on the effort of Member States to reduce their greenhouse gas emissions to meet the Community's greenhouse gas emission reduction commitments up to 2020 [2009] OJ L140/136.

[17] European Commission, 'Proposal for a Regulation amending Regulation (EU) 2018/842 on binding annual greenhouse gas emission reductions by Member States from 2021 to 2030 contributing to climate action to meet commitments under the Paris Agreement' COM (2021) 555.

The Effort Sharing Framework does not specify which mitigating actions will have to be taken to achieve the binding reduction targets; it is left to the decision of MSs. There is always a risk that GHGs reductions in agriculture will not be sufficient, which has been underpinned by the European Court of Auditors' report, which found out that CAP has so far been ineffective in reducing farm-related emissions, including methane.[18] Emissions in agriculture have not changed significantly since 2010, despite the fact that climate action has been one of the major objectives of CAP and that EUR 100 bn in CAP funds were attributed to climate action between 2014–2020. The 2020 Farm to Fork Strategy,[19] and the forthcoming legislative proposals, are expected to fill this gap.

2. The Farm to Fork Strategy and the new CAP: 2023–27

The reduction of methane emissions from agriculture is also subject to a non-binding Farm to Fork Strategy for a fair, healthy and environmentally-friendly food system. It recognises the role of farmers in reducing methane emissions from livestock by installing anaerobic digesters for biogas production from agriculture waste and residues, such as manure. The strategy recognises that other sources of waste can also be used for biogas production, including waste from the food and beverage industry, sewage, wastewater and municipal waste.

The strategy includes a couple of other measures, which could foster methane reduction, such as: placing feed additives on the market and the promotion of 'carbon-efficient' methods of livestock production. The strategy suggests a number of behavioural measures related to dietary shift through customers' empowerment and a sustainable food labelling framework, improved availability and price of sustainable food, and, potentially, tax incentives to nudge the European consumers towards more sustainable and healthy diets, for example by reducing tax rates for organic food. The strategy suggests using the EU tax system as a tool, helping to ensure that the prices of different foods reflect all the costs, including the environmental externalities.

However, the abovementioned objectives are not fully aligned with the new CAP, as the shift towards more sustainable and healthier diet implies a reduction in livestock. According to some studies, the attainment of the European

---

[18] European Court of Auditors, 'Common Agricultural Policy and Climate. Half of EU Climate Spending but Farm Emissions Are Not Decreasing' (2021).

[19] European Commission, 'A farm to fork strategy for a fair, healthy and environmentally-friendly food system' COM (2020) 381.

Green Deal objectives stipulated in the Farm to Fork Strategy is expected to lead to a decrease in livestock production by 10–15%.[20]

B. Waste

1. Waste Framework Directive

The Waste Framework Directive (WFD) is a fundament of EU waste management acquis. It defines key concepts (e.g. 'waste', 'by-product'), establishes major principles (e.g. precautionary principle, the principle of proximity[21]) and allocates responsibilities between key stakeholders. Other pieces of waste law regulate specific waste streams (e.g. batteries and accumulators, packaging waste) or forms of waste management (e.g. landfilling).The legal basis of the WFD is Article 192(1) of the Treaty on the Functioning of the EU (TFEU),[22] hence EU waste management law is part of the EU environmental policy framework.

The first WFD was adopted in the 1970s and has undergone several revisions since then. The latest revision introduced by Directive 2018/851 aligned waste management with the framework for sustainable production and consumption – circular economy.[23] This led to much more focus on waste prevention. For instance, the amended WFD prescribes the reduction of food waste by halving the per capita global food waste at the retail and consumer levels and by reducing food losses along production and supply chains by 2030.

Moreover, the WFD introduced a five-step 'waste hierarchy': prevention, reuse, recycling, recovery for other purposes (e.g. energy) and disposal as the last resort.[24] According to the EU waste hierarchy, anaerobic digestion of organic waste resulting in the production of biogas and of digestate is regarded as recycling and one of the key waste-to-energy processes promoted in the EU.[25] However, while the reduction in landfilling of biodegradable waste and the production of waste-derived biogas can lead to lower methane emissions,

---

[20] J Bremmer and others, 'Impact Assessment Study on EC 2030 Green Deal Targets for Sustainable Food Production: Effects of Farm to Fork and Biodiversity Strategy 2030 at Farm, National and EU Level' (Wageningen University & Research 2021) https://edepot.wur.nl/555349/.

[21] The principle of proximity implied that waste should be treated as close to its source as possible.

[22] Consolidated versions of the Treaty on European Union and the Treaty on the Functioning of the European Union [2016] OJ C202/1 ('TFEU').

[23] Directive (EU) 2018/851 amending Directive 2008/98/EC on waste [2018] OJ L150/109.

[24] WFD (n 14) art 4.

[25] European Commission, 'The role of waste-to-energy in the circular economy' COM (2017) 034.

it is equally important to prevent methane leaks from biogas facilities resulting from inadequate design or maintenance.[26]

Thanks to the new targets concerning municipal waste recycling (at least 55% of municipal waste by weight will have to be recycled by 2025, 60% by 2030 and 65% by 2035) and separate collection of biowaste set out in the WFD,[27] as well as the application of requirements specified in the Landfill Directive presented below, the production of biogas derived from waste, which could be used in cogeneration, injected into the gas grid, and used in transport fuels, is expected to increase in the EU. The 2021 European Biogas Association data confirm that, as of 2013, the share of biogas derived from energy crops is decreasing in favour of agriculture substrates, municipal waste and sewage sludge.[28]

2. Landfill Directive

Directive 1999/31 on the landfill of waste (Landfill Directive) is the building block of the EU waste policy. The Directive does not directly address the issue of methane emissions, but it sets out a broader aim of preventing, and if that is not possible, reducing the negative impact of landfills on the environment, in particular on surface water, groundwater, soil, air and human health. The aim is to be achieved by introducing more stringent operational and technical requirements for waste and landfills.

The directive introduces basic definitions, for example of 'waste' and 'landfill', and three categories of landfill sites: landfills for hazardous waste; landfills for non-hazardous waste (municipal waste) and landfills for inert waste (waste that will not decompose or burn, e.g. sand and stone). It mandates that EU countries implement national strategies to decrease the amount of biodegradable waste disposed of in landfills and sets out new requirements for landfill site operators. They must apply for permits and provide additional information, including operating, monitoring and control plans, and details of closure and after-care procedures.

The Landfill Directive was amended by Directive 2018/850 to facilitate the transition to a circular economy.[29] The Directive introduces new restrictions on landfilling of waste from 2030 and aims to limit the share of municipal waste landfilled to 10% by 2035. Additionally, it sets out rules on

---

[26] ibid.

[27] WFD (n 14) art 11.

[28] European Biogas Association (EBA), 'EBA Statistical Report' (European Biogas Association 2021) https://www.europeanbiogas.eu/eba-statistical-report-2021/ accessed 25 August 2022.

[29] Directive (EU) 2018/850 amending Directive 1999/31/EC on the landfill of waste [2018] OJ L150/100.

the calculation of the attainment of municipal waste targets, quality control and a traceability system for municipal waste landfilled. EU members are required to send reports on the implementation of the Landfill Directive to the European Commission every three years, based on a predefined questionnaire. Moreover, the European Commission and the European Environment Agency (EEA) are required to prepare early warning reports identifying shortcomings in the attainment of the targets and recommending corrective action three years before each deadline. Lastly, the revised Landfill Directive allows MSs to apply economic instruments and other measures to promote the application of the waste hierarchy introduced by the WFD.

3. Non-binding Guidance on Landfill Gas Control

The non-binding Guidance on Landfill Gas Control provides clarity on landfill gas management and establishes key criteria for the collection, treatment and use of landfill gas.[30] In particular, the Guidance suggests that methane captured can be injected into the gas mains, and thus used to generate electricity and heat or utilised directly as fuel.

C. EU Methane Strategies

The 2020 EU strategy to reduce methane emissions is currently the key document setting out a broad EU vision for the reduction of 'the other GHG'.[31] The strategy is part of the EU long-term climate strategy, the European Green Deal. The legal basis for the EU methane strategy proposal is Article 16 of Regulation 2018/1999 on the Governance of the Energy Union, which requires the EU Commission to take into account the objectives of a circular economy.[32]

Like the first EU methane strategy published in 1996,[33] the document concentrates on three major sources of emissions, indicating energy, agriculture and waste as the sectors with the highest needs for methane emissions abatement. However, in contrast to the first strategy document, the 2020 strategy does not propose any reduction targets. It only notes that meeting

---

[30] European Commission, 'Landfill Waste' https://environment.ec.europa.eu/topics/waste-and-recycling/landfill-waste_en accessed 25 August 2022.

[31] 'On an EU strategy to reduce methane emissions' (n 12).

[32] Regulation (EU) 2018/1999 on the governance of the energy union and climate action, amending Regulations (EC) 663/2009 and (EC) 715/2009, Directives 94/22/EC, 98/70/EC, 2009/31/EC, 2009/73/EC, 2010/31/EU, 2012/27/EU and 2013/30/EU, Council Directives 2009/119/EC and (EU) 2015/652 and repealing Regulation (EU) 525/2013 [2018] OJ L328/1.

[33] European Commission, 'Strategy paper for reducing methane emissions' COM (96) 557.

the upgraded 55% GHG reduction target by 2030 requires stepping up reductions of methane by an additional 6–8% in comparison to current policies on non-CO_2 emissions. In other words, EU methane emissions need to be reduced by 35–37% by 2030 compared to 2005 levels.

Another difference is that in the new document the EU executive recognises the synergies and trade-offs related to the reduction of methane emissions from the three key sources, especially in terms of biogas production. Moreover, the EU Commission puts much more emphasis on the monitoring, reporting and verification (MRV) of methane emissions. Third, the 2020 strategy recognises that the EU has a limited impact on global emissions. Therefore, it suggests intensified collaboration with other countries and international organisations to promote further reduction of methane emissions globally.

The strategy suggests a series of sectoral measures to manage methane emissions. The approach to reduce farm-related emissions is founded on 'a balance of technologies, markets and dietary changes [and] reduced fossil hydrocarbon inputs', ensuring business opportunities for farmers, and the cornerstone of EU food policy, the Farm to Fork Strategy. Therefore, the EU Commission has suggested the following measures:

- creation of an expert group on life-cycle methane emission metrics (in the first half of 2021);
- development of the inventory of best practices and available mitigation technologies and innovative technologies, focusing on the most effective ways to reduce emissions from enteric fermentation (by the end of 2021);
- encouraging MSs to include methane reduction schemes in their strategic plans for the CAP, for example carbon farming initiatives;
- revision of the Effort Sharing Regulation;
- targeted research – technology and nature-based solutions leading to a reduction of methane emissions and dietary shift (Horizon Europe Strategic Plan 2021–2024);
- potentially, bringing cattle rearing within the scope of the Industrial Emissions Directive.

Given the significant reductions in GHGs from the waste sector, the EU actions are likely to focus on the enforcement of existing legal requirements (targets for biodegradable waste, treatment of biodegradable waste prior to disposal) and:

- reviewing the Landfill Directive in 2024: improving landfill gas management, reducing climate effects and using synergies related to clean energy production;
- adopting conclusions on best available techniques for landfilling;

- targeted research on waste to biomethane technologies (Horizon Europe Strategic Plan 2021–2024);
- potentially, reviewing the Urban Waste Water Treatment Directive to reduce emissions from sewage sludge.

IV. PRODUCTION OF BIOMETHANE: OPPORTUNITIES AND RISKS

The production of biogas from organic waste could contribute to reducing methane emissions from agriculture and waste, but also to the broader EU circular economy objectives and decarbonisation of the gas sector. Biowaste from households, plant by-products, animal by-products, industrial and municipal organic wastes and sludges, wood by-products and sequential crops could provide considerable feedstock for biogas production. There are calls for rapid scaling up of biogas and biomethane production[34]. The European Commission estimates a potential of 350 TWh per year for 2030 of biogas produced from sustainably harvested biomass.[35] That could cover up to 10% of gas consumption. For 2050 the potential could reach 1,000 TWh.

Biomethane is now substantially cheaper than natural gas and with the increasing carbon price this tendency can be sustained. Biomethane is produced locally, strengthening security of supply and creating jobs. It has the potential to make a significant contribution to a sustainable energy supply, replacing fossil fuel and avoiding methane emissions from manure and waste. Biomethane could be used in industry, power generation, transport and buildings. It can be stored easily, helping to deal with demand and supply fluctuations. Biomethane use in combination with carbon capture and storage could provide for negative emissions helping to achieve carbon neutrality. To achieve all this, potential substantial scaling up of production and upgrade of biogas for biomethane and its injection in the grid are needed.

European legislation provides important safeguards that the biomass used for biogas production should be produced in a sustainable manner.[36] The use of bioenergy should fulfil the sustainability and GHG emissions saving criteria. Still, the issue of methane emissions is not sufficiently addressed.

---

[34] Gas for Climate, 'Biomethane Declaration' https://gasforclimate2050.eu/news-item/new-analysis-report-explores-the-future-role-of-biomethane/.

[35] European Commission, 'A clean planet for all – a european strategic long-term vision for a prosperous, modern, competitive and climate neutral economy' COM (2018) 773.

[36] Directive (EU) 2018/2001 on the promotion of the use of energy from renewable sources [2018] OJ L 328/82 ('RED II').

A recent study analysing fugitive emissions from biogas plants finds that fugitive losses related to biogas production can be as high as 9%,[37] suggesting that more efforts are necessary to regularly monitor and prevent such emissions. The proposed methane legislation covers biomethane use in pipelines, but not the production facilities. To avoid methane leakages in biogas installation the mirroring of MRV from the fossil energy sector could be considered and obligations for regular leak detection and repair programmes requested. Technologies are available both for the monitoring and prevention of fugitive emissions, but legal frameworks would guarantee that they are applied.

V. FILLING THE GAPS: POLICY RECOMMENDATIONS

Awareness of the impact of methane emissions on global warming has led to improved methane policies in many countries. By the end of 2021 over 100 countries representing 70% of the global economy joined the Global Methane Pledge (GMP). The GMP is a collective aim to reduce global methane emissions by at least 30% from 2020 levels by 2030. GMP signatories also commit to improving inventory methodologies to quantify methane emissions, particularly from high emitting sources. Current policies are mostly focused on fossil methane emissions, where mitigation measures are largely not producing net costs. As fossil fuel use will decrease as a result of climate policies, attention should now turn to methane emissions from the agriculture and waste sectors.

Mitigation of methane emissions is still the main target, but improving waste and agricultural production related methane emission management can be one way of producing sustainable energy. 'Sustainable biogas systems include processes for the treatment of waste, for protection of the environment, for conversion of low value material to higher value material, and for the production of electricity, heat and advanced gaseous biofuel', believes the International Energy Agency (IEA).[38] Existing gas infrastructure can be fully used to transport biomethane to customers to provide energy services in all consumption sectors. Such an approach will provide opportunities to create jobs in rural areas and support farmers' incomes. As agricultural activities absorb GHGs through the process of photosynthesis, responsible management of methane emissions from the agriculture and waste sectors would provide an import source for the circular economy. To achieve this, activities should

---

[37] Semra Bakkaloglu and others, 'Quantification of Methane Emissions from UK Biogas Plants' (2021) 124 Waste Management 82.

[38] Anton Fagerström and others, *The Role of Anaerobic Digestion and Biogas in the Circular Economy* (IEA Bioenergy Task 37 2018) https://www.ieabioenergy.com/blog/publications/the-role-of-anaerobic-digestion-and-biogas-in-the-circular-economy/.

focus on four areas: MRV in the agriculture and waste sectors; applying best practices to mitigate methane emissions; advancing the sustainable production of biomethane; and the responsible operation of biomethane plants.

A. Measurement, Reporting and Verification of Methane Emissions from the Agriculture and Waste Sectors

Monitoring, verifying and reporting methane emissions from the agriculture and waste sectors is more complex than in the energy sector. The EU Methane Strategy has announced an ambition to make Tier 3 methane reporting more widespread across the EU.[39] To report methane emissions, UNFCCC has developed a three-tier reporting framework, from simple estimations in Tier 1 to modelling based on measurements in Tier 3. In many cases, reporting on a Tier 1 basis seriously underestimates methane emissions and these data are difficult to verify. For serious policy measures, the point of departure is good knowledge of real emissions. The European Commission proposes in the Strategy a temporary objective of applying Tier 2 approaches with disaggregation of EFs in the agricultural sector because of the high number of stakeholders involved. In the waste sector, improvements should be made regarding wastewater to achieve Tier 3 level. The quality of reporting of waste disposal in landfill sites is considered satisfactory. Even with the temporary lower ambition for the agriculture sector, it is clear that all methane emission reporting in the EU should reach Tier 3 level. The transition will be supported by considerable development in methane emission measurement technologies. The scope of various technologies is already broad. Data provided by measurement and modelling are needed to decide on the scope of mitigation actions.

The potential measures that the EU Commission could consider to achieve this objective include: introducing a methane emissions monitoring requirement for industrial livestock production sites; continual improvement of EU reporting to UNFCCC (through methodological improvements and emission measurement campaigns) and better coordination between UNFCCC reporting and the International Methane Observatory (IMEO).

B. Applying and Continuing to Improve Best Practices to Mitigate Methane Emissions

Methane emission mitigation could be achieved by more sustainable production through innovation and technology. Improvement of animal diets, herd management and manure management are instruments that are proven.

[39] 'On an EU strategy to reduce methane emissions' (n 12).

The biggest potential for reducing methane intensity is in novel approaches to feeding (improving the mix of feed materials like incorporating seaweed in cattle feed, feed additives, feeding techniques). There are still many challenges. Targeted research on the different factors that lead to methane emission reduction will help, as will setting up a life-cycle methodology on overall emissions from livestock. Methane emissions from rice fields can be reduced by appropriate agricultural practices (rewetting, drying). To facilitate emission mitigation at the farm level, in 2022 the European Commission intends to provide a digital carbon navigator template and guidelines on common pathways for the quantitative calculation of GHG emissions and removals. Dissemination of best practices and cooperation among farmers are important factors to mitigate methane emissions from agriculture. To facilitate this, an inventory of best practices and available technologies is being developed. Technological developments are being supported by the European Innovation Council (EIC).[40] The EIC Accelerator Challenge 'Technologies for "Fit for 55"' supports the development and scaling up of sustainable agriculture, including abatement of methane emissions.

In waste management, landfill operators are legally required to use landfill gas to generate energy or flare it. The obligation to collect biodegradable waste separately and an overall limit on landfilling of waste should considerably decrease methane emissions from landfills. Collecting and treating wastewater in centralised facilities helps prevent significant methane emissions. However, there are still no legal requirements on mitigating methane emissions from wastewater and sewage sludge. The revision of the relevant legislation could propose measures to mitigate methane emissions. The application of new technologies and incentives to convert waste to biomethane could provide a step change in dealing with human waste. Only 2% of the 105 billion tonnes of organic waste produced globally each year is treated and recycled. Efficient treatment of this waste could decrease GHG emissions by 10% by 2030.[41]

A significant reduction in methane emissions is unlikely without behavioural changes such as dietary shifts. A recent study[42] demonstrates the co-benefits of shifting to a sustainable diet (e.g. where animal-sourced proteins constitute a limited part of the diet and it includes more plant-sourced protein) in terms of both health outcomes (reduced cancer incidence rates) and reduc-

---

40 European Innovation Council (EIC), 'European Innovation Council Accelerator' (2021) https://eic.ec.europa.eu/eic-funding-opportunities/eic-accelerator_en#ecl-inpage-136 accessed 19 January 2022.

41 European Commission, 'Sustainable carbon cycles' COM (2021) 800.

42 Jessica E Laine and others, 'Co-Benefits from Sustainable Dietary Shifts for Population and Environmental Health: An Assessment from a Large European Cohort Study' (2021) 5 The Lancet Planetary Health e786.

ing greenhouse gas emissions and land use. Measures at the EU level could start with awareness-raising campaigns and food labelling encouraging better consumer choices.

C. Sustainable Production of Biomethane

Non-recyclable human and agriculture waste and residues can be used to produce biogas. The biogas produced can be used directly to generate heat and electrical power or be upgraded to biomethane, which has a very broad application range. Sustainable biogas production has an important potential to support the decarbonisation of the EU's economy and cost-efficiently mitigate methane emissions from the waste and agriculture sectors. The technological process also produces digestate, which could replace mined fertilisers as a sustainable soil improver. It is essential for biogas production to be based on waste or residues as biogas derived from food or feed crops increases methane emissions. This could require incentives to collect and use high methane emitting organic waste and residues. The measures to support biogas production should be carefully designed in line with the general criteria for bioenergy and to avoid creating perverse incentives, which could lead to an overall increase in waste. Monitoring and verification of the sustainability of the biomethane produced should accompany these developments.

D. Responsible Operation of Biomethane Plants

The biogas industry uses anaerobic digestion to produce methane emissions from waste and agricultural residues. While anaerobic digestion helps to avoid methane emissions, the methane emissions from the process should also be avoided from biomethane plants. The potential leaking components are quite well known. Emissions in the receiving stage can be avoided by tightly covering open tanks and controlling the temperature and pH value. Diffusion through gas holder membranes can be considerably reduced by performing regular maintenance of foils. Gas holders should not be filled above 50% to avoid emissions from safety valves. The residual biogas should be kept in gas-tight covered digestate storage tanks that are connected to the gas system. During biogas utilisation methane emissions can occur in a biogas plant. In the case of a malfunction of a Combined Heat and Power plant, the excess gas must be burned by flaring, so that the methane is converted to carbon dioxide and water. All plants need to have leak detection and repair programmes to address the leaks identified.

The growing size of the global population and the climate change threat require an accelerated approach to the circular economy. Methane emissions are part of the food and waste sectors. Untreated they do much harm, but with appropriate policies in place they could provide value. In the waste sector some steps have been taken, while in the agriculture sector we are still at the beginning of this process. A step change could be achieved by putting activities related to the mitigation of methane emissions from all sectors into Nationally Determined Contributions (NDCs). This would provide a more focused and stable policy framework.

Beside a regulatory framework, incentives to promote biogas and biomethane production are needed because there is direct competition with fossil fuels. An increased carbon price could lead to an unsubsidised market, but still much attention will be needed to monitor the sustainability of value chains. The EU taxonomy has recognised anaerobic digestion of biowaste and sewage sludge as economic activities substantially contributing to climate change mitigation.[43] This regulation also established technical screening criteria for the construction and operation of dedicated facilities for the treatment of separately collected biowaste through anaerobic digestion, with the resulting production and utilisation of biogas and digestate and/or chemicals. This requires monitoring and contingency plans to minimise methane leakage at facilities and requirements on the input feedstock. Input feedstock should be source segregated and collected separately and the share of food and feed crops should be limited to 10%. The biogas produced could be used directly to generate electricity and heat or upgraded to biomethane and injected into the gas grid.

In 2020 combined biogas and biomethane production covered 4.6% of the gas demand in the EU and had created 210,000 jobs. The industry believes that volumes of sustainably produced biogas and biomethane could at least double by 2030. The EU is clearly embarking on the path to a circular economy by using methane produced from waste. However, this is only the beginning.

VI. CONCLUSION

The European Climate Law establishes a binding objective for the EU to reach climate neutrality by 2050.[44] The pathway includes phasing out fossil fuels, starting with coal followed by oil and gas. However, society will continue to

---

43 Commission Delegated Regulation (EU) 2021/2139 supplementing Regulation (EU) 2020/852 by establishing the technical screening criteria for determining the conditions under which an economic activity qualifies as contributing substantially to climate change mitigation or climate change adaptation and for determining whether that economic activity causes no significant harm to any of the other environmental objectives [2021] OJ L442/1.

44 Regulation (EU) 2021/1119 establishing the framework for achieving climate neutrality and amending Regulations (EC) 401/2009 and (EU) 2018/1999 [2021] OJ L243/1 ('European Climate Law').

need carbon even with a decreased demand. This carbon should be sustainably sourced from our ecosystems and our industries. Particular attention should be focused on recycling carbon from waste streams. Methane emissions are very much related to this and agricultural production. There are many opportunities to substantially reduce these emissions, but a large part of them could be used to generate electricity and heat, as vehicle fuel or as feedstock in the chemical industry. Carbon dependency could be at least partially solved with a sustainable carbon cycle based on capture and sustainable production of biogas and biomethane. Establishing a sustainable carbon cycle in the EU economy and ecosystems is a long-term endeavour that requires coordinating action now.[45] Some of the actions require innovative technologies, but to avoid any pitfalls robust MRV must be established for all anthropogenic methane emissions.

LEGISLATION

Consolidated versions of the Treaty on European Union and the Treaty on the Functioning of the European Union [2016] OJ C202/1 ('TFEU')

Directive 1999/31/EC on the landfill of waste [1999] OJ L182/1 ('Landfill Directive')

Directive (EU) 2018/850 amending Directive 1999/31/EC on the landfill of waste [2018] OJ L150/100

Directive (EU) 2018/2001 on the promotion of the use of energy from renewable sources [2018] OJ L 328/82 ('RED II')

Directive 2008/98/EC on waste and repealing certain Directives [2008] OJ L312/3 ('Waste Framework Directive'; 'WFD')

Regulation (EU) 2018/842 on binding annual greenhouse gas emission reductions by Member States from 2021 to 2030 contributing to climate action to meet commitments under the Paris Agreement and amending Regulation (EU) 525/2013 [2018] OJ L156/26 ('Effort Sharing Regulation'; 'ESR')

Regulation (EU) 2021/1119 establishing the framework for achieving climate neutrality and amending Regulations (EC) 401/2009 and (EU) 2018/1999 [2021] OJ L243/1 ('European Climate Law')

Regulation (EU) 2018/1999 on the governance of the energy union and climate action, amending Regulations (EC) 663/2009 and (EC) 715/2009, Directives 94/22/EC, 98/70/EC, 2009/31/EC, 2009/73/EC, 2010/31/EU, 2012/27/EU and 2013/30/EU, Council Directives 2009/119/EC and (EU) 2015/652 and repealing Regulation (EU) 525/2013 [2018] OJ L328/1

Delegated Regulation (EU) 2021/2139 supplementing Regulation (EU) 2020/852 by establishing the technical screening criteria for determining the conditions under which an economic activity qualifies as contributing substantially to climate change mitigation or climate change adaptation and for determining whether that economic activity causes no significant harm to any of the other environmental objectives [2021] OJ L442/1

---

45 'Sustainable Carbon Cycles' (n 41).

Decision 406/2009/EC on the effort of Member States to reduce their greenhouse gas emissions to meet the Community's greenhouse gas emission reduction commitments up to 2020 [2009] OJ L140/136

PART III

Cross-Sectoral Issues

9. The Energy Tax Directive reform

Álvaro Antón Antón[1]

I. INTRODUCTION

The European Green Deal establishes the objective of 'zero net-emissions' by 2050. The achievement of the objective will require a greenhouse gas (GHG) emissions reduction of 55% by 2030.[2] This political commitment has become a legally binding obligation as a result of Regulation 2021/119 (the 'Climate Law').[3] This Regulation sets out a binding objective of climate neutrality in the European Union (EU) by 2050 in pursuit of the long-term temperature goal set out in point (a) of Article 2(1) of the Paris Agreement,[4] and provides a framework for achieving progress in pursuit of the global adaptation goal established in Article 7 of the Paris Agreement. The Regulation also sets out a binding Union target of a net domestic reduction in GHG for 2030. According to Article 2.2 of the 'Climate Law', the relevant EU institutions and the Member States (MSs) shall take the necessary measures at Union and national level, respectively, to enable the collective achievement of the climate-neutrality objective. According to the Regulation, the objective must be achieved considering the importance of promoting both fairness and solidarity between MSs and cost-effectiveness in order to achieve this objective.

Within this broader package, the chapter focuses on the Energy System Integration Strategy, which is meant to move the EU towards a more integrated energy system.[5] Such a system would be more energy efficient and circular,

---

1 This chapter is the result of research completed under the Research Project Environmental tax reforms for a fair green and digital recovery: Spain in the European context (PID2020-119151RB-I00).

2 European Commission, 'The European Green Deal' COM (2019) 640.

3 Regulation (EU) 2021/1119 establishing the framework for achieving climate neutrality and amending Regulations (EC) 401/2009 and (EU) 2018/1999 [2021] OJ L243/1 ('European Climate Law').

4 Council Decision (EU) 2016/1841 on the conclusion, on behalf of the European Union, of the Paris Agreement adopted under the United Nations Framework Convention on Climate Change [2016] OJ L282/1.

5 See also Chapter 1 in this volume.

stimulate further renewables-based electrification and further use of renewable and low-carbon fuels in those sectors where electrification is not yet a viable option. This would require reusing waste heat and biomass wastes and residues, promoting renewable-based electrification in sectors such as transport, buildings, industry and promoting the use of renewable and low-carbon fuels.[6]

Pricing instruments could play a fundamental and complementary role in the context of the described roadmap, which, in turn, is related to others such as the Circular Economic Action Plan,[7] particularly regarding the objectives related to the conversion of biological waste and residues into biofuels and biogas. For example, getting the price of fossil fuels right will encourage the switch to advanced biofuels and other renewable energy products. The use and development of advanced biofuels[8] will be essential not only for the transition to a carbon-neutral economy as planned by the European Green Deal, but also for the transition to a green economy in line with the objectives of the EU NextGeneration Recovery Plan.[9] In fact, the International Energy Agency (IEA) has stated that replacing fossil fuels with advanced biofuels is one of the primary ways to decarbonise the transport sector, especially in the initial phases of the transition to a neutral emission mobility. Advanced biofuels in particular will play a fundamental role by presenting the advantage of being functionally equivalent to fuels derived from petroleum and compatible with the existing fuel infrastructure.[10]

Despite their pivotal role in low-carbon scenarios, advanced biofuels are produced on a limited scale. Scholars have stated that, from the perspective

---

[6] European Commission, 'Impact Assessment of the Renewable Energy Directive (EU) 2018/2011 on the promotion of the use of energy from renewable sources' SWD (2021) 621.

[7] European Commission, 'A new Circular Energy Action for a cleaner and more competitive Europe' COM (2020) 98.

[8] Advanced biofuels are energy products produced from non-food-crop feedstocks (wastes, residues and dedicated crops that are produced in a way that does not compete with food crops – such as crops grown on marginal land). Capable of delivering significant lifecycle GHG emissions reductions compared with fossil fuel alternatives, they are considered sustainable as they do not directly compete with food and feed crops for agricultural land or cause adverse sustainability impacts. In the specific case of the EU, Directive (EU) 2018/2001 (on the promotion of the use of energy from renewable sources [2018] OJ L328/82 ('RED II')) defines advanced biofuels as biofuels that are produced from feedstocks listed in its Annex IX. See, Adam Brown and others, 'Advanced Biofuels – Potential for Cost Reduction' (Task 41, IEA Bioenergy, 2020).

[9] The use and supply of biomass will not only reduce emissions and dependence on imported fossil fuels, but might also create employment in rural areas.

[10] See David Chiaramonti and others, 'The Challenge of Forecasting the Role of Biofuel in EU Transport Decarbonisation at 2050: A Meta-analysis Review of Published Scenarios' (2021) 139 Renewable & Sustainable Energy Reviews.

of end use and its introduction in the market, advanced biofuel faces both challenges related to economic aspects (appropriate prices) and technical challenges such as: (i) fuel quality; (ii) the compatibility of the engine; and (iii) the improvements required in the infrastructure to process, store and sell said fuels.[11] From an economic point of view, the main challenge of advanced biofuels it that their production costs are currently higher than conventional biofuels and the fossil fuels they are intended to replace.[12] From this perspective, the support of public policies will be necessary to allow these technologies to mature, either by internalising the positive externalities of these products and, therefore, adding value to low-carbon fuels; or by adding a significant carbon cost to fossil fuels by removing subsidies to these products or by internalising their negative externalities through carbon pricing policies. For that reason, if the objective of the European Green Deal is to radically reduce the EU's climate impact, it is imperative to incorporate the transport sector and household emissions into carbon pricing tools.

In recent years, both scholars and international institutions have supported well-designed carbon pricing instruments, which could help States steer their economies towards and along a carbon-neutral growth path.[13] Carbon pricing instruments are efficient and effective policies to achieve climate goals and support a green recovery. Setting an explicit price on carbon can translate into changes in behaviour and direct companies and consumers towards less polluting alternatives while mobilising resources to achieve the budgetary and environmental objectives of the States.[14] Emissions trading systems, on the one hand, and carbon or CO_2 taxes, on the other, have become the main economic instruments to introduce price signals of this kind.[15]

In the EU, economic instruments already in force, such as the EU Emissions Trading System (ETS) and the Energy Tax Directive (ETD),[16] could play a sig-

---

[11] Calliope Panoutsou and others, 'Advanced Biofuels to Decarbonise European Transport by 2030: Markets, Challenges, and Policies that Impact their Successful Market Uptake' (2021) 34 Energy Strategy Reviews.

[12] The costs of producing advanced biofuels is estimated in the range of 62 €/MWh to 158 €/MWh for production based on biomass feedstocks, and 48 to 104 €/MWh for waste-based production. This indicates a significant cost gap with the price of the fossil fuels of between 12 €/MWh and 128 €/MWh. See Brown and others (n 8).

[13] OECD, *Taxing Energy Use for Sustainable Development: Opportunities for Energy Tax and Subsidy Reform in Selected Developing and Emerging Economies* (OECD 2021).

[14] OECD, *Effective Carbon Rates. Pricing CO2 through Taxes and Emissions Trading Systems* (OECD 2016).

[15] World Bank, *State and Trends of Carbon Pricing 2020* (World Bank 2020).

[16] Directive 2003/96/EC restructuring the Community framework for the taxation of energy products and electricity [2003] OJ L283/31 ('ETD').

nificant and complementary role in carrying out this intervention for carbon pricing and make advanced biofuels cost-competitive. However, to date, none of these instruments seems to have been effective in introducing an adequate price signal to favour renewable energy products. In fact, studies by the European Commission show that there is clearly scope to apply the 'polluter pays principle' (PPP) more rigorously through an expansion of environmental taxation and other economic instruments in the EU because, currently, the costs of pollution and environmental damage greatly exceed the revenues generated from taxes and other economic instruments to tackle polluting activities.[17] As a matter of fact, as the European Court of Auditors (ECA) has confirmed, many opportunities for a more rigorous application of the PPP in the EU have still been missed.[18]

The EU ETS, a cap-and-trade system, is the key tool for reducing GHG emissions cost-effectively in the EU. It applies a carbon price set by the market, mainly on emissions from installations in the power generation sector and from energy-intensive industries.[19] However, the EU ETS only covers around 40% of the EU's GHGs and sets free emission allowances for some sectors as a safeguard for the international competitiveness of industrial sectors at risk of carbon leakage. The EU is working on the revision of its climate, energy and transport-related legislation under the so-called 'Fit for 55' package and has proposed a comprehensive set of changes to the existing ETS. The proposal notably aims to phase out free allocation of emission allowances to sectors that are to be covered by the carbon border adjustment mechanism and create a new self-standing emissions trading system for buildings and road transport.

Explicit carbon pricing, via emission trading systems or carbon taxes, is not the only way to achieve climate goals. There are numerous levers and indirect ways to create incentives for 'decarbonisation': energy taxes, car registration taxes and circulation (for example, on automobiles powered by combustion engines), the elimination of subsidies on fossil energy products or product standards and regulations. This range of instruments has the potential to emit implicit signals in carbon prices.

---

17 The external costs of air pollution and GHG amount approximately to €720 billion per year –around 5% of EU GDP – of which just 44% is internalised. See David Mottershead and others, *Green Taxation and Other Economic Instruments. Internalizing Environmental Costs to Make the Polluter Pay* (Publication Office of the European Union 2021).

18 European Court of Auditors (ECA), *The Polluter Pays Principle: Inconsistent application across EU environmental policies and actions* (Special Report 12/2021, ECA 2021).

19 Directive 2003/87/EC establishing a system for greenhouse gas emission allowance trading within the Union and amending Council Directive 96/61/EC [2003] OJ L275/32 ('ETS').

In this context, the ETD could play a key role in the field of climate and energy policy. However, the current ETD is not aligned with the rest of the objectives of the European Green Deal and is an inefficient instrument both for setting carbon prices and for discouraging the consumption of fossil fuels. For this reason, the 'Fit for 55' package also includes a proposal to review the ETD to align energy taxation with the energy, environmental and climate policies of the EU.

Considering the described context, this chapter will analyse the role of energy taxes in the EU's Energy System Integration Strategy. Specifically, it will consider whether the European Commission's proposal to review the ETD is in conformity with the Strategy in so far as it can create incentives to produce advanced biofuels. The remainder of this chapter is structured as follows: Section II discusses the environmental aspects of energy taxes. Section III sets out the EU's energy taxation framework, which forms the basis of the analysis in Section IV as to the divergence between the EU's energy taxation policies and the Green Deal. Section V analyses the proposal presented by the European Commission in 2021 to modify the ETD to align it with the objectives of the European Green Deal. Section VI concludes.

II. ENERGY TAXES: ENVIRONMENTALLY DRIVEN TAXES?

Apart from pricing mechanisms such as the ETS, the European Green Deal shows a continuing commitment to environmental taxes. Principally, the so-called 'environmental taxes' seek to provide the right price signals to the market and promote changes in the national tax systems. Therefore, environmental taxes are instruments of environmental policy that can contribute to achieving more efficient tax systems and a higher level of protection of the environment. Thus, well-designed environmental taxes might form part of the group of policy reforms to deliver on the EU's increased ambition in the climate and energy areas. Apart from the internalisation of externalities through effective carbon pricing instruments and the precise application of the PPP, these price-based instruments are meant to create the right environment for green innovation. As the Court of Justice of the European Union (CJEU) pointed out, we are talking about taxes that must present a structure (specifically, with respect to their tax base, taxable event and type of tax) designed in such a way that either they emit a sufficient price signal between the most polluting alternatives or with worse environmental behaviour so that taxpayers orient their behaviour towards more sustainable alternatives, or they directly promote the use of other products with less harmful effects on the environment via tax advantages.[20]

In this sense, it must be taken into account that organisations such as the Organisation for Economic Co-operation and Development (OECD) or the EU define environmental taxes as those 'whose tax base is a physical unit (or a similar physical unit) of some material that has a proven and specific negative impact on the environment'.[21] According to this definition, the environmental nature of a tax depends largely on the configuration of the essential elements that compose it and, specifically, on its tax base. Therefore, when the link between the tax base and damage to the environment is weak, the tax runs the risk of not having the desired impact and, in parallel, of introducing unnecessary distortions and costly production and consumption decisions. Problems related with the configuration of the tax base could however be solved by setting the rest of the structure of the tax so that other elements of it consider the impact that different products have on the environment. Thus, for example, a tax that includes in its scope of application both fossil and renewable energy products could maintain an environmental character – despite including the sustainable alternative in its tax base – if it sets a preferential tax rate, a differentiated price signal, for products with better environmental performance.

At the same time, a tax classified as environmental due to the configuration of its tax base may not be useful to achieve the intended environmental objective, for example, because the tax rate is not adequate to inducing a change in behaviour. In relation to this issue, it must be considered that carrying out an adequate quantification of the tax rate is essential so that the environmental objective is not relegated to the background, becoming only a stable collection instrument. This issue is usually appreciated in the stability of the collection levels obtained through these taxes, because most polluters subjected to the tax end up paying it to continue maintaining the same level of pollution.[22]

Therefore, the 'official' definition of environmental tax becomes too broad when we bear in mind that many of the so-called 'environmental taxes' neither pursue a genuine environmental objective, nor are they correctly designed in accordance with environmental principles such as the PPP. In fact, some energy taxes are classified as 'environmental taxes' based exclusively on the configuration of their tax base, only because their tax base is a polluting sub-

---

[20] Case C-82/12, *Transportes Jordi Besora SL v Generalitat de Catalunya* ECLI:EU:C:2014:108 [2014].

[21] Regulation (EU) 691/2011 on European environmental economic accounts [2011] OJ L192/1.

[22] Iñaki Bilbao Estrada, 'El sistema tributario como complemento de los instrumentos económicos previstos en el protocolo de Kioto' (2009) 113 Seguridad y medio ambiente 52.

stance or activity.[23] Thus, they will maintain the environmental qualification despite responding to an eminently fiscal objective or resulting in a preferential tax regime for certain non-sustainable energy products; in many cases, to mitigate the possible loss of competitiveness of companies or sectors most affected by the price increase associated with the tax or, in many others, to mitigate the impact of the cost increase on households. Consequently, although some taxes, especially in the field of energy and transport, are classified as environmental, the reality is that their design is not always aligned with the achievement of these objectives.[24]

Energy-related taxes are often included among mechanisms designed to protect the environment. However, these energy taxes are, above all, collection taxes that may include certain non-fiscal elements, in this case, aimed at protecting the environment. Therefore, in a broad sense, energy taxation would encompass all tax measures that affect the energy sector.[25] Specifically, the energy taxation family would include all the excise taxes levied on certain energy products, electricity or production technologies (nuclear, solar, wind, hydraulic) in any of their production phases (extraction, generation, distribution). In general, energy taxes are based on energy products for transportation (such as gasoline, diesel, natural gas, kerosene, or fuel oil) or on energy products for stationary applications (such as fuel oil, natural gas, coal, coke, biofuels and electricity). In most cases they take the form of excise taxes on fuel consumption and usually apply a tax rate per physical unit (litre or kilogram) or energy unit (kilowatt hour or gigajoule).

However, while energy taxes cannot be classified *per se* as environmental taxes, the structure of certain energy taxes would allow them to fit into both categories.[26] Likewise, it should be taken into account that, although they cannot be qualified as 'environmental taxes' in the strict sense, it is possible to introduce 'environmental tax elements' in energy taxes to force their internal logic towards an environmental purpose – i.e., by introducing tax incentives or

---

[23] Alice Pirlot, 'Exploring the Impact of EU Law on Energy and Environmental Taxation' in Christiana HJI Panayi, Werner Haslehner and Edoardo Traversa (eds), *Research Handbook in European Union Taxation Law* (Edward Elgar 2020).

[24] Federica Pitrone, 'Design of Energy Taxes in the European Union: Looking for a Higher Level of Environmental Protection' in Pasquale Pistone and Marta Villar Ezcurra (eds), *Energy Taxation, Environmental Protection and State Aids: Tracing the Path from Divergence to Convergence* (IBFD 2016).

[25] Marta Villar and Federica Pitrone, 'The Concept of "Environmental Taxes" in the Energy Sector: Possible Solutions in a State Aid Context' in Marta Villar Ezcurra (ed), *State Aids, Taxation and the Energy Sector* (Thomson Reuters-Aranzadi 2017).

[26] Marta Villar and Pernille Wegener Jesses, *Energy Taxation and Key Legal Concepts in the EU State Aid Context: Looking for a Common Understanding* (CEU Ediciones 2015).

tax modulations into their structure or quantification elements. In this regard, the European Green Deal emphasises that the energy taxation framework should support the clean energy transition, contribute to sustainable and fair growth, and reflect social equity considerations.

Particularly, energy taxes could play this complementary role as long as they are designed in such a way that they give the correct price signals in order to modify the behaviour of economic agents (households and companies): either by introducing incentives for eco-friendly behaviours through tax incentives, or by introducing disincentives to discourage harmful ones by taxing more heavily activities that negatively affect the environment (negative externalities).

Consequently, a well-designed rule for energy taxes (based on well-designed tax rates, a correct configuration of the tax base and an adequate use of revenues) has the potential to lower emissions by reducing the demand for carbon-intensive energy products while increasing demand for carbon-efficient ones (since their lower tax burden will reflect their positive externalities in terms of GHG reduction).

A fiscal system based on taxes of these characteristics can represent not only a good climate policy but also a good fiscal policy in the context of a green tax reform.[27] Fundamentally, considering that environmental taxes are: (i) effective instruments for the internalisation of environmental externalities; (ii) efficient and effective instruments for the achievement of the climate and energy objectives assumed by the EU (promoting innovation and structural changes); (iii) an additional source of public revenue; and (iv) incentives to modify the behaviour of consumers and producers towards more efficient guidelines.

Therefore, energy taxes have the potential to guide behaviours towards the use of energy produced from renewable and recycled sources such as biofuel or biogas. Consequently, they are suitable instruments not only in the field of energy or climate policies, but also in circular economy (CE) strategies. However, only tax measures that aim to protect the environment and are designed accordingly can be classified as true 'environmentally driven taxes' and, therefore, be useful instruments to achieve non-fiscal objectives.[28]

To consider that a real environmental element has been incorporated into an energy tax, its structure must be designed in such a way as to encourage the use of products with better environmental performance. However, energy taxes introduced by some MSs present the following design problems: (i) tax quanti-

---

[27] Floren Flues and Kurt van Dender, 'Carbon Pricing Design: Effectiveness, Efficiency and Feasibility: An Investment Perspective' (2020) OECD Taxation Working Papers, n. 48.

[28] Pirlot (n 23).

fication elements are not configured, defined or directly linked to the negative environmental externalities they could correct; and (ii) the tax base is aligned with the concept of environmental taxes but tax rates are insufficient to issue corrective signals or do not introduce differentiated tax treatments according to the environmental performance of each product.

These shortcomings converge in the case of the ETD, making it an inefficient instrument both for setting carbon prices and for discouraging the consumption of fossil fuels. Therefore, despite its potential to contribute to the objectives of the European Green Deal, in some MSs energy taxation remains imperfect to achieve such a complementary role.

In general, many of the deficiencies indicated are caused by the lack of a correct balance between the collection and environmental purposes of the energy taxes introduced by the MS. In this sense, it must be borne in mind that energy taxation has historically been an instrument for MSs to collect tax revenues, and has been part of existing national tax measures since long before the recognition of its role in achieving environmental objectives. In fact, energy taxes range from 3.5% to 9% of total national revenues and, in most MSs, do not pursue an explicit and well-defined CO_2 reduction objective.[29]

In recent years, the European Commission itself has recommended the use of indirect taxation, such as energy taxes, over direct taxation, doing so because it considers that, from an economic perspective, indirect taxes can raise revenues in a less distortive way than direct taxation and have a less detrimental impact on growth.[30] At the same time, the main issues associated with the design of energy taxes in some MSs are attributable to the current configuration of the ETD. Therefore, if the European Commission is serious about deploying its European Green Deal a new restructured ETD should send the right pricing signals to influence behaviour and investment towards sustainable energy sources.

III. THE EU ENERGY TAXATION FRAMEWORK

The ETD sets minimum levels of taxation for energy products used for motor fuel, heating and electricity, while allowing MSs to apply a national rate above these minimum rates, as well as introducing additional taxes. This structure makes it a potentially suitable instrument for these products to reflect in their prices the cost to society of the CO_2 emissions derived from their use.

---

29 European Commission, 'Impact Assessment report. Accompanying the document. Proposal for a Council Directive Restructuring the Union framework for the Taxation of Energy Products and Electricity' SWD (2021) 641.

30 ibid.

Precisely, the idea was that the ETD would become an instrument so MSs could use taxation policy in support of environmental protection and the achievement of international climate-related commitments, energy efficiency or transport policies.

However, the reality after almost 20 years since its approval is that this instrument is not correctly aligned with the objectives of the European Green Deal, mainly because its environmental objectives were relegated to its main one: harmonising the minimum levels of taxation of electricity and energy products used as heating or motor fuel to ensure the proper functioning of the internal market. The priority became to avoid the harmful effects of tax competition on energy, since the market was threatened by the diversity of prices of energy products between MSs.

As stated above, energy taxation has been part of the existing national tax measures since long before the existence of the ETD. In fact, prior to the ETD, there was an energy taxation framework in the EU, although limited to mineral oils – Directives 92/81[31] and 92/82[32] (the so-called 'Mineral Oils Directives'). The ETD replaced those Directives while retaining their structure based on minimum levels of taxes expressed in volume terms but broadening the scope to avoid distortions between competing energy sources (such as electricity). It also set new minimum rates for new products under the expanded scope and increased rates for previously covered mineral oils.

Therefore, the EU's priority became the creation of a common framework for the taxation of energy products and electricity, and not the introduction of a single harmonised framework for environmental tax. Bearing in mind the exact objective of the ETD, its lack of coherence with the European Green Deal goals can be explained by looking at its legislative history and, specifically, the requirement of unanimity to approve indirect fiscal measures under Article 113 of the Treaty of the Functioning of the European Union (TFEU).[33]

To reach unanimity, the current ETD sacrificed its environmental potential in exchange for further progress in the harmonisation of energy taxation, even though the role of taxation in reducing CO_2 emissions has been on the EU political agenda since the 1990s. However, the different Commission proposals failed to garner the required unanimous backing of the Council and were

---

[31] Directive 92/81/EEC on the harmonization of the structures of excise duties on mineral oils [1992] OJ L316/12.

[32] Directive 92/82/EEC on the approximation of the rates of excise duties on mineral oils [1992] OJ L316/19.

[33] Legal basis for the harmonisation of indirect taxes and, therefore, current legal basis of the ETD: Consolidated versions of the Treaty on European Union and the Treaty on the Functioning of the European Union [2016] OJ C202/1 ('TFEU').

withdrawn.[34] Due to successive rejections, as of 1997, the idea of establishing an EU environmental tax was abandoned and efforts were focused on protecting the internal market.

For that reason, the environmental aspects of the ETD were far different to those proposed in 1992 and 1995, including numerous transition periods, and the ability of the MSs to establish exemptions and differential taxes, even setting them below the minimum level. Proof of this is that Article 2.4 of the ETD excludes some of the most polluting industries from its scope (such as glass, ceramics and fibreglass production; sectors which are included in the EU ETS). The only positive aspect at that time was the updating of EU minimum tax levels (although below the rate of inflation).

Under the current framework MSs must tax all forms of energy products regardless of their behaviour in terms of CO_2 emissions and positive contribution to the objectives of the European Green Deal. In particular, and as regards the objective scope of these taxes, it should be noted that, in accordance with Articles 1 and 2 of the ETD, MSs have had to tax the manufacture and import of electricity and energy products intended for use as heating fuel or motor fuel regardless of their fossil or renewable origin. Consequently, the inherent logic of the ETD is to include in its scope of application all energy products regardless of their environmental performance.

For this reason, it could be said that the ETD did not really introduce a harmonised framework for 'environmentally driven taxes' in the field of energy, but rather a framework for the implementation of 'energy-related taxes'. That is, taxes collected on all forms of energy regardless of their environmental performance. Precisely, 'energy-related taxes' are defined by the fact that the tax base (the taxed product) includes some form of energy. Therefore, we are talking about taxes whose internal logic responds to a primarily collection purpose, which means that its internal logic is to tax all energy products regardless of their environmental performance.[35]

The ETD provided an opportunity for MSs to correct the situation described. Specifically, it left to the discretion of the MS the decision to introduce energy taxes into their national tax system with a true environmental purpose to comply with the minimum rates. MSs had the possibility to establish energy taxes designed to take into account the different environmental performance

[34] See, for example, European Commission Proposals: 'Proposal for a Council Directive introducing a tax on carbon dioxide emissions and energy' COM (92) 226; 'Amended Proposal for a Council Directive introducing a tax on carbon dioxide emissions and energy' COM (95) 172; 'Proposal for a Council Directive on restructuring the community framework for the taxation of energy products' COM (97) 30.

[35] Janet Milne, 'Carbon Taxes in the United States: The Context for the Future' (2008) 10 Vermont Journal of Environmental Law.

of each energy product or to include environmental tax elements in the form of tax exemptions in their traditional energy taxes. Specifically, several MSs have introduced tax figures to issue explicit signals on the price of carbon (for example, Denmark, Finland, France, Ireland, Iceland, Norway, the Netherlands, Portugal, the United Kingdom, Sweden and Switzerland), in many cases, to complete the EU ETS and compensate for the fact that the ETD does not establish tax rates on energy sources based on carbon content.[36] This means that a coherent and harmonised explicit signal is not being issued in relation to the price of CO_2 in the EU, especially in sectors excluded from the EU ETS.

The high degree of flexibility of the ETD brought with it not only a clear lack of efficiency from the environmental point of view, but also an additional problem directly related to the facultative nature of the fiscal measures adopted by the MS to provide energy taxes with greater environmental coherence.

The inherent logic of the ETD, transposed by many MSs to their internal taxes, is to tax electricity and energy products regardless of their fossil or renewable origin and their sustainability.[37] Any deviation from this logic to achieve environmental goals must be introduced by the MS through fiscal measures such as differentiated rates or tax relief. These measures, in turn, must be previously authorised by the Commission when they meet the elements to constitute State aid in accordance with Article 107 of the TFEU, which usually happens when a measure is introduced in favour of sustainable energy products, since they are considered selective advantages for departing from the reference framework and internal logic set by the ETD (that is, taxing all energy products).[38] As confirmed by the CJEU, the objective pursued by State measures is not sufficient to exclude those measures outright from classification as 'aid' for the purposes of Article 107 TFEU.[39] These objectives, however, can be invoked when the Commission analyses their compatibility with the Treaty and, therefore, authorises their implementation.

---

[36] Macarena Larrea, 'La fiscalidad sobre el carbono en Europa. principales desarrollos y tendencias' (2021) 111 Revista de la Facultad de Derecho 1.

[37] Álvaro Antón and Marta Villar, 'Inherent Logic of EU Energy Taxes: Toward a Balance Between Market Protection and Environment Protection' in Larry Kreiser and others (eds), *Environmental Taxation and Green Fiscal Reform: Theory and Impact, Critical Issues in Environmental Taxation* (Edward Elgar 2014).

[38] Álvaro Antón and Iñaki Bilbao, 'State Aid and the EU Council Directive 2003/96/EC: The Case for Augmenting the Environmental Component' in Claudia Dias Soares and others (eds), *Critical Issues in Environmental Taxation: International and Comparative Perspectives* (Oxford University Press 2010).

[39] See, *inter alia*, Case C-342/96, *Spain v Commission* [1999] ECR I-2459; and Case C-75/97, *Belgium v Commission* [1999] ECR I-03671.

An example of the above State aid issues can be found in Article 16 of the ETD, which authorises the MSs to apply, under fiscal control, exemptions or reduced tax rates to energy products derived from biomass, including biofuels.[40] According to the European Commission, any tax reduction or exemption introduced in these taxes to favour biofuels' market penetration entails a deviation from the general structure of the tax system.[41] In fact, the well-established doctrine of the European Commission is to consider that the reduction of the excise tax on biofuels meets the criteria of Article 107(1) and is thus deemed to constitute State aid.[42]

It is true that the European Commission may declare such aid of an environmental nature as compatible with Article 107.3 of the TFEU, as long as they meet the criteria set out in *soft law* documents such as the Environmental Aid Guidelines and the sustainability criteria provided in Article 29 of RED II.[43] However, it is also true that the current framework allows MSs to grant exemptions and reductions to energy products for reasons unrelated to energy efficiency or net reduction of CO_2 emissions, and, in some cases, without requiring European Commission validation.[44]

IV. DIVERGENCE BETWEEN EU ENERGY TAXATION POLICY AND THE EU GREEN DEAL

The current structure of the ETD creates incentives that are in contradiction with the European Green Deal objectives by *de facto* favouring fossil fuels over those with better environmental performance (i.e., promoting the use of coal as heating fuel). In this regard, the European Commission stated that the current ETD does not provide incentives or even price signals to encourage alternative energy and encourage consumers to save energy.[45] In fact, it can be

---

[40] Álvaro Antón, 'Energy Taxes and Promotion of Renewable Energy Sources (RES): Combination of Excise Reliefs and Supply Obligations of RES' in Pascuale Pistone and Marta Villar (eds), *Energy Taxation, Environmental Protection and State Aids: Tracing the Path from Divergence to Convergence* (IBFD 2016).

[41] Joined Cases C-106/09 P and C-107/09 P, *Commission and Spain v Government of Gibraltar and United Kingdom* [2011] ECR I-11113.

[42] European Commission Decisions on State aid: NN 61/04 – Spain: Excise duty exemption to biofuels C (2006) 2993 final, N 57/2008 – Poland: Operating aid for biofuels C (2009) 7140; and N 63/2008 – Italy: Excise duty reduction for biofuels C (2008) 4589 final.

[43] RED II (n 8).

[44] Antón and Villar (n 37).

[45] European Commission, 'Smarter energy taxation for the EU: Proposal for a revision of the Energy Taxation Directive' COM (2011) 168.

said that the current approach of the ETD even prevents it from fulfilling its main objective – to ensure the proper functioning of the internal market.

In this sense, the ETD has allowed, respecting the minimums established within it, the proliferation of asymmetric tax rates among MSs. The configuration of the ETD tax base does not ensure the desirable degree of consistency in the tax treatment of basic fossil fuels and electricity. In this sense, taking into account the energy content of each energy product, the levels of taxation vary substantially according to the product. Thus, for example, in the case of fuel use for transport, the minimum tax rate set for gasoline is 359 euros/1000 litres compared to the 330 euros/1000 litres set for diesel. The lower minimum tariffs for diesel further reinforce the natural advantage that diesel has over gasoline due to its high energy content. Moreover, the current minimum price according to energy content is 9.4 euros/gigajoule for diesel and 10.9 euros/gigajoule for gasoline, without this difference being justified from the point of view of the fight against climate change, since diesel has a worse performance in terms of GHG emissions.[46]

The main responsibility for these deficiencies must be attributed to the very structure of the ETD: (1) configuration of the tax base (taxation of fuels based on volume); (2) outdated relevance of the minimum rates levels over time; (3) outdated coverage of energy products; and (4) presence of sector-specific energy tax exemptions or reductions.

The tax base configuration of the ETD does not ensure the desirable degree of consistency in the treatment of the basic fossil energy sources and sustainable ones. According to the European Commission, when the energy content of the various products is considered, the minimum levels of taxation vary substantially depending on the product in question.

A classic broad-based energy tax would define the tax base in terms of the energy content of the identified range of energy sources. However, the ETD applies the minimum tax rates on the volume of the energy product consumed. This option is not the most appropriate way to give an environmental character to energy taxes since this parameter does not reflect the energy content and CO_2 emissions of each product.[47]

According to the Commission, this configuration results in an inefficient use of energy and a distortion of the internal market. Moreover, taxation according to volume discriminates against renewable fuels. For example, this results

---

[46] Impact assessment report. Accompanying the document. Proposal for a Council Directive restructuring the Union framework for the taxation of Energy Products and Electricity (n 29).

[47] Smarter Energy Taxation for the EU: Proposal for a Revision of the Energy Taxation Directive (n 45).

in a situation where, as long as the minimum rates are respected, renewable energy can be taxed at a higher rate than a competing fossil fuel.

In particular, the volume parameter does not conform to the characteristics of products such as biofuels and other sustainable products, since: (1) biofuels have lower energy content and, therefore, a higher volume of these products is required to produce the same amount of energy as products with a higher energy content, such as fossil fuels; and (2) the same tax rates are applied to sustainable and unsustainable energy products. In this sense, it must be considered that, although the objective of the EU legislator was to tax hydrocarbons, the reality is that, in order to avoid distortions, Article 2 of the ETD implemented the same tax treatment for biofuels and for fossil fuels.

The sum of these two factors leads to a potentially higher tax burden on biofuels compared to the same volume of the fossil fuel with which it competes and which it would have to replace. Specifically, since the current minimum rate for gasoline is 359 euros/1000 litres, its current minimum rate according to its gigajoule content is 10.9 euros/gigajoule, while the current minimum rate according to its gigajoule content of renewable fuel that can replace it, bioethanol, is 17 euros/gigajoule, since, as we have anticipated, despite having a lower energy content, the Directive reserves the same tax treatment as gasoline, 359 euros/1000 litres. For its part, the current minimum rate for diesel, 330 euros/1000 litres, means that its minimum rate according to its energy content is 9.4 euros/gigajoule, while that of biodiesel is 11.7 euros/ gigajoule. Furthermore, the ETD ignores the better performance of advanced biofuels in terms of the environment, security of supply and reduction of CO_2 emissions.[48]

Another problem with the ETD is that it does not send a sufficiently strong signal to bring changes in behaviour aligned with the objectives of the European Green Deal, specifically because its minimum tax rates are not high enough to discourage the consumption of fossil energy products, thus indirectly encouraging sustainable ones. The absence of an increase in its minimum rates for more than a decade has eroded the tax-induced price signal necessary to encourage investment in energy-efficient technology and behaviour, and also undermined their contribution to the proper functioning of the internal market (minimum tax rates have lost their convergence effect with national tax rates).[49] In fact, in the last decade, some MSs have increased their national level of taxation while others have not. As a result, there is a risk of growing distortion of competition in the Single Market and an erosion of the

---

[48] European Commission, 'Proposal for a Council Directive restructuring the Union framework for the taxation of energy products and electricity' COM (2021) 563.

[49] Furthermore, the minimum rates are not indexed to external developments such as inflation or a CO_2 benchmark – i.e., the EU Allowance (EUA) price (price of 1 tonne of CO_2 in the EU ETS).

tax base in high-taxing countries (e.g., in the case of motor fuels that can be easily and legally transported across borders).

The problems described are long-standing; already in 2011, the European Commission proposed to change the scope and structure of the ETD.[50] The fundamental premise behind this proposal was based on the belief that the ETD structure has the potential to deliver both explicit and implicit carbon price signals. The fundamental pillars of the proposal were the introduction of an explicit distinction between, on the one hand, energy taxation specifically linked to CO_2 emissions (CO_2-related taxation) and, on the other hand, taxation linked to energy consumption (general taxation of energy consumption), in the latter case, with a component based on the energy content of the products. However, the unanimity requirement established by Article 113 TFEU once again acted as a barrier and, after four years of negotiations with MSs without progress, the European Commission withdrew the proposal in 2015.

More recently, in 2019, the Commission presented an initiative to review the ETD in 2021 as part of the European Green Deal, with the objectives of: (i) aligning the taxation of energy products and electricity with the European Green Deal's objectives; and (ii) preserving the EU internal market by updating the scope and structure of rates as well as by rationalising the use of optional tax exemptions and reductions by MSs. The main novelty of the initiative presented was not only in its content, but also in the legal basis on which the European Commission intended to base its adoption. According to the Commission, since the proposed review of the ETD focuses on environmental issues, it would be possible to avoid the requirement of unanimity set by Article 113. In particular, the Commission proposed as a legal basis for its adoption Article 192 of the TFEU (environmental measures including measures of a fiscal nature), which allows the adoption of proposals in this field by the ordinary legislative procedure (qualified majority instead of unanimity).[51]

V. ENERGY TAXATION IN THE CONTEXT OF THE EU GREEN DEAL OBJECTIVES

In July 2021, the European Commission presented the package 'Fit for 55' to adapt the EU policies on climate, energy, transport and taxation to European

---

50 European Commission, 'Proposal for a Council Directive amending Directive 2003/96/EC, restructuring the Community framework for the taxation of energy products and electricity' COM (2011) 169.

51 European Commission, 'A more efficient and democratic decision making in EU energy and climate policy' COM (2019) 177.

Green Deal objectives.[52] The package proposes to review a number of elements of the EU climate legislation – including the EU ETS or the ETD – to establish in real terms how the EU aims to achieve these goals. These measures follow the tenets of the European Green Deal, in which the need to make national budgets 'greener' is defended through tax figures and pricing systems that, in addition to providing income, send the right price signals to encourage/discourage certain types of consumption or production.

The package is composed of interconnected legislative proposals, which seek to: (i) set a price on carbon in sectors excluded so far (i.e., road transport and buildings) and generate additional income to guarantee a just transition; (ii) support a greater use of renewable energies and energy savings; (iii) facilitate the acquisition of cleaner vehicles and fuels for transportation; and (iv) offer security to the industry to promote investment and innovation. The set of proposals includes the belief that effective carbon pricing and the removal of incentives for fossil fuel consumption are needed to deliver the GHG emission reductions together with other regulatory measures.

However, according to the EU Commission, a balance between carbon pricing policies and regulatory mechanisms is necessary, on the one hand, since carbon pricing would not be sufficient to overcome either persistent market failures or non-carbon-related barriers, and, on the other hand, because an over-reliance on regulatory policies would lead to unnecessarily high economic burdens. For example, the Commission has stated that a possible extension of carbon pricing instruments alone might not be enough to drive the development of advanced biofuels in all cases. The Commission recognises that pricing instruments, such as the ETD or the EU ETS, are important to promote the shift to mature low-carbon technologies but may not be sufficient by themselves to deliver an optimal investment signal for developing new innovative technologies. Such reversal signals could also continue to drive up costs to consumers from carbon taxes and the ETS. Thus, the early stage of technological development together with its high costs could slow down its penetration in the market if specific incentives for its development are not introduced.[53]

For this reason, the package combines regulatory mandate and control mechanisms with economic or market instruments to achieve a certain balance

---

52 European Commission, '"Fit for 55": Delivering the EU's 2030 climate target on the way to climate neutrality' COM (2021) 550.

53 Impact Assessment of the Renewable Energy Directive (EU) 2018/2011 on the promotion of the use of energy from renewable sources (n 6).

between pricing policies/instruments, environmental objectives, standards and support measures. The package introduces the following proposals:

- Mandate and Control: (i) Stronger standards for CO_2 emissions for cars and vans; (ii) new infrastructure for alternative fuels; (iii) ReFuelEU – more sustainable aviation fuels: (iv) FuelEU – cleaner fuels for maritime transport; (v) updating the Effort Sharing Regulation; (vi) updating the Land Use and Forestry Regulation; and (vii) updating the Renewable Energy Directive.
- Economic or market instruments: (i) Strengthening the EU ETS, including the aviation sector; (ii) extension of the EU ETS to maritime and road transport, and buildings; (iii) updating the ETD; and (iv) a mechanism for border carbon emissions adjustment.

The economic instruments envisaged focus on introducing and applying the PPP to tax energy sources in line with climate targets and to price carbon in excluded sectors that generate additional income.

In particular, the revised EU ETS would require: (i) Reducing GHG emissions by 61% in sectors already subject to it; (ii) gradually expanding its application to the maritime sector; and (iii) gradually eliminating free emission rights of the aviation sector. Furthermore, it is proposed establishing in 2026 a specific EU ETS for the so-called diffuse sectors (road transport and buildings), which are currently excluded from the EU ETS due to the difficulty and cost of controlling their emissions.

Along with these measures, the Commission also proposes the amendment of the ETD. Considering the set of proposals, it could be argued that the objectives of the 'Climate Law'[54] could theoretically be achieved without the contribution provided by the ETD. In fact, the European Commission recognises that the main role in the decarbonisation of the EU economy will essentially fall to the revised ETS and the Effort Sharing Regulation.

However, it must be borne in mind that the ETD would have to be revised to address other shortcomings presented above, especially those related to the proper functioning of the internal market. Moreover, the revision is necessary to align the ETD with environmental issues and eliminate the incentives that fossil fuels receive under the current framework.

Furthermore, the European Commission considers it essential that the ETD be more consistent with other 'Fit for 55' proposals and instruments; for example, because, without the contribution of the ETD, other initiatives would have to contribute more, which could result in a higher price in the context of

[54] European Climate Law (n 3).

the ETS. Therefore, a proper coordination of the ETD and ETS could help to reach the goals in 2030 in a more cost-effective way.

As indicated, taxes could play a complementary role and help achieve the objectives of the European Green Deal by creating the right incentives both to change the behaviour of producers and consumers and to create a proper environment for eco-innovation.

This can be achieved by eliminating the disadvantages of sustainable technologies and introducing higher taxation for inefficient and polluting fuels, thereby ensuring that energy taxes better reflect the impact that each energy product has on the environment and health. This tax reform seems even more urgent in the transport sector, which is associated with a greater increase in emissions. In this area, tax measures and financial incentives (i.e., subsidies to purchase electric vehicles) could be useful complementary instruments to promote the use of alternative fuels and electric vehicles.

Unlike previous proposals, the European Commission tries to achieve these objectives by means of simplification.[55] To that end, it proposes to move from a volume-based tax to an energy-content-based tax, which would eliminate the *de facto* advantage that currently exists for fossil fuels. It dismisses the idea of introducing a component on CO_2 emissions as foreseen in its 2011 proposal, mainly because it intends to extend the EU ETS to sectors such as transport and buildings and, therefore, these emissions would already have a carbon pricing instrument.

Furthermore, it intends to introduce a classification of tax rates based on environmental performance. Specifically, it proposes to simplify the tax structure by grouping energy products and electricity into categories, and introducing a classification based on their environmental performance:

- Group 1 (Highest rate): Fuels with the worst performance in environmental terms (conventional fossils – diesel and petrol);
- Group 2 (Reduced rate – two-thirds of the reference rate – for a period of 10 years): Fossil fuels with lower environmental impact and greater potential to contribute to decarbonisation (natural gas, LPG and hydrogen);
- Group 3 (Reduced rate – half of the reference rate): Renewable products such as biofuels that, despite meeting sustainability criteria, cannot be considered as 'advanced biofuels';
- Group 4 (Super reduced type): Electricity (regardless of use), advanced biofuels, bioliquids, biogas and hydrogen from renewable sources.

[55] Proposal for a Council Directive restructuring the Union framework for the taxation of energy products and electricity (n 48).

The change in the tax base together with the setting of differentiated tax rates would eliminate the advantage that fossil fuels currently receive and, at the same time, would introduce preferential tax treatment to products with better environmental performance. This will help integrate energy taxation into green tax reforms aimed at achieving a balance between environmental and fiscal sustainability.

The planned reform will introduce a tax advantage for products such as biofuels. However, and unlike what happens with the tax benefits adopted by virtue of Article 16 of the current ETD, the advantage may not be classified as State aid in accordance with Article 107 of the TFEU. The application of differentiated rates would be mandatory for States. Given that the States would have no margin of discretion, the advantage could not be considered an intervention by the State or granted through State resources, and, therefore, it would not cumulatively meet all the elements required by Article 107 to qualify as State aid.

It is true that a tax system must be neutral, however, is also true that a neutral tax system is not always efficient.[56] Sometimes the intervention of the State will be necessary to promote some behaviour with a high social return or the discriminatory treatment of certain activities could be justified. These are scenarios in which the disadvantages of moving away from neutrality, complicating the tax system, must be weighed against the advantages in terms of greater efficiency that could derive from this departure.

Notwithstanding the above, in a context such as the current one of rising energy prices and economic crisis, it could be difficult to adopt the new ETD, mainly due to the difficulty of reaching an agreement between MSs. The potential impact of the new ETD on competitiveness and households could lead some MSs to reject the proposal. This would prevent reaching the unanimity required by Article 113 of the TFEU and, consequently, would frustrate the plans of the Commission. Article 113 of the TFEU requires unanimity to adopt harmonisation measures in the area of indirect taxation and has already acted in the past as a barrier to adopting proposals to modify the ETD, such as the one presented by the Commission in 2011.

Faced with this barrier, the Commission could try to avoid the unanimity requirement by arguing that, given that the proposed revision of the ETD focuses on environmental issues, it is possible to activate one of the so-called 'passerelle clauses' provided for by the TFEU itself. In particular, the Commission could propose Article 192 TFEU (environmental measures including measures of a fiscal nature) as the legal basis for the adoption of its

---

56 Åsa Hansson and Cécile Brokelind, 'Tax Incentives, Tax Expenditures Theories in R&D: The Case of Sweden' (2014) 6 World Tax Journal 2.

proposal, an article that allows the adoption of proposals in the field of environmental protection through the legislative procedure ordinarily provided for in Article 116 (qualified majority instead of unanimity). The qualified majority foreseen in Article 116 implies that the proposals presented must be approved by a vote in favour of 55% of the MSs and that they represent at least 65% of the EU population (double majority rule). However, activating the 'passerelle clauses' would require, once again, a unanimous agreement by the Council on the proposal presented by the Commission and not much progress has been made in this area.

Another possibility to deal with this possible reluctance of some of the MSs would be related to paying special attention to the distributional impacts and to competitiveness linked to environmental taxation, specifically through the introduction of mechanisms that mitigate and compensate said effects on certain social groups and economic sectors. In this sense, and as the economic doctrine has defended, compared to regulation or command and control instruments, environmental taxes have the advantage that the additional income obtained through them can be used for distributive compensation measures and/or mechanisms to mitigate the loss of companies' competitiveness. The Commission is aware that while introducing carbon price signals for fossil fuels and fuels in the transport or heating sector constitute powerful incentives for behavioural change, in the short-term consumers may not be able to easily change their consumption patterns when it affects an important part of their income. For this reason, in its proposals the EU Commission considers the impact that its approval could have on the most vulnerable sectors and competitiveness.[57]

Regarding this last issue, the economic literature argues that, according to the double dividend hypothesis, it is possible to obtain both economic and environmental benefits with environmental taxes. Specifically, collection could be increased through these taxes while simultaneously reducing the tax burden of other pre-existing (distortionary) taxes in a neutral income framework.[58] However, in recent years we have witnessed the new generation of green tax reforms, known as reforms of third generation – particularly following the 2008 crisis, and with the consequent increase in public revenue needs and distributive and competitive concerns. The recent green tax reform

[57] See Álvaro Antón, 'Environmental and Energy Taxation in the Context of the EU Green Deal and the Recovery Plan: The case of Spain' in Stefan E Weishaar and others (eds) *Green Deals in the Making: Perspectives from Across the Globe* (Edward Elgar 2022).

[58] Francisco J Delgado, Jaume Freire-González and Maria J Presno, 'Environmental Taxation in the European Union: Are there Common Trends?' (2022) 73 Economic Analysis and Policy.

waves no longer universally pursue a 'double dividend' (financial and environmental dividend), but seek to put in place new legal packages including financial measures to support those in vulnerable situations. These tax reforms are characterised by a more flexible and heterogeneous use of tax collection adapted to the new socio-economic environment – distribution programmes, energy efficiency, support for renewables, etc. This means that the tax revenue obtained through these taxes could be recycled, for example, in policies for the development of advanced biofuels or to compensate the most vulnerable sectors.

VI. CONCLUSIONS

Energy taxes have the potential to guide behaviours towards the use of sustainable energy products such as advanced biofuel or biogas. By getting the price of fossil fuels 'right', these taxes can encourage the switch to advanced biofuels and other renewable energy products. Therefore, they are suitable instruments in the field of the European Green Deal and CE strategies.

Despite their potential, not all the energy taxes can be classified as true 'environmentally driven taxes'. To consider that a real environmental element has been incorporated into an energy tax, its structure must be designed in such a way as to encourage the use of products with better environmental performance. In that sense, energy taxes introduced by some MSs present the following design problems: (i) tax quantification elements are not configured, defined or directly linked to the negative environmental externalities they could correct; and (ii) the tax base is aligned with the concept of environmental taxes but tax rates are insufficient to issue corrective signals or do not introduce differentiated tax treatments according to the environmental performance of each product.

The main shortcomings associated with the design of energy taxes in some MSs are attributable to the current configuration of the ETD. In particular, ETD's tax base configuration (taxation of fuels based on volume) does not ensure the desirable degree of consistency in the treatment of the basic fossil energy sources and sustainable ones. Therefore, if the European Commission is serious about deploying its European Green Deal a new restructured ETD should send the right pricing signals to influence behaviour and investment towards sustainable energy sources.

LEGISLATION

Consolidated versions of the Treaty on European Union and the Treaty on the Functioning of the European Union [2016] OJ C202/1 ('TFEU')

Directive 92/82/EEC on the approximation of the rates of excise duties on mineral oils [1992] OJ L 316/19
Directive 2003/87/EC establishing a system for greenhouse gas emission allowance trading within the Union and amending Council Directive 96/61/EC [2003] OJ L275/32 ('ETS')
Directive 92/81/EEC on the harmonization of the structures of excise duties on mineral oils [1992] OJ L316/12.
Directive 2003/96/EC restructuring the Community framework for the taxation of energy products and electricity [2003] OJ L283/32 ('ETD')
Directive (EU) 2018/2001 on the promotion of the use of energy from renewable sources [2018] OJ L328/82 ('RED II')
Regulation (EU) 2021/1119 establishing the framework for achieving climate neutrality and amending Regulations (EC) No 401/2009 and (EU) 2018/1999 [2021] OJ L243/1 ('European Climate Law')
Regulation (EU) 691/2011 on European environmental economic accounts [2011] OJ L192/1
Council Decision (EU) 2016/1841 on the conclusion, on behalf of the European Union, of the Paris Agreement adopted under the United Nations Framework Convention on Climate Change [2016] OJ L282/1
European Commission Decision on State aid N 63/2008 – Italy: Excise duty reduction for biofuels C (2008) 4589 final
European Commission Decision on State aid NN 61/04 – Spain: Excise duty exemption to biofuels C (2006) 2993 final
European Commission Decision on State aid N 57/2008 – Poland: Operating aid for biofuels C (2009) 7140
Joined Cases C-106/09 P and C-107/09 P, *Commission and Spain v Government of Gibraltar and United Kingdom* [2011] ECR I-11113.

CASES

Belgium v Commission (Case C-75/97) [1999] ECR I-03671
Spain v Commission (Case C-342/96) [1999] ECR I-2459
Transportes Jordi Besora SL v Generalitat de Catalunya (Case C-82/12) ECLI:EU:C:2014:108 [2014]

10. EU law and policy shaping supranational and national investment in biofuel and biogas transition

Agnieszka Smoleńska[1]

I. INTRODUCTION

To make a net zero future a reality and deliver on the goals of the Green Deal, the European Union (EU) needs to mobilise a wide range of technologies and transformations across value chains through bold regulatory incentives and unprecedented amounts of investment in electrification, improving energy efficiency and further developing wind and solar energy. The implications of Russian aggression on Ukraine, with the concomitant impact on EU's energy security, make transition away from fossil fuels all the more imperative. Certain types of bioenergy have an important dual role in helping the EU realise its objectives and face its challenges. First, biofuels can help decarbonise high-emitting transport. Second, the development of bioenergy from waste contributes to meeting another EU environmental objective, that of creating a circular economy (CE).[2]

Given bioenergy's potential contribution to a net zero future, forecasts predict growth in demand, with the production of biogases and biofuels tri-

[1] Research for this chapter was supported by a National Science Centre grant (UMO-2021/40/C/HS5/00134).

[2] International Energy Agency (IEA), 'Outlook for Biogas and Biomethane: Prospects for Organic Growth' (IEA 2020) 15. This chapter follows the definitions outlined in the Introduction to this volume, whereby biogases and biofuels are defined as renewable energy sources produced from biomass (to be distinguished from renewables produced from non-biological origins). Biomass in this context encompasses biowaste (residues in agriculture, food and forestry) as well as dedicated agricultural and forestry crops. This chapter focuses on the EU's current support for the conversion of biological waste into biofuels and biogases, using the roles of EU law and policy in shaping the financial support for fuel crops as evidence of the significance of the EU's legal framework for shaping the investment climate in bioenergy.

pling globally in a net zero scenario.[3] The starting point, however, is quite low and telling in terms of challenges faced by this market segment. Furthermore, as discussed in this chapter, traditional biofuels obtained from dedicated crops (e.g. corn or trees) dominate over the more sustainable advanced biofuels derived from biowaste, which reveals the long shadow of previous public policies.[4] With more attention on the sustainability of bioenergy and its competition with other land uses (e.g. for food production), policymakers are looking more favourably towards the production of bioenergy from waste, which has so far remained marginal and therefore has significant growth potential. Regulatory interventions, discussed in other parts of this book, seek to facilitate the development of sustainable biogases and advanced biofuels, *inter alia*, through clearer standards and opening up the gas market and infrastructure to alternative fuels such as biomethane.

So far, given the limited economic viability of bioenergy technologies,[5] their uptake in the EU has been driven by the public financial support made available in order to fulfil the EU renewable energy targets.[6] Only since the late 2000s has the focus shifted to subsidising the development of advanced technologies, as concerns about sustainability came to the fore. Private investment in the area of bioenergy remains more limited than for other renewable energy technologies such as wind or solar, but the scale of EU investment needed makes attracting private capital to biogas/biofuel indispensable. The imperative of supporting the role of bioenergy in the EU's energy mix was emphasised in the 2022 REPowerEU strategy of the European Commission to

---

[3] International Energy Agency (IEA), 'World Energy Outlook' (IEA 2021) 223; SP Andersen, SB Allen and GC Domingo, 'Biomass in the EU Green Deal: Towards Consensus on the Use of Biomass for EU Bioenergy' (Institute for European Environmental Policy (IEEP) 2021) 19.

[4] The IEA (n 3) projects that with the stated policies scenario the use of biofuels will double from 2020 levels by 2030. For a net zero world, such production would have to triple (to circa 5.5 mboe/d) with a significant development of advanced biofuels (biojet, biodiesel, ethanol). Biogas (biomethane) production is projected to increase from 2 EJ today to over 5 EJ in a net zero scenario, predominantly through the development of upgrades to biomethane IEA (n 3) 215 and 238.

[5] Note that the lack of economic viability is partially the result of continued subsidies and privileged market access by fossil fuel producers.

[6] Biogases and biofuels are produced from biomass and allow the production of low-carbon substitutes for conventional fuels used for electricity production and transport. Definitions of biogases and biofuels are set in the Renewable Energy Directive (Directive (EU) 2018/2001 on the promotion of the use of energy from renewable sources [2018] OJ L328/82 ('RED II')). Biogases include biomethane (natural gas), which allows for the biogas to be blended into gas networks or used as transport fuel. The terminology in the chapter follows the EU regulation. The ambiguity and significance of term definitions are addressed in Section V.

wean the EU off Russian energy, *inter alia* by increasing by 50% (to 35 bcm) the targets for biomethane in EU's energy mix by 2030.[7]

This chapter analyses how EU laws and policies shape the availability of financing for the development of biofuels and biogases produced from biological waste from agriculture, food and forestry along three financing streams: directly at EU level, by shaping Member State (MS) policies, and through regulating sustainable finance. To this end, Section II focuses on EU-level policies and provides an overview of EU budget programmes distributed at the EU and MS levels, which can contribute to the development and implementation of bioenergy technologies. Section III turns to the MS stream and examines how EU law (e.g. binding Renewable Energy Sources targets and State aid rules) shapes the national financing schemes. Section IV explains the role of EU policies in driving the role of private capital in financing transition ('sustainable finance'). To explore the commonalities and differences between the three streams, Sections II–IV identify the amounts of funds available, the type of financing and potential beneficiaries across the different instruments. Section V problematises the role of EU law and policy in shaping the financing framework, focusing in particular on the (in)coherence of spending priorities and regulatory treatment of biogases/biofuels from biowaste across the framework, as well as its flexibility across a number of MSs' institutional contexts. Section VI concludes.

II. FINANCIAL SUPPORT TO BIOGAS AND BIOFUELS AT EU LEVEL

Unprecedented investment is necessary for the EU to achieve its climate neutrality and CO_2 emission reduction goals. In 2020, the European Commission announced its ambition to mobilise 1 trillion euros by the end of 2030 through the EU budget to achieve the objectives of the EU Green Deal.[8] The Sustainable Europe Investment Plan (SEIP) is realised through the 2021–2027 Multiannual Financial Framework (MFF) and the pandemic Recovery Fund, totalling almost 2 trillion euros.[9] Since financing the EU's Green Deal is a major transversal objective of the new EU budget, over 600 billion euros are to be dedicated to green projects across the MSs over the next few years.[10]

---

[7] European Commission, 'REPowerEU: Joint European action for more affordable, secure and sustainable energy' COM (2022) 108.

[8] European Commission, 'Sustainable Europe Investment Plan: European Green Deal Investment Plan' COM (2020) 21 (henceforth 'SEIP').

[9] Current prices are used throughout the chapter.

[10] 'Green mainstreaming' is set between 30% and 37% of different EU funds within the EU 2021–2027 Multiannual Financial Framework (MFF).

What constitutes 'green' in this context is quite broad. Nonetheless, a number of budgetary instruments are of particular relevance in the context of driving the uptake of biofuels and biogases. Such funds are distributed and managed at two levels. First, the EU-level programmes finance projects through competitive tenders run by the EU's new climate-oriented agency, CINEA (European Climate, Infrastructure and Environment Executive Agency). The two largest of these programmes are LIFE (facilitating project implementation) and Horizon Europe (research funding). In addition to these European-Commission-managed funds, the EU budget guarantees investment in green projects via the European Investment Bank (EIB) through the InvestEU programme. Second, a large amount of EU funds is being distributed at the MSs level (cohesion funds, the post-pandemic Recovery and Resilience Fund) on the basis of national priorities and strategies of transition. Additional EU funds are likely to be mobilised to support the EU's objective of accelerating its energy independence from Russia, *inter alia* through investment in bioenergy, as part of the 2022 REPowerEU strategy.

A. EU-level Programmes

The primary EU-wide programme dedicated to implementing the EU's environmental objectives and supporting the implementation of related policies is LIFE (Programme for the Environment and Climate Action), endowed with a total of 5.4 billion euros over 2021–2027. Biogas- and biofuels-related projects could benefit from less than half of these funds: primarily through the sub-programme 'Clean Energy Transition' (1 billion euros), less so – based on the indicated scope of the financed projects – the 'Circular Economy and Quality of Life' sub-programme (1.3 billion euros). Since the projects financed from LIFE are intended to facilitate the implementation of policies, the grants cover up to 60% of eligible costs.[11] LIFE is open to all legal entities, though SMEs and start-ups are especially encouraged to apply for funding. In the area of bioenergy, priorities of the European Commission for the first part of the 2021–2027 funding cycle include: the collection and recycling of biowaste (including anaerobic digestion), using waste heat in buildings, and the general development of renewable energy sources. LIFE funds are also intended to support administrative capacity in MSs and implementation of EU legislation in the area of clean energy. Under the 2014–2020 MFF, LIFE financed projects

---

[11] The remainder having to be covered by the beneficiary from other sources. Regulation (EU) 2021/783 establishing a Programme for the Environment and Climate Action (LIFE), and repealing Regulation (EU) No 1293/2013 [2021] OJ L172/53.

related to use of waste as energy, such as a dryer for energy recovery from sewage sludge and manure (biowaste) and electricity/heat cogeneration.[12]

Much larger funds are available through EU's flagship research programme Horizon Europe, which boasts a total of 95.5 billion euro for the 2021–2027 period.[13] Relevant from the perspective of biofuel and biogas projects are two thematic clusters: 'Climate, Energy and Mobility' and 'Food, Bioeconomy, Natural Resources, Agriculture and Environment', for which a total of 20 billion euro is available. With Horizon Europe funds are generally distributed as grants covering all costs incurred (100% of eligible costs), and the funding conditions are also more favourable than in the case of programmes such as LIFE. The difference is explained by the fact that whereas LIFE largely supports the implementation of EU policies, technology development – critical in the case of biofuels/biogases – including research and innovation for clean energy transition, is to be funded through the Horizon Europe programme. Such a differentiation is in line with the general EU policy, whereby scientific projects receive more favourable funding conditions than those that are closer to being marketed and therefore can access co-financing from financial institutions. Horizon Europe sets specific biofuel/biogas spending priorities, such as research on the sustainability of such energy sources (e.g. carbon-negative sustainable biofuel production), the development of value chains and the scaling up of technology, and the production of innovative biomethane and biogas in agriculture, including 'in a circular approach for soil nutrients and carbon'. As will be further explored in Section V, in this respect, the Horizon Europe thinking appears most advanced in terms of integration of and synergy across environmental priorities.

Synergies in this respect seem to be largely also driven by centralisation of the responsibility for administering the funds, with the CINEA established in 2021 to manage a total of 56 billion euro across different supranational programmes and with the precise aim of improving coordination across dedicated EU energy transition policies.[14] In addition to administering European funds, CINEA is also to provide further assistance to renewable energy made available by MSs through the EU renewable energy financing mechanism (RENEWFM). This programme allows CINEA to support cross-border pro-

---

12 European Commission, LIFE Project database (n.d.) https://webgate.ec.europa.eu/life/publicWebsite/search/ last accessed 16 May 2022.

13 Regulation (EU) 2021/695 establishing Horizon Europe – the Framework Programme for Research and Innovation, laying down its rules for participation and dissemination, and repealing Regulations (EU) No 1290/2013 and (EU) No 1291/2013 [2021] OJ L170/1.

14 Other funds administered by CINEA with a potential impact on biogas/biofuels include the Innovation Fund and Just Transition Fund.

jects in renewable energies being developed to ensure that MSs meet the relevant trajectory for RES use in their power mix. Such efforts should be funded predominantly through MS contributions and private finance (blended finance).[15]

A third relevant EU-level programme that explicitly covers investment in the transition to biofuels/biogases is InvestEU. The programme, which is a successor to the European Fund for Strategic Investments (EFSI, so-called 'Juncker Fund') established in the aftermath of the sovereign debt crisis, leverages the EU budget guarantee of 26 billion euro with the goal of mobilising 372 billion euro of investments in 2021–2027. Within InvestEU's broad remit, the production and supply of biofuels and biogases (in accordance with the objectives of Directive 2018/2001 ('RED I')) are identified as a distinct priority area.[16] InvestEU investments further have to be Green Taxonomy compliant; that is, only projects deemed as contributing to meeting the EU's environmental objectives would be eligible for this financing.[17] At the same time, and differently from LIFE or Horizon Europe, projects financed through this EU programme are intended to be profit-making and the financing provided is to be repaid by the beneficiary. Any complementary financing is to be meanwhile provided commercially by financial institutions. The 'public support' element resides in the favourable terms (lower price than market financing). Furthermore, the InvestEU's financing through the EIB is intended to have a higher risk appetite, favour European SMEs and have a long-term perspective.

B. Member-State-level EU Financing Programmes

In nominal terms the most EU support to projects related to renewable energy and the CE will flow through the cohesion funds and the new post-pandemic Recovery and Resilience Facility (RRF), administered by MSs in accordance with their specific needs.[18] Within the scope of national priorities, climate change is to be streamlined and spending devoted to mitigating it tracked in accordance with a common methodology.

---

[15] Implementing Regulation (EU) 2020/1294 on the Union renewable energy financing mechanism [2020] OJ L303/1.

[16] Annex II on eligible projects, Regulation (EU) 2021/523 establishing the InvestEU Programme and amending Regulation (EU) 2015/1017 [2021] OJ L107/30.

[17] See further Section IV on the Green Taxonomy.

[18] Structural funds are jointly managed by the European Commission and the Member States on the basis of jointly adopted strategic documents. RRF funds meanwhile are disbursed on the basis of National Recovery Plans (NRPs) prepared by Member States and endorsed by the European Commission and the EU Council.

Cohesion policy (including the European Regional Development Fund) accounts for just over 30% of the EU's 1.2 trillion 2021–2027 budget, with the largest beneficiaries in nominal terms being Poland (75 billion euro), Italy (42 billion euro) and Spain (35 billion euro).[19] These funds are distributed across the EU MSs' regions in accordance with local income and are oriented at facilitating growth and development. Investment priorities are decided *ex ante* in Operational Programmes jointly approved by the MSs and the European Commission. Whereas in the past cohesion policy supported largely infrastructural projects, the policy is now oriented more towards human capital investment and accelerating socio-economic transformation towards climate neutrality. Cohesion green spending – given the climate change mainstreaming requirements – is therefore to amount to around 100 billion euro and the transition to a green and circular economy pursued largely through actions under Policy Objective 2 ('A low carbon and greener Europe'). In addition to general greenhouse gas (GHG) emission reduction aims, financing investments in distribution networks, including the retrofitting of gas transmission, to make them 'ready for adding renewable and low carbon gases, such as hydrogen, biomethane and synthesis gas' is explicitly allowed.[20] Concrete priorities are however set at the national and regional levels. In the past, biogas projects have featured for example in the operational programme of the French Bourgogne; however, a recent overview shows that for the 2014–2020 MFF, renewable energy investment (including biomass) ranged between 8% and 19% of total allocations across regions.[21] The Cohesion Fund has also been used to finance a number of projects enabling municipal energy production from waste (e.g. in Gdańsk, Poland).[22]

The RRF is the EU's economic response to the pandemic. It makes 724 billion euro available to MSs to rapidly invest and introduce reforms oriented at stimulating growth and improving economies' capacities in the face of health sector pressure, recurring lockdowns and social instability caused by COVID-19. Increasing resilience to climate change and pursuing environmental objectives closely linked with the pandemic's causes (e.g. decreasing

---

[19] European Commission, 'Cohesion Policy amounts by Member States' (2021) https://ec.europa.eu/info/sites/default/files/about_the_european_commission/eu_budget/1_table_breakdown_of_cohesion_policy_current_prices.pdf accessed 16 May 2022.

[20] Regulation (EU) 2021/1058 on the European Regional Development Fund and on the Cohesion Fund [2021] OJ L231/60.

[21] European Commission, 'Notice – Technical guidance on the climate proofing of infrastructure in the period 2021–2027' C (2021) 5430.

[22] At the time of writing, 2021–2027 Partnership Agreements between the European Commission and MSs were still under development, consequently a consistent overview of the bioenergy-related priorities of MSs was not possible.

biodiversity) are a major target for the RRF funds. While at least 268 billion euro (37% of total funds) must be allocated to green objectives, all spending must not be harmful to the EU's environmental aims, following the approach introduced by the Green Taxonomy regulation.[23] For the purpose of calculating the green target of RRF spending, only biomass projects entailing high GHG reductions are treated as helpful for mitigating climate change, meanwhile the contribution to other environmental objectives (such as a CE) is set at a coefficient of 40%, meaning that the CE contribution is not meaningfully acknowledged, with the exception of favourable treatment of waste heat in high-efficiency cogeneration.[24] Specific guidance on biomass projects is limited to specifying the GHG savings necessary in the context of production of electricity and heat (80% savings) and of biofuels (65% savings).[25] The resulting framework creates more favourable conditions for investment in other renewable energy sources than bioenergy. MSs seem to have presented few biogas/biofuel projects as part of their National Recovery Plans (NRPs), focusing rather on low hanging fruit (railway) or trends (hydrogen). The German NRP even includes a commitment to reducing land use for biomass for bioenergy purposes, in line with the stricter framework for land use.[26] The French NRP, however, does provide for financing measures promoting innovation for the ecological transition (e.g. sustainable fuels strategy), in line with the national energy transition plan. Likewise, the Lithuanian NRP plan will support biomass-based renewable schemes (including biofuel and biomethane). Nevertheless, as made clear in the European Commission's first review of the NRPs finalised by March 2022, it is evident that MSs have focused on wind and solar energy as the prime renewable energy sources.[27]

The Common Agricultural Policy (CAP), which accounts for the largest part of the EU budget, has historically played a key role in the development of biofuels from crops. This support has been subsequently more limited as sustainability and land use concerns gained centre stage. Nonetheless, bioeconomy development is to be one of the focal points of the new Strategic Plans developed by MSs from 2023 under the new CAP regime. Circular and

---

[23] The so-called 'do no significant harm' (DNSH) principle, see further Section IV.

[24] Regulation (EU) 2021/241 establishing the Recovery and Resilience Facility [2021] OJ L57/17, Annex VI.

[25] European Commission, 'Guidance to Member States Recovery and Resilience Plans' SWD (2021) 12 https://ec.europa.eu/info/sites/default/files/document_travail_service_part1_v2_en.pdf last accessed 16 May 2022.

[26] Andersen, Allen and Domingo (n 3) 37, see further Section V on the significance of the evolving regulatory context.

[27] European Commission, 'Report on the implementation of the Recovery and Resilience Facility' COM (2022) 75.

renewable energy constitutes an important contribution to climate change mitigation, a horizontal objective of the CAP.[28] Small gas plants allow farmers to use their waste products (manure, crop residue) as an additional source of income. However, support for bioenergy was not initially supported under the framework as a rule, but rather left for MSs.[29] Rather, as the CAP legal framework makes clear, the EU wanted to support development of 'new rural value chains' in the 'emerging bio-economy' through innovative financing instruments, namely InvestEU following the EU's 2018 Bioenergy Strategy.[30] This deferential approach, discussed further below, is likely to be supplemented with further guidance from the EU level in the aftermath of the Russian invasion of Ukraine and new EU strategies to establish energy independence, in particular through biomethane. The European Commission's REPowerEU strategy already indicates that CAP Strategic Plans will be used to specifically 'channel funding to biomethane produced from sustainable biomass sources, including in particular agricultural wastes and residues'. While further details are to follow through 2022, this marks an important shift in policy.[31]

III. EU LAW AND POLICIES SHAPING MEMBER STATE SUPPORT FOR BIOENERGY

EU budgetary support for biogas, either through EU- or MS-level programmes (cohesion policy, RRF), are however only a fraction of the public funds available to bioenergy projects. In fact, as the International Energy Agency (IEA) 2020 Outlook on Biogas emphasises, 'in Europe most biogas plants to date have been built to capture feed-in tariffs and other forms of support for renewable power generation'.[32] As this section explains, the main drivers of such public support are the EU-level targets for renewable energy set by RED as well as favourable GHG treatment for biomass, while the available forms of aid are determined by the applicable State aid rules.

---

[28] Regulation (EU) 2021/2115 establishing rules on support for strategic plans to be drawn up by Member States under the common agricultural policy (CAP Strategic Plans) and financed by the European Agricultural Guarantee Fund (EAGF) and by the European Agricultural Fund for Rural Development (EAFRD) and repealing Regulations (EU) No 1305/2013 and (EU) No 1307/2013 [2021] OJ L435/1.

[29] Janusz Wojciechowski, 'Zielony Ład i WPR Szansą dla zrównoważonego rolnictwa' (Magazyn Biomasa, listopad/grudzień 2021) https://magazynbiomasa.pl/porozumienie-sektorowe-juz-jest-czy-rozpedzi-branze/ last accessed 16 May 2022.

[30] European Commission – Directorate-General for Research and Innovation, *A Sustainable Bioeconomy for Europe: Strengthening the Connection between Economy, Society and the Environment* (Publication Office of the EU 2018).

[31] SEIP (n 8) para 2.1.2.

[32] IEA (n 2) 50.

Bioenergy is treated as a 'renewable energy source' (RES) under the RED II, and consequently, expanding its uptake allows MSs to meet the set targets. Under the 2018 reiteration of the Directive, the EU committed to deriving at least 14% of energy from renewable energy sources, while transport fuel is to comprise at least 3.5% of advanced biofuels.[33] Learning from past mistakes, the contribution of biofuels produced from food and feed crops was limited to 7% of transport energy consumption in 2020, while high indirect land-use change (ILUC) risk biofuels are to be gradually phased out.[34]

The previous RED framework, which included first generation biofuels in the RES targets, incentivised growing crops for biogas. This regulatory effect is evident where the high share of crops use in the EU can be contrasted with the situation in China or the US, which – though producing significantly less biogas – thus far have relied mostly on animal manure or municipal solid waste.[35] To develop biofuels MSs such as Germany, Denmark, France, Italy or the Netherlands spent significant public funds, totalling as much as 15 billion euros a year.[36]

The EU shapes such spending in two ways. On a general level, the EU fiscal rules set a constraint on public budget spending at 60% debt and 3% deficit to GDP ratio. The review of these limits, launched in 2020, may lead to the introduction of a 'green golden rule', which would exempt certain types of green investment – presumably also in the area of bioenergy defined as sustainable under the EU framework – from the applicable ceilings. More concretely, EU rules on Environment and Energy State Aid shape the subsidies which the MSs may offer to local bioenergy producers.[37] Under these Guidelines, the European Commission allows for a derogation from the Treaty State aid prohibition

---

[33] Note ongoing work to further adjust the EU's biofuel framework as part of the 'Fit for 55' legislative agenda, and specifically European Commission's 'Proposal for a Regulation on the deployment of alternative fuels infrastructure, and repealing Directive 2014/94/EU of the European Parliament and of the Council' COM (2021) 559.

[34] Note ongoing work to further adjust the EU's Regulation on the inclusion of GHG emissions and removals from land use, land use change and forestry (LULUCF) as part of 'Fit for 55'.

[35] Seventy per cent of the biomethane used in Europe in 2020 came from energy crops, see: IEA (n 2) 59.

[36] IEA (n 2); European Parliamentary Research Service, 'Cohesion and Climate' (2021) PE 690.514 https://www.europarl.europa.eu/RegData/etudes/ATAG/2021/690514/EPRS_ATA(2021)690514_EN.pdf/; Camilla Hodgson, 'The EU's Biomass Dilemma: Can Burning Trees Ever Be Green?' *Financial Times* (London, 1 July 2021)

[37] Relevant rules on energy taxation and public procurement are also harmonised in the EU. Guidelines for State aid in the agricultural and forestry sectors and in rural areas apply to aid granted for the development of biofuel capacities for farmers' own consumption.

where such aid allows for the development of economic activities related to environmental protection.[38] The applicable Guidelines were reviewed in 2021 to *inter alia* include more favourable treatment of CE schemes such as the reuse of waste heat or recycling of waste.[39] Since the EU State aid rules evolve in tandem with changing priorities, new guidelines encourage bioenergy that avoids competition with food or feed production.[40] Specifically, only support for biofuels and biogases deemed sustainable under RED II can be approved.[41] Under the 2021 E&E State Aid Guidelines, MSs can support biofuel/biogas projects that aim to reduce or remove GHG, in cases – as the European Commission phrases it – where the carbon price does not force market actors to fully internalise the costs of emissions.[42] State support must comply with the principles of necessity, appropriateness and proportionality, compliance with which is ensured in the following way: the rules generally favour schemes under which biogas producers apply for support in a competitive process. Small projects (e.g. involving energy below 1 MW or implemented by SMEs) and cross-border ones are exempt from this rule. Competitive certificate or supplier obligation is allowed where the MS can prove that the aim of the scheme is to stimulate demand and consistency with the mass balance system documentation under RED II.[43] Such aid has proven indispensable for the economic viability of biogas projects given the high cost differential (about 20%) between biofuels and conventional liquid energy sources.[44]

IV. EU LAW AND POLICIES SHAPING PRIVATE INVESTMENT IN BIOENERGY

By some estimates 70% of the funding necessary to secure a net zero future will have to come from private investors.[45] In this vein, mobilising private capital to invest in green projects is at the heart of EU action. The EU's funding plan

---

38 Consolidated versions of the Treaty on European Union and the Treaty on the Functioning of the European Union [2016] OJ C202/1 ('TFEU'), art 107 (3)(c).

39 European Commission, 'Guidelines on State aid for climate, environmental protection and energy 2022' COM (2022) 481, OJ C80/1 ('Environmental State Aid Guidelines'). Aid for use of waste for energy production is treated under the conditions for aid for activities lowering GHG emissions (point 224).

40 See further Chapter 11 in this volume.

41 Environmental State Aid Guidelines (n 39) point 80.

42 ibid point 89.

43 ibid point 108.

44 IEA (n 3) 222.

45 ibid.

for the green transition[46] commits to regulation forcing polluters to internalise the value of the damage they cause. As long as the carbon pricing does not work efficiently, however, the bulk of the EU's regulatory and policy efforts is directed at making investing in 'green' projects easier and less risky for private capital.[47] Such 'ease' is to come for example through common classification frameworks, which clarify the required sustainability standards for technologies (e.g. the Green Taxonomy, discussed further below). Furthermore, EU funds similarly seek to facilitate private investment in renewables, including sustainable bioenergy (see Table 10.1). For example, the regulation establishing the LIFE programme declares its aim as being to: '[m]ainstream and de-risk energy efficiency and renewable energy investments with a particular focus on private finance stakeholders, by contributing to already existing practices or through new approaches filling well identified gaps'.[48]

The clarity of the regulatory framework for biogas production is important as bioenergy is deemed the riskiest of the renewable energy sources by investors, in particular if it uses waste or manure. The reason is that such energy production does not scale easily (it is not viable to transport waste long distances); the supply of waste may not be stable (precluding long-term delivery contracts), while the gas content is lower than in the case of dedicated crops.[49] Nonetheless, it is a growing market, in particular with regard to upgrading biogas to biomethane, which is reflected in the EU's framework for sustainable finance.

The EU Green Taxonomy[50] is the centrepiece of the EU's sustainable finance agenda, where it creates a common classification system to determine

---

[46] European Commission, 'Strategy for financing the transition to a sustainable economy' COM (2021) 390.

[47] See to this end: IEA (n 3) 73 calling for such common frameworks; European Commission, 'LIFE Programme List of Priority Topics for 2021–2024' (n.d.) https://ec.europa.eu/info/funding-tenders/opportunities/docs/2021-2027/life/wp-call/2021-2024/priority-topics_life-2021-2024_en.pdf/, p. 30. See further Agnieszka Smoleńska and Jens van 't Klooster, 'A Risky Bet: Climate Change and the EU's Microprudential Framework for Banks' (2022) Journal of Financial Regulation 51 and Daniela Gabor, 'Wall Street Consensus' (2021) 52 Development and Change 429.

[48] See Section II.

[49] European Energy Futures, 'Making biogas work: a financial perspective' (Webinar, 2021) https://www.youtube.com/watch?v=RO_kooffXnc last accessed 16 May 2021.

[50] Regulation (EU) 2020/852 on the establishment of a framework to facilitate sustainable investment, and amending Regulation (EU) 2019/2088 [2020] OJ L198/13 ('Green Taxonomy Regulation'). See further: Smoleńska and van 't Klooster (n 47); Christos Gortsos, 'The Taxonomy Regulation: More Important than Just as an Element of the Capital Markets Union' (2021) https://papers.ssrn.com/abstract=3750039/ accessed 16 May 2022.

whether a given business activity is sustainable, that is: (a) it contributes to one of the EU's six environmental objectives;[51] (b) it does not significantly harm the other five (DNSH principle); and (c) it meets minimum standards of good governance. Such activities cover the majority of current GHG emissions in the EU (manufacturing, transport, energy production). In a highly granular fashion, the delegated acts to the Taxonomy Regulation set thresholds (e.g. CO_2 emissions) for 'green' investments. As such, the framework is essentially a technology for translating the findings of climate change science (and other environmental sciences in the context of other sustainability objectives) into the language of finance and business activity. The regulation is foundational, because it enables other rules such as labels and disclosures; it is also used as a benchmark for assessing EU spending.[52] In particular, as has already been discussed in Section II, the Green Taxonomy increasingly informs the spending framework for EU funds such as the Recovery Fund and InvestEU, albeit with caveats. These reflect the fact that the Green Taxonomy framework is still under development and its full and extended use in the context of the 2021–2027 MFF would undermine legal certainty. So far, only the rules relating to climate change mitigation and adaptation have been published, with the CE-promoting investments to be defined by 2023. Further extended taxonomy frameworks, covering for example activities which help to accelerate transition, but are not themselves sustainable, are also to be developed.[53]

Within the Green Taxonomy framework, a special place is foreseen for bioenergy, in particular the advanced biofuels made from forestry residue and food waste. Taxonomy also emphasises the potential of anaerobic digestion for reducing methane emissions.[54] In line with the emerging narrower definitions on biofuel sustainability, transport biofuels derived from crops fit for human

---

51 These are: climate change mitigation; climate change adaptation; sustainable use and protection of water and marine resources; transition to a CE; pollution prevention and control; and protection and restoration of biodiversity and ecosystems.

52 See Section II.

53 Platform on Sustainable Finance, 'The Extended Environmental Taxonomy: Final Report on Taxonomy extension options supporting a sustainable transition' (2022).

54 European Commission Delegated Act supplementing Regulation (EU) 2020/852 by establishing the technical screening criteria for determining the conditions under which an economic activity qualifies as contributing substantially to climate change mitigation or climate change adaptation and for determining whether that economic activity causes no significant harm to any of the other environmental objectives [2021] OJ L442/1 ('Green Taxonomy Delegated Act'), rec 32.

and animal consumption – such as wheat and corn (food and feed crops) – are not considered 'green'.[55]

There are a number of categories of sustainable activities related to biofuel and biogas. For example, the manufacture of renewable energy technologies is an enabling activity for climate change mitigation.[56] Likewise, the manufacture of biogas for use in transport, the generation of electricity and the cogeneration/production of heat and power from biogas, bioliquid fuel and waste heat, as well as anaerobic digestion, are activities which under certain conditions are defined as contributing to mitigating climate change under the 2021 Green Taxonomy Delegated Act.[57] Specific thresholds relate to consistency with a wider regulatory framework (i.e. with RED II) and GHG savings (e.g. at least 80% less than the fossil fuel comparator for cogeneration of heat, 65% for biofuels used in transport).[58] Anaerobic-digestion-related activities must minimise methane leakage and the produced biogas must be used directly for the generation of energy/heat or upgraded to biomethane. To contribute to climate change adaptation, activities related to biogas/biofuel must be durable in the face of physical risks with a proof and analysis of climate risk and vulnerability. Consistency with local, sectoral, regional or national adaptation plans and strategies is required, although how this requirement is to be verified is unclear.

Taxonomy's classification is only the first step, however. The EU policymakers intend to incentivise financial institutions to invest in green investment through further regulatory actions (e.g. disclosure rules, microprudential regulation). As a result, green projects are intended to benefit from cheaper capital. Such impact will occur through a number of channels. First, Taxonomy-mandated disclosures will negatively impact the reputation of

---

[55] The lack of consistency with RED II raised by some biofuel producers does not seem well founded in this respect, cf. Sean Goulding Carroll, 'Biofuel Makers Protest against EU's Green Investment Taxonomy Rules' (Euractiv 27 May 2021) https://www.euractiv.com/section/biofuels/news/biofuel-makers-protest-against-eus-green-investment-taxonomy-rules/ last accessed 16 May 2022. Note however the explicit consistency concern expressed in this regard by the European Commission in the Green Taxonomy Delegated Act (n 54), rec 30. High politicisation of biofuels in the Taxonomy is also evident by the number of dedicated responses to the Delegated Act with the topic receiving one of the highest number of dedicated comments. Furthermore, a number of the business activities related to advanced biofuels in public road and water transport were dropped in the final version of the Act. See Annex to: Franziska Schütze and Jan Stede 'The EU Sustainable Finance Taxonomy and its Contribution to Climate Neutrality' (2021) Journal of Sustainable Finance & Investment.

[56] Green Taxonomy Regulation (n 50) art 10(1)(i).

[57] Green Taxonomy Delegated Act (n 54).

[58] Compare Green Taxonomy Delegated Act (n 54) rec 30 and the thresholds for 'climate tagging' under the Recovery and Resilience Facility discussed in Section II.

high emitters, and improve the credibility of green companies. Already some energy companies, such as Shell, are developing green projects in the area of biogas production that fall within the Taxonomy criteria to benefit from the reputational gains.[59] Second, and this is more relevant from the perspective of small-scale biogas/biofuel activities, such regulations will incentivise banks to dedicate more funding to green projects, with increased competition resulting in a 'greenium' (green premium), that is, a lower cost of capital for Taxonomy-compliant projects. Given the cost differential with traditional fossil fuel production, such greeniums can constitute a welcome incentive when offered by private financial institutions or public development banks.[60] Third, where the Taxonomy will have to be adopted by financial institutions across Europe, it will create a transparent framework for business activities related to bioenergy, which – according to IEA at least – was not well understood by financiers. Fourth, the Taxonomy informs the public spending framework in particular with regard to the EU funds, although with the caveats discussed above. Consequently, the DNSH criterion will restrict the availability of EU funds for bioenergy projects. Given the significant market and public finance impact, the scope and granular thresholds of the Taxonomy are highly politicised, also in areas relevant from the point of view of developing biogas/biofuel technologies. In addition to the exclusion of unsustainable bioenergy production, maritime transport and aviation are not included in the current rulebook.[61]

V. CHALLENGES IN THE EU FRAMEWORK FOR BIOGAS/BIOFUEL TRANSITION FINANCING

Bioenergy market development in Europe provides clear evidence of how EU law and policy shape the financing available for new (sustainable) tech-

---

[59] See Schütze and Stede (n 55), pp. 2–3, 7. On the Shell biomass project see: Albert Sikkema, 'How Sustainable is Shell's New Biomass Plant? – WUR Experts Deliver their Verdict' (WUR Resource, 6 November 2021) https://www.resource-online.nl/index.php/2021/11/06/how-sustainable-is-shells-new-biomass-plant/?lang=en accessed 16 May 2022.

[60] Schütze and Stede (n 55) mention German KfW's SME loan programme 'Klimaschutzoffensive für den Mittelstand' which disburses 'climate grants' on the basis of the Green Taxonomy.

[61] However, this does not preclude specific action being taken by individual MSs, for example Spain in its NECP commits to developing aviation biofuel. By contrast, in Germany the definition of sustainable aviation fuels does not cover advanced biofuels. IEA Bioenergy, 'How Can Biomass/Bioenergy Aid the Transformation Towards Carbon Neutrality & What Actions Are Needed' (webinar, 9 December 2021) https://www.youtube.com/watch?v=6zUfrUc2FCc accessed 16 May 2022.

Table 10.1 *Overview of financing sources for biogas/biofuel transition in the EU*

Financing type	Amount (euro)	Beneficiary	Purpose	Priorities	Conditions
EU: LIFE-grants	2.3 billion (2021–2027)	Legal persons	Implementation of environmental protection laws	Collection and recycling of biowaste, waste heat in buildings, development of RES	Grants covering 60% of eligible costs
EU: Horizon Europe	20 billion (2021–2027)	Research institutions	(Basic) research	Sustainable biofuel production, scaling up of technology, innovative biomethane and biogas in agriculture	Grants covering 100% of eligible costs
EU: InvestEU	[fraction of] 372 billion (2021–2027)	Legal persons	Growth and competitiveness	Production and supply of biogases/biofuels	Loans & other types of financing
EU-MS: cohesion policy	100 billion (2021–2027)	Legal persons (including municipalities)	Social, economic cohesion	Set at national/ regional level around the set priorities (including green economy)	Grants covering 40–75% of costs (variable depending on region)
EU-MS: RRF	268 billion (2020–2026)	Legal persons (including municipalities)	Recovery and resilience (reforms and investments)	Set at national/ regional level around the set priorities (including green economy)	Grants
MS-subsidies	15 billion (2018 only, all MS)	Biomass energy production	Fulfilling RES targets	In line with State aid rules	Subsidies (e.g. through a certificate system)
Private finance	EU	Legal persons (including municipalities)	Sustainable investments (Green-Taxonomy-aligned)	Lowering GHG emissions, biomethane	Loans & other forms of financing for project finance covering 70–80% of costs at 2–4% interest (but with a 'greenium')

Source: Author's own compilation. MS - Member States, RES - renewable energy sources, RRF - Recovery and Resilience Facility.

nologies. In this particular case, as shown in this chapter, the EU does so less by providing dedicated funds, but rather by creating regulatory incentives (e.g. 'RES' classification of biomass), which shape the decisions of MSs and private actors. The flows of subsidies to biofuel projects, in particular in countries like Germany, are oriented at ensuring that the RES targets are met quickly and at the lowest (short-term) cost.[62]

From the perspective of overall policy coherence and effectiveness, two problems emerge from the preceding analysis of EU support to biogas/biofuel transition financing. First, notwithstanding a level of harmonisation of rules and the inclusion of the development of bioenergy among the priorities of EU green transition spending, whether or not the technology is supported lies with decisions of individual MSs and their particular policy preferences. Second, although a certain level of policy coherence is assured via the ample references to RED II across all analysed financing streams, evidently bioenergy is treated predominantly through the lens of climate change mitigation rather than that of a CE.

A. Member States Lead on Bioenergy

As production of energy from traditional biomass became increasingly controversial in the last decade, a hesitant approach – largely deferential to MS preferences – followed, and can now be observed across the EU financing support framework. In fact, beyond the refined RED II definitions, most biofuel/biogas action takes place at the national level. Even with regard to plants for the production of biogas from waste in agriculture, across financing policies (CAP, cohesion, RRF) MSs have the last word. As a result, biogas capacities across the EU vary greatly.[63] Furthermore, scalability issues in the production of biogas from waste make large-scale and cross-border EU projects difficult. Rather, the EU defers seeking to shape private financing available to firms (InvestEU, Green Taxonomy). Such an approach is of course not surprising in the light of the MSs' retained competence to define their own energy mixes.[64]

As a result of this approach, however, though the EU institutions use certain assumptions about future biogas consumption in their future scenarios, these

---

62 On the ambiguities and unintended consequences of the EU's biomass framework see especially Juan J Cadillo-Benalcazar and others, 'Why Does the European Union Produce Biofuels? Examining Consistency and Plausibility in Prevailing Narratives with Quantitative Storytelling' (2021) 71 Energy Research and Social Science.

63 Renewable Gas Trade Centre in Europe (REGATRACE), 'Mapping the state of play of renewable gases in Europe' (2020).

64 TFEU (n 38) art 174.

remain unclear as to the specific role which biofuel and biogases from waste are to play long-term apart from a prediction of increased use of the advanced biofuels in high-emitting transport sectors for which electrification (primary decarbonisation strategy) is not possible, in line with the RES targets.[65] Absence of a clear vision for bioenergy at the EU level explains why the bulk of EU financing is dedicated to Research and Innovation (R&I), rather than implementation or direct support to existing technologies which are uncompetitive under the current carbon pricing regime.

Meanwhile, financing the development of technologies and their implementation requires a complex navigation of many unknown unknowns and in particular the interplay between various policy scenarios and the complex energy system undergoing change.[66] Given the plethora of green technologies and strategies (hydrogen, electrification, synthetic fuels), ambiguity within the framework and absence of technology deployment trajectories effectively discourages investment. Without such guidance, the private finance framework in particular is unlikely to become a meaningful driver of the development of biowaste sources of energy. Small (private) biogas producers will look only to State subsidies financing, while large multinational corporates (e.g. Shell) will use the system to offset and – potentially – greenwash.

The market development will therefore remain contingent on national action, rather than EU financing programmes. In this respect, significant differences across MSs persist, which are not easily explained by inherent capacity: the number of biogas plants in the EU ranges from over 130 per 1 million persons in Germany, to fewer than five in Spain, Bulgaria and Romania.[67] Differences in biomethane production capacities and uses are even starker. Biomethane uptake is already high in Sweden, with new fuel blending obligations introduced in Italy.[68] The new EU targets regarding biomethane deployment are likely to result in a stronger role for the EU level. As has already been mentioned, REPowerEU, the flagship programme to shore up the EU's energy independence foresees a special role for CAP in accelerating biomethane production. To this end, further upfront investment (biodigesters, smaller-scale units) and EU guidance on the supporting framework (feed-in

---

[65] Anouk van Grinsven and others, 'Research for European Parliament TRAN Committee – Alternative fuel infrastructures for heavy-duty vehicles' (European Parliament, 12, 2021) https://www.europarl.europa.eu/RegData/etudes/STUD/2021/690901/IPOL_STU(2021)690901_EN.pdf.

[66] Smoleńska and van 't Klooster (n 47).

[67] European Biogas Association (EBA), 'EBA Statistical Report 2020' (2021).

[68] IEA (n 2) 62, cf. Asha Singh, Thomas Christensen and Calliope Panoutsou, 'Policy Review for Biomass Value Chains in the European Bioeconomy' (2021) 3 Global Transitions 13.

tariffs, industrial policy support) is needed. The EU should also provide more direct support across value chains and facilitate the emergence of scaleable 'biohubs' (regional biomass depots), which would allow for the 'commoditification' of biomass.[69]

B. Partial Systems-Thinking

The EU legal framework for bioenergy is highly complex, as discussed throughout this volume. An effort to streamline and ensure consistency with respect to the financing framework is nonetheless visible. RED II is a clear starting point for all currently applicable frameworks for financing streams for biofuel/biogas development. In terms of ensuring synergy across environmental policy objectives, a new role is to be played by the EU agency CINEA.

The key challenge seems to be, however, settling the question of the sustainability of bioenergy production, and in particular decoupling the discussion on biofuels from biowaste from those using dedicated crops, such as trees or corn.[70] With the sustainability question dominating the discussion (and scholarship on EU biomass policy), the dual usefulness of biogas production from the perspective of the EU's environmental policies (i.e. for both climate change mitigation and CE development), does not attract enough attention. Two examples elucidate the resulting problem. First, under the RRF, projects related to waste reuse are not considered in the light of climate change mitigation, while those using biomass (including biowaste) for the production of energy are considered to only partially contribute to the CE objective. Similarly, a siloed approach is visible in the context of the Green Taxonomy. While the principle of DNSH is meant to ensure consistency across the different objectives, there is no method for tracking synergies (i.e. where an investment contributes to two environmental objectives at the same time). The problem is horizontal: also under the LIFE programme discussed in Section II.A it is not *a priori* clear where biogas projects fit best.

Though green projects contributing to two objectives are perhaps more likely to find investors (who have different green preferences), the lack of a synergetic approach withholds a significant regulatory incentive which

---

[69] Wolter Elberssen, 'To Be or Not to Be a Biobased Commodity – Assessing Requirements and Candidates for Lignocellulosic Based Commodities' (Webinar, 30 November 2021) https://www.ieabioenergyconference2021.org/wp-content/uploads/2021/12/02-03_ELBERSEN.pdf accessed 16 May 2022.

[70] European Commission, 'Proposal for a Directive amending Directive (EU) 2018/2001 Regulation (EU) 2018/1999 and Directive 98/70/EC as regards the promotion of energy from renewable sources, and repealing Council Directive (EU) 2015/652' COM (2021) 557.

would prioritise such projects. Political economy factors may explain such a lack of a systems-based approach, given the highly politicised process of developing sustainability classifications as well as 'different policy interests and initiatives leading to isolated incentives and demands'.[71] A key open question will be the impact of the REPowerEU agenda on the EU (and MS) approach in this regard. Evidently there is a strong case to be made that CE policy objectives are well aligned with a strategy oriented at reducing the EU's dependence on external suppliers.

VI. CONCLUSION

This chapter has provided an overview of the financial support available for the development of biogas and advanced biofuel production from biowaste in the EU. In the context of a general increase in funding available to green projects across the EU and ambitions of accelerating the energy transition, the analysis revealed continued hesitancy about biomass use and difficulty in integrating into the siloed framework synergies across projects pursuing multiple environmental objectives. Focus is placed on integrating the energy system (and its decarbonisation), rather than on broader planetary boundary terms. Discussion of the overall framework reveals the critical role of EU law and policy – in addition to different streams of EU funds – in shaping the availability of (public and private) support for transition. The hesitancy about biomass use, which spills over to biogases/biofuels, has led the EU to largely defer to MSs in this regard. Consequently, given the heterogeneity of starting points and government policies, the biogas/biofuel sector is likely to face highly heterogenous access to finance across the EU MSs, both with regard to State and EU public funds, as well as private investment. Such a result is unsatisfactory in particular given the multi-purpose role which biogas could play in a more flexible and decentralised circular energy system. Nevertheless, as part of a renewed push to wean the EU off Russian fossil fuels, which foresees a greater role for biomethane in the energy mix in the short term, further convergence is necessary. This entails complementing the EU-level focus on R&D in the field of bioenergy with marketing and infrastructure investment through direct national and EU funding (e.g. CAP).

LEGISLATION

Consolidated versions of the Treaty on European Union and the Treaty on the Functioning of the European Union [2016] OJ C202/1 ('TFEU').

---

[71] Andersen, Allen and Domingo (n 3).

Directive (EU) 2018/2001 on the promotion of the use of energy from renewable sources [2018] OJ L328/82 ('RED II')
Regulation (EU) 2021/695 establishing Horizon Europe – the Framework Programme for Research and Innovation, laying down its rules for participation and dissemination, and repealing Regulations (EU) No 1290/2013 and (EU) No 1291/2013 [2021] OJ L170/1
Regulation (EU) 2020/852 on the establishment of a framework to facilitate sustainable investment, and amending Regulation (EU) 2019/2088 [2020] OJ L198/13 ('Green Taxonomy Regulation')
Regulation (EU) 2021/523 establishing the InvestEU Programme and amending Regulation (EU) 2015/1017 [2021] OJ L107/30
Regulation (EU) 2021/783 establishing a Programme for the Environment and Climate Action (LIFE), and repealing Regulation (EU) No 1293/2013 [2021] OJ L172/53
Regulation (EU) 2021/241 establishing the Recovery and Resilience Facility [2021] OJ L57/17
Regulation (EU) 2021/2115 establishing rules on support for strategic plans to be drawn up by Member States under the common agricultural policy (CAP Strategic Plans) and financed by the European Agricultural Guarantee Fund (EAGF) and by the European Agricultural Fund for Rural Development (EAFRD) and repealing Regulations (EU) No 1305/2013 and (EU) No 1307/2013 [2021] OJ L435/1
Regulation (EU) 2021/1058 on the European Regional Development Fund and on the Cohesion Fund [2021] OJ L 231/60.
Implementing Regulation (EU) 2020/1294 on the Union renewable energy financing mechanism [2020] OJ L303/1
European Commission Delegated Act supplementing Regulation (EU) 2020/852 by establishing the technical screening criteria for determining the conditions under which an economic activity qualifies as contributing substantially to climate change mitigation or climate change adaptation and for determining whether that economic activity causes no significant harm to any of the other environmental objectives [2021] OJ L442/1 ('Green Taxonomy Delegated Act')

11. Energy State aid

Allard Knook

I. INTRODUCTION

State aid law has gained an unprecedented amount of attention in recent years. But there are hardly any areas of State aid law which have become as relevant recently as energy aid – not only because of the hundreds of billions of euros earmarked for the energy transition as a result of the Green Deal, but also because of the need to become less dependent on Russian gas as a result of the Russian-Ukrainian War, which is also illustrated by the REPowerEU plan of the European Commission.

In a nutshell, within the European Union (EU), providing State aid is prohibited by virtue of Article 107(1) Treaty of the Functioning of the European Union (TFEU).[1] Most State aid rules deal with the exceptions to this rule. For many years, typical of virtually every State aid test when it came to energy aid was finding the right balance between protecting the environment and avoiding market distortions. In the words of Commissioner Vestager, in the accompanying press release to one of the decisions by which the Commission approved the German Renewable Energy Act: 'I want to strike a balance between several needs: to promote renewable energy and ensure its stable financing. At the same time, we need to protect the competitiveness of European industry. Today's decision achieves this'.[2]

Providing energy aid has always been about striking the right balance between these two values: in essence between finding the right balance between economic integration and protecting the environment. This is clearly reflected in the Climate, Environment and Energy Aid Guidelines (CEEAG), which entered into force in January 2022 and which serve as an important instrument to achieve the goals of the European Green Deal. With the Green

---

1 Consolidated versions of the Treaty on European Union and the Treaty on the Functioning of the European Union [2016] OJ C202/1 ('TFEU').

2 European Commission, 'State aid: Commission approves German aid scheme for renewable energy (EEG 2012); orders partial recovery' (25 November 2014) https://ec.europa.eu/commission/presscorner/detail/en/IP_14_2122/.

Deal, the EU aims to transform the Union into a resource-efficient and competitive economy. The Commission has estimated that achieving the Green Deal targets will require EUR 390 billion of additional annual investment compared to the levels in 2011–2020, with a further EUR 130 billion a year for the other environmental objectives estimated previously. Cleary, the State aid rules needed significant adjustments to allow for such investments. For this reason, the Commission adopted the CEEAG. This chapter will assess to what extent, as a result of the Green Deal, the balance between the energy transition and avoiding market distortion, which has developed over the years (Section III) into a seemingly fixed equilibrium (Section IV), has now been altered significantly by these guidelines (Section V). However, since this question is only relevant when State aid is involved, it will first be discussed when a measure of a Member State (MS) constitutes energy aid (Section II).

II. WHEN THE BALANCE IS IRRELEVANT: NO AID INVOLVED

There is no need to find the right balance between renewable energy and market distortion when an MS measure constitutes State aid within the meaning of Article 107(1) TFEU is involved. This, in short, is the case when three cumulative criteria are met:

1. Does the measure amount to a transfer of State resources?
2. Is a selective, non-market advantage granted to (an) undertaking(s)?
3. Is the measure liable to distort competition and affect trade between MSs?

These three conditions will now be discussed.

A. Does the Measure Amount to a Transfer of State Resources?

State resources may be granted either directly by the State or through an entity which administers the funds from which the aid is granted. The fact that a State aid measure is not financed directly by a State but by an entity created or appointed by a State can still lead to a transfer of State resources.[3] It is irrelevant whether the origin of the resources is public or private, or whether the contributions to be made are voluntary or compulsory.[4] On the other hand, the private nature of the entity in question may play an important role in the question of the imputability of the aid measure to the State. However, this in

[3] Case 78/76 *Steinike & Weinlig* ECLI:EU:C:1997:52 [1977], para 21.

[4] See also: Case T-139/09 *France v Commission* ECLI:EU:T:2012:496 [2012], paras 63–64.

itself is not decisive. In addition to the private nature of the entity managing the funds in question, it may also be relevant whether that entity manages purely private funds. However, that fact alone is not decisive either.[5] If, for example, the funds originate from compulsory charges, there may still be a transfer of public resources even if those funds do not originate from a public authority.[6] The case law of the Court of Justice (ECJ) and the General Court as well as the decision-making practice of the European Commission show that several factors can determine the existence of a transfer of public resources.[7] In the context of energy aid, the *PreussenElektra* judgment of 2001 and the *Essent* judgment of 2008 are still determinative.

The *PreussenElektra* judgment concerned an obligation imposed on private electricity supply undertakings to purchase electricity produced from renewable energy sources at fixed minimum prices higher than the actual market value. The purpose of the scheme was to encourage German producers to produce green electricity. The ECJ ruled that this did not result in a transfer of State resources to the producers of such electricity. Indeed, according to the Court, the undertakings concerned had not been designated by the public authorities to administer an aid scheme. Therefore, the funds they managed could not be considered State resources.[8]

In contrast, it follows from the *Essent* judgment that there is only a transfer of public resources if these resources come under public control before they are directly or indirectly transferred to the beneficiaries. The difference with the *PreussenElektra* judgment is relative, but important. The *Essent* judgment also involved levies imposed on private undertakings. The difference with *PreussenElektra*, however, was that in *Essent*, the undertakings in question had been designated by law to collect the charges on behalf of the government and to pass them on to the beneficiaries. The private companies could not use the proceeds of these levies for purposes other than those provided by law. In addition, there was a certain degree of public control. According to the Court, this was sufficient for them to be considered State resources.[9] The Court followed a similar line of reasoning in the *Iride* judgment in relation to an Italian stranded costs compensation measure. The funds in question were first collected from private consumers of energy and then transferred to private undertakings. However, this was done by a public body appointed by the Italian Government to deliver the reimbursement of the stranded costs to

---

5 Case C-83/98 *Ladbroke* [2000] ECR I-3271, para 50.

6 Case T-358/94 *Air France* [1996] ECR II-2109, para 65–67.

7 European Commission Decision on State aid SA.39042 – Romania: RES support reduction for energy-intensive users C (2014) 7287, para 50.

8 Case C-379/98 *PreussenElektra* [2001] ECR I-2099, paras 59–62.

9 Case C-206/06 *Essent* [2008] ECR I-5497, para 70.

the beneficiary undertakings. The Court of First Instance therefore considered that, in those circumstances, there was a transfer of State resources.[10]

B. Is a Selective, Non-market Advantage Granted to (an) Undertaking(s)?

The concept of advantage within the meaning of Article 107(1) TFEU covers any advantage that an undertaking would not have obtained, either directly or indirectly, without State intervention.[11] The question of whether an advantage is involved is usually determined by whether the Market Economy Operator (MEO) principle is complied with: in short whether a market conform advantage is provided. For example, in June 2015, the European Commission ruled, on the basis of a benchmark, that the tariffs applied by the Romanian public company Hidroelectrica were an advantage on market terms.[12]

In the context of energy aid, the 'EDF decision' of 2000 and the 'EDF judgment' of 2012 are determinative in respect of this second condition. Although two completely different issues were involved, this judgment and this decision well reflect the playing field within which a government needs to operate in order to comply with the MEO principle.

In the 'EDF decision', the European Commission ruled that the application of preferential tariffs by the French state-owned company Electricité de France (hereafter EDF) to the supply of electricity to paper mills equipped with so-called electrically-powered infrared dryers complied with the MEO principle. At the time, EDF had surplus capacity from nuclear energy. The European Commission considered that, in the case of overcapacity, a private investor in a market economy would normally seek to maximise profits and would therefore sell an additional quantity of its product, without covering all the costs for this additional quantity. Therefore, according to the European Commission, the application of a preferential electricity price for the additional consumption resulting from the installation of electric dryers could be considered an accept-

---

[10] Case T 25/07 *Iride and Iride Energia* [2009] ECR II-245. The appeal in this case was declared partly inadmissible and partly manifestly unfounded: Case C-150/09 P *Iride and Iride Energia* ECLI:EU:C:2010:34 [2010] ECR I-5.

[11] Case C-39/94 *SFEI* [2016] ECR 1996 I-3547, para 60; Case C-342/96 *Spain v Commission* [1999] ECR 1999 I-2459, para 41.

[12] European Commission Decision (EU) 2017/501 on tariffs applied by Hidroelectrica of Romania to S.C. ArcelorMittal Galaţi, S.C. Alro SA, S.C. Alpiq RomEnergie S.R.L., S.C. Alpiq RomIndustries S.R.L., S.C. Energy Financing Team Romania S.R.L. (EFT), S.C. Electrica SA, S.C. Electromagnetica SA, S.C. Energy Holding S.R.L., S.C. EURO-PEC SA, S.C. Luxten-Lighting Group SA, S.C. Electrocarbon SA Slatina and S.C. ELSID Titu SA – SA.33623 (2012/C), SA.33624 (2012/C), SA.33451 (2012/C) and SA.33581 (2012/C) [2017] OJ L83/1.

able commercial approach. In the Commission's view, this was in line with the MEO principle.[13]

The 2012 EDF judgment, as indicated, concerned a completely different matter. The French State – as sole shareholder – had waived a tax claim of just under €900 million in corporate tax due when EDF was restructured. The French State argued that such a waiver should be seen as comparable to an investment that a private investor would have made in the context of the restructuring of EDF. The European Commission did not follow this view and ordered recovery of the aid.[14] However, the ECG[15] and the ECJ[16] ruled that the MEO principle had been respected. The Court ruled that if it could be demonstrated unequivocally, on the basis of objective and verifiable data, that a private shareholder would have acted in the same way, a waiver could be regarded as a market-based investment. This information had to show that the public authority concerned had already determined, before making the investment, to what extent the company was profitable or otherwise justify its investment.

With regard to the question of when a *selective* advantage is involved, in particular tax incentives to promote sustainability are regularly considered to be non-selective. For example, the European Commission considered that a general Dutch exemption from energy tax for green electricity was not selective,[17] but a partial exemption from this energy tax for Dutch waste incinerators was.[18] The first decision concerned a tax exemption for companies that purchased green electricity. The European Commission ruled that this scheme applied equally to 'all undertakings and all sectors'. At the same time, the European Commission noted that the exemption did give the producers of green power an advantage compared to producers of grey power. The second decision concerned a partial exemption from the same energy tax for Dutch waste incineration plants that produced energy from burning organic material. The European Commission found that this fiscal measure only applied to a selective group of electricity producers. Therefore, the measure constituted a selective measure.

---

[13] European Commission Decision 2001/274/EC on the measure implemented by EDF for certain firms in the paper industry [2001] OJ L95/18.

[14] European Commission Decision 2005/145/EC on the State aid granted by France to EDF and the electricity and gas industries [2005] OJ L49/9.

[15] Case T-156/04 *EDF v Commission* [2009] ECR II-4503.

[16] Case C-124/10 P *Commission v EDF* ECLI:EU:C:2012:318 [2012].

[17] European Commission Decision on State aid NN 30/B/2000 and State aid N 678/2001 – zero tax rate for green electricity (28 November 2001).

[18] European Commission Decision on State aid N 239/2001 – partial exemption from energy tax for waste incineration plants (11 December 2001).

These decisions show that in order to determine whether there is a selective advantage, it is not only the possible aid recipients that must be considered. Also, third parties may possibly receive a selective advantage within the meaning of Article 107(1) TFEU.

C. Is the Measure Liable to Distort Competition and Affect Trade Between Member States?

As regards the construction of distribution networks, the European Commission has, to date, on three occasions found that such aid did not fulfil the last two criteria of Article 107(1) TFEU. These three decisions concerned successively a distribution network for the sale of natural gas, a similar network in the Italian city of Bolzano[19] and in the Italian region of Piedmont[20] for the propulsion of motor vehicles, and the already mentioned Amsterdam subsidy scheme in so far as it concerned subsidies for the purchase of electric charging points.[21] At the same time, due to the fast growing (European) market for electric cars, it is (still) very questionable whether the construction of distribution networks for electric cars can still be considered as local aid.

If a measure constitutes State aid within the meaning of Article 107(1) TFEU – in other words, all three criteria discussed in this section have been met – the GBER is, in practice, the most logical way to bring the aid measure into line with State aid law. A notification to the European Commission is then not necessary: despite the fact that there is State aid, it is exempt from notification. If the GBER does not apply, the measure involved must be notified to the European Commission, which will then assess that measure on the basis of the CEEAG. The next sections will discuss the significance of these Guidelines against the background of their historical background (Section III).

III. THE EARLY RULES: FINDING THE RIGHT BALANCE BETWEEN RENEWABLE ENERGY AND MARKET DISTORTION

The balance described in the introduction to this chapter clearly tilted in favour of environmental protection in the first State aid framework on environmental

---

[19] European Commission Decision on State aid case N275/08 – Refuelling infrastructure for natural gas-powered vehicles (18 August 2008).

[20] European Commission Decision 2006/63/EC on the aid scheme which Italy (Region of Piedmont) is planning to implement for the reduction of airborne pollution in its territory [2006] OJ L32/82.

[21] European Commission Decision on State aid SA.34719 – the Netherlands: Electric Transport Scheme in Amsterdam C (2013) 7886 final.

aid from 1974.[22] This framework, which was renewed with some amendments in 1980[23] and again in 1986[24] and 1993,[25] provided that aid could be authorised (already) if it was for investments by firms that were necessary to comply with certain mandatory environmental standards. Under these guidelines, State aid could even be granted to cover regular costs of companies. The emergence in the 1980s of the 'polluter pays' principle led to a different approach. Although the guidelines allowed State aid to be provided for the promotion of environmental protection measures, they could not be used to support companies which were already under a legal obligation to take these measures. This was reflected in the requirement that environmental and energy aid should primarily benefit society as a whole, not merely the undertaking concerned. In other words, such aid had to have a wider impact than merely on the undertaking concerned.

The 1994 framework, which was extended (unamended) in 1999[26] until 30 June 2000 and then again until 31 December 2000,[27] was finally replaced by a new framework in 2001.[28] The focus was again on balancing environmental protection on the one hand and preventing market distortion on the other. In addition, as a result of the Kyoto Protocol in 1997, the European Commission emphasised more than ever that, on the basis of Article 6 of the EC Treaty (now Article 11 of the TFEU), environmental policy had to become an integral part of all European policy areas, thus also of European State aid policy.[29] The

---

[22] Letter to the Member States (6 November 1974) SEC (74) 4264 and European Commission, *IVth Report on Competition Policy* (Publications Office of the European Union 1975), paras 175 to 182.

[23] Letter to Member States (7 July 1980) SG (80) D/8287 and European Commission, *Xth Report on Competition Policy* (Publications Office of the European Union 1977), paras 222 to 226.

[24] Letter to Member States (23 March 1987) SG (87) D/3795 and European Commission, *XVIth Report on Competition Policy* (Publications Office of the European Union 1990), para 259. For the extension in 1993 see letters to Member States dated 18 January and 19 July 1993.

[25] Council Recommendation regarding cost allocation and action by public authorities on environmental matters [1975] OJ L194/1. This principle is codified in Article 192(2) TFEU.

[26] European Commission, 'Extension of the validity of the Community guidelines on State aid for environmental protection' [2000] OJ C14/8.

[27] European Commission, 'Extension of the validity of the Community guidelines on State aid for environmental protection' [2000] OJ C184/25.

[28] European Commission, 'Community guidelines on State aid for environmental protection' [2001] OJ C37/3.

[29] See, *inter alia*, European Commission, 'The Cologne Report on Environmental Integration' SEC (99) 777 and European Commission, 'From Cardiff to Helsinki and Beyond: Report on the integration of environmental concerns and sustainable development into Community policies' SEC (1999) 1941.

granting of State aid was therefore seen as an important means of achieving the objectives of the Kyoto Protocol. At the same time, in the introductory recitals of the 2001 guidelines, it was stated that the European Commission was trying to clarify the guidelines: '... to what extent and under what conditions may aid measures be necessary to ensure environmental protection and sustainable development without having disproportionate effects on competition and economic growth'.[30]

The 2001 Energy and Environmental State Aid Guidelines (EEAG) were replaced in 2008 with a new aid framework. Again, the main objectives of this framework were to ensure that energy aid led to a higher level of environmental protection which would not be reached without the aid. Furthermore, a large number of categories of aid in the EEAG were simultaneously included in the – then new – GBER. As a result, since 2008 there have been complementary regulations: for many categories of environmental aid included in the GBER there is an equivalent in the EEAG. The main difference is that under the EEAG the aid must be notified to the European Commission, while under the GBER the aid is exempt from notification. Obviously, for this reason, the possibilities under the General Block Exemption Regulation were more limited; for example, the aid intensity under the GBER is generally lower. Both the GBER and the EEAG focused on the 'balancing test' included in the State Aid Action Plan 2008.[31] This test must lead to the aid actually being granted when it promotes environmental protection, is directed and proportional; but has only a limited effect on competition. The purpose of the balancing test is to ensure that environmental aid is genuinely targeted at remedying market failures that are harmful to the environment. Since 2008, the balancing test has played an important role in the European Commission's decision-making practice in the field of environmental aid.

IV. THE EQUILIBRIUM IN THE 2014 GBER AND THE 2014 EEAG

Both the EEAG and GBER have formed an important basis for granting aid in the energy sector. As a result of the modernisation of State aid law, the balance between environmental protection and the avoidance of market distortions became the focus of the EU2020 policy and the resulting Energy2020 policy. One of the three so-called basic pillars of the modernisation programme was that the new State aid policy should contribute to 'sustainable, smart and inclu-

---

[30] Community guidelines on State aid for environmental protection (n 28) point 5.

[31] European Commission, 'State Aid Action Plan 2008. Less and better targeted state aid: a roadmap for state aid reform 2005–2009', SEC (2005) 795.

sive growth ... in a competitive internal market'.[32] In particular, following the modernisation of State aid law, environmental aid rules should be seen as an important tool to promote initiatives contributing to the EU2020 policy. Both the amended provisions on environmental aid in the General Block Exemption Regulation and the new EEAG are therefore explicitly designed with the EU 2020 policy in mind.

Due to this emphasis on EU2020 policy, the possibilities under the GBER and the EEAG were further extended. In addition, new categories of aid were included in the GBER, such as aid for energy infrastructure and operating aid for the production of electricity from renewable energy sources. The EEAG also contained new categories, namely support for energy infrastructure, support for energy-intensive users and support for security of supply. In the explanatory documents, the amendments to the EEAG referred explicitly to the Energy 2020 policy. More specifically, reference was made to the most important principle of this policy, namely that efforts must be made to achieve energy efficiency throughout the energy chain.

At the same time, the new EEAG clearly aimed to avoid market distortion, or rather to stimulate market forces with respect to electricity from renewable energy sources. For example, feed-in tariffs were seen by the European Commission as distorting the market. For this reason, they are to be gradually replaced by public bidding procedures. During a transitional phase in 2015 and 2016, support for at least 5% of planned new electrical capacity from renewable energy sources had to be granted through a competitive bidding procedure based on clear, transparent and non-discriminatory criteria. As of 1 January 2017, State aid for this category had to then be awarded in full on the basis of a public bidding procedure.[33]

Next to the GBER and the EEAG, the Emission Trading Scheme guidelines aim to reduce the impact of CO_2 costs for electricity-intensive businesses, based on the idea that this is necessary for these businesses to remain globally competitive (unlike other businesses that also had CO_2 costs due to greenhouse gas emissions trading). The guidelines can be used to provide support to companies as part of the implementation of the European Directive regulating

---

[32] European Commission, 'EU State Aid Modernisation (SAM)' COM (2012) 209.

[33] Only three exceptions to this rule are possible, namely if it can be demonstrated:

A. that only one or a very limited number of projects or sites can be considered;
B. that a competitive bidding process would result in higher aid levels (e.g. to deter strategic bidding), or
C. that a competitive bidding process would result in a lower percentage of projects being implemented.

emissions trading (the ETS Directive).[34] The aforementioned balancing test is also central to these Guidelines. This means that the State aid must be necessary to attain the environmental objectives of the ETS Directive, while at the same time the aid must be limited to the minimum necessary to achieve the environmental protection objective pursued, without unduly distorting competition and trade in the internal market. Aid based on the Guidelines must be notified to the European Commission but can be authorised if the conditions of the EEAG are fulfilled.[35]

Also relevant is the 2001 Commission Communication relating to the methodology for analysing State aid linked to stranded costs.[36] This Communication contains specific rules with regard to tariffs or other long-term arrangements that are usually fixed for a longer period. Now that the legal basis (in Directive 96/92)[37] has expired with the entry into force of Directive 2009/72,[38] the question is to what extent this Communication can still be applied, although the European Commission still seems to apply the principles underlying this Communication in its decision-making practice.

V. THE EQUILIBRIUM DISTORTED? STATE AID AS A MEANS TO ACHIEVE THE GREEN DEAL

As mentioned, in order to support the MSs in achieving the Green Deal objectives, the State aid rules clearly required amendment. The first step was taken by amending the EEAG, now dubbed the CEEAG. The CEEAG entered into force on 27 January 2022. It is generally expected that the drastic amendments of the CEEAG – providing for an unprecedented flexibility when it comes to energy aid – will be reflected in the new GBER, a draft version of which will be published in the summer of 2022. The scope *ratione materia* of the CEEAG has been considerably extended. In short, they now apply to all technologies that reduce greenhouse gases and improve energy efficiency. Another new element is the treatment of measures in the field of support for clean mobility, support for improving the energy and environmental performance of buildings

---

34 Directive 2009/29/EC amending Directive 2003/87/EC so as to improve and extend the greenhouse gas emission allowance trading scheme of the Community [2009] OJ L140/63.

35 European Commission Decision on State aid SA.37084 – the Netherlands: Compensation of indirect EU ETS costs C (2013) 6636.

36 Letter to Member States (6 August 2001) SG (2001) D/290869.

37 Directive 96/92/EC concerning common rules for the internal market in electricity [1997] OJ L27/20.

38 Directive 2009/72/EC concerning common rules for the internal market in electricity and repealing Directive 2003/55/EC [2009] OJ L211/55.

and support for the transition to a circular economy. The flexibility created by the CEEAG is also illustrated by the fact that they offer the possibility, under certain conditions, of compensating the entire funding gap of a project. This does require that the reimbursement is limited to the minimum necessary for the implementation of the activity and that a competitive bidding process has been organised.

Importantly, the CEEAG furthermore allow for many new State aid instruments. For example, the so-called *contracts for difference* have been introduced, where the beneficiary is compensated for the difference between the actual market prices and a fixed reference price in order to ensure a stable revenue stream. The new CEEAG covers a wide range of support measures that are relevant to the Green Deal. A number of important themes, the so-called *flagship areas*, receive special attention. These include, in particular, the energy performance of buildings and clean mobility. The CEEAG explain in detail under which conditions support for these objectives can be allowed.

Given these significant changes, does this mean that the balance between finding the right balance between renewable energy and market distortion has altered significantly. Perhaps it is too early to tell? It will depend on how the CEEAG will be applied in practice. The new CEEAG do introduce mechanisms to increase the effectiveness of aid and to prevent distortions of competition. In this context, for example, the participation of stakeholders in the design of large aid measures will be increased. Under certain circumstances, a public consultation on the main features of the envisaged scheme is to be held, something which the previous EEAG did not refer to. Furthermore, CEEAG also stress that a competitive bidding procedure should be the standard way of providing aid in order to avoid overcompensation and market distortions. Save for a few exceptions, such bidding procedures must be open to the maximum extent possible for competing technologies in the MS that can achieve the emissions reduction target. The selection criteria used to allocate the State aid should, as a rule, relate the contribution to the main objective of the measure directly or indirectly to the amount of support requested by the applicant. This can, for example, be expressed in terms of aid amount per unit of environmental protection. This would ensure that the aid is used in the most efficient way, although one might wonder how easy it is in practice to express this numerically, let alone in a way that allows a genuine comparison between different bids.

VI. CONCLUSION

The CEEAG serve as an important means to achieve the Green Deals goals, by allowing a wide array of State aid instruments, with high State aid intensities and with a very broad scope of *ratione materia.* At the same time, however, the Commission aims to ensure these unprecedented amendments will not lead to an undue distortion of the competitiveness of the EU, for instance by creating a competitive bidding procedure, already introduced by the previous Guidelines as means to replace feed-in tariffs, and now the standard way of awarding aid in a proportionate way. The proof of the pudding will be in the eating. At the time of writing, no decisions of the European Commission have been published in which the CEEAG had been applied. However, the Commission has ensured that clear mechanisms have been inserted in the CEEAG to ensure that the equilibrium between sustainability and market distortion will not tilt significantly.

LEGISLATION

Consolidated versions of the Treaty on European Union and the Treaty on the Functioning of the European Union [2016] OJ C202/1 ('TFEU')

Directive 96/92/EC concerning common rules for the internal market in electricity [1997] OJ L27/20

Directive 2009/72/EC concerning common rules for the internal market in electricity and repealing Directive 2003/55/EC [2009] OJ L211/55

Directive 2009/29/EC amending Directive 2003/87/EC so as to improve and extend the greenhouse gas emission allowance trading scheme of the Community [2009] OJ L140/63

European Commission Decision 2006/63/EC on the aid scheme which Italy (Region of Piedmont) is planning to implement for the reduction of airborne pollution in its territory [2006] OJ L32/82

European Commission Decision 2005/145/EC on the State aid granted by France to EDF and the electricity and gas industries [2005] OJ L49/9

European Commission Decision 2001/274/EC on the measure implemented by EDF for certain firms in the paper industry [2001] OJ L95/18

European Commission Decision on State aid SA.37084 – the Netherlands: Compensation of indirect EU ETS costs C (2013) 6636

European Commission Decision on State aid SA.34719 – the Netherlands: Electric Transport Scheme in Amsterdam C (2013) 7886

European Commission Decision on State aid N 239/2001 – partial exemption from energy tax for waste incineration plants (11 December 2001)

European Commission Decision on State aid case N275/08 – Refuelling infrastructure for natural gas-powered vehicles (18 August 2008)

European Commission Decision on State aid SA.39042 – Romania: RES support reduction for energy-intensive users C (2014) 7287

European Commission Decision on State aid NN 30/B/2000 and State aid N 678/2001 – Zero tax rate for green electricity (28 November 2001)

European Commission Decision (EU) 2017/501 on tariffs applied by Hidroelectrica of Romania to S.C. ArcelorMittal Galați, S.C. Alro SA, S.C. Alpiq RomEnergie S.R.L., S.C. Alpiq RomIndustries S.R.L., S.C. Energy Financing Team Romania S.R.L. (EFT), S.C. Electrica SA, S.C. Electromagnetica SA, S.C. Energy Holding S.R.L., S.C. EURO-PEC SA, S.C. Luxten-Lighting Group SA, S.C. Electrocarbon

SA Slatina and S.C. ELSID Titu SA – SA.33623 (2012/C), SA.33624 (2012/C), SA.33451 (2012/C) and SA.33581 (2012/C) [2017] OJ L83/1

CASES

Air France (Case T-358/94) [1996] ECR II-2109
Commission v EDF (Case C-124/10 P) ECLI:EU:C:2012:318 [2012]
EDF v Commission (Case T-156/04) [2009] ECR II-4503
Essent (Case C-206/06) [2008] ECR I-5497
France v Commission (Case T-139/09) ECLI:EU:T:2012:496 [2012]
Iride and Iride Energia (Case T 25/07) [2009], ECR II-245
Iride and Iride Energia (Case C-150/09 P) ECLI:EU:C:2010:34 [2010] ECR I-5
Ladbroke (Case C-83/98) [2000] ECR I-3271
PreussenElektra (Case C-379/98) [2001] ECR I-2099
SFEI (Case C-39/94) [2016] ECR 1996 I-3547
Spain v Commission (Case C-342/96) [1999] ECR 1999 I-2459
Steinike & Weinlig (Case 78/76) ECLI:EU:C:1997:52 [1977]

12. Renewable support schemes and Guarantees of Origin applied to renewable energy regulation

Alberto Pototschnig and Ilaria Conti

1. INTRODUCTION

With the European Green Deal,[1] the European Union (EU) has committed to reach climate neutrality by 2050.[2] To achieve this ambitious goal, greenhouse gas (GHG) emissions will have to be reduced by at least 55% by 2030,[3] with respect to 1990 levels. Renewable energies will continue to play a key role in decarbonising the energy sector, with the European Union having now set a target for their share in final energy consumption of 42.5% by 2030, with an ambition to reach 45%.[4]

The achievement of these ambitious environmental targets requires a change of pace in many sectors of the economy. As has been the case so far,[5] the electricity sector will be called on to provide a more than proportional contribution

1 European Commission, 'The European Green Deal' COM (2019) 640. In reality, a strategic long-term European vision for a prosperous, modern, competitive and climate neutral economy, which would lead to net-zero GHG emissions by 2050 had already been outlined in the Communication: 'A Clean Planet for all – A European strategic long-term vision for a prosperous, modern, competitive and climate neutral economy' COM (2018) 773.

2 Regulation (EU) 2021/1119 establishing the framework for achieving climate neutrality and amending Regulations (EC) 401/2009 and (EU) 2018/1999 [2021] OJ L243/1 ('European Climate Law') art 2.

3 ibid art 4.

4 European Commission, 'Proposal for a Directive amending Directive (EU) 2018/2001, Regulation (EU) 2018/1999 and Directive 98/70/EC as regards the promotion of energy from renewable sources, and repealing Council Directive (EU) 2015/652' COM (2021) 557 ('Proposal for RED III').

5 Against a 20% renewable target for 2020, in 2019 renewables already accounted for 34.1% of gross final electricity consumption in the EU-27.

to the achievement of the renewable penetration target.[6] Indeed, it is likely that, by 2030, two-thirds or more of final electricity consumption will be met by renewable generation.[7]

The gas sector will also be called on to play its role, no longer as a mere back-up for renewable electricity generation, but as a conveyor of renewable energy via molecules, albeit in a way consistent with the overall decarbonisation objectives.[8] The decarbonisation strategy in Europe is based on increased electrification, since in this way there will be greater potential to use renewable energy: renewable electricity is expected to be available in greater volumes than, for example, renewable gaseous or liquid fuels and greater efficiency will be achieved, since in most cases the use of electricity avoids an additional energy transformation. However, not every sector or process can be easily or economically 'electrified', and low-carbon gases[9] will be needed in some applications, both as energy carriers and as feedstock.

On the other hand, the large majority of incentives or support schemes to renewable energy has so far addressed only renewable *electricity*, while renewable and low-carbon gases such as biogas or biomethane and even renewable hydrogen would require financial support in order to develop and upgrade to a meaningful level. This chapter focuses on how to promote renewable *energy* (hence clean electrons and molecules) in an efficient manner. The most suita-

---

[6] It is widely expected that, against a 40% penetration target for renewables in final energy consumption by 2030, renewables will account for 65–70% of electricity generation in that year.

[7] Beyond the increase in the share of renewable-based generation in final electricity consumption, the absolute volume of renewable-based generation is likely to increase, as the extensive electrification of many sectors of the economy – including transport and heating – is likely to overweigh the reduction in electricity demand due to increased energy efficiency (European Commission – Directorate-General for Energy, Directorate-General for Climate Action and Directorate-General for Mobility and Transport, *EU Reference Scenario 2016 – Energy Transport and GHG Emission Trends to 2050* (Publication Office of the European Union 2016) https://ec.europa.eu/energy/sites/ener/files/documents/ref2016_report_final-web.pdf/; Climate Action Network (CAN) Europe and European Environmental Bureau (EEB), 'Building a Paris Agreement Compatible (PAC) Energy Scenario' (June 2020)).

[8] In the recently published 'Hydrogen and decarbonized gas markets package' the European Commission proposed, for the first time, a set of provisions aiming at the definition and integration of 'renewable' and 'low carbon gases' (European Commission, 'Proposal for a Directive on common rules for the internal markets in renewable and natural gases and in hydrogen' COM (2021) 803).

[9] It has long been discussed which gases can be classified as 'renewable' and which ones as 'low-carbon'. The Florence School of Regulation (FSR) has also contributed to the debate with a proposal on a taxonomy of green gases (Ilaria Conti, *How Many Shades of Green? An FSR Proposal for a Taxonomy of 'Renewable' Gases* (European University Institute 2020) https://cadmus.eui.eu/handle/1814/66356/).

ble instrument to achieve this goal would be the Guarantees of Origin (GOs), an already existing instrument which, if enhanced in its scope, could lead to an efficient achievement of the renewable energy penetration target.

It is worth highlighting at this point that, since the GHG reduction target and the renewable energy penetration target are separate, albeit related, targets,[10] they will need two separate, if possibly interrelated, policy instruments.

This chapter proposes an approach, based on a wider role of GOs, to deliver the EU renewable penetration target at least cost and in a way that traces the renewable characteristic of energy through transformations. As the renewables penetration target becomes more ambitious, it will likely be more expensive to reach, and achieving it at the least cost becomes increasingly important. Moreover, a circular economy and integrated energy system, characterised by a larger share of biogas and other renewable energy sources, would benefit from a renewables support approach which could trace the renewable characteristic of energy through transformations.

Last but not least, using GOs for this purpose would perfectly help to fulfil the European Commission's vision, outlined in its Energy System Integration Strategy, for 'trustworthy and efficient markets [to] guide customers towards the most energy-efficient and cheapest decarbonisation option, on the basis of prices that properly reflect all the costs of the energy carrier used'.[11]

To do this, Section II reviews the way in which renewable energy has been promoted so far in the EU. Then, Section III briefly illustrates the current EU legislation on GOs before presenting, in Section IV, the proposed renewables support scheme based on GOs and some implementation aspects. Section V provides an assessment of the proposed scheme in the context of the circular energy system. Section VI contains some conclusions.

---

10 Since the 2020 Climate and Energy Package (Eur-lex, '2020 Climate and Energy Package' (*eur-lex.europe.eu*, 10 September 2015) https://ec.europa.eu/clima/eu-action/climate-strategies-targets/2020-climate-energy-package_en/ accessed 19 September 2022), the EU has set separate targets for GHG emissions reduction and the penetration of renewable energy in final energy consumption. From a purely decarbonisation perspective, renewables have so far represented an 'expensive' way to reduce GHG emissions. However, the setting of a separate renewables target has been justified by the additional benefits that this type of energy brings – including security of supply and the reduction in other harmful emissions – and by the fact that renewables will definitely have to play a role in a climate-neutral world and these technologies required a long lead time for technological development and deployment at scale. For example, only recently some more mature renewable technologies, such as on shore wind generation, have achieved economic viability, after almost thirty years of incentivisation in many Member States.

11 European Commission, 'Powering a climate-neutral economy: An EU Strategy for Energy System Integration', COM (2020) 299, s 3.4, p 14.

II. RENEWABLE SUPPORT SCHEMES

Since the mid-2000s, the EU policy approach to decarbonisation has had as its main pillar the Emission Trading System (ETS).[12] The EU ETS aims at promoting a reduction in GHG emissions by putting a price on them.[13] By working through a price signal, the EU ETS promotes the least-cost approach to achieving any emissions reduction target. However, while promoting decarbonised/low-carbon energy vectors[14] by charging their fossil-based competitors, the EU ETS alone will not likely ensure that the penetration of renewable energies meets the renewable penetration policy goal.[15] A further, more targeted tool is needed.

The EU has been setting increasingly ambitious renewables penetration targets.[16] Experience with renewable energy support in Europe is fairly varied. In the electricity sector, most jurisdictions have so far relied, above all, on feed-in tariffs (FITs), which are being replaced by feed-in premiums (FIPs).[17] Only

---

[12] The EU ETS was originally established by Directive 2003/87/EC (establishing a scheme for greenhouse gas emission allowance trading within the Community and amending Council Directive 96/61/EC [2003] OJ L275/32 ('ETS')).

[13] In reality, the ETS covers carbon emissions from the burning of fossil fuels. For example, carbon emissions from the use of biogas or synthetic gas are not charged under the ETS.

[14] An 'energy vector' is an entity that facilitates the transfer of a given quantity of energy in a particular time and place, and hence makes it available for use. Energy vectors include, *inter alia*: fossil fuels – oil and derivatives, natural gas and derivatives, coal and derivatives; electricity; hydrogen and other synthetic fuels.

[15] As the GHG abatement targets and the renewables penetration targets are separate goals, two instruments are needed. The EU ETS (and carbon levies for sectors not included in the EU ETS) promotes the achievement of the GHG emission reduction targets. National support schemes, mostly of the price-based type, i.e. providing incentives in terms of higher prices or price top-ups, have been used so far to promote the achievement of the renewables penetration target. The scheme proposed in this chapter is an alternative – or possibly – complementary one, of the quantity-based type.

[16] These targets have been typically defined in terms of the share of renewable energy sources in final energy consumption. The 2020 Climate and Energy Package (n 10) set a 20% target to be achieved by 2020. The 2019 Clean Energy for All Europeans Package (European Commission – Directorate-General for Energy, *Clean Energy for All Europeans* (Publication Office of the European Union 2019)) set a 32% target for 2030. More recently, the European Commission has proposed to increase this target to 40% in the 'Fit for 55' Package (European Commission, '"Fit for 55": delivering the EU's 2030 Climate Target on the way to climate neutrality' COM (2021) 550) and to 45% in the REPowerEU Plan (European Commission, 'REPowerEU Plan' COM (2022) 230). The co-legislators eventually agreed on a binding target of 42.5%, with an ambition to reach 45%.

[17] Where this happens, FITs may be maintained for smaller installations.

a handful of jurisdictions have implemented Tradable Green Certificate (TGC) schemes.[18] While FITs are typically administratively set, an increasing number of jurisdictions are using tendering procedures to assign the right to FIPs and to fix their levels. Providing certainty to investors has been a major consideration in the choice of support instruments.[19]

In the gas sector, support for renewable gases has been much more limited,[20] as has been the penetration of these gases. In this context, it is now clear that, if renewable gases are needed to replace natural gas for heating and cooling, for electricity generation and as feedstock in industrial processes, they will have to be more effectively promoted. It is also clear that any decarbonisation scenario would require the gas sector – and conceivably renewable and decarbonised gases – to support the greater penetration of renewables in the electricity sector. To do so, they would need to provide flexibility in the forms of storing energy over longer periods of time and of transporting energy over longer distances.

Therefore, the question arises: what is most effective instrument for promoting the development of renewable gases, including renewable hydrogen, taking stock of the long experience gained in supporting renewable-based electricity?

Table 12.1 classifies the main instruments used to support renewable energies (mainly electricity), according to whether they aim at promoting

---

[18] According to the 'Status Review of Renewable Support Schemes in Europe for 2016 and 2017' of the Council of European Energy Regulators, of the 27 jurisdictions surveyed, 17 were using FITs and 16 were using FIPs in 2017. In contrast, in the same year, only six were using TGC systems ((*CEER* 2021) Ref: C20-RES-69-04 https://www.ceer.eu/documents/104400/-/-/ffe624d4-8fbb-ff3b-7b4b-1f637f42070a/).

[19] However, failures in the design of support schemes forced at least one MS to adjust retroactively the level of support granted to renewables, greatly affecting investors' confidence. This led to the inclusion, in RED II, of provisions on the stability of financial support for renewable energies, specifying that 'the level of, and the conditions attached to, the support granted to renewable energy projects are not revised in a way that negatively affects the rights conferred thereunder and undermines the economic viability of projects that already benefit from support' (art 6(1)) and that 'Member States may adjust the level of support in accordance with objective criteria, provided that such criteria are established in the original design of the support scheme' (art 6(2)). Directive 2018/2001 (on the promotion of the use of energy from renewable sources [2018] OJ L328/82 ('RED II')).

[20] RED II (n 19) art 4 governs 'Support schemes for energy from renewable sources'. However, while para 1, which contains a general provision regarding the possibility of MSs applying support schemes, refers to 'energy', paras 2 to 6 only relate to renewable-based electricity.

Table 12.1 Main instruments for the support of renewable energies

	Price-based	**Quantity-based**
Capacity-based	Investment grants Tax incentives	Tendering systems for capacity
Energy-based	Feed-in tariffs Feed-in premiums Contracts for differences Tax incentives	Quota obligation based on traded certificates

renewable generation capacity or energy, and to whether they are price-based or quantity-based.[21]

A detailed assessment of the performance of the different instruments is beyond the scope of this chapter. Suffice it to note here, as is well known, at least in theory that:

- Price-based mechanisms are better suited where the main concern is the total cost of the support afforded to renewable energies, while there is some flexibility on the achievement of the target penetration level. In fact, in this case, the policymakers set the level of support, while the resulting penetration of renewables in the energy sector depends on the reaction of renewable project promoters to the available incentives. Only by predicting these reactions can policymakers set the level of support that delivers the target penetration level, but there is clearly scope for missing or overshooting the target and repeatedly having to adjust the level of support;
- Quantity-based mechanisms are better suited where the main concern is the achievement of a quantitative renewables penetration target (e.g. the 40% penetration of renewables in EU final energy consumption by 2040). Quantity-based mechanisms might however result in high compliance costs, even though there are ways in which this can be avoided, albeit at the expense of not achieving the target.[22]

[21] Price-based instruments promote renewables by providing them with a higher price or a price top-up. In this case, the outcome of implementation of the instrument, in terms of the volume of renewables being developed, depends on the response of investors to the higher prices and/or price top-ups. Quantity-based instruments, instead, typically define a quantity target, possibly applied as an obligation for a certain cohort of market agents, then leave the market to determine which incentives are needed to achieve the set target. In this case, if compliance with the instrument can be ensured through effective enforcement, the achievement of the target is guaranteed, but the cost of the instrument depends on the costs of the actions required to achieve the target.

[22] For more on this, see sub-section V.D.

As indicated above, most Member States (MSs) have historically used price-based support instruments – FITs and FIPs, despite the EU and MSs having committed to quantitatively-defined renewable penetration targets.[23] This apparent contradiction can be explained by the volatility of the price of TGCs, which, like the price of any traded instrument, depends on the interplay of demand and supply. It is therefore not surprising that renewable generation promoters have preferred, and better reacted to, FITs and FIPs than to TGCs. In reality, the volatility of the TGCs' price could have been addressed with the development of hedging instruments, as is common practice in financial markets. However, in many jurisdictions, TGCs were abandoned before such hedging instruments could be developed and their market achieved sufficient liquidity over suitable time horizons.

Going forward, the challenge of designing the most effective renewable support instruments should consider:

- The need to promote the achievement of the renewable penetration target at least cost – and the need for least-cost solutions will be greater with more ambitious renewables penetration targets;
- The need to trace renewable energy through transformations, including in the context of a circular energy system.

In this respect, GOs could play a key role.[24]

III. THE EU LEGISLATION ON GUARANTEES OF ORIGIN

GOs were introduced by the first Renewable Energy Directive (RED I)[25] and their use extended by the second Renewable Energy Directive (RED II).[26] In both Directives, the purpose of GOs is defined as, and limited to 'demonstrating to final customers the share or quantity of energy from renewable sources in an energy supplier's energy mix and in the energy supplied to consumers

---

23 A review of the renewable support instruments used by EU MSs can be found in CEER 2021 (n 18). For a brief summary of EU renewables penetration targets, see n 16 above.

24 Such a role was first proposed by the authors in Alberto Pototschnig and Ilaria Conti, 'Upgrading Guarantees of Origin to Promote the Achievement of the EU Renewable Energy Target at Least Cost' (European University Institute 2021) https://fsr.eui.eu/publications/?handle=1814/69776/.

25 Directive 2009/28/EC on the promotion of the use of energy from renewable sources and amending and subsequently repealing Directives 2001/77/EC and 2003/30/EC [2009] OJ L140/16 ('RED I').

26 RED II (n 19).

under contracts marketed with reference to the consumption of energy from renewable sources'[27] (disclosure purpose). RED I limited the use of GOs to electricity and heating and cooling from renewable sources. RED II extended their use to all types of energies from renewable sources, therefore including renewable gases. Under RED II, MSs may also arrange for GOs to be issued for energy from non-renewable sources. Therefore, GOs can now be issued with respect to energies from all sources. In this way, suppliers will be able to document the sources of all electricity delivered to their customers. Since GOs specify the energy source against which they are issued, those issued against renewable-based electricity can play a role in supporting such production.

In fact, despite restricting the use of GOs for disclosure purposes, legislation admits that GOs might have a market value, prescribing that such a value 'is taken into account appropriately in the relevant support scheme'.[28] In this way, GOs are recognised as contributing to supporting the deployment of renewable energies.

Clearly, a GO has no fixed price, and its value depends on market demand and supply. Therefore, in this respect, GOs face the same challenges as the TGCs.[29] However, GOs have been in circulation for more than 20 years,[30] even though their use is still purely voluntary, and producers of energy from renewable sources can decide whether or not to request the issuing of GOs.

Article 19 in RED II lists the minimum information that GOs must include, that is: '[information] concerning the installation where the energy was produced; whether the installation or the unit of energy benefited from investment support or from a national support scheme; the date on which the installation

27 RED II (n 19) art 19(1).

28 ibid art 19(2), third sub-para.

29 In the context of renewable support schemes, TGCs are certificates representing the renewable nature of the energy against which they are issued. TGCs are traded separately from the underlying energy, which is traded as a commodity product. A promotion scheme based on TGCs typically imposes an obligation on a cohort of market agents – for example, generators using non-renewable sources of energy – to acquire and submit to a competent authority TGCs equivalent to a pre-defined share of the electricity produced from non-renewable sources. The challenges referred to in the text arise from the variability of the price of the TGCs, which is a source of risk for both the renewable producers – who are exposed to the possibility that the TGC price could be lower than expected – and the obligated agents – who are exposed to the possibility of a higher TGC price and therefore to higher costs for fulfilling their obligation.

30 The Association of Issuing Bodies (AIB), the first of its kind in Europe, was established in 2002. The AIB aims to develop, use and promote a standardised system of energy certification for all energy carriers: the European Energy Certificate System (EECS). Since then, two other certification systems have been established: ERGaR (European Renewable Gas Registry) and CertifHy (focusing on hydrogen).

became operational; the date and country of issue and a unique identification number'.

IV. ACHIEVING THE RENEWABLE ENERGY PENETRATION TARGET AT LEAST COST

As noted above, the EU renewable energy penetration target for 2030 is expressed in terms of the share of renewable energy in final energy consumption; a sub-target is only envisaged for the transport sector, into which renewable fuels have traditionally found it more difficult to penetrate, at least in some MSs.[31] For the other sectors, the target could conceivably be achieved with any combination of renewable shares for the different energy vectors.[32] The question, therefore, arises of which combination of renewable penetration levels for the different vectors delivers the overall target at least cost and whether the resulting mix of renewable energies is acceptable from an energy policy perspective.[33]

---

[31] The 2020 Climate and Energy Package (n 10) set a 10% target for each MS, for the share of renewable sources in all energy used in transport, to be achieved by 2020. Sustainability criteria were also introduced for biofuels in order for them to count towards the renewable energy share. In 2020, 10.2% of the total energy used in transport in the EU was from renewable sources, following a steady increase in this share since 2005, when it was just under 2%. This indicates that the 2020 target of 10% was reached at the EU level. However, progress has varied significantly across MSs, with the 10% target being achieved by less than half of EU MSs. The overall EU target was reached thanks to overachievement in a handful of countries. Also see European Environment Agency (EEA), 'Use of Renewable Energy for Transport in Europe' (*eea.europa.eu*, 2022) https://www.eea.europa.eu/ims/use-of-renewable-energy-for/ accessed 19 September 2022.

[32] Even though a 'normalisation rule' for accounting for electricity generated from hydropower and wind power is provided in Annex II of RED II (n 19). However, this normalisation rule does not alter the fact that the overall renewable penetration target could be achieved through different combinations of renewable energy vectors. Rather, it implies that the power generated by some technologies should be 'normalised' before it is taken into account for the achievement of the overall target.

[33] Policymakers might have views regarding the renewable vector mix which most effectively and efficiently delivers the 2050 EU carbon neutrality goal, and the intermediate renewable penetration targets in earlier years. As such, they might, therefore, be tempted to steer the energy sector towards that mix. However, policymakers should be aware that steering the energy sector away from the mix which is delivered by a technology-neutral market mechanism might increase the overall cost of achieving the target. A different aspect is the effort-sharing among EU MSs, where a political agreement – based on the concerns of some MSs to limit the cross-border transfer of the benefits accruing from the development of renewable energies – might lead to a departure from the EU-wide least cost solution for meeting the 2050 carbon neutrality goal and the related intermediate targets.

It is a straightforward matter to show that the least-cost solution for meeting the overall renewable energy penetration target is the one for which the marginal cost of replacing a vector in its conventional, but decarbonised form with its renewable alternative is the same across all vectors. The remainder of this chapter will refer to the replacement of a vector in its conventional decarbonised form with its renewable alternative as 'greening' the vector.[34] Therefore, an instrument which promotes the achievement of the overall renewable energy target at least cost should provide signals to equalise the marginal costs of greening the different vectors.[35]

With the use of such an instrument, the actual renewable shares for the different vectors will be determined by the market on the basis of the relative costs of 'greening' the different vectors. Vectors for which the cost of greening is lower – due to an abundance of renewable sources and/or cheaper technology available to produce them – will likely make a larger contribution to the achievement of the overall renewable energy penetration target. For example, it is accepted that electricity is cheaper to 'green' than other vectors, and therefore it is expected that in 2030, against an overall renewable target of 42.5–45% in final energy consumption, renewable electricity will account for approximately two-thirds to three-quarters of final electricity consumption.

If the limitation of their use to disclosure purposes is removed, GOs could represent the best instrument to promote the equalisation of the marginal cost of 'greening' across the different vectors and therefore the minimisation of the cost of achieving the overall renewable energy target, subject to the limitations which will be discussed in sub-section IV.B.

A system based on GOs would also allow the tracing of renewable energy through transformations, including in the context of a circular energy system. Section V will discuss this latter aspect in more detail.

Finally, it is worth noting that an approach based on GOs will not deliver, by itself, a pre-defined renewable share for any of the vectors.[36] In order to achieve that, additional support for specific vectors/technologies might be needed. In this respect, it is important to clarify that an approach based on GOs could be accompanied by additional targeted support, to promote, for example, the development of infant technologies. It should be clear, though, that this kind of additional support, to the extent that it leads to a deviation from the

---

[34] However, this clearly does not mean, and cannot mean, that the same electron or molecule changes their source and becomes renewable-based.

[35] It is worth emphasising that equalising the marginal cost of 'greening' the different energy vectors does not correspond to equalising the marginal cost of producing the different vectors from renewable (green) sources.

[36] Unless the instrument is applied separately to the different vectors.

mix of renewable energies delivering the renewable energy penetration target at least cost, might increase the cost of achieving that target.[37]

A. How the Mechanism Could Work

For GOs to play an enhanced role, they would need to contain additional information. In particular, they would have to indicate whether the energy against which they have been issued qualifies as 'renewable' according to legislation. Any GOs issued against the production of energy from renewable sources could then be referred to as Guarantees of Renewable Origin (GROs).

Therefore, GOs could be issued on all energy produced in the EU – including energy produced from non-renewable sources.[38] But only those issued against energy produced from renewable sources would qualify as GROs. The other GOs would only be used for disclosure purposes.

In this respect, it is important here to stress that the same GROs could be used both for disclosure purposes and as an instrument to promote renewable energies. But how would the proposed mechanism based on GROs work?

First of all, GROs would need to become statutory[39] instruments. GROs would be issued to energy producers against their energy production from renewable sources. As the renewable energy penetration target is expressed in terms of final energy consumption, an obligation would be imposed on energy consumers, or, in the case of small consumers buying from suppliers, on the suppliers serving them, to procure an amount of GROs equal to a pre-defined share of the final energy consumption for which they are responsible.[40] In the following, this obligation will be referred to as the 'GRO obligation'. This pre-defined share defining the GRO obligation might be the same for all types of consumers and energy vectors,[41] or, if policymakers so decide, differentiated by consumer category and/or energy vector. It is important to stress that the ability of the GRO-based mechanism to achieve the renewable

---

[37] See also n 33.

[38] As already allowed by art 19(2) of RED II (n 19) 'Member States may arrange for guarantees of origin to be issued for energy from non-renewable sources'.

[39] In the sense that the instrument would provide the basis for the promotion of renewable energies and will be mandatory within its geographical scope.

[40] In this description, an aspect is neglected, which will have to be addressed at the implementation stage: the losses during transportation of an energy vector. Losses of energy during transformation processes (e.g. Power to Gas) will, instead, be taken into account by the surrendering of GROs related to the vector used in the transformation and the issuance of GROs on the vector resulting from the transformation. See Section V.

[41] In this case, to achieve a 38–40% renewable energy penetration target, the obligation would be set at this level for all consumers and energy vectors.

energy penetration target at least cost is not affected by the way in which the GRO obligation is allocated across different consumer categories and energy vectors. This would only affect the way in which the cost of achieving said target is shared among different consumers.

Large consumers and suppliers would be able to procure the required GROs directly from renewable energy producers or on the market. In fact, it would assist the efficiency of this mechanism if a market were established where GROs could be traded between renewable energy producers, large consumers and suppliers, as well as intermediaries and market makers, thus increasing its liquidity.

Large consumers and suppliers would be able to demonstrate the fulfilment of their obligations by surrendering the required quantity of GROs to an entity responsible for operating, monitoring and enforcing the mechanism. Once surrendered, these GROs would be cancelled. GROs which are not surrendered within a pre-defined period after being issued would expire and would, therefore, be automatically cancelled.

The way in which GROs would be issued, traded, surrendered and cancelled might emulate the current practice for GOs used in voluntary schemes.[42] To illustrate how the mechanism might work, consider the following example. The mechanism is introduced, imposing a 40% GRO obligation. A supplier subject to such an obligation would have to procure and surrender GROs representing an amount of renewable energy equal to 40% of the energy supplied to its customers. However, on the basis of the surrendered GROs, the supplier would also be able to inform its customers that 40% of the energy that it supplies to them is of renewable origin. In fact, the supplier might want to lay claim to a larger share of renewable energy and therefore procure (and surrender) more GROs than those required by its GRO obligations. Or the supplier might decide, in procuring the GROs it needs, to favour local renewable energy producers and, in doing so, to claim that it supports local renewable production.

From this example it is clear that, as already indicated, there is no conflict between the use of GROs for meeting a possible GRO obligation and their use for disclosure purposes, as at present.

B. The GRO Granularity and Trading

As indicated in sub-section A, a mechanism based on GROs, by promoting the equalisation of the marginal cost of greening across different vectors, would

42 Cf. RED II (n 19).

help to reduce, and possibly minimise, the cost of achieving the renewable energy penetration target.

In this context, there are a number of dimensions which need to be considered in designing such a mechanism:

- The geographical scope of the mechanism;
- The cross-vector dimension; and
- The time granularity.

The design choice on each of them determines the extent to which the mechanism is able to reduce the costs of achieving the defined renewables penetration target. In all cases, the wider the perimeter within which the mechanism operates and within which GROs could be traded – in terms of participating jurisdictions, energy vectors and time granularity – the greater the flexibility offered (to large consumers and suppliers) to meet the(ir) GRO obligations. And greater flexibility should lower the cost of achieving the renewable energy penetration target. However, greater flexibility also means that the obligation related to the final energy consumption of one vector at a specific time in a specific jurisdiction could be met by renewable energy of a different form, produced in a different jurisdiction and/or at a different time.

While until now in this chapter it has been implicitly assumed that the GRO mechanism would operate across different vectors – hence the reference to the equalisation of the marginal costs of greening the different vectors – the exact perimeter and structure of the mechanism would need to be carefully designed. The mechanism could also apply to a subset of vectors and jurisdictions, separately or as part of the same mechanism.

C. The Geographical Scope

Different MSs are endowed with different renewable energy resources and, therefore, are likely to have different costs of renewable energies compared to their conventional decarbonised equivalents. Therefore, significant savings in achieving the renewable energy penetration target might be obtained by producing more renewable energies where their cost differentials (with respect to conventional, decarbonised equivalents) are lower, using them also to fulfil the renewable energy obligations in jurisdictions characterised by higher 'greening' costs. This opportunity would require the cross-border tradability of GROs. This, however, would imply that the renewable energy obligations in one jurisdiction could be met by renewable energy production in another jurisdiction. Thus, while large consumers and suppliers in the former jurisdiction would face the (somewhat lower) cost of meeting their GRO obligations, the local benefits of renewable energy production (e.g., in terms of job creation) would accrue to a different jurisdiction.[43]

In deciding the geographical scope of a GRO mechanism, a trade-off would have to be considered between:

- The minimisation of the costs of achieving the overall renewable energy penetration target, which would call for the widest possible geographical scope;
- Maintaining the local benefits of renewable energy production in the proximity of those large consumers and suppliers who pay for greening the energy, which would suggest a more limited geographical scope of the mechanism or its segmentation into different geographical markets.

In fact, the proposed mechanism is totally flexible in terms of the geographical scope of its implementation. It might be implemented across the whole EU, perhaps including also EEA states, or at a regional level. Alternatively, the mechanism might be implemented, in parallel, in different sub-regions, with trading between them subject to specific conditions and limitations.

Finally, in order to avoid any double counting of the renewable energy produced and consumed in a jurisdiction, the GRO mechanism would have to become the mandatory instrument for accounting for renewable energy for the achievement of the renewable penetration target within the participating jurisdictions. This, however, does not exclude the possibility that some renewable energy technologies are further supported by more targeted mechanisms, with the caveat that this would likely result in a deviation from the least-cost solution for achieving the overall renewable energy penetration target.

D. The (Cross-)Vector Dimension

There are significant differences in the costs of 'greening' the different vectors. For electricity, generation from a number of renewable technologies – such as

---

[43] This kind of decoupling of the accrual of the costs and benefits of an increasing share of renewables led MSs to reject the Commission's proposal in 2007 for an EU system of Certificates of Origin. However, the statistical transfers envisaged in art 8 of RED II (n 19) and the EU renewable energy financing mechanism, being launched by the European Commission, also provide some flexibility in the way in which overall EU renewable energy penetration targets and the individual MS contributions are achieved. In particular, in its EU renewable energy financing mechanism infographics, the European Commission emphasises that the mechanism will bring benefits to a 'contributing' MS in terms of 'potentially lower direct and indirect costs than deployment of installations at home' and 'access to potentially cheaper or otherwise unavailable renewable energy sources'.

onshore wind and solar PV – is increasingly commercially viable even without subsidies. This is not (yet) the case for renewable gases. The costs of biogas and renewable hydrogen are still substantially higher than their decarbonised, but not renewable, equivalents.[44]

Therefore, the cost of achieving the overall renewable energy penetration target could be significantly reduced if there were flexibility in the renewable energy mix which is used to meet these targets. As already noted in Section I, there is an expectation that, at least until 2030 and probably also afterwards, electricity will contribute more than proportionally to the achievement of the renewable energy penetration target, as its 'greening' cost is currently lower than for other vectors. But it could be left to the market to determine the exact way in which each vector will contribute to the overall renewable energy penetration target.

In practice, this would require large consumers and suppliers to be able to meet their GRO obligations related to the final consumption of one vector by procuring and surrendering GROs issued vis-à-vis the renewable-based production of another vector. For example, a large industrial consumer of hydrogen might be allowed to meet its GRO obligation with GROs issued in respect of the production of any renewable vector, including, for example, electricity.

The implications of this kind of flexibility would be a greater supply of GROs issued *vis-à-vis* the renewable-based production of those vectors where the greening costs are lower. As a result, the renewable-based production of these vectors would be greater than the quota imposed on their final consumption, while the reverse would happen for those vectors whose greening costs are higher.

Alternatively, the mechanism might require that the GRO obligation related to the final consumption of one energy vector be met by surrendering GROs issued vis-à-vis the renewable-based production of the same vector. That would lead to a vector-wise segmentation of the GRO market and cost minimisation would only be achieved within each vector. This is what happens, for example, with TGC schemes, which apply only to electricity and in which cost minimisation is only achieved among the different renewable-based electricity production technologies.

---

44 See, in this regard, International Energy Agency (IEA), 'Outlook for Biogas and Biomethane: Prospects for Organic Growth' (IEA, 2020) and Christopher Jones, James Kneebone and Andris Piebalgs, 'Cost-effective Decarbonisation Study 2022' (European University Institute 2022) https://cadmus.eui.eu/bitstream/handle/1814/73658/QM-01-22-010-EN-N.pdf?sequence=4&isAllowed=y/.

In deciding the (cross-)vector dimension of a GRO mechanism, a trade-off would, therefore, have to be considered between:

- The minimisation of the costs of achieving the overall renewable energy penetration target, which would call for the mechanism being applied across all vectors;
- Ensuring that a pre-defined quota of renewable-based production is achieved for each vector, which would suggest that the mechanism is applied separately to the different vectors.

E. The Time Granularity

Legislation requires MSs to meet their renewable energy penetration target on an annual basis.

This means that, within a GRO mechanism, the obligation on large consumers and suppliers could also be imposed annually. However, it is possible that MSs would prefer to have shorter periods within which the renewable energy penetration quota has to be achieved.

A GRO mechanism could be designed with any desired time granularity. Large consumers and suppliers might be required to fulfil their GRO obligations with respect to their final energy consumption in a quarter or a month – or even a week or a day – with GROs issued vis-à-vis renewable-based energy production in the same quarter or month – or week or day. Clearly, the longer the period of time over which the obligation applies, the greater the opportunities for producing renewable-based energy at lower costs (just by extending the options) and, therefore, the lower the cost of meeting the obligations. However, longer periods would weaken the physical link between final energy consumption and a quota of it being renewable-based.

The time granularity of the GRO mechanism would also affect the deadline for surrendering the GROs to demonstrate the fulfilment of the obligation and the moment in which non-surrendered GROs are cancelled. A GRO mechanism operating over a year, for instance, might require surrender by a deadline at some stage in the following year and the cancellation of non-surrendered GROs thereafter. At the other extreme, a GRO mechanism operating on a daily basis would require surrendering within a much shorter timeframe and cancellation thereafter.

In deciding the time granularity of a GRO mechanism, a trade-off would, therefore, have to be considered between:

- The minimisation of the cost of achieving the overall renewable energy penetration target, which would call for the mechanism having the lowest time granularity, i.e. being applied over longer periods;

- Maintaining some sort of – albeit loose – physical link between the final consumption on which the obligation is imposed and the corresponding quota of renewable-based energy production, which would suggest that the mechanism is applied with a greater granularity, i.e. over shorter periods of time.

V. PROMOTING RENEWABLES IN A CIRCULAR ENERGY SYSTEM

One further aspect relates to the way in which the GRO-based mechanism could support a circular energy system. A circular energy system is characterised, *inter alia*, by the transformation of energy, from one vector to another, as explained in the European Commission's vision for an integrated energy system.[45] In such a context, it would be important to trace the renewable nature of the energy through these transformations. The GRO-based mechanism would facilitate such tracing.

Consider, as an example, the production of renewable hydrogen. Hydrogen cannot be found as such in nature and should be produced through chemical processes, typically requiring energy. In this context, renewable hydrogen can be produced by using renewable-based energy.[46] For example, renewable hydrogen produced by electrolysis would require the use of renewable electricity.

Within the GRO mechanism outlined above, electrolysis will produce renewable hydrogen, against which GROs would be issued, only if the electricity used in the process is accompanied by an equivalent amount of GROs. The operator of the electrolyser would then have to surrender these GROs to have the electricity used in the process qualified as renewable, and would be issued with GROs in respect to the hydrogen output.

In its Hydrogen Strategy,[47] the Commission seems to imply that renewable hydrogen would be produced by electrolysers directly connected to solar-

---

45 European Commission, 'EU strategy on energy system integration' (*energy.ec.europa.eu*, n.d.) https://energy.ec.europa.eu/topics/energy-systems-integration/eu-strategy-energy-system-integration_en/ accessed 19 September 2022.

46 In art 2(4) of the proposal for a 'Commission Delegated Regulation supplementing Directive (EU) 2018/2001 by establishing a Union methodology setting out detailed rules for the production of renewable liquid and gaseous transport fuels of non-biological origin' (European Commission, Ares (2022) 3836651) 'renewable hydrogen' is defined as 'hydrogen derived only from renewable energy sources other than biomass'.

47 European Commission, 'A hydrogen strategy for a climate-neutral Europe' COM (2020) 301 ('the Hydrogen Strategy').

and wind-powered electricity generators.[48] Requiring electrolysers producing renewable hydrogen to be physically linked to renewable-based electricity generators, to ensure that the hydrogen will be produced with renewable electricity, would limit the capacity utilisation of the electrolysers to the production pattern of the linked generators. In most instances this will limit the load factor of electrolysers, thus increasing the cost of renewable hydrogen.

An alternative approach could be to use the GROs to qualify the electricity used in electrolysers as renewable. In such a case, the hydrogen produced by the electrolyser would be qualified as renewable only if GROs were procured and surrendered corresponding to the total electricity consumption of the electrolyser. This approach, while consistent with using GROs for accounting renewable energy production against final energy consumption, could be criticised for creating only a 'virtual' correspondence between the electricity produced from renewable sources and the electricity consumed by the electrolysers. In this context, it is to be noted that some of the flexibility mechanisms currently allowed by legislation – such as statistical transfers – also rest on a 'virtual' or accounting correspondence. Moreover, what should matter the most is that the renewable energy penetration target is achieved at the EU level, with each MS making its contribution, and that this is done in the most cost-efficient way.

In this context, concerns have been raised that, unless electrolysers are physically linked to renewable electricity generators, their demand for renewable electricity would lead to an increase in electricity demand which could be met by marginal, possibly non-renewable or non-decarbonised sources, thus leading to an increase in the electricity sector carbon footprint. This is clearly a serious concern. However, as long as the GRO mechanism is adopted as the basic statutory mechanism, as outlined in this chapter, it would guarantee that the renewable electricity against which the GROs procured by the electrolysers are issued is additional to the renewable energy required to meet the renewable penetration target with respect to final electricity consumption.

In fact, the demand for GROs by an electrolyser, for its energy to be defined as renewable, would be on top of the demand for GROs by electricity con-

---

[48] ibid, s 3. Cf. s 3 (p 7) 'From now to 2030, investments in electrolysers could range between €24 and €42 billion. In addition, over the same period, €220–340 billion would be required to scale up and *directly connect* 80–120 GW of solar and wind energy production capacity to the electrolysers to provide the necessary electricity' (emphasis added). However, in n 28 of the Hydrogen Strategy, the Commission recognises that renewable hydrogen could also be produced by electrolysers not directly connected to renewable electricity generators as long as 'certain conditions are met, including the additionally of the renewable electricity used'. This additionality criterion could be easily addressed by the GRO mechanism outlined in the text.

sumers and suppliers subject to GRO obligations. This increased demand for GROs could only be met by the additional production of energy from renewable sources.

Another transformation in relation to which a GRO-based mechanism could ensure the tracing of the renewable quality of energy is the use of biomass and biomethane in pyrolysis.

Differently from electrolysis, where the feedstock used is water, hence a renewable source by definition, different types of feedstock can be used in the process of pyrolysis. Within the GRO mechanism outlined above, pyrolysis will produce renewable hydrogen, against which GROs would be issued, only if the electricity and the feedstock[49] used in the process is accompanied by an equivalent amount of GROs. The operator of the pyrolysis hydrogen plant would then have to surrender these GROs – to have the electricity and the feedstock used in the process qualified as renewable – and be issued with GROs in respect of the hydrogen output.

A. Statute and Governance

For the GRO mechanism outlined above to become the basic instrument for promoting the development of energies from renewable sources and for tracing the renewable quality of energy through transformations in the context of a circular energy system, it would have to acquire statutory status, i.e. it would have to be mandated by legislation.[50] The same GRO mechanism might also be used for counting the renewable-based energy production towards the achievement of the EU-wide penetration target and contributions by MSs.

While a statutory GRO mechanism could take advantage of the experience gained by the current voluntary GO schemes, a number of design features would have to be defined in legislation. A detailed design and implementation plan is beyond the scope of the present chapter; however, in what follows three aspects are highlighted, which would definitely need to be addressed in such a design:

- The issuing of GROs;
- The trading of GROs;
- The tracing of GROs and enforcement.

---

[49] According to the current legislative framework, the only feedstocks to be used in the pyrolysis process which would qualify for GROs are biogas and biomass.

[50] As indicated in s III above, GOs are currently issued only as part of voluntary schemes and there are currently no legal provisions for any statutory role for them.

The experience of the EU ETS could help with the design of all three points. In fact, while the GRO mechanism outlined above would play a different role from the EU ETS in the decarbonisation of the EU economy, the GROs would share several features with the EU ETS allowances (EUAs):

- GROs, like the EUAs, would be the basic statutory instrument for promoting a specific energy/climate objective;
- GROs, just as the EUAs, would provide the 'common currency' instrument for promoting the equalisation of marginal costs across different opportunities to pursue the energy/climate objective.

B. The Issuing of GROs

It would be appropriate that in each MS or region one entity is entrusted with issuing GROs once it has verified that the energy production against which they are issued is accurate in its quantity and that it is of a renewable source, as defined in legislation. It might be possible to entrust more than one entity in each MS or region with issuing GROs, as long as care is taken to avoid the double issuing of GROs for the same energy. Common standards for the verifications required for issuing GROs would be needed to ensure a level playing field across the EU.

C. The Trading of GROs

GRO trading should, instead, be allowed on the widest possible terms. While the liquidity of the GRO market might be promoted by the concentration of trading in a few marketplaces, this should be the result of market forces and it seems inappropriate to introduce limitations to the freedom of trading, beyond those required to avoid double counting or fraud.

D. GRO Tracing and the Enforcement of the Mechanism

For the proper functioning of the GRO mechanism, it would be imperative that GROs be traced throughout their lifecycle, from their issue, to their transfer and trading, to their surrendering and cancellation, or withdrawal or expiry.

One option for ensuring the proper tracing of GROs would be the establishment of a single EU Registry, similar to the one established for the EU ETS. All issued GROs could be recorded in this Registry, along with any subsequent lifecycle event. Large consumers and suppliers subject to the GRO obligation would have to ensure that, by the given deadline, they have the required quantity of GROs under their name in the Registry. Their obligation would be met by surrendering the required quantity of GROs for cancellation.

An alternative solution would be to allow several Registries to operate in parallel. This would require common standards, as well as interoperability rules which would ensure seamless transfer and trading of GROs, as well as their surrender, irrespective of the Registry in which they are recorded. Clearly, the single-registry solution would be easier to implement, even though it would mean a radical departure from the multiple voluntary GO systems operating at present. A single-registry approach could also act as the accounting system for measuring the quantity of energy from renewable sources produced in each MS and, therefore, in the EU as a whole.

The design of the GRO mechanism would also require enforcement provisions. A penalty for non-compliance with the GRO obligation would have to be defined. As in other similar mechanisms, the non-compliance penalty would have a double role. It would promote compliance. However, it would also act as a cap on the price of GROs: no party would be willing to pay a price for GROs higher than the penalty, since, if such a price exceeded the penalty, it would be cheaper to pay the latter. The penalty would then be necessarily fixed at a level at which policymakers are ready to concede that the achievement of the renewable penetration objective is becoming too expensive and, therefore, that the objective could be relaxed. In a sense, the two roles of the penalty are complementary. For GRO prices up to the penalty level, the penalty promotes compliance. For GRO prices above the penalty level, the penalty represents a safety valve to prevent the pursuit of the renewable energy penetration target becoming overly expensive for the economy.

E. The International Dimension

RED II envisages the possibility of joint projects between MSs and third countries for the production of electricity from renewable sources. RED II sets a series of conditions which have to be met in order for the electricity from renewable sources produced in a third country to be taken into account for the purposes of calculating the renewable energy shares of the MSs.[51] Thus, it seems appropriate that, when these conditions are met, GROs could be issued against any renewable energy produced in a third country.

VI. CONCLUSIONS

The GRO mechanism outlined in this chapter aims at achieving the EU renewable energy penetration target at least cost. This mechanism is politically very ambitious, as it encompasses different types of renewable energies, across

---

51 RED II (n 19) art 1.

vectors and across jurisdictions. Such a mechanism would however also facilitate the development of a circular energy system, by allowing the tracing of the renewable nature of energy throughout the transformations.

In order to deliver its full benefits, the GRO-based mechanism would require some degree of flexibility in the mix of renewable energies and on the location of their deployment. This latter dimension of flexibility was turned down by MSs when the European Commission envisaged an EU market for Certificates of Origin, as part of its legislative proposal which led to RED I.

However, the mechanism outlined in this chapter starts from the basic consideration that the renewable energy penetration target is collective for all Europe, hence it would be worth thinking of an EU-wide mechanism to achieve it.

Moreover, the current target for 2030 will be more than twice as high[52] as the 20% one for 2020, set by the 2009 Directive. Therefore, the costs of achieving this higher target are likely to be much more substantial and the benefits of achieving it at the least cost correspondingly greater. As a result, MSs may now look more favourably at a scheme that will ensure a least-cost solution.

The GRO-based mechanism could then act as the main, basic support mechanism for renewable energies. As indicated in Section IV, policymakers might decide to complement this mechanism with additional targeted support schemes, for example for promoting infant technologies, being aware that such additional support might increase the costs of meeting the renewable energy penetration target. In this sense, the proposed mechanism might be considered as 'supplementing' other additional support schemes.

LEGISLATION

Directive 2009/28/EC on the promotion of the use of energy from renewable sources and amending and subsequently repealing Directives 2001/77/EC and 2003/30/EC [2009] OJ L140/16 ('RED I').

Directive 2018/2001 on the promotion of the use of energy from renewable sources [2018] OJ L328/82 ('RED II').

Regulation (EU) 2021/1119 establishing the framework for achieving climate neutrality and amending Regulations (EC) 401/2009 and (EU) 2018/1999 [2021] OJ L243/1 ('European Climate Law')

Directive 2003/87/EC establishing a scheme for greenhouse gas emission allowance trading within the Community and amending Council Directive 96/61/EC [2003] OJ L275/32 ('ETS')

[52] As indicated in n 16, the 32% renewable energy penetration target set by RED II (n 19) for 2030 has been increased to 42.5%, as agreed by the co-legislators in RED III, and in line with the increase in the GHG emission reduction target from 40% to 55%, by the same year, envisaged in the European Climate Law (n 2).

13. The (in)coherence–(in)effectiveness nexus of the EU's circular energy system

Lucila de Almeida and Josephine van Zeben

I. TRANSITIONING TOWARDS A CIRCULAR ENERGY SYSTEM

In moving towards energy system integration, including through the creation of a circular energy system, the European Union (EU) faces a plethora of economic, social, and legal challenges. This volume sets out some of the impacts of these ambitions on different, though ultimately interrelated, policy areas with a view to considering whether the EU's legal framework is 'fit for purpose' vis-à-vis the energy transition. Since the measures proposed under the Green Deal cross various domain areas and sectors, the related legal reforms are proposed by, and debated in, expert groups or committees that rarely dialogue with each other. The resulting 'silo-thinking' engenders incoherence between measures proposed in different silos, which ultimately leads to the ineffectiveness of the Green Deal.

In this Conclusion, we first provide an overview of the key findings of the preceding chapters, after which we consider to what extent these confirm the existence of an incoherence–inefficiency nexus.

A. From Waste to Biofuels and Biogas[1]

Waste-to-energy implicates at least three EU policy areas: the energy union; environmental policy (especially air quality regulation and climate change law); and waste regulation.[2] The key sectors to this transition – agriculture,

[1] This section highlights the main findings of Part 1 of the volume.

[2] J Malinauskaite and H Jouhar, 'The Trilemma of Waste-to-Energy: A Multi-Purpose Solution' 129 Energy Policy 636.

food, and forestry – all deal with waste in different ways.[3] The current environmental and sectoral regulations of these industries do not envisage, and often actively discourage, circularity within the production process. Moreover, an effective circular energy system depends on strengthening cooperation between supranational, national, regional, and local authorities to enable the reuse of biowaste, biofuel, and biogas production and consumption. For instance, while the management of organic waste is usually a concern for local authorities, the definition of by-waste falls under national authorities' competence, and the classification of biofuels and biogas that counts towards Member States' renewable energy targets is established at the European level. The compatibility of these legal frameworks is fundamental to our ability to 'fuel' the transition to a circular energy system.

To complicate matters further, achieving a 'complete' cycle of design, production, consumption and recovery/recycling is virtually impossible due to the Second Law of Thermodynamics. This law implies that the purity of materials will eventually decline over time and repeated recycling without external energy sources or new materials is impossible. Every transition through the material cycle requires energy, which results in material losses. In addition, for a 'sustainable' circular economy, energy should come from renewable resources. While reducing energy usage levels is beneficial to circularity, only renewable energy sources can ensure true sustainability within the circular economy – an aspect which has been largely overlooked.

Within this debate, the use of arable land for biofuel and biogas production has been contentious, as it may direct fertile soil away from food production and towards energy production, resulting in indirect land-use change (ILUC).[4] To address this concern, the EU's Renewable Energy Directive 2018/2001 (RED II) recently introduced regulations regarding ILUC, emphasising the use of crop residues and animal manure as primary substitutes for bioenergy generation. In addition, RED II has established binding targets for bioenergy development. However, despite this, the Common Agricultural Policy (CAP) grants Member States (MSs) considerable flexibility with regard to this domain – indicating a gap between RED II and CAP regulations.

It is evident that both RED II and the CAP have a political motivation to endorse bioenergy but, unfortunately, the EU does not have specific binding rules which promote utilising agricultural waste products either in RED III or in the National Strategic Plans of the CAP. Therefore, it is essential to further research ways of using these frameworks cleverly to enhance the utilisation of agricultural waste streams and reach a more circular energy economy

---

[3] For an overview, see van Calster, Chapter 2.
[4] See in detail Alessandrini, Alblas and Batten, Chapter 3.

while also addressing ILUC issues. One potential solution could be producing energy crops only on contaminated soil – which would require exploiting legal and regulatory frameworks to cause constructive changes within an energy transition.

To sum up, employing arable lands for bioenergy creation is a controversial problem that needs thoughtful consideration. While RED II and the CAP reveal political aims to back up bioenergy endeavours, the lack of precise obligatory rules could pose obstacles to achieving a circular economy. Therefore, future research should focus on optimising those frameworks effectively so we can develop a more responsible course of action with regard to bioenergy production that considers ILUC factors.

With respect to food law, policies and regulations have increasingly offered incentives for diverting food waste towards energy recovery, leading to an increase in infrastructure investment by businesses across the EU to facilitate this valorisation.[5] However, food waste used for bioenergy generation may not be regarded as a desirable form of valorisation from a food policy standpoint, as this biomass contains valuable elements such as nutritionally or biologically significant compounds that might be lost in the process.

The European Union Joint Research Centre has set out EoW (end-of-waste) criteria for a variety of materials, but the EU-level criteria only exist for iron scrap, copper scrap, and glass cullet. Decisions on when a waste material ceases to be considered waste for most other materials are left to the discretion of each MS. This ruling by the Court of Justice implies that food waste valorisation through energy recovery in the EU is reliant on how each MS interprets and enforces related legislation.

In the area of forestry, much change has also been afoot:[6] the Proposal for RED III addresses some issues by partially extending the sustainability criteria for agricultural biomass to forest biomass and strengthening the forest biomass criteria, particularly with respect to soil quality, biodiversity, and primary forests. However, further improvements are still necessary.

The sustainability and LULUCF (land use, land-use change, and forestry) criteria have been considered insufficient and weak, particularly when compared with those relevant to agriculture. The forest criteria lack safeguards for carbon stocks and the protection of critical environmental features compared to those set for agricultural biomass. The current forest criteria require the existence of laws and monitoring or management systems at the forest sourcing area level, focusing on formality rather than actual sustainability standards.

---

5 See Rao, Bast and de Boer, Chapter 4.
6 See in detail Cavallin, Chapter 5.

The draft RED II implementing act also appears to be primarily concerned with the formal legality of harvesting, rather than actual sustainability standards.

Promoting the use of residues and waste over primary wood for energy production is paramount in the new proposal. Member States are obligated to consider the cascading principle when designing their support schemes for bioenergy. Furthermore, they are prohibited from granting support for the production of energy from sawlogs, veneer logs, stumps, and roots, all of which serve as potential residues and waste materials that should remain in situ. Additionally, MSs cannot grant support energy production from waste incineration if rules on separate collection have not been adhered to or for practices that contradict the cascading principle as established by the future new Delegated Act.

B. The Use of Biofuel and Biogas in the Circular Energy System[7]

Alongside regulating the supply side of the circular energy system, structuring the potential uptake of biofuel and biogas by different sectors is equally important. One crucial sector is of course that of heating. An analysis of EU policies and legislation that encourage, or limit, the growing use of biogas produced from biowaste in the provision of heating and electricity along with cogeneration of heat and power shows that there is significant variance between National Energy and Climate Plans.[8] As the consumption of biogas is expected to continue to increase, a focus on sustainable development for production is needed to ensure its most sustainable use. In this regard, high-efficiency cogeneration based on waste biogas appears to be an appealing solution. This, however, requires conditions including regulatory mechanisms to ensure its optimal use in the process of energy transformation.

In the transport sector, there are currently no provisions solely dedicated to promoting the use of biofuels and gaseous biomass fuels from biowaste.[9] Instead, there are various layers of regulations that encourage the use of sustainable biofuels and gaseous biomass fuels, each with different scopes:

1. Minimum shares in the RED II and RED III for replacing fossil fuels with advanced biofuels in the transport sector, where multipliers further incentivise MSs to exceed the specific advanced biofuel targets and meet overall transport-related renewable energy targets;
2. Obligatory shares for deploying sustainable aviation fuels in the aviation transport mode;

---

7 This section highlights the main findings of Part 2 of the volume.

8 See Sokołowski, Chapter 6.

9 See in detail dos Reis, Lugmayr and Gomado, Chapter 7.

3. Targets for reducing greenhouse gas intensity of energy used in the transport sector in RED III and the Fuel EU Maritime Initiative;
4. Targets for the penetration of renewable energy into the energy system in RED II and RED III;
5. Exemption from surrendering ETS allowances for installations using sustainable biofuels and gaseous biomass fuels in compliance with the sustainability and GHG emissions saving framework of RED II and RED III, according to the 2018 EU ETS Directive, its revision, and the revision of the EU ETS Directive for aviation;
6. The zero-rating of emissions from bioenergy towards the Effort Sharing Regulation (ESR) annually binding emission limits for each Member State in the 2018 EU ESR Regulation and its revision.

The final contribution to this part of the volume relates not to a specific sector but rather to the emissions of a specific greenhouse gas, methane.[10] As a particular potent GHG, its reduction is a priority. However, methane could also be used for energy production, as vehicle fuel or as feedstock in the chemicals industry. This would reduce dependency on carbon. The 2020 EU Strategy to reduce methane emissions set out an extensive framework addressing methane emissions from the key sources: agriculture, waste, and energy. The strategy combines cross-sectoral actions (e.g. measurement and reporting of methane emissions by companies, biogas production) with sector-specific measures. While negotiations on a legislative framework for energy-related methane emissions are ongoing, the EU Commission has yet to revise the existing framework addressing two main sources of methane emissions in the EU: agriculture and waste. There are many opportunities here for technological solutions only if a robust monitoring, reporting, and verification scheme is put in place.

C. Cross-Sectoral Issues[11]

Apart from traditional regulation, the transitions needed for the circular energy system's success can be further encouraged through economic instruments. Energy taxes can encourage the use of sustainable energy products such as advanced biofuels and biogas by appropriately pricing fossil fuels.[12] This makes energy taxes a suitable instrument in line with the European Green Deal and Circular Economy strategies. However, in some MSs, energy taxes are designed inadequately, which can lead to insufficiently corrective signals,

---

10 See Olczak and Piebalgs, Chapter 8.
11 This section highlights the main findings of Part 3 of the volume.
12 See Antón, Chapter 9.

or a lack of differentiated tax treatment for products with diverging environmental performances. These design flaws can be attributed to the current configuration of the Energy Tax Directive (ETD), which taxes fuels based on their volume and thus lacks consistency in the treatment of both fossil and sustainable energy sources. To address these shortcomings and effectively deploy the European Green Deal, a new restructured ETD is needed to send the right pricing signals and encourage behaviour towards sustainable energy sources.

In addition to pricing, subsidies and other type of funding can also be used as catalysts of the transition. However, a number of inconsistencies and gaps remain across key EU funding programmes, State aid rules, and sustainable finance regulation, which hinder a more significant role for biowaste in European energy supply.[13] The absence of a clear vision for bioenergy at EU level explains why the bulk of EU financing is dedicated to research and innovation, rather than implementation or direct support to existing technologies which are uncompetitive under the current carbon pricing regime.

In the area of State aid, the Climate, Environmental and Energy Aid Guidelines (CEEAG) provide a broad range of State aid instruments with the ability to contribute to the goals of the Green Deal.[14] Within the EU, providing State aid is the exception to the rule that, in principle, to ensure market integration, State aid is prohibited. Given the broad scope and reach of the exceptions under the CEEAG, the Commission is keeping a close eye on making make sure that they will not lead to undue distortion of the competitiveness of the EU. No Commission decisions have thus far been taken related to the CEEAG, but the Commission has stressed that it aims to maintain the equilibrium between sustainability and market distortion.

Finally, there is the aim of achieving the EU's renewable energy penetration target in a cost-effective manner. A key role in this process has been given to Guarantees of Renewable Origin (GROs), which would allow for the penetration of renewables at least cost. GROs treat renewable energy in a non-discriminatory way, making no distinction between biofuels and biogases.[15] They aim to include various types of renewable energy sources across different sectors and jurisdictions and to facilitate the creation of a circular energy system by enabling the tracking of renewable energy from its source through various transformations. Importantly, GROs also promote the equalisation of the marginal cost of 'greening' across different vectors, which is particularly relevant in light of the targets of renewable shares in the energy mix for 2030. A GRO-based mechanism could provide key support for increasing the market

13 See Smoleńska, Chapter 10.
14 See Knook, Chapter 11.
15 See Pototschnig and Conti, Chapter 12.

share of renewable energies, with policymakers considering additional targeted support schemes to complement it, such as promoting nascent technologies.

II. THE (IN)COHERENCE–(IN)EFFECTIVENESS NEXUS

The aim of this volume was to provide an analysis of whether, and how, replacing natural gas and fossil fuels with biogas and biofuel produced from biowaste would contribute to decarbonising the energy sector. And importantly, how the EU's legal framework would be able to facilitate this transition, and conversely, where possible regulatory gaps or conflicts might arise.

Although the impacts and implications of the transition to a circular energy system are expressed very differently in different policy areas, two common themes emerge. First, the horizontal fragmentation between EU institutions of competences related to the regulation of circular energy system, or of sectors closely linked to the system, such as agriculture, food, and forestry, leads to incoherence in policy goals and measures. Second, this lack of coherence is compounded by vertical divergence in the transposition and implementation strategies of the Member States.

A telling example of this incoherence–inefficiency nexus can be found by comparing the conclusions from experts on waste regulation from the food, forestry, and agriculture sectors with energy regulation scholars. On the one hand, waste measures aim to reduce biomass or reuse for various purposes, while energy remains a low priority in the 'waste hierarchy'. At the same time, the gas sector reform proposes measures to ensure access to biofuel and biogas for infrastructure and end-users. These measures assume that the supply of biofuels will increase, which is highly unlikely without additional reforms of waste regulation. The same level of incoherence can be seen with respect to the use of the economic instruments aimed at accelerating the energy transition. Energy taxes and GROs, although both sector-related economic mechanisms designed to leverage renewables, are applied to renewables indistinctly. Inconsistencies and gaps remain across key EU funding programmes, State aid rules, and sustainable finance regulation. The absence of a clear vision for bioenergy at EU level explains why the economic incentives are not leading investments to boost energy circularity.

The EU's Green Deal ambitions are important and potentially transformative, leading to long-term sustainability in the European MSs and possibly beyond. A circular energy system is central to achieving these aims while maintaining quality of life. However, it is not surprising to find that bringing about such a transformation requires merging, or at least achieving mutual acknowledgement and awareness, of a range of policy areas that have long been siloed. The highly technical nature of these fields related to the circular energy system further complicates this ambition as it requires collaboration between different legal fields, as well as between lawyers and engineers, as evidenced by this volume.

Index